PLAYBOY'S HOST & BAR BOOK

PLAYBOY'S HOST & BAR BOOK

By Thomas Mario

A PLAYBOY PRESS BOOK

P❦P

CONTENTS

INTRODUCTION

That the bouquet of freshly decanted Barolo wine once reminded a drink connoisseur of rain-drenched violets is the kind of verbal effusion the modern American male will no longer buy. For not only *doesn't* Barolo smell of violets, very few people in the Western Hemisphere are at all likely to have violets on the brain when they drink it. Of infinitely more interest to the young host planning a dinner is the knowledge that Barolo—a red wine of northern Italy that ages gracefully—will glorify roast ribs of beef as well as veal *piccata* or sautéed venison chops.

This desire for knowing how to combine fine food and drink has grown from the isolated hobby of a few to a basic part of every man's liberal education. The old family patriarch may or may not have known that his Welsh rabbit needed to be liberally doused with strong ale. Today's host lights the lamp under his own fondue pot, selects his own Emmentaler and Gruyère cheeses, pours his own white wine and kirsch and tells his guests when they can begin spearing the chunks of French bread into the velvety fondue itself. Today's host knows—or wants to learn—that while his wafer-thin slices of Smithfield ham should be completely unadorned, his Polynesian cocktails should be rich with rums, mangoes, limes and floating orchids.

In the time since Repeal, while the great American bourbons were coming of age, the American drinking man also matured. The Jamaican may know his rums, the Frenchman his cognacs and the Scot his single malts, but the American in the last three decades has been able to become expert in judging the worldwide range of bibulous pleasures from vodka to Van der Hum and from tequila to *Trockenbeerenauslese.* And the cosmopolitan host is naturally an urbane host. He no longer feels it necessary to boast of how much liquor he can hold; instead he takes pride in the variety and quality of the liquors in his cabinet.

There was a time, not so long ago, when martini drinkers in this country would meekly accept any combination of gin and vermouth the bar waiter happened to deliver. Today a man will specify that his martini must contain proportions ranging from 3-to-1 to 30-to-1. Or he may demand that his glass be swirled with Pernod before the martini is poured; he'll want his drink on the rocks or straight up, with a twist of lemon, with an olive, neither or both. In his home, he may use a vermouth atomizer or vermouth dropper. In any case, his choice has little if anything to do with snobbism. Make no mistake—the martini drinker today isn't just a conspicuous fusspot. The years have refined his martini sense. His taste buds are imbued with the same kind of informative sensitivity an Italian enjoys when he drinks one of the wines he's known ever since he was old enough to hold a glass in his hands.

In the art of mixing drinks, the author assumes that the accomplished amateur will often outshine his professional counterpart when it comes to originality and enthusiasm. While the barkeep at the corner pub will dole out cocktails and highballs to the crowd—all made from a spate of recipes he can probably write on one shirt cuff—his standard bill of fare is beer and polite banter. Not so with the host at home. He not only mixes and pours—he entertains. With immense relish he becomes the director of a zestful drama every time he offers drinks—whether he's entertaining drop-ins after the game or guests at a black-tie dinner. In the spotlight of his own home, he is the man who wants his screwdrivers to stop the show, his bourbon to be 100 proof in pleasure and his V.S.O.P. cognac worthy of any critic's acclaim. And he fits his refreshments to the mood. His vodka and clear turtle consommé on the rocks, he's convinced, are perfect for his noontime party; the only fitting send-off at his *bon-voyage* party will be *blanc de blancs* champagne. Over the years, he runs his progressive dinner parties and his theater parties, his big open-house parties and his I've-finally-reached-you parties, selecting for each the drink to fit the merriment. His May wine is a very different compound from the cocktails at his June bachelor dinner, the daiquiris on his cabin cruiser or the holiday punch he brews for waving out the old year and welcoming the new. In a drinking sense, he's a man truly for all seasons.

Of course, there is much the amateur can pick up from the pro—his speed, his icemanship, glassmanship and, above all, his orderly bar habits, even when the fling is at its wildest. *Playboy's Host and Bar Book* is planned as a *mariage de convenance* of both amateur enthusiasm and professional competence—it is intended to be a method school for the modern man at his liquor cabinet.

Articles about whiskeys, gins, rums, vodkas, brandies, wines and beers have been a regular feature in PLAYBOY since it first appeared. While they form the basis of this book, it has been enlarged to contain much that is new. Several hundred previously published recipes have here grown to nearly 800. Comprehensive liquor lists, suggestions for wine cellars, a wine-terminology glossary, descriptions of bar equipment, and essays on the fact and lore of liquor history are also newly

written. It is hoped that the compendium of contemporary
parties, outlines for organizing them, plus comment on today's
code of conviviality enrich the book's value beyond the scope of
the conventional collection of bar recipes.

Playboy's Host and Bar Book is not for the solitary drinker
or wine archivist. Rather, it is written in the belief that whenever
two or more persons touch glasses, both the liquor and
something else begin stirring up fun. That something else is the
young appetite for life and for the varied means of enjoying
it—PLAYBOY's reason for existence and the reason for this book.

PART ONE
how to earn maximum returns
on your liquid assets

1

THE CODE OF CONVIVIALITY

Meticulous planning, comfortable digs, elaborate platters may be important to your reputation as a host, but *vital* to it is your understanding that every prearranged drinking session calls for two kinds of alchemy: The first is mixing potables; the second, mixing people.

Whether your drinks are as potent as arrack or as gentle as fino sherry, whether they be frosty coolers or steaming punches, their purpose is to create fun and amity. As for guests—whether lads or lassies, foreigners or natives, celebrities or aspirants, anecdotists or listeners—all should be carefully blended in your mind beforehand, and during the party reblended—like a true Spanish solera—in the most stimulating proportions. To this end, as a good host you need, first and always, to be a resourceful mind reader.

You should start with the proposition that friends who are warm toward you are not necessarily warm toward each other. Mindful of this kind of sensitive interplay, you'll naturally choose for small gatherings guests who'll be as compatible as gin and tonic. For larger parties, two or three abrasive acquaintances may provide just the catalytic force needed to transform a low-key soirée into an uninhibited revel—like yeast in small quantities, they often guarantee the lively but controlled fermentation on which good parties rise. In any event, guests—however diverse—who share wisely chosen libations do become *simpatico.* Arriving whether as friends or strangers, they leave with a glowing feeling, having found and fathomed the same warm company.

After drawing up your guest list, it's best, except for the most formal parties, to telephone invitations or to make them in person. Not only are they warmer and more immediate, but they make it possible to convey additional information about the nature of the party—how many people will be there, what to wear and if a meal will be served. It always is advisable to send those few dreamy acquaintances in every crowd a written follow-up.

Most guests at a party will unbend only if the host himself can relax. You should take care of all preliminaries hours before or, if possible, the *day* before the event. Amassing ice cubes, polishing brandy snifters, shopping, cooking, marinating, table setting, choosing disks for the stereo, setting out cocktail napkins and cigarettes, or hiring party help to do it for you—these are some of the jobs that must be attended to beforehand if you want to enjoy yourself at your own party.

If it's going to be a smallish get-together for no more than five or six couples, you'll probably be able to handle the drinks and food yourself, without having to spend half your time in the kitchen or behind the bar. But if you're planning a grand gala for more than 12, you'll be well advised to arrange for outside help—unless you want to make do with premixed punch and prepared finger food.

A few duties may have to be held off to the last moment. If, for instance, on a cold day you're planning to serve Irish coffee, buy the usquebaugh, the fresh coffee and heavy cream the day before. The cream should be whipped and stored in the refrigerator about a half hour before the guests arrive; the coffee should be ground at the same time; the coffeemaker should be filled and ready to go but not plugged in until the last moment.

Another key to relaxation for the thoughtful host is simply rehearsing. If, for instance, you're concocting a wine cup you've never made before, or a punch, it's a good idea to swizzle up a half pint or so the day before the party. Even if you're going to use a tried and tested recipe, a quick run-through can be useful; you may be using a different gin than you formerly used, or the lemons may not be as tart in the fall as in the spring. The practice run gives you the polish and assurance that every skillful host enjoys.

If you're planning a bacchanalia to start at three o'clock on a weekend afternoon, set your bedside alarm for an early hour in the morning rather than noontime; it'll take longer than you think to wrap up all the last-minute details. You'll be doing yourself and your guests another favor if you not only write out a work agenda beforehand, but consult it long before partytime. But all such schedules are only worth the paper they're written on unless they're checked and carried out. And make sure those bunches of watercress that were so hard to find are actually decorating the platters of cold cuts and not buried in the refrigerator for you to stumble over next week.

When the revelers arrive, remind yourself that no matter how busy the whirl, everyone appreciates a congenial word of welcome at the door. Shake the hands of the men *and* the women, a charming European custom that American men should adopt. And a gracious kiss is not inappropriate for those ladies who are old acquaintances.

Expect that each guest will arrive with parched throat and ravenous appetite—and offer drinks within moments, trays of hors d'oeuvres within minutes. Since the greeting of guests at the door and first-round dispensing of drinks is always fast-moving, it's a good idea to have a friend or inamorata act as cohost. The load is lightened, of course, if you've hired a bartender.

Introductions depend entirely on the size of the party. At small gatherings, it may be feasible to introduce newcomers all the way around, but in a larger crowd, introducing each new arrival to all present becomes increasingly time-consuming and stiff; names and faces usually become a blur after four or five exchanges. If possible, make two or three strategic introductions for latecomers—preferably to those with whom they'll have something in common—or, if this means fighting your way across the room, introduce them to whoever is nearest at hand. Again, a cohost can ease your burden.

Hosts, like verbs, are either active or passive, with the active much to be preferred. The passive host is one who feels obliged only to line up his bottles of liquor and then point the way. However pleasant this may be for him, it's not appreciated by the guest who must then do battle with a half-dozen other eager drinkers, all vying for the bottle of Scotch. (There *are* times when a self-serve bar is welcome—at the end of a long, cold drive, for drop-ins at an impromptu drinking party, when the host is unavoidably shunted elsewhere.) For a planned festivity, an active host enjoys doing rather than merely waiting on the sidelines, whether he's offering his own mint juleps, his Rhine-wine punch or his midnight fondue. He'll naturally spot the dwindling rocks in an old-fashioned glass and offer renewals. His vigilant eye, undeterred by his own double Scotch, will tell him that a coaster is needed here, a napkin there. He'll check the air conditioning in the summer or toss an extra log on the fire in the winter. Instead of emptying ashtrays, his or his waiter's sleight of hand will simply put fresh ashtrays in place while the old unobtrusively disappear. Even if he sponsors a catered party, he sees to it that the caterer's drinks provide a special éclat that sets them off from the routine drinks poured at committee meetings or the straight firewater tossed down at nightly commuters' bars. Every active host has a simple test for his drink offerings: Will his guests spot their special excellence? In almost everyone's drinking career, one is bound to meet up sooner or later with a memorable potable—a Ramos gin fizz in New Orleans, an outsize derby daiquiri on a tropical beach, a special champagne cocktail under countless stars. Such drinks don't just happen; the drinkmaster thoughtfully calls the shots or creates them. There are many hosts who, when it comes to food, will turn heaven and every gourmet shop in the hemisphere if necessary to serve a barbecued blue-ribbon shell of aged beef, a platter of braised pheasant in sour cream or a curry of fresh Maine lobster; the active host at his bar will do no less.

Talk about active hosts—in the South there are partisans who specialize in old-fashioneds. Before partytime they'll line up their old-fashioned glasses. In the bottom of each glass, lemon peel, sugar and a trickle of boiling water are worked and reworked by hand with a muddler until the zest of the peel and the syrupy liquid in each glass turn to a rich, almost aged mellowness, when the best bourbon in the land is added. The glasses are stashed in the refrigerator or freezer for further ripening until the guests pile in, and then rocks are placed in each glass just before serving. A host with an aide or two will think nothing of building up 2 or 3 dozen glasses in this manner. Neither he nor his guests ever need an excuse for toasting. They drink to the drink itself.

But while a host should be active and should generously offer his punches, his pitchers or trays of cocktails, he should remember at the height of his wassailing that he's a host and not a hustler. The host should rely on his sixth sense to tell him that bibbers here and there are getting too much of a glow on and the moment has arrived when the restoratives of food and hot coffee are needed to provide the mellow slowdown in which every good drinking party basks. Guests know their own capacities. Let them be pleased with, not plied with, drinks.

A talented drinking host, the kind who's born with a barspoon in his mouth, always feels free to create his own drinking customs. Guests will invariably stretch out their hands to welcome his offerings at almost any hour of the day or night. If a man decides to serve champagne at 11 o'clock in the morning rather than at midnight, his guests will hail the novelty as the host's inalienable right. Generations ago, a bottle of vintage port would be opened late at night, before a fireplace and under the frowns of ancestors preserved in oil and canvas. But a host today, if he wishes, may tap his vintage port after 18 holes of golf, or carry it to his ski lodge, or sip it in a secluded picnic spot, in each case with mellow contentment. Bachelors these days frequently find themselves serving breakfast or brunch. Few if any guests would question the host's judgment in mixing his fresh orange juice with vodka or light rum or Pernod. If called upon, the host could cite numerous precedents for serving spirits in the morning. John Adams regularly took a tankard of hard cider before breakfast. The Germans now, as of yore, serve their Steinhäger gin or schnapps and their thin Westphalian ham on a wooden plate as regular matutinal fare. Novelty for novelty's sake is hardly the aim of the modern host at his bar. But novelty which becomes an unexpected pleasure turns everybody on.

As for tradition, that, too, has its place. Take toasting: No host in his right mind would rise like a stuffed phoenix from the dining table and toast a guest just because his renowned pedigree or station in life made him theoretically toastable. But if one of his guests had just stepped into a new job, was about to fly to the other side of the globe, had just completed his Ph.D. thesis, was just engaged or just married, a toast in his honor would add to the general merriment.

Inviting guests for drinks is a perfect way for a man living alone to entertain. His bachelor apartment may be comparatively small, but if his food and drink are keyed for intimate fun, his friends will happily embrace the chance to crowd into his cozy quarters. More and more hosts nowadays—bachelors as well as nonbachelors—are getting away from the stodgy notion that parties attended must be parties repaid, like meeting a bank note on a certain date. The whole idea isn't to load your guests down with both liquor and an obligation to return the liquor, but simply to achieve fun and friendship.

2

GLASSWARE— THE LONG & SHORT OF IT

Because fine glasses make drinking surprisingly more pleasurable, you should acquire those that are both functional and elegantly shaped. They should be so handsome that the mere sight of the sparkling, clear glasses on the shelf makes you want to pour liquor into them and begin quaffing. In choosing them, it isn't necessary to spend months delving into either the drinking custom of Roman nobles, who fashioned wine cups after the most beautiful breasts of the day, or the practice of old warriors who quaffed mead from the skulls of their enemies. It is helpful, however, to understand a few basic terms.

Crystal—genuine crystal—is glassware that contains lead, and the lead gives it not only a musical tone and magnificent sheen but also a magnificent price. Crystal is seldom tinted or opaline. (The rather common ruby-tinted and green-tinted glasses of just a few years back, originally conceived to hide the cloudiness of wine, are rapidly finding their way into the hands of glass antiquarians. Modern methods have made the great Rhine wines and other white wines almost transparent.)

Glassware labeled "hand-blown" is usually the guide to the handsomest of all beverageware. *Hand-blown* simply refers to the method wherein the glassmaker dips a long tube into a pot of molten glass, picks up a blob at one end of his pipe and then, with his lips and breath as tools, blows until the bowl takes shape. He twists, turns, rubs and paddles the blown bubble until it reaches its final perfect curve. *Blown* glassware is similar but made by machine. *Pressed* glassware—the least expensive—is made by pouring molten glass into molds from which it takes its shape. Today you can find drinkware of pressed glass with heavenly lines and limpid forms. Finally there's *cut glass,* that is, glass cut or engraved and polished to reflect as much prismatic light as possible—the darling of conservative drinkers, now growing semiobsolete. Whatever glassware you choose, buy it if possible from open stock so that matching replacements or additions can always be had.

Regardless of the quality of glassware you decide on, you'll find it available in two basic shapes: tumbler and stemware. The latter is more gracious to the eye and easier on furniture, since condensation on the cold glass rarely makes its way down to the base. But tumbler glasses are less formal, more secure and usually less expensive.

If you want to limit yourself to only two kinds of glasses, the first one to buy is the on-the-rocks glass. It's simply an old-fashioned-cocktail glass, with or without a short stem. In our time it's become the liquid bearer for any potable from ale to zinfandel. It's practical not only for cocktails but for whiskey, rum, gin and vodka, and every now and then—to everyone's intense surprise—it is used for the old-fashioned cocktail of bourbon or Scotch, the drink for which it was originally designed. The other most sought-after glass is the tulip-shaped wineglass, holding from 8 to 11 ounces, allowing ample space for swirling and releasing the wine's bouquet. It, too, has leaped way beyond its birthright and is now the vehicle for any liquid from champagne to stout. Oddball hosts, game for anything, have even been known to pour water into it.

You'll want to supplement your glass supply with such specialized vessels as sour glasses, steins and Pilsners, highball glasses, ponies, jiggers and hollow-stemmed champagne glasses (see the array of glittering glassware in the color section). But it's no longer necessary to stock an infinite variety of glassware. Although it was once customary for the proper host to set out an assortment of glasses at the dinner table in anticipation of the wines that were offered with each course, now, even at black-tie dinners, you seldom see four different kinds of wineglasses arrayed like four empty-headed guardsmen. Nine times out of ten there will be one all-purpose glass for one carefully chosen wine. If a sauternes or champagne is passed with the dessert or if port follows the demitasse, another appropriate glass can be brought on at that time.

It's also unnecessary to have all your glassware in the same pattern. Matching beverageware should be used at the dining table, but before or after dinner, the patterns may vary. Dry sherry on the rocks can be poured on your patio in lightweight old-fashioned glasses; whiskey and soda by the hearth in stately, heavy-bottomed highball glasses.

How many glasses should you own? It depends on the maximum number of people your pad can comfortably contain at any one time. Double it for drop-ins and for normal glassware breakage. Thus, if you normally invite eight for a party, stock 16 of each kind of glass you'd most likely use.

The higher mathematics of whether a drinking glass should hold 6 or $8^{1}/_{2}$ or $10^{5}/_{8}$ ounces isn't important if you're pouring punch from a bowl, or beer from a bottle or keg. You merely pour until you have what your thirst says is a reasonable amount and stop. But if you're concocting a particular cocktail following a particular recipe and the ingredients are designed to fill a $4^{1}/_{2}$-ounce cocktail glass and your glass holds a miserly 3 ounces, you'll find yourself with more drinks than you intended or with seconds that slush around with ice until they're too weak to serve. If you're buying champagne for a party and you don't know whether your glasses hold $5^{1}/_{2}$ ounces or 7 ounces, you can miscalculate badly. For special concoctions and for mass drinking, you really should know the capacity of the drinking vessels you own. If necessary, fill them with water and pour the contents into a measuring glass or beaker from the chem lab. Make a note of their capacity and use it as a guide for the next party.

There are a few practical rules to follow for taking care of your glassware. Wash glasses as soon as possible after each use—in warm water, with a detergent. If they're stemware, wash by hand. Glasses used for sticky liqueurs should be soaked before washing. If two glasses have been stacked together and are locked, place the bottom glass in warm water and fill the top with cold. The resulting expansion and contraction should separate them safely. After washing, rinse in scalding-hot water. Dry with a lint-free towel or, better yet, if thirsty guests aren't waiting for another round of drinks, let them drain dry, turned upside down on a ridged draining surface. Never stack or pile them in the sink, where they're likely to break, scratch or nick. And store them upside down on the shelf—each size in a row, front to back.

After the glasses have been stowed away, check your liquor closet to see what needs to be replenished for the next party.

Among offbeat drinking vessels you may want to consider, there are special glasses emblazoned with hens, tomatoes or oranges designed for hosts who respectively specialize in bullshots, bloody marys and screwdrivers; for the aquatic cocktail hour there are swimming-pool glasses that float; glacier tumblers with walls that retain the cold can be prechilled in the freezing section of your refrigerator for long icy chills of gin and tonics, cuba libres, etc.; Moscow-mule copper cups are available for husky drafts of ginger beer and vodka; the Irish-coffee goblet with thick stem is designed for comfortably grasping the hot brew of coffee, Irish whiskey and cream; for warm wassail in the wintertime, you'll need capacious beverage mugs with handles that stay cool; finally for extra large parties of 50 to 100 people, particularly outdoor bashes, you'll probably want the disposable, well designed, very thin plastic drinkers with no fear of insufficient glasses or clean-up problems. How many kinds of specialized beverageware you'll need depends entirely on your potable life style.

3

KEEP YOUR SPIRITS UP

Let's assume you're planning to stock a home bar and you don't as yet own an ounce of straight stuff. Like many men acquiring the rudiments of the *ars bibendi,* you'll probably think automatically of whiskey, gin and vermouth, the trio that is usually built into the three standard drinks for satisfying the thirsts of 20th Century man—martinis, manhattans and highballs. One kind of gin will do as a starter. You'll need two kinds of vermouth, sweet and dry. When it comes to whiskey, however, you'll need four kinds: American blended whiskey (usually misnamed rye), bourbon, Scotch and Canadian. Thus, a bottle of each, seven in all, would be a possible kickoff. But in less time than it takes to say daiquiri or screwdriver, you realize that rum and vodka would rapidly complete the starting lineup. These, then, are the potables that all barkeeps, public as well as private, constantly reach for, the ones you'd want whether you're host or guest.

Presumably, you won't be drinking alone but often with friends socializing casually with you. For this kind of dropping by and drinking, you must allow for individual tastes in your own neck of the woods. Every host soon learns that a special Scotch provides a warm afterglow for some of his comrades, a certain bourbon is preferred by others. Knowing these choices, you'll stock the kinds of liquor which are most congenial for your own solidly knit friends. Finally, if you entertain at small dinner parties, you'll want a modest supply of postprandial liqueurs and brandy. Allowing, then, for all these liquid pastimes, a typical founding supply might reasonably consist of the following bottled goods in approximately these proportions, in quarts or fifths:

2 Bourbon
3 Blended whiskey, U.S.
3 Scotch whisky
1 Canadian whisky
3 Gin
2 Rum
3 Vodka
1 Dry vermouth
1 Sweet vermouth
1 Brandy
3 Assorted liqueurs (fruit, coffee, crème de menthe, etc.)
Total cost: about $100.

As your spirit world expands, you'll begin to think of diversifying this basic closet with a variety of other potables. If, for example, your basic gin is American, you'll add English imported gins, or perhaps a bottle of Holland genever gin. If you started with light Puerto Rican rum, you might want to add the aged Puerto Rican *añejo* rum or one of the 151-proof rums. Thus, your starting repertory might reasonably be expanded to include varieties like these:

Gin—American, English, Holland, German Steinhäger
Rum—Puerto Rican, Martinique, Virgin
      Islands, Jamaican, Añejo, 151-proof, Hawaiian
Bourbon—86- and 100-proof, bonded,
Scotch—light, heavy-bodied, 12- to 20-
      to 30-year-old
Vodka—80-proof, 100-proof, zubrovka
Brandy—California, cognac, Armagnac,
      calvados, German, Greek Metaxa
Liqueurs—from straight flavors like
      peach to proprietary brands
      like Southern Comfort, Grand

Marnier, Chartreuse, Drambuie,
Benedictine, Cherry Heering,
etc.

Going still further, one might wish to add:

Whiskey—Irish
Unaged brandies—aquavit, slivovitz,
    kirsch
Apéritifs—Campari, Dubonnet, Byrrh,
    Amer Picon

For the average bar host, $80 would cover a reasonable
selection from the two preceding categories. Also available are
30-year-old Scotches that go for about $35 a bottle,
special-reserve rums at about $9 and hoary old cognacs for about
$40. But these are in a rarefied drinking realm and should be
bought only if your connoisseurship really qualifies you to judge
them appreciatively.

Having stocked your bar with potables calculated to satisfy
the tastes of your most sophisticated guests, you may wonder
whether, under any circumstances, you should consider stocking
and serving any of the growing list of bottled premixed cocktails.

Premixed drinks are especially useful if you're hiring a
bartender of doubtful talent for an evening's work. At the end of
a long, dusty day, you may not have fresh lemons for your
tom-collins thirst; the bottled gin sours made into tall drinks
with ice and club soda will perform well as understudies, while
bottled whiskey sours elongated with ice and soda are quickly
transformed into whiskey collinses. On boat trips, in cramped
galley quarters, at wayside picnics, for tail-gate bars at football or
ski sites, the premixed partymates are most welcome. But the
fact is that little labor is saved by using them. If you're serving a
bottled martini, for example, you still have to prechill the
glasses, take ice out of the freezer, mix and stir the makings in a
shaker, pour them and adorn each martini with an olive or a
lemon twist.

Nevertheless, effort aside, there are some premixed cocktails
that will serve you well. The number of such potables cramming
the shelves in liquor stores has grown from a few standard
combos to such specialty items as mai tais and stingers—and a
few of them are actually first-rate. Among the best of the lot is
the bottled manhattan, which may be even better than the one
you make yourself. When the two ingredients—whiskey and
vermouth—not only mingle but marry, as they do in the bottle,
the result is as superior to the fresh-made mixture as a curry on
the third or fourth day. And no one would presume to fault—or
imitate—the excellence of English Pimm's No. 1 Cup, the

definitive premixed base for a gin sling; or the subtlety of that aristocrat of after-dinner drinks, B & B, an epicurean admixture of brandy and Benedictine.

But be warned that there are limits to these distillery-born combinations. While manufactured manhattans, martinis, rob roys and black russians may turn up winners, the great majority of premixes made with fruit juice draw an average to poor grade, simply because bottled orange or lemon juice can't begin to match the fresh.

Our advice: Be as selective about the premixes you purchase as you are about the appropriate occasions to serve them. For most purposes—and people—it's more fitting (and more fun) to do it yourself.

There will be times when your normal bar supply will be temporarily expanded for mass drinking—a big cocktail celebration, a holiday blowout or similar affair where the number of heads and the possible number of drinks must be estimated. In such cases, the slide rule works like this: A fifth of hard liquor will be enough for 17 1½-ounce (standard-size) drinks. A quart will provide 21 drinks. At a dinner party, count on two to four jiggers of hard liquor per person, dispensed in either straight or mixed forms. At a bachelor party, allow from three to six jiggers.

Finally, a few sensible reminders to all custodians of liquor:

Your bar may be a movable one on wheels, a built-in piece of sectional furniture, the shelves above a clothes closet, a tea wagon or a wicker hamper in the back of your station wagon. Reserve supplies may be stashed away wherever it's convenient—in cellars or attics. But within easy reach, close to your mixing counter, there should be one bottle of each commonly used liquor. Your inventory isn't an old-rock collection to be hunted behind bookshelves, nor is a host normally able to pop fifths Houdini-like out of a silk hat. Keep everything arranged so conveniently that you can find the liquor you're looking for without fumbling or squinting at labels. For big blowouts, punch-bowl and holiday parties, fill in your stock well in advance of the fest itself. Don't get caught scrounging for replacements at the eleventh hour.

A host may commence many things; he may finish few. But every host at his home-bar base learns that the one thing that always gets finished is liquor. Still, you may now and then find an odd bottle which has reached the aged-in-the-coffin stage. Take such oddments, supplement them with fresh liquors and turn them into coolers, pitchers or punches. It's fun to invent them and to make room simultaneously for new liquors that may readily become a going concern.

Filling a wine rack or a wine cellar is a separate avocation dealt with under chapter 15.

4

ALL THE TRIMMINGS

The applied art of mixing alcoholic drinks depends on many things that aren't alcohol. There would be no screwdrivers without orange juice, no daiquiris without limes, and Irish coffee without coffee and whipped cream would be just a glass of whiskey. Alcohol must be made tart, sweet, rich, bitter, foamy and, in countless other ways, congenial to sophisticated taste buds. Frequently it's garnished in a manner that accents a drink's appearance as well as its flavor and aroma, as with the olive in the martini, the cucumber peel in the Pimm's Cup or the strawberry in the champagne cocktail.

Quantities of accessories for mixing will depend upon whether you're going in for mass drinking or for more modest quenching. As a rule, small containers of seasonings like bitters are less likely to lose their zest than larger bottles that hang around on the shelf too long. Large bottles of syrups like Falernum or red-currant syrup will lose their bright color and flavor if untouched for months. If this occurs, don't hesitate to discard the old stock and buy fresh replacements. Fruits or other perishables should be emphatically fresh.

The checklist which follows should be consulted not only for setting up a basic bar stock but every time you're hosting a drinking party of sizable dimensions. Normal bar items which belong in any basic bar are differentiated from those less frequently used by an asterisk.

Almonds   Use them whole for Scandinavian glögg, sliced or julienne for floating on punches and tall summer drinks.

Almond syrup   Called orgeat when made in France, orzata when made in Italy.

Apple juice   Often found in congenial company with vodka. The spacesaving frozen concentrated variety is handy for parties. (See also **cider.**)

Apricots   Whole peeled canned apricots are better than the fresh for velvety blender drinks.

Bananas   Should always be speckled ripe for bar purposes. They're turned to best account in banana daiquiris.

*Bitter lemon   A superior mixer in high esteem among the gin-and-tonic crowd.

*Bitters   Best known is Angostura from Trinidad, but orange bitters are better for drinks that benefit from a soupçon of citrus. It's a good idea to keep Peychaud's bitters on hand for making New Orleans sazeracs.

Butter   Use fresh sweet butter for a mellow glow in hot buttered rum.

Cassis   This black-currant syrup—*simpatico* with vermouth—is similar to crème de cassis, except that it contains no alcohol.

*Cherries   Most common are the maraschino, with or without stems. Mint-flavored cherries provide a green decorative note; brandied pitted red cherries and pitted black cherries, with or without rum flavor, complete the cherry constellation.

Cider   In groceries, *apple cider* and *apple juice* are synonymous terms for pasteurized juice of the apple. Country cider, sold at roadside stands, is often partially fermented apple juice. Hard cider is apple juice fermented to the wine stage.

Cinnamon sticks   Used for both stirring and flavoring hot mulled mixes.

Cloves   Add them whole (not ground) to hot winter wassail.

*Club soda   Buy it in splits for individual drinks, the 12-ounce size for several highballs, and quarts for parties or punch bowls. Most national brands have good bite and can keep their fizz locked up overnight or even several days. Generally, club soda provides more zing than seltzer water despite the convenience of the siphon.

Cocktail mixes   (Not to be confused with bottled premixed cocktails.) Nonalcoholic mixes are never the equal of the fresh ingredients, but many hosts like to keep them on hand as reserve ammunition. Mixes for the bloody mary, daiquiri, mai tai, manhattan, navy grog, scorpion and whiskey sour have become standard items in many home bars. While all bottles have specific mixing directions on them, try varying the alcohol-mix ratio to suit your own taste.

Coffee   Brew it fresh and strong for steaming Irish coffee.

Cranberry juice   Adds brilliant color and eye-opening tartness to punches and vodka drinks.

Cream   Use heavy sweet cream for alexanders and dessert drinks.

Currant syrup   Red currants (rather than black cassis berries) go into this tart extract. It's not a substitute for grenadine but a flavoring component in its own right.

Eggs   There would be no nog without them—nor a number of frothy confections such as clover clubs, silver fizzes and the like.

Falernum   A delightful West Indian syrup made from almonds and spices.

*Fomee or Frothee   A few dashes of either of these will give drinks the creamy head supplied otherwise by egg whites; however, the head tends to disappear faster than an egg-white head. Both eliminate the taste of albumen from which some drinkers shy.

*Ginger ale   The drier the better for modern tastes.

Ginger beer   The second-fiddle catalyst in a moscow mule.

Grape juice   One of vodka's many compatible consorts. The frozen concentrated form is a spacesaver.

Grapefruit juice   The one fruit juice that's better canned or frozen than fresh, undoubtedly because the latter is often so insipid and varies so much in flavor. The unsweetened variety is best for drink making.

Grenadine   A bright-red syrup made from the pulp of pomegranates, it's used in jack rose, clover club, bacardi, and many other cocktails, as well as in punches and tall drinks. Unlike most additives, it can be stored on the shelf for long periods without losing its tint or tartness.

Guava jelly   Melted down to a syrup, it's used for sweetening Caribbean rum drinks.

Honey   Use a light-colored honey for bar purposes. If granulation occurs, place the jar in hot water for a few minutes and then stir until the granules disappear.

*Lemons   They should be firm and green-stemmed. The size of the fruit is not too important, since most recipes using lemon juice are most successful following ounce measurements.

Lemon juice   The bottled juice, whether in glass or plastic containers, never equals the fresh-squeezed variety and should be kept on hand for emergency use only.

*Limes   A far from silent partner in almost all rum drinks. Choose limes with smooth green skin rather than yellow.

Lime juice   As with lemon juice, the bottled product should be used only in emergencies.

*Lime juice, Rose's   Actually a tart syrup rather than a substitute for fresh lime juice, it's the essential ingredient in a gimlet.

Mangoes or mango nectar   An exotic ingredient in certain tall rum drinks.

Maple syrup   Occasionally used as a drink sweetener.

Milk   Essential in many brandy drinks, milk punch and eggnogs.

Mint   Fresh mint leaves are best if taken from the mint patch directly to julep cups or glasses. In buying them, choose mint leaves that are deep green rather than yellowed, small tender leaves rather than large.

Nutmeg   For flips, nogs, mulls and other hot cold-weather drinks, buy the whole nutmeg for grating rather than the ground.

*Olives   Although the small pitted variety is a standard bar ingredient, many martini men prefer the unpitted, stuffed colossal or supercolossal. There are also almond-, anchovy- and onion-stuffed olives, all of which are delightful; and even pitted black olives are used in certain martini-type drinks. Be sure to store opened jars in the refrigerator; olives should be kept in their own brine and washed just before serving.

*Onions, cocktail or pearl   The *sine qua non* of the gibson cocktail. Buy them in small jars and store in the refrigerator after opening.

Orange-flower water   An essential ingredient in the Ramos gin fizz, it's available in drugstores as well as some liquor stores.

*Oranges   Juice from fresh oranges is always better than frozen juice or the kind that comes in cartons or bottles, even though the fresh fruit varies widely in sweetness and color during the year. (Frozen juice also varies widely in quality from one brand to the next. If you must use it, say, for large blowouts, select the best brand you can find.)

Orange slices   Actually wedges rather than slices, they're packed in syrup in jars. They provide a rich garnish for old-fashioneds.

Orgeat   (from France) or
orzata (from Italy) Nonalcoholic almond syrups.

Papaya syrup or nectar   One of the tropic juices occasionally called for in Polynesian rum drinks.

Passion-fruit juice   A pleasantly tart nectar often used in rum drinks.

Peaches   Sliced fresh in season, they make an elegant adornment for champagne, sparkling Rhine wine and wine cups. Elbertas—frozen or canned—are best for crushed-ice blender drinks.

Pineapple   When buying, check for ripeness: The leaves should

come out easily and the fruit should have a heavy, musky
pineapple aroma. Pineapple cocktail sticks in syrup are a
pleasant cocktail garnish.

Pineapple juice   Best for bar purposes is the frozen concentrated
juice, canned unsweetened next. If canned juice is stored in the
refrigerator after opening the can, be sure to pour it into a glass
jar tightly covered to ward off other refrigerator aromas.

Quin-tessence   A concentrate for making quinine water by
adding to siphon water or club soda, it's useful on boats and in
other cramped bar quarters.

*Quinine water   A staple bar item that you should keep on
hand in quantity for warm-weather drinks.

Raspberries   Use fresh or frozen in summer wine cups, punch
bowls and blender drinks.

Raspberry syrup   This bar sweetener, not as tart as grenadine,
has its own distinctive fruit-with-a-punch flavor.

Seltzer water   Fizz from a seltzer bottle seldom has the
liveliness of club soda, but it's convenient. A cartridge charge for
permanent siphon equipment is a modern spacesaver.

*Seven-up   The most popular of all light carbonated lemon
drinks, this one can be mixed with almost any conceivable
potable.

Soft drinks   Besides cola drinks and ginger ale, such flavors as
pineapple, coffee and grapefruit are pleasant tall-drink extenders.

Strawberries   Fresh berries make a colorful garnish for May
wine, wine cups, fancy drinks and summer fruit bowls. Frozen
ones can be used in blender drinks with crushed ice.

Strawberry syrup   One of the brightest members of the family of
red bar sweeteners. Be sure it's a natural, not artificial, fruit
flavor—and don't keep it too long on the shelf.

*Sugar   For bar purposes, superfine sugar, which dissolves
quickly, is preferred to plain granulated; but if kept too long after
the box is opened, it will tend to lump, in which case it should
be put through a fine sieve. Do not use confectioners' sugar.
Brown sugar is rarely called for except in hot mulled drinks.

Sugar syrup   The commercially prepared kind is usually too
thick for blending easily; make your own (see page 32).

5

SAY WHEN

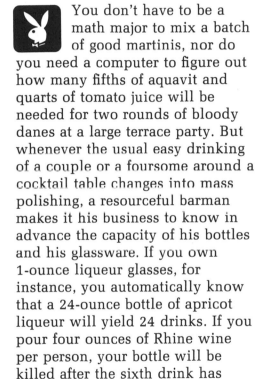 You don't have to be a math major to mix a batch of good martinis, nor do you need a computer to figure out how many fifths of aquavit and quarts of tomato juice will be needed for two rounds of bloody danes at a large terrace party. But whenever the usual easy drinking of a couple or a foursome around a cocktail table changes into mass polishing, a resourceful barman makes it his business to know in advance the capacity of his bottles and his glassware. If you own 1-ounce liqueur glasses, for instance, you automatically know that a 24-ounce bottle of apricot liqueur will yield 24 drinks. If you pour four ounces of Rhine wine per person, your bottle will be killed after the sixth drink has been served.

The bar measurements below will provide you with the information needed to plot your way from dash to demijohn. They'll also help you take a single drink recipe and magnify it at will or reduce a giant punch-bowl recipe to the desired amount of swig.

Tea   Punch bowls of colonial times, now happily being revived, often called for brewed tea as part of the liquid. Brew it for five minutes; then let it cool at room temperature to prevent the drink from clouding.

*Tomato juice   The base for bloody marys and many other pick-me-ups. Buy straight tomato juice rather than tomato-juice cocktail. Jars, rather than cans, are best for refrigerator storage.

Vegetable juice   Sometimes preferred to tomato juice in a bloody mary because its blend of flavors provides a somewhat livelier, more subtle flavor to the drink.

*Water   At out-of-the-way picnic nooks and lonely beach sites, a jar of this offbeat ingredient is sometimes desirable as an additive to Scotch. In localities where tap water is rusty or has a pronounced taste of chlorine, use bottled spring water.

Worcestershire sauce   A snappy accent for prairie oysters, bloody marys and the like.

Dash For all drink recipes in this book, a dash means ¹/₈
teaspoon; two dashes will thus fill a ¹/₄-teaspoon measure.
Theoretically, a dash is the amount of liquid that squirts out of a
bottle equipped with a dash stopper. Stoppers, however, vary in
size, and to different liquor dispensers a dash means anything
from three drops up; but dashes have potent flavor or they
wouldn't be dashes, so it's important to be as accurate as
possible. Thus, if you're making sazeracs for 16 people and you
need 16 times a dash of Pernod, a little calculating will quickly
tell you that you need two teaspoons of Pernod, and it's best to
measure it exactly rather than to take a clumsy guess.

Teaspoon ¹/₃ tablespoon, or ¹/₆ ounce. Use a measuring
teaspoon, not a long-handled barspoon, which is designed for
mixing rather than measuring.

Tablespoon 3 teaspoons, or ¹/₂ ounce.

Pony 1 ounce, or the small end of a double-ended measuring
jigger. Also the usual capacity of the liqueur glass or the
pousse-café glass. Miniature liquor bottles usually contain 1
ounce, or ¹/₁₆ pint.

Jigger 1¹/₂ ounces. Also called a bar measuring glass, it's the
standard measure for mixing individual drinks, though generous
hosts use a 2-ounce jigger. Although jiggers are supposed to
provide exact measurements, they're sometimes grossly
inaccurate, so it's a good idea, if possible, to check any new
jigger you buy with a lab measuring glass.

Wineglass Used as a measuring term, it means 4 ounces, which
is the old-fashioned wineglass filled to the brim. Though today
wine is generally served in a much larger glass—one-third full to
permit the wine to be swirled for releasing its
bouquet—*wineglass* as a 4-ounce measure still appears in some
drink recipes and in food recipes.

Split or nip 6 to 8 ounces. Eight ounces is ¹/₂ pint, or the
contents of a standard measuring cup. One refers to a split of
champagne, but the same quantity of stout is called a nip.

Pint 16 ounces; ¹/₂ quart; 2 standard measuring cups. Many
bottles listed on bar menus as a pint of champagne or a pint of
wine are actually half of a fifth, or 11 to 13 ounces, and many
small bottles of liqueur are in a no-measure land. Strega, for
instance, is sold in both 10-ounce and 11¹/₂-ounce sizes;
Chartreuse contains 11.8 ounces; Triple Sec is ⁴/₅ pint, or 12.8
ounces. *Moral:* Read all bottle labels carefully before you buy.

Fifth   25.6 ounces; $^4/_5$ quart; $^1/_5$ gallon. Many bottles of still wine don't quite reach the fifth size and frequently hold only 24 ounces. Champagne (traditionally called quarts on wine lists) may vary from 24 to 26 ounces per bottle.

Quart   32 ounces; 2 pints; 4 measuring cups; $^1/_4$ gallon. Not to be confused (in Canada and England) with the imperial quart, which is 38.4 ounces or (in continental Europe) with the liter, 33.8 ounces. Most imported vermouths come to the U.S. in a "quart" bottle containing a stingy 30 ounces.

Magnum   52 ounces; the double-size champagne bottle.

Half gallon   64 ounces. In some states, hard liquors are sometimes sold in the full 2-quart size; the bottles are a bit unwieldy but they're usually sold at a price advantage.

In the U.S., bottles larger than a half gallon are infrequently seen, although occasionally you'll notice a monster bottle of wine or champagne displayed in a liquor-store window. It's more a conversation piece than the kind of container you'd want to carry home to your apartment-size liquor cabinet. The larger specimens are listed below:

Jeroboam   104 ounces, or a little more than 4 fifths. It's the largest domestic champagne bottle.

Tappit-hen   About 77 ounces, or 3 fifths.

Rehoboam   About 160 ounces, or $1^1/_5$ gallons.

Extremely large bottles of wine seen in Europe are seldom shipped to the U.S. Because of the difficulties of making huge bottles in uniformly exact capacities, the following measurements are all approximations.

Methuselah   208 ounces; about $1^3/_5$ gallons. The largest-size champagne bottle exported from France.

Salmanazar   312 ounces; about $2^1/_2$ gallons.

Balthazar   416 ounces; about $3^1/_3$ gallons.

Nebuchadnezzar   520 ounces; about 4 gallons with a slight plus.

Demijohn   From 1 to 10 gallons.

For the quantities of liquor, mixers, etc., to buy for party purposes, see "Drink Calculator," chapter 23.

6

BARMANSHIP

 Given a choice selection of spirits, fresh and flavorful mixing ingredients and attractive glassware, the host at home is still several steps away from the professional bartender's finesse, an art which is public property for every drinker astride a barstool to behold. It looks deceptively easy, especially to the eye that's been mellowed by two or three dry martinis. But there are skills, tricks of the trade and tips in creating and serving drinks—icemanship, mixing, stirring, garnishing and others—which can be briefly explained in the same way that a pro on the golf course can make a detailed analysis of each of the strokes and positions he's carefully mastered. Familiarize yourself with the basic barman's skills that follow, consult them for special potables, and every time you pour drinks, you'll generate among your guests the mood described superlatively by Fielding as "one universal grin."

Icemanship   There was a time when rocks were really rocky, when a bartender armed with an ice pick hacked away at his block of ice until it eventually disappeared. On a summer's day you'd ask for a gin rickey and it would come to you with one or two tottering crags of ice. It looked cool, but it couldn't possibly stand up to a contemporary gin rickey, because of a simple undisputed fact: Ice is now much colder than it once was. Frozen water may be 32° F. or, just as possibly these days, –32° F. Most of the cubes in the present ice age range from 0 to −10° F. Needless to say, for fast cooler-offers, the colder the ice the better. Crushed ice or cracked ice is chillier in a bar glass than the cubed variety, because more cooling ice surface comes into intimate contact with the drink.

The number of muscle-powered as well as plug-in ice crushers seems to have kept pace with the population explosion. There are ice crushers, used as blender attachments, that can reduce a tray of ice cubes to crushed ice or snow ice in 20 to 30 seconds. Even simple ice trays are now designed not only for cubes but for ice slices, 38 to a tray, and, perhaps most useful of all, for cracked ice. Lacking this equipment, a man needn't find the technique for cracking or crushing ice too difficult. Simply place the ice cubes in a canvas bag designed for this purpose or in a large, clean kitchen towel (wrap the towel around the ice so that there is a double thickness of cloth); on a carving board, bang the bag or towel with a mallet or the smooth side of a meat tenderizer. Keep your banging somewhat restrained if you want fair-sized pieces of cracked ice; for crushed ice, whack away with abandon.

Every barman—amateur or pro—should insist that his ice be clean, hard and dry and should make each drink or batch of drinks with fresh ice. Hoard your ice in the freezing section of your refrigerator until you actually need it. Use ice buckets with vacuum sides and lids; plastic-foam ice tubs are convenient for throwaway service. When you empty your ice trays, don't run water over them unless it's absolutely necessary to spring the ice free. Running water causes them eventually to stick together after they're put into the bucket. Most new ice trays, especially those with no-stick surfaces, discharge their cargo with a single swift yank. There are refrigerators that not only make ice cubes automatically but turn them out and store them night and day—a comforting thought when one is party-planning. If the water in your fiefdom is heavily chlorinated, use bottled spring water for ice. Finally, as a host, be the most prodigal of icemen. If you're gambling on the fact that you may just possibly get by with two buckets of ice at a summer fling, don't gamble. Provide at least three or four bucketfuls for supercooling your crowd. If your ice-making equipment is somewhat limited, find out before your rumpus takes place just where you can buy or borrow additional ice.

Punch-bowl ice There are still commercial icehouses where you
can buy a chunk of ice tailored to fit your punch bowl. But you
can make your own ice floe by filling a deep pot or plastic
bucket with water—at least a day in advance of the party—and
placing it in the freezer. The top of the ice may congeal in a
hump as the water expands. When you're ready to use it, run
warm water over the sides of the pot and invert it, permitting the
round glacier, with its smooth bottom upright, to slide into your
bowl.

Aquavit in ice At smorgasbord parties, it's a delightful custom
to serve a bottle of aquavit (or sometimes straight vodka) encased
in a block of ice. The job's simple: Place the bottle of liquor in
an empty 2-quart paper milk container with the top removed; fill
the container with water; then set it in the freezer. The alcohol
will keep the liquor from solidifying as the surrounding water
freezes. Finally, tear off the paper or remove it with a knife. The
long robe of ice with its rectangular sides should be partly
covered with a napkin for serving and then returned to the
freezer to preserve it for second skoals.

Frappéed ice cap After-dinner frappés—refreshing alternatives
to cloying desserts—are made by drizzling a liqueur or liqueurs
over finely crushed ice in a saucer champagne glass. A cool and
convenient variation is to make them beforehand and store them
a few hours or even overnight in the freezer. In time the liqueur
settles to the glass bottom, and the ice forms a solid cap on top;
after you remove it from the freezer, the cap will loosen slightly,
allowing the icy liqueur to be sipped from the rim of the glass
sans straw.

Chilling glasses Every cocktail glass should be chilled before
it's filled. There are three ways: (1) Before drinking time, store
glasses in the refrigerator or freezer until they're cold. (2) Bury
the glasses completely in cracked ice. (3) Fill them with cracked
ice and stir the ice a few times before pouring drinks.

Frosting glasses For a longer-lasting frost, dip the glasses into
water and, while still dripping, place them in your refrigerator's
freezer section (set at its coldest point) for 2 or 3 hours.

Sugar-frosting glasses Glasses for appropriate cocktails, coolers
and liqueurs can be made more fascinating to the eyes and lips
by frosting their rims with sugar. To administer this fancy
finishing touch, make sure, first of all, that you use superfine
sugar—not the regular granulated or confectioners'. Moisten the
rim of each glass, inside and out, to a depth of about 1/4 inch
before dipping into sugar. There are four easy rites: (1) Anoint
the rim with a small wedge of lemon or orange; invert the glass

to shake off extra juice; dip into sugar. (2) Rub rim with lemon or orange peel, using the outside of the rind; then dip into sugar. (3) Dip rim into grenadine, Falernum or any other syrup—or any desired liqueur—then into sugar. (4) Moisten rim with coffee liqueur; then dip into a mixture of 3 teaspoons superfine sugar mixed well with 1 teaspoon powdered instant coffee.

The contents of all sugar-frosted glasses, needless to add, should be sipped without benefit of a straw. For party purposes, a large number of glasses may be sugar-frosted and stored in the refrigerator or freezer until drinktime.

Preparing peel   Lemon or orange peel should be cut just before using to save volatile oils. Use a lemon-twist cutter or a very sharp paring knife for the job. And, if possible, avoid cutting a large amount of peel before partytime.

Simple syrup   In many drinks, such as the whiskey sour, some barmen prefer sugar syrup to loose sugar, since it makes drinks velvety smooth and—because alcohol is a notoriously poor solvent for sugar—is often easier to use because it blends without prolonged stirring or shaking. Others object to syrup on the grounds that, in such potables as the daiquiri, sugar adds to the bite of the drink. In the final analysis, your own taste should dictate the sweetener best suited for your drink.

To make a batch of simple syrup, bring 1 cup water to a boil and stir in 1 cup sugar; simmer for 1½ minutes. By that time, the mixture will have been reduced to approximately 1 cup, making it possible to substitute equal amounts of syrup for sugar in any bar recipe where it may be preferred. Pour it into a bottle or syrup container and store at room temperature. After a while, there may be some crystallization of sugar, but it won't affect the syrup's usefulness.

The dairy bar   As indicated earlier, cream for drink making, particularly as an ingredient in liqueur cocktails for dessert, should be heavy, not light. And if it's been standing for a day or two, check it for freshness. Note that when it's mixed with lemon juice, as it is in a clover-club cocktail, it tends to turn after a few minutes; that is, while not actually spoiling, it does become thickish and somewhat clotted. Therefore, when using cream with tart fruit juices, mix your drinks as closely as possible to serving time. Like cream, milk for eggnogs and milk punch should be checked for freshness; ditto for butter in hot buttered rum.

A good egg   When a whole egg is used in a single drink, its richness is sometimes overpowering, particularly in one as small as a sherry flip. To avoid this, use a small pullet egg for a single drink or two large eggs for three drinks. Eggs, of course, must be

strictly fresh; to double-check, empty the egg into a dish before
dropping it into the shaker or blender. If it's fresh, the yolk will remain whole and the white will be thick, not runny.

To separate whites from yolks, place two small dishes or cups on your working surface. Holding the egg over one dish, crack the shell in the center with a knife; then pour the yolk back and forth between shell halves while the white slips into the dish below. Drop the yolk into the second dish. Occasionally the yolk alone is used in a drink; it may also be saved for an omelet or hollandaise sauce or other use.

Filling the shaker   Ice should always go into the shaker first, alcohol last; by giving ice first place, all the ingredients that follow will be cooled on their way down. Furthermore, once you acquire the habit of adding the liquor last, it's unlikely that you'll inadvertently double the spirits or, worse yet, forget them altogether, both possible errors for hosts taking jolts along with their guests. The order of ingredients between ice and alcohol follows no dogmatic ritual; whether sugar should precede the lemon juice or vice versa isn't important as far as the final drink is concerned. Another useful control for drinking hosts is to put the correct number of glasses for the needed drinks in front of the shaker before adding *anything*—a clear reminder of how many dashes of bitters, how many spoons of this or jiggers of that are necessary. Finally, never fill a shaker to the brim; allow enough room for all ingredients to be tossed back and forth, to set up the clear, pleasant rattle of ice.

Measuring   Guests at a pour-it-yourself bar should feel free to pour as many fingers as they please, but if the host himself is preparing any kind of mixed drinks, he should trust the jigger rather than his eye, just as the best professional barmen always do. In simple drinks such as Scotch and soda, as well as in more complicated tipple, too much liquor can be unpleasant and, in a way, as inhospitable as too little.

Stirring   To keep their icy clarity, cocktails such as martinis, manhattans, rob roys and gimlets should always be stirred, not shaken (though it's no major disaster if you unwittingly shake rather than stir a martini; it will turn cloudy, but only for a few minutes). For proper dilution, stir every batch of cocktails at least 20 times. When carbonated water is added to tall drinks, stir as briefly as possible; most of the liquor rises to the top automatically, and excessive stirring only dissipates the sparkle in the water.

Shaking   Shake the shaker, not yourself. Don't just rock it—hold it well out in front of you and move it diagonally from lower left to upper right, or in any other convenient motion, with a pistonlike rhythm. In time the cold, icy feel of the cocktail shaker will tell you that the drinks have a creamy head and are ready for pouring. Shake one round of drinks at a time and rinse the shaker thoroughly after each use.

Pouring When drinks are shaken, pour them at once; don't let the cocktail shaker become a watery grave. If extra liquid is left in the shaker, strain it off at once; the so-called dividends left standing in ice will be weak replicas of the original drinks. Never pour drinks higher than 1/4 inch from the rim of the glass. In the case of wine, a large glass should never be more than one-third to one-half full to permit swirling of the wine and liberation of its aromas. In large brandy snifters, a 1 1/2-ounce drink is the maximum. When garnishes such as orange slices and pineapple sticks are being used, allow sufficient room to add them without causing the drink to overflow. When pouring more than one mixed drink, line up the glasses rim to rim, fill them half-full, then pour again to the same height in each glass.

Horse's neck Drink recipes sometimes call for the peel of an entire orange or lemon in one continuing spiral. To prepare it, use a small, sharp paring knife (not a lemon-twist cutter) and, starting at the stem end, cut a continuous 1/2-inch swath around the fruit; avoid breaking the "neck" as the piece becomes longer.

Floating liqueurs Drinks are sometimes served with a spoonful of liqueur or 151-proof rum floating on top; usually such toppings are merely poured slowly from the spoon against the side of the glass. The pousse-café, on the other hand, is a multilayered after-dinner drink whose rainbow effect can be created in any one of four ways: (1) First pour the heaviest liqueur slowly against the side of the glass, following it in turn with progressively lighter liqueurs, a procedure that can be learned by trial and error or by following the drink recipes on page 264. (2) Pour the liqueurs over an inverted small spoon held at the top of the glass. (3) Pour the liqueurs down the side of a mixing rod held in the glass. (4) Pour liqueurs slowly into the glass in any sequence you desire, place the glass in your refrigerator, and in time each liqueur will find its own weight level, forming distinct layers.

Flaming liquors Occasionally brandy or liqueurs are set aflame in a drink (see Blue Blazer, page 277). For this bit of showmanship, the liquor should be preheated briefly—not boiled, which causes the alcohol to evaporate, but simply made hot enough so that when a flame is held to the liquor, it will begin quietly to blaze.

Drink garnishes   There are two kinds. Some, like the twist of lemon in the martini or the cucumber peel in the Pimm's Cup, actually transform the drink's aroma and savor; others are frankly adornments for bedecking the festive glass but, like neckties, which are also dispensable, should be tastefully chosen. Some of the main garnishes—like the cherry in the manhattan—are purchased in bottles or jars and are listed in chapter 5. The guide below tells you how to prepare your own drink garnishes and put them to best use.

Almonds   Sliced almonds or almonds julienne are sometimes floated on tall drinks or punches. They're best if toasted beforehand and slightly cooled: Spread the almonds in a shallow pan with a small amount of melted butter. Toast them in a moderate oven 10 to 15 minutes or until light brown, stirring from time to time to avoid charring; then sprinkle generously with salt and cool before adding to drinks.

Bananas   Cut firm, ripe bananas into slices and immediately dip into tart fruit juice to keep the fruit from darkening. Slices cut from rim to center and fastened onto the rim of a glass make a delicious adornment for banana daiquiris.

Fresh cherries   Remove the stems from fresh Bing or Royal Anne cherries; then remove the pits with a sharp-pointed paring knife or cherry pitter.

Whole coconut   Like the whole pineapple, the whole coconut is sometimes used as a bearer for rum potations. The end *opposite* the eyes should be cut off. Holding the eye end in one hand, strike the opposite end a sharp, glancing blow with a heavy French knife. Pour off liquid. Place the coconut cup in a deep dessert dish with cracked ice to keep the cup in a stable position.

Cucumber peel   A cool complement to Pimm's No. 1 Cup as well as wine cups and other slakers of summer thirsts. Using a sharp paring knife or a lemon-twist cutter, slice the peel about $1/2$ inch wide, but use it sparingly; it's surprisingly pungent.

Flowers   The exotic fragrance of tame or wild orchids, gardenias, roses and hibiscus blossoms not only ornaments drinks but also enhances the flavors of rum and fruit juices in tall potables as well as summer punch bowls.

Lemon, lime or orange slices   Cut the fruit crosswise just before adding to your drinks. Whenever possible, place the slice on the rocks so that the nostrils almost meet the fruit when the drink is sipped. Or you may cut each slice from rim to center and affix it to the rim of the glass.

Melons   Any thick, ripe melon, such as honeydew, Persian, casaba or Cranshaw, may be cut into round balls (using a parisienne-potato cutter).

Mint leaves   You may not be able to reach out of your penthouse window and grab fresh mint leaves, but mint should be as close to garden-fresh as possible, with tender young, rather than overgrown, leaves. The leaves may be dipped into syrup and then into superfine sugar before planting in drinks.

Nutmeg   Though most spices for hot winter drinks, like cinnamon sticks, whole cloves and whole allspice, are simply dropped into the drink, nutmeg is generally ground. You can buy it that way, but for best effect, buy it whole and grate it fresh, either by using a nutmeg grater or by rubbing it over the fine side of a square metal grater.

Pineapple   Like the coconut, pineapple can serve both as a garnish and as a fancy substitute drinking vessel for outsize rum drinks—when the fruit is part of the drink. To prepare whole pineapple as a drinking vessel, lop off the leafy top and cut out the deep cone of fruit with a long narrow-bladed knife or meat-boning knife; then remove more of the interior with a grapefruit knife—but be careful not to pierce the shell, or your drink will spring a leak.

For making pineapple sticks or wedges, start by lopping the cap off, using a heavy, sharp knife, removing the leaves with one slice. Then cut off and discard a bottom slice about $1/2$ inch thick. Holding the fruit upright, slice off the skin from top to bottom and gouge out the remaining pieces with a pointed paring knife, making sure that the outside is completely edible. Finally, cut it in half from top to bottom, place fruit flat side down and cut lengthwise into equal wedges of any desired thickness; then slice off the core end of each wedge. Cut each long wedge into smaller ones—about $2 1/2$ inches to make pineapple sticks, $3/4$ inch thick to make chunks.

If the fruit is very tart, sprinkle it heavily with sugar and marinate 3 to 4 hours, or even overnight, before using in drinks.

Pomegranate seeds   In drinks made with grenadine, a few seeds of the pomegranate, from which the syrup is made, are sometimes added for their tart succulence.

Strawberries   Some prize strawberries come with their own long stems, perfect for plucking from a bar glass. Strawberries may be dipped into red syrup such as grenadine or into beaten jelly. Outsize berries may be cut in half through the stem end.

Tropical fruit For rum libations, fresh mangoes or papayas may be cut into long pieces like pineapple sticks or into chunks about ³/₄ inch thick.

Finally, a note on retrieving fresh-fruit garnishes: No strict code of etiquette, fortunately, exists; small pieces of fruit like melon balls, strawberries, etc., may be dropped directly into a drink and later retrieved with a spoon, cocktail spear or, for that matter, the bare hand. But for convenience as well as eye appeal, the fruit may be affixed to a cocktail spear, which can then be placed into the end of a straw (if the drink is a tall cooler) or across the rim of the glass.

PART TWO

delineating the delights and
distinctions of spirits, wine and beer

7

WHISKEY— PROOF POSITIVE

Bobbie Burns, liquordom's Scottish laureate, left no doubt about the wellspring of his inspiration when he said, "O whisky, soul o' play and pranks,/ Accept a bardie's gratefu' thanks." Americans say thanks not in verse but in the gallonage they drink. Three out of every four bottles of the distilled spirits with which they now commune are whiskey. Most of it, of course, is really whiskey spelled with an e—perhaps for excellence—an added tribute which the thrifty Scots and Canadians have never found essential.

Any knowledgeable owner of a liquor cabinet knows that he can get by with one kind of gin, one kind of vodka, one kind of brandy and one, maybe two kinds of rum. But when it comes to whiskey, he should be able to dispense at least four—and preferably five— different kinds: U.S. blended, bourbon, Canadian, Scotch and Irish. And if his whiskey outlook is liberal, he'll offer two from each class.

The making of whiskey in all countries follows steps that are essentially the same: A mash is made of grain, malt turns it to sugar, yeast turns it to alcohol, heat vaporizes the alcohol, it cools into whiskey, and wood ages it. But the subtle variations in the finished product are virtually limitless.

There are whiskey disciples, for example, who still believe that what's very old is naturally superior to what's contemporary. You can test the theory by sipping a jigger of pre-Prohibition whiskey, if you can find one like Gibson's Ancient Special Reserve Pure Rye Whiskey, distilled in 1916. Among playboys of the day, its heavy rye flavor and pungent straw overtones held pride of place. But drinking it today makes a man feel about as relaxed as he would be dressed in a long duster, cap and goggles, negotiating a potholed back road at the wheel of a 1916 Cadillac. It's a perfectly preserved specimen of a type of whiskey against which drinkers have successfully rebelled in the intervening years, championing in its stead the lighter proofs, flavors and bodies—and by body we mean quantity of flavor, not quality.

In distinguishing the lighter from the heavier whiskeys, you'll note, after a little practice, that both types create an aftertaste of sorts. The light whiskey leaves a pleasant small glow that seems to linger in the back of the mouth, while a heavier whiskey's taste hangs around the front of the tongue and the lips and usually overstays its welcome. Don't, incidentally, let color influence your judgment—it has nothing to do with what we mean by lightness. Some whiskeys receive their tint from the casks in which they're aged; others, with the outstanding exception of bourbon, from added caramel coloring.

Lightness in the mouth is only one good feature of a whiskey's profile. The things that make up whiskey flavor, that give it its essence, are called congeners, or products other than alcohol resulting from distillation. To recruit the pleasant congeners and stave off the poor ones is the real science and sorcery of whiskey making. In a fifth of whiskey there is, all told, only about a teaspoon of congeners, but without them it would be plain alcohol and water. Some congeners are born in the kind of grain used. Others owe their genes to the yeast's paternity. They must be controlled during the whiskey's stormy adolescence in the big fermenting vats, and in the still they're carefully hoarded by drawing off the liquor at low proofs. By federal regulation, bourbon, the principal whiskey in this country, must be taken out of the still at 160 proof or less. Actually, most of it is drawn off at considerably lower proofs and is cut to drinking strength later. The higher the proof when the liquor leaves the still, the weaker the flavor. If liquor trickling out of the still goes above 190, much of the gusto of the grain simply disappears. You then have grain neutral spirits, the basis for vodka or gin. It's like a steak cooked rare retaining its magnificent flavor and a steak cooked well done losing its juices. The comparison must be amended, however, because whiskey begins to flash its good stuff only when the congeners become mellow—after long aging in the wood.

Let us hastily add, however, that you can't judge a whiskey's personality exclusively by age. Some whiskeys mature earlier than others. Weaker-flavored spirits age more quickly than stronger ones. Whiskey in a large hogshead takes longer to mature than the same whiskey in a small cask, because less of it's in contact with the wood. If certain whiskeys are left too long in the wood, for age's sake alone, they sometimes begin to show the "casky" flavor of old age.

Whiskey flavor is coaxed out of a grain mash by either a pot still or a column still. The pot still isn't a yawning soup pot but a huge onion-shaped metal flask having a blazing fire beneath it and a narrow outlet at the top for trapping and delivering the whiskey vapors into a coil where they're cooled back to a liquid. Some pot stills in Ireland today are monsters holding over 20,000 gallons each. The other, more modern utensil is the column still, a lanky affair three or four stories high in which the alcohol is wheedled out by live steam inside the column rather than by flames beneath it. Column stills are like modern coffeemakers—the slave of science rather than art—producing a suave, controlled flavor. Pot stills are like old-fashioned enamel coffeepots in which the ground beans have been dumped into the boiling water and swirled around to bring out all the robust coffee essence, a technique that could throw the amateur. But those who handle both the pot stills and the column stills in the big-name distilleries today are pros, highly disciplined in the virtuosity and the chemistry of spirits.

Some bourbons today are made, as they were generations ago, in pot stills. Others flow from the column stills. Most of the Scotch and Irish whiskeys exported to this country are now combinations of pot- and column-stilled spirits.

U. S. WHISKEYS

For all practical purposes, American whiskey production falls into three categories:

Straight whiskey Whiskey distilled at 160 proof or less and aged for at least two years. Bourbon is a straight whiskey, concocted from a grain mixture that is at least 51 percent corn, aged only in charred new oak barrels; bourbon's counterpart, rye whiskey, is similarly made from a mixture of at least 51 percent rye.

Blends of straight whiskey Two or more straights united to combine their best features, some for mellowness, some for strength, some for aroma.

Blended whiskey A blend of about one-third straight whiskey at 100 proof (the law says one-fifth is enough) and two-thirds neutral spirits; it's often misnomered "rye."

Like a stubborn gate-crashing ghost, the word *rye* keeps weaving in and out of bars and drinking parties when what's really meant is blended whiskey. Actually, less than one-half of 1 percent of the whiskey wetting American throats is straight rye. In the finer liquor stores you may still find a distinguished old bottling of straight rye, but that is decidedly the exception. To be sure, rye, the grain, is used in many American whiskeys as a minor ingredient along with other grains such as wheat and barley, but to call for rye in a bar today is as illogical as asking for an onion stew when you really want beef, on the grounds that onions are used for seasoning purposes.

At the end of World War Two, three out of four jiggers of whiskey were the neutral-flavored blended whiskey. Shortly thereafter, bourbonmen began to cut their traditional 100-proof liquors down to 86. Many of them started to spin out lighter flavors. But it was still bourbon, made from the seraphic oils of the corn, its new, easier flavor as perfectly burnished as ever. Bourbon sales blasted off and have now eclipsed blended whiskey. Its first well-known distiller was a Baptist minister, the Reverend Elijah Craig. It was named after a section of northeastern Kentucky called Bourbon to honor Louis XVI of France for his help in freeing the colonies from Britain.

For those seeking special whiskeys, bottled in bond is the most eminent and can be spotted by its green, rather than red, stamp. It must be a straight whiskey (and is almost always bourbon) produced by a single distillery in one year, at least four years old, bottled at 100 proof and kept under more or less constant surveillance. During its slumber it's tax-free, and during this time it's watched by Internal Revenue men who look upon their quarry as something of a cross between the *Pietà* of Michelangelo and the man at the head of the F.B.I.'s ten-most-wanted list. Theoretically, it can be a very poor whiskey and still be bottled in bond; the revenuers don't care about quality. Actually, most of the prominent bottled in bonds are the very cream of the present bourbon dynasty.

The terms *sweet mash* and *sour mash* can stand clarification. A sour-mash bourbon is produced when the grain mixture contains some "spent" beer from a previous run of whiskey. Like the chunk of leftover dough bakers use for their sour rye bread, it's the kind of leftover that up- rather than down-grades the new batch of whiskey. Sweet-mash bourbon starts off with a clean slate. Almost all U.S. whiskey now distilled is sour mash. The amount of leftover mash used varies, and those whiskeys which indicate sour mash on their label usually contain a larger proportion from the still, resulting in a unique flavor.

Finally, there's corn whiskey. It's made up and distilled like bourbon but must contain at least 80 percent corn, as compared with bourbon's minimum of 51 percent. It's aged in uncharred or reused oak barrels and lacks the deep mellowness of bourbon, although it has its faithful Southern following.

SCOTCH WHISKY

Young drinkers who take their first sip of Scotch are sometimes torn between what they think they should like and what they actually like. But something of a mellow note draws them back, and before long they're in tune with the great Highland fling.

In 1908, a royal commission looking into British whisky tastes had warned that the drinking public wanted a whisky "of less marked characteristics." They were talking about the classical unblended Scotch malts made with barley as the sole grain, dried over peat smoke and sent through a pot still. These malts are still the foundation of the Scotch-whisky industry. Although the method of making them has changed somewhat over the years—the famed peat fires are now mostly coal, partly because of the high cost of peat (in Scotland) and partly because the heavy peat "reek" is simply too strong for Scotsmen themselves—they're still made in the old distilleries, each of which depends for its lifeblood on the small stream of water flowing beside it. Although the unblended Scotches called "single malts" were for a long time almost unknown in this country, a small but powerful oligarchy of whisky judges both in the British Isles and here has never stopped singing their praises. Two of the most prestigious, the 12-year-old Glenlivet and the 10-year-old Glenfiddich, among others, are available in the States. When you taste them the very first time, you may be inclined to withdraw at first from their volatile Highland flavor; you know at once that what you're drinking isn't to be trifled with. But the champions of single malts know that if only you're exposed to these rare generous whiskies long enough, you, too, may just find the true faith.

But the malts are now only half the picture. The rest are light whiskies made from a combination of barley, corn and rye and sent through modern column stills at high proofs, as light as thistledown, approaching the borderline of neutral spirits

—something like vodka. But unlike vodka, they're then aged until they acquire a gentle whisky flavor.

Scotches coming to this country are blends not of one heavy malt whisky with one light grain, but of as many as a dozen heavies with a dozen lights. Some Scotch blends imported in the U.S. are now 80 percent light grain whisky and 20 percent heavy malt whisky; the average is perhaps 60 and 40. (Men who keep an assortment of Scotches in their liquor cabinet sometimes assume that most of the light Scotches are now leveled out to a common plateau where one light Scotch doesn't differ noticeably from another. It's a mistaken conclusion, and the host who tastes one light versus another at the same sipping session will discover that any Scotch, no matter how light, shows its own strong profile. The malt still dominates the whisky in the same way that onions dominate an onion soup—you can use one, two or three cups of onions in the same pot; it will still emerge as onion soup and not a colorless consommé.) Whatever the relative amounts of heavies and lights, the breeding and crossbreeding of these whiskies is a process so refined and complex that it can rightly be called a Scottish art. And what's amazing is that, year after year, Scottish shippers, some of whom blend their whisky but don't own a distillery, can turn out a spirit that seldom varies, as purebred in flavor as bottles of a vintage wine from the same grapes on the same hillside of the same château.

Some Scotches, particularly the less expensive ones, are now bottled at 80 rather than the usual 86 proof. *Caveat emptor:* The reduced proof means not merely that alcohol has been taken away but that Scotch whisky itself has been removed and water added.

Before World War Two, almost all Scotches coming to this shore were at least eight years old. U.S. law says they must be a minimum of four years old; i.e., the youngest of the blend must be four years old. Now they're running between five and seven years, even though many labels indicate no age at all. If you're in a mood for taste exploration, try the same brand of Scotch in an 8- and a 12-year-old version. The satiny smoothness of the older Scotch is roamin' in the gloamin' at its best. Now and then a label will read, "Liqueur Scotch Whisky." It's not a sweet liqueur in the literal sense, but indicates an older Scotch which the shipper presents as his gilt-edged potation.

CANADIAN WHISKY

If, in spelling *whisky,* the Scot in the Canadian seems to have taken charge, in distilling it the French-*canadien* is obviously the creative force—for Canada turns out the world's lightest, most delicate of spirits, a marvelous balance of corn, rye and barley. While every bottle of Canadian whisky seems to reflect the icy clarity of the arctic, you can depend upon its eventual effect to be as warming as any 86-proof potable in the world.

Like their famous liquor, our neighbors to the north may appear a bit cool until you get to know them, and their public attitude toward drinking seems positively standoffish. There are few Canadian cities where you'll find men and women drinking together in a cocktail room. A barmaid is unknown. A man carrying a bottle from a government liquor store can be jailed if the wrapper should accidentally drop off his fifth. The queen's health is even toasted in ice water at state dinners. But while the puritan seems all-powerful in public, in the privacy of the great old distilleries, the government is the soul of leniency. Canadian liquormen are subject to only a fraction of the rules besetting distillers in the States. For example, since 1800, when every miller in Canada was also a distiller, the whisky taste makers have used charred or uncharred oak barrels as they pleased. Their own self-imposed code of excellence is responsible for the light, brilliant spirits, at least six years old, now sent into the States. But the liquor they keep at home may be better still; travelers in Canada often notice that in its native habitat, Canadian whisky seems even softer than in the States. The simple explanation is that in Canada many of the best-known brands are sold at a supersmooth 80 proof, rather than the usual 86.

IRISH WHISKEY

In sharp contrast to the light Canadian spirits are Ireland's hearty whiskeys. After a few sturdy drams, amateur whiskey genealogists often trace Irish whiskey to its first maker, Patrick, patron saint of Ireland. When literal-minded whiskey historians insist that Saint Patrick in the Fifth Century was a brewer of beer rather than a distiller of whiskey, Irishmen aren't in the least bit rattled. They simply point out that whiskey is only distilled beer, just as brandy is distilled wine. And the whole history of distilling, they add, from the ancient Arabs onward, is such a barmy tale that Saint Patrick might just as well be credited as less worthy benefactors.

When impertinent Sassenachs claim that Irish whiskey is like Canadian but more robust, they make a comparison that may be partly true but is nevertheless odious to any true Irishman, who can point out that the very word *whiskey* is a derivative of the Gaelic *uisge beatha,* "water of life." For there's something regal in the flavor of Irish whiskey that sets it apart not only from Canadian but from any other whiskey in the world. As best described in Holinshed's *Chronicles* in 1577, "Trulie it is a

soverigne liquor if it be orderlie taken." Like Scotch, its base is
barley with oats and other grains for additional flavoring. It's
dried over closed fires and, unlike Scotch, smoke never gets in
its eyes. A second difference from Scotch is that while Scotch is
made from all malted barley, only half the barley in Irish
whiskey is malted or sprouted. Straight Irish whiskey today is
sent through pot stills three times before it's finally set aside to
age. Most of it reaching this country is at least five years old;
some of it is ten years or older.

To meet the contemporary appetite for lighter spirits, the
principal Irish distillers recently started to blend their whiskeys
with a small amount of grain neutral spirits. Instead of the
phrase *Irish Whiskey* on the label, you'll now read on many
bottles *Blended Irish Whiskey.* As far as mixability is concerned,
the new Irish whiskeys leave the old ones far behind. The
best-known mixture in which Irish whiskey is "orderlie taken"
is, of course, Irish coffee—a drink as good cold as hot (see page
282).

In the whiskey world, the most significant shift in recent
years is that, as far as aging is concerned, Scotch and American
whiskeys are moving closer all the time. Scotch whisky is a
blend of about 20 or 30 whiskies, all of them aged. At one time
the best blended whiskey made in this country was about
one-third straight whiskey or bourbon and two-thirds straight
white eye—that is, raw white alcohol, just as it came from the
still, cut to drinking strength. It's this two-thirds that's now
transformed. U.S. whiskeymen, in an effort to turn out the best
blended whiskey, have begun to age all of it. A good blended
whiskey in this country, such as Seagram's 7 Crown, is made up
of about 75 different spirits, all of them mellowed by long years
in the wood.

Drinking tastes are always in ferment or they wouldn't be
tastes. Where future whiskey tastes are destined is any bar
philosopher's guess. But learned whiskeymen believe that in the
years just ahead, many of the 86-proof whiskeys will probably be
offered in 80-proof versions—several have already appeared
—and that the lighter whiskey flavors will become even lighter
still. A new whiskey to be called "Light American Whiskey" by
government definition will join the U.S. whiskey family in 1972.
It will be distilled at proofs higher than the 160 to which
bourbon is now limited and may be aged in used rather than
new charred oak barrels in which all bourbon now grows to
manhood. The new product is expected to compete with the
light Canadian whiskies.

But be it heavy in flavor or light, 86 proof or 80, the real
proof of any whiskey is in the drinking. And having discovered
this, more and more men find themselves in felicitous accord
with the canny Scotsman who said, "There's whusky and there's
guid whusky, but there's nae bad whusky."

8

GIN—THE MASTER MIXER

The next time someone asks, "Who is Sylvius?" be prepared with the answer: He was the inventor of gin. Sylvius's proper name was Franciscus de la Boë. He was a professor of medicine at the Dutch University of Leiden, and the pure lab alcohol which Dr. Sylvius distilled with the oil of juniper berries was intended as a blood cleanser for sale in apothecaries rather than taverns. It was the 17th Century, when drinking most distilled liquors snapped the neck and left a lingering ball of fire in the throat. The professor's comparatively smooth and inexpensive nostrum soon not only cleansed the blood of countless native Hollanders but also juiced up the minds and bodies of English soldiers campaigning in the Lowlands. Englishmen brought the new Dutch formula back to their cold, foggy isle, and a great mass warming of an entire nation took place over the next several centuries.

Beginning in England with the reign of William of Orange, gin drinking became a mark of the highest patriotism. The number of amateur gin makers mushroomed until eventually every fourth house in London was a ginshop; English workmen were even paid a share of their wages in gin. In the late 19th Century, the elaborate gilded and mirrored Victorian gin palaces came into being, and gin rose to a peak of glamour, reaching its apex with the introduction to England of the American cocktail; not even Prohibition's bathtub gin, generations later, nor the runaway rise of vodka could cause gin to fall again.

All dry gins are created equal; that is, they all start out as neutral spirits made from grain. But they're later redistilled in the presence of juniper berries and other forms of flavor sorcery, such as coriander, bitter almonds, cardamom, cassis bark, angelica and lemon and orange peel. It's this second flavoring step which reveals the gin maker's art and which accounts for most of the differences in gins.

Deepest-flavored of all is the imported Holland gin called genever or Hollands. (The English word *gin* is a contraction of the Dutch *genever,* which means "juniper.") Holland gin makers use fresh juniper berries chopped and added right into the fermenting mash before distillation takes place, and they distill their gins at rather low proofs. This technique imparts an odd, impressive flavor which is so assertive that Hollands is seldom used in a mixed drink; it's always taken biting cold and neat. While the first gulp is always somewhat surprising to Americans, it leaves a rich aftertaste much like an old *eau de vie.* Like Germany's Steinhäger gin—which is very much like it in flavor—genever is sold in stone crocks.

English gins differ from each other just as American gins do. The gin gap between the two countries, however, seems to be closing, although many English gins are still distinguished by a 94 proof as against the American 90 or less. The English starting spirits, before they're juniper-flavored, often have somewhat more body than those used for American gins. Some gins in both England and the United States are now distilled under vacuum, permitting the flavors of the botanicals to be liberated at low temperatures rather than the pugnaciously high temperatures of normal stills, which sometimes cause flavors to be rough. Still other gins are flavored, not by immersing the botanicals right in the still, but by passing the finished alcohol vapors, as they come from the still, through a separate chamber where the juniper and other spices convey a pleasant subtlety to the spirits before they're condensed. How "ginny"—how vividly flavored—you like your gin is purely a matter of personal taste.

Whatever the manner in which they're flavored, both American and English gins are considered to be dry. Until recently that meant unsweetened, but virtually all gins today are unsweetened. When barmen speak of dry gin these days, they mean one which is more muted in flavor, though not pallid, and above all, smooth. Actually, the only nondry gin is English Old Tom, which is made with added sugar as a sweetener and is exported mostly to the Orient. There are also a few fruit-flavored gins on the market, but they're not a significant segment of the gin world. And sloe gin isn't gin at all but a liqueur made with the sloe plum of the blackthorn.

In addition to being dry, most gins in England and America are unaged, but a few in both countries are mellowed in the wood for further blending and flavor development. Although American liquor laws don't permit gin labels to carry any statement of age, these elder statesmen can be recognized by their clear straw color.

Over the centuries, English gin drinkers have created their own terminology, and some of it has spilled across the ocean. Pink gin, for instance, is simply gin with a dash of Angostura bitters; "gin and it" is a blend of gin and Italian vermouth; and the gin sling, which has been a British standby since General Gordon drank it at the officers' mess in Khartoum, will probably outlast the final expiration of the Empire. It's sold bottled as Pimm's No. 1 Cup.

Wherever it comes from and whatever company it keeps, Sylvius's venerable and versatile nostrum remains among the best possible medicines for the treatment of the common thirst. It is written that Elijah the prophet once derived sublime comfort from sitting under a juniper tree. It's not surprising that most men today prefer to take their juniper through the lips in the comfort of an armchair.

9

VODKA—THE BREATHLESS BEVERAGE

 Vodka, according to the ads, will leave you breathless. This pitch has always made a particular appeal to those executives who sometimes return to the office after an important business lunch with a breath strong enough to carry freight, and, in a sense, it's true. Vodka will leave you breathless. It will also, if you drink enough of it, leave you speechless and motionless.

Originally, in this country, vodka was a drink for people who were looking for just this combination—fireworks without flavor. But, while there are still people who love the effects but hate the taste of most strong liquors, a sizable segment of the American drinking population now loves vodka for vodka's sake.

By federal definition, vodka must be so treated "as to be without distinctive character, aroma or taste." Why not, then, buy the cheapest vodka—on the assumption that they're all alike—and be done with it? Because distilling is a most complicated art involving all kinds of sophisticated equipment, and two distillers, like two chefs, will seldom come up with the very same end product—even when they follow the same recipe. Furthermore, nothing that passes over our taste buds is truly tasteless, and the ingredients—water, grain and yeast—that go into the original vodka mash produce an infinite variety of low-key flavors. If you were to "nose" and then sip in succession three or four prominent brands of vodka at room temperature, you would detect certain definite minor differences in taste. And if you were to compare American or English vodkas with those from central Europe and Russia, you'd notice another breed of cat altogether.

Still, though some Russian vodka was once distilled from potato mash, the best of it, even in the czar's day, was and is distilled the same way we make ours—from grains such as corn, rye or wheat. The pure grain neutral spirits are taken from the stills at 190 proof or higher, bearing in mind that the higher the proof, the less the flavor. The process is very much like the first step in making gin. But while gin is redistilled with juniper berries and other flavorings to give it its characteristic flavor, vodka is then processed to *remove* as much flavor as possible.

Vodkamen have two ways of eradicating flavor. The first is to distill it with such artful care that only the smoothest, purest fraction of spirits from the still is accepted for vodka; the balance of the run is rejected. The second is a finishing process wherein the liquor is sent through columns of charcoal until it emerges clean, satiny and as tasteless as technology can make it. The dozens of kinds of charcoal used by various distillers—and the woods from which they're made (hickory, oak or cherry)—produce subtle differences in flavor that are detectable by the educated palate. Obviously, the variations within both methods of vodka polishing are wide enough to permit all kinds of good-natured alcohols to emerge.

For those few who like vodka but still want some semblance of flavor, there are lemon, orange, lime, mint, grape and other flavored specimens. And perhaps the most distinctive of all flavored vodkas is the one from central Europe called zubrovka. Its liqueurlike flavor is developed by steeping buffalo grass, an herb which gives it an offbeat but extremely pleasant taste, in the vodka.

Although all vodka is distilled at a skull-popping 190, it's cut to proofs ranging from 80 to 100 before bottling, and most brands are offered in a choice of 80 or 100. The higher proofs, with less water in the bottle and thus a more distinctive "tastelessness," are preferred in such potent swizzle as the vodka martini. But the lower-proof vodkas are smoother and more soothing in such preprandial potables as a screwdriver.

Mixed vodka drinks fall into three categories: First of all

there are the conventional mixed drinks in which vodka takes the place of gin, whiskey or other liquors: vodka martinis, vodka and tonic, vodka-and-ginger-ale highballs, vodka old-fashioneds and the like. The second group consists of those fruit-juice compounds in which the juice delivers the flavor while the vodka provides the punch. Best known is the screwdriver, but other fruit-juice combinations—apple juice, grapefruit juice, grape juice, loganberry juice, pineapple juice or cranberry juice—all demonstrate vodka's amazing mixability. The final category includes those mixed drinks that originated with vodka specifically and for which vodka is most famed, such as the bloody mary (vodka and tomato juice, lemon juice and spices), the moscow mule (vodka and ginger beer) and the bullshot (vodka and consomme).

The Scandinavians, particularly the Finns, have cultivated the art of drinking vodka straight as an aperitif. It's an art we highly recommend. When the Finnish bartender reaches for the vodka, he brings out a bottle robed in a thick blanket of ice. (To make the ice robe, see page 31.) The Finn then pours the biting-cold vodka into an iced glass and downs the contents with a single chugalug. As a chaser, he nibbles a tidbit of plump herring fillet that obliterates the intensity of the drink. In a moment or two, he feels a yearning for another shot, following it this time with a bite or two of smoked salmon. After the third, he may munch a slice of hot sausage on rye. And so on. Then the Finn's taciturn nature turns into slow, ecstatic colloquy. If you keep pace with him, you'll soon see your own private display of northern lights.

Another aftereffect—even if it's taken in moderation—is an expansive sense of well-being and companionability that enhances not only food but fun. Host and guest could ask for little more.

10

AND A BOTTLE OF RUM

 One of rum's most memorable qualities is that it never lets you forget where it comes from. Bourbon, Scotch or gin drinkers don't necessarily think of corn-covered prairieland, peat bogs or verdant groves of juniper shrubs while imbibing their pet potations. But as soon as the first drop of rum is poured, tropical touches inevitably begin to appear—plump mangoes, passion fruit, ripe papayas, green limes, cool coconut milk, and pineapples heavy and musky as the jungle itself. Even without such exotic persuasions, there's something in the sheer aroma and brandylike smoothness of distilled sugarcane that spurs every mixmaster's imagination.

While making rum is an art, the secret of which is well guarded by the few who hold it, the basic steps in the process can be described simply: Remember, first of all, that rum is a by-product of sugar. Sugarcane is crushed; it turns to cane juice; it's boiled down; part of the rummish stew turns to crystallized sugar and is removed; the rest, the "mother liquor" or molasses, is first fermented, then distilled; finally, all rums are aged. The youngest blend coming to this country now is usually three years old, but rums run in age up to ten years or older, and some rank with the rarest of velvety old brandies in flavor. In some aging warehouses, rums are handled in a solera system, where a cask is never completely emptied; part of the old rum always remains to mingle with the new in such proportions that the new merges with the old and takes on its best features.

Most of the yo-ho-ho sold in the States is Puerto Rican, a light, dry spirit in favor with contemporary freebooters. An oligarchy of Puerto Rican distillers take more pride in their rum formulas than a Kentucky colonel takes in his bed of mint leaves. Warehouses in which the rum is kept for aging are patrolled day and night by armed government guards. The lock to each warehouse contains two keyholes, one for the owner and one for the government guard, so that neither can tamper with the sleeping golden distillate. And the government, in cooperation with the University of Puerto Rico, carries on a research program to keep the rum *ne plus ultra* in every drop that leaves the island.

Light Puerto Rican rum is recognized by its white or silver label. It's usually two to five years old and finds its way automatically into daiquiris, rum sours, rum tonics and similar drinks. In the next category are the golden rums, darker in color and aged usually from five to eight years. These are the mainstays of rum and Coke, the rum collins and other drinks with slightly heavier rum body. A third group includes the aged rums about 10 to 15 years old like the Bacardi añejo or the Don Q Eldorado. Like sippin' whiskey, you take them straight in dock glasses or brandy snifters. Then there are the medium- to heavy-bodied rums from Jamaica and elsewhere, many of which are still simmered to their rich flavor in old-fashioned pot stills. Their eventual homes are in rum swizzles, planter's punch, winter punch bowls and in mixed tropical drinks combined with lighter rums. There are 151-proof rums now offered by all major Puerto Rican distilleries. At one time the best-known representative of this particular form of kill-devil was the Demerara rum from British Guiana, designed primarily to thaw the frozen veins of Canadian lumberjacks. Today 151-proof rums serve more urbane needs; their high proof makes them perfect accents for any dessert from *baba au rhum* to crêpes flambée. In mixed drinks the 151-proof rums, in small quantities, add a piquant note of concentrated rumminess. A bottle belongs in every man's rum library.

The personality of every rum, no matter how old it may be, depends upon its birthplace. Thus:

Puerto Rican rum   Known for its light body, delicate dry flavor.

Virgin Islands rum   Although in the light, dry class, its molasses flavor is more pronounced than Puerto Rican.

Jamaican rum   Full and pungent in flavor, dark mahogany in color. London dock rums are Jamaican rums sent to London for special aging in Thames warehouses, where damp air favors the slow ripening of the rum's best qualities.

Barbados rum   Midway generally between light Puerto Rican rums and their heavier Jamaican cousins. It's pot-stilled.

Demerara rum   Heavy-flavored and a shade less assertive than Jamaican. Much of it arrives in the U.S. at 151 proof.

Haitian rum   Deep-flavored but mellow. A perfect partner for lighter rums in elaborate Polynesian drinks.

Batavian arak   A pungent, dry rum distilled and aged on the island of Java. Its offbeat flavor is due to special molasses, local water and the Javanese rice used in the fermenting tubs.

Hawaiian rum   The newest, softest and lightest (80 proof) rum on the market. Extremely pleasant with orange juice as a brunch starter; equally companionable with tonic water and ice on a sultry summer's day.

New England rum   A rum of intermediate body made from West Indies molasses. It's a straight rum rather than a blend, ideally suited for hot winter grog.

Rum has often been called the one-bottle bar. It's particularly true of the light, dry rums. The best way to demonstrate their versatility is to serve them without any preliminary fanfare in the standard bar drinks calling for whiskey, as well as in the gin and vodka concoctions. Rum manhattans, rum old-fashioneds, rum martinis and rum screwdrivers are not only great cooling agents but serve equally well any time of the year as catalysts for warm comradeship.

Any young man today who has learned to wet his lips with something other than water knows that rum has a peculiarly persuasive effect. Whiskey makes a girl stop arguing. Beer soothes her. Gin disarms her. But rum cajoles. No one has described the effect better than William James when he philosophized about alcohol: "It is in fact the great exciter of the Yes function in man. It brings its votary from the chill periphery of things to the radiant core."

GLASSWARE FOR THE BAR

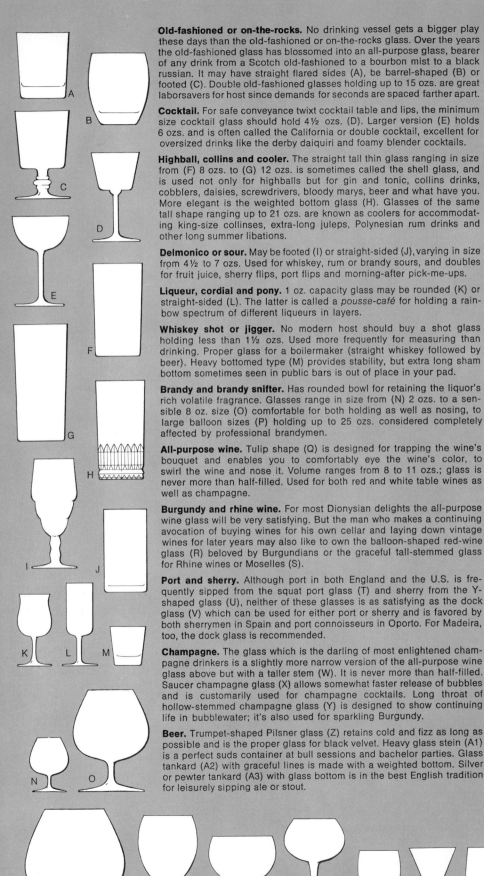

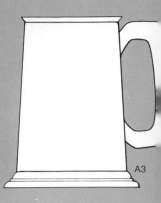

Old-fashioned or on-the-rocks. No drinking vessel gets a bigger play these days than the old-fashioned or on-the-rocks glass. Over the years the old-fashioned glass has blossomed into an all-purpose glass, bearer of any drink from a Scotch old-fashioned to a bourbon mist to a black russian. It may have straight flared sides (A), be barrel-shaped (B) or footed (C). Double old-fashioned glasses holding up to 15 ozs. are great laborsavers for host since demands for seconds are spaced farther apart.

Cocktail. For safe conveyance twixt cocktail table and lips, the minimum size cocktail glass should hold 4½ ozs. (D). Larger version (E) holds 6 ozs. and is often called the California or double cocktail, excellent for oversized drinks like the derby daiquiri and foamy blender cocktails.

Highball, collins and cooler. The straight tall thin glass ranging in size from (F) 8 ozs. to (G) 12 ozs. is sometimes called the shell glass, and is used not only for highballs but for gin and tonic, collins drinks, cobblers, daisies, screwdrivers, bloody marys, beer and what have you. More elegant is the weighted bottom glass (H). Glasses of the same tall shape ranging up to 21 ozs. are known as coolers for accommodating king-size collinses, extra-long juleps, Polynesian rum drinks and other long summer libations.

Delmonico or sour. May be footed (I) or straight-sided (J), varying in size from 4½ to 7 ozs. Used for whiskey, rum or brandy sours, and doubles for fruit juice, sherry flips, port flips and morning-after pick-me-ups.

Liqueur, cordial and pony. 1 oz. capacity glass may be rounded (K) or straight-sided (L). The latter is called a *pousse-café* for holding a rainbow spectrum of different liqueurs in layers.

Whiskey shot or jigger. No modern host should buy a shot glass holding less than 1½ ozs. Used more frequently for measuring than drinking. Proper glass for a boilermaker (straight whiskey followed by beer). Heavy bottomed type (M) provides stability, but extra long sham bottom sometimes seen in public bars is out of place in your pad.

Brandy and brandy snifter. Has rounded bowl for retaining the liquor's rich volatile fragrance. Glasses range in size from (N) 2 ozs. to a sensible 8 oz. size (O) comfortable for both holding as well as nosing, to large balloon sizes (P) holding up to 25 ozs. considered completely affected by professional brandymen.

All-purpose wine. Tulip shape (Q) is designed for trapping the wine's bouquet and enables you to comfortably eye the wine's color, to swirl the wine and nose it. Volume ranges from 8 to 11 ozs.; glass is never more than half-filled. Used for both red and white table wines as well as champagne.

Burgundy and rhine wine. For most Dionysian delights the all-purpose wine glass will be very satisfying. But the man who makes a continuing avocation of buying wines for his own cellar and laying down vintage wines for later years may also like to own the balloon-shaped red-wine glass (R) beloved by Burgundians or the graceful tall-stemmed glass for Rhine wines or Moselles (S).

Port and sherry. Although port in both England and the U.S. is frequently sipped from the squat port glass (T) and sherry from the Y-shaped glass (U), neither of these glasses is as satisfying as the dock glass (V) which can be used for either port or sherry and is favored by both sherrymen in Spain and port connoisseurs in Oporto. For Madeira, too, the dock glass is recommended.

Champagne. The glass which is the darling of most enlightened champagne drinkers is a slightly more narrow version of the all-purpose wine glass above but with a taller stem (W). It is never more than half-filled. Saucer champagne glass (X) allows somewhat faster release of bubbles and is customarily used for champagne cocktails. Long throat of hollow-stemmed champagne glass (Y) is designed to show continuing life in bubblewater; it's also used for sparkling Burgundy.

Beer. Trumpet-shaped Pilsner glass (Z) retains cold and fizz as long as possible and is the proper glass for black velvet. Heavy glass stein (A1) is a perfect suds container at bull sessions and bachelor parties. Glass tankard (A2) with graceful lines is made with a weighted bottom. Silver or pewter tankard (A3) with glass bottom is in the best English tradition for leisurely sipping ale or stout.

(Preceding page) Before any host drops a single silver onion into a Gibson or decorates a tall glass with a long orange horse's neck or pulls the cork of his favorite bottle of Bordeaux, he should scan the assortment of small hand tools now available for serving spirits and wine. On the opposite page is an A-to-Z tableau of bar gadgetry showing some of the most useful implements for the conveniences and pleasures of party drinking.

1. Small glass compote dish is convenient vessel for cherries, olives and onions.

2. Long tongs snugly grip ice cubes although in many wet circles of society hands are now *de rigueur* for picking up rocks from an ice bucket.

3. Ice pick may be used for chipping large ice block into suitable size for punch bowl and is also useful for unsticking ice cubes in ice bucket.

4. Small citrus squeezers which come in sets of 6 are handy for squeezing wedges of lemon or lime into drinks and double as lemon squeezers for fish course at dining table.

5. Handled jigger with ½ and 1½ oz. measures is useful for pouring liquor into shaker as well as into rows of glasses lined up for party drinks prepared *en masse.*

6. Coil-rimmed strainer for cocktail mixing glass is good trap against ice floe tumbling into cocktail glass.

7. Olive or cherry grabber will find its mark in most stubborn bottle.

8. Long-handled bar spoon-stirrer is used either in a cocktail mixing glass or as a substitute for glass martini stirrer, as well as for stirring all long, deep potations—coolers, pitchers, punches and zombies.

9. Sturdy metal bottle stopper is less likely to get lost than common plastic disk. Keeps anything from club soda to bitter lemon sparkling from one night to the next.

10. Cork bottle stopper with no-drip pouring end is useful for dispensing anything from créme de cassis to vermouth.

11. Chrome pourer cap measures exactly one jigger.

12. Nutmeg grater is welcome for long, year-end partying when flips, nogs, grogs and glöggs are flowing.

13. Heavy duty lime or lemon squeezer is indispensable for squeezing fruit and dropping shell into fizzes, tonics and other tall mixtures with juniper juice.

14. Push-button olive, cherry or onion grabber. In relatively sober hands it works.

15. The open-all gadget is planned for unscrewing stubborn tops of jars and bottles of varying sizes as well as flipping lids.

16. The trouble with most shoddy coasters isn't that they disappear but that they don't disappear fast enough. Both drinking glass and drink look better when placed in these no-skid coasters.

17. A sharp well-balanced French knife is best for slicing fruits.

18. Sturdy capacious cutting board is less likely to warp than small thin version; board doubles as kitchen equipment.

19. Fang of heavy duty beer can opener easily sinks into metal.

20. Bottle cap opener is the husky type providing good leverage.

21. Stainless steel knife *cum* opener has pronged edge for stabbing fruit and other garnishes.

22.. Set of standard measuring spoons is indispensable in formulas calling for small quantities of flavoring liqueurs, juices and bitters.

23. Rx martini dropper is both fun and useful for passing among guests to add vermouth to taste to their martinis; narrow dropper easily fits into neck of vermouth bottle.

24. Folding flat waiter's corkscrew is good for itinerant bartenders carrying pocket equipment to beaches and mountain sites for fun and games.

25. Corkscrew is self-opening; one motion pulls the cork out by simply turning in the same direction.

26. Wing type corkscrew permits you to use both hands in extracting stubborn corks. (Many hosts recently have abandoned the conventional corkscrew in favor of the CO_2 bottle opener. A small charge of CO_2—which has no effect whatever on a wine's flavor—gently raises the cork out of the bottle without wrenching muscles.)

11

TEQUILA— VIVA MAGUEY!

 When Christopher Columbus wrote about an Indian drink made from the "marrow of the maguey," a cactuslike plant, he may have been referring to the heady beer which the Mexicans now call *pulque* or the distilled beverage called tequila. Quibblers may argue that the art of distillation was introduced to the New World from the Old, but scholars of potable spirits aren't so sure; some believe the Mexican Indians may indeed have discovered distillation independently, and if they did, tequila was undoubtedly the drink they used to conquer their Spanish conquerors. Tequila today is made from maguey, grown in the foothills of the Sierra Madre.

For some time now, American liquor manufacturers have been importing tequila, aging it in the United States and energetically bottling a good portion as the premixed margarita—the cocktail of tequila, orange liqueur and lime juice served in a salt-rimmed glass, which Americans find as memorable as a visit to the bullring.

In flavor tequila bears an uncanny resemblance to Dutch
genever gin, the type in which the juniper berry is ground right
into the original mash. Indeed, Dutch gin drinkers might well
think that tequila is simply an interesting variation of their own
native product, although the two liquors are produced from
completely different raw materials.

The tall tales poured out by American visitors to Mexico,
comparing tequila to a fierce white lightning delivered with the
impact of a thousand blackjacks, are little more than a myth—the
kind that some Mexicans themselves foster and enjoy
immensely. If you can slough off the hair-raising tales of tequila's
fiery potency and forget free assocations with the stinging flavor
of Mexican chilies and guacamole, with their explosive effect on
the taste buds, you can accept tequila as a new kind of
brandy—for the maguey is a fruitlike plant, and like distillations
of the grape, the apple, the plum and other fruits, tequila is the
essence of this tropical fruit. It takes ten years for the maguey to
mature, during which time the plant reaches chunky
five-by-five-foot dimensions. At this point, the pointed leaves of
the plant are lopped off and the cores of the plants, looking like
monster pineapples, weighting from 50 to 200 pounds, are
carried to the distillery where they're steam-cooked, ground,
pressed, fermented and pot-stilled.

Those who describe the aftereffects of tequila as akin to
tramping on a third rail should be told that it's distilled at an
amazingly low 104 proof. The Mexican government enforces this
low proof in order to retain the natural flavors that are lost at
higher proofs. Like other liquors, such as whiskey, vodka, gin
and rum, tequila is then further cut with water. The best-known
brands coming to this country are bottled at 80 to 100 proof, a
very civilized range for any hard liquor.

In Mexico most tequilas are unaged, like our own vodkas
and gins, but a small fraction is aged in the wood and is called
gold tequila. Those shipped to the United States are aged four to
five months in Mexico and are then further aged for about a year
and a half in this country. The additional aging gives them a
rounded finish, which makes them very compatible in tequila
sours, tequila and tonic and tequila martinis.

Although tequila has come into wide use as a cocktail base,
Mexicans and other tequila purists still toss it down using their
famed here's-blowing-the-lid routine. Before hoisting the glass,
the *aficionado* bends his head back, squints in the direction of
the camera, the spotlights or the sun, and squeezes the juice
of the sourest lime he can find directly into his mouth; and
sometimes he actually eats part of the lime. Then he swallows
his straight tequila in a lightning chugalug and finally laps up a
dab of salt from the soft flesh between thumb and first finger.
Sometimes the order is reversed, with the salt first and the lime
last. But however the ritual is performed, all he's actually bolted

down is a straight jigger of liquor with less potency than an American boilermaker—a shot of whiskey followed by beer.

As much fun as it is to indulge in such drinking histrionics, tequila is equally enjoyable if it's sipped and rolled about in the mouth just as though you were tasting a new brandy. To some men the flavor is reminiscent of the aroma of freshly ground pepper; to others there's a reminder of salt and sugar. But like Danish aquavit or German Steinhäger gin, it can easily become an acquired taste, and as a mixer it has sumptuous possibilities. Whatever the associations the taste of tequila brings to you, however you choose to drink it, the pleasant aftereffects are always *muy simpatico.*

12

APÉRITIFS— PREPRANDIAL POTATIONS

Too often in the conviviality of the cocktail hour, drinks are gulped as indifferently as one clinks ice in a highball. But apéritifs, straight or mixed, are never taken for granted. Observe, for example, the Frenchman in his natural habitat, as each afternoon he sits at his favorite café table and partakes of his Byrrh, Amer Picon or vermouth cassis with attentive enjoyment. To him each day's apéritif is an excitingly different experience. He observes its color, savors its scent and samples it with a relish one usually associates with newfound pleasures. His senses then undergo the most salutary of metamorphoses: Taste buds tingle in anticipation of the evening repast; the local scenery becomes more vivid; and the passing *mesdemoiselles,* though they may be the same *jeunes filles* who promenade daily past his table, are surveyed with fresh appreciation.

Even the etymology of apéritif evokes its appetite-awakening effects. Though the word is French, it's best understood by going back to its Latin source, *aperio,* meaning "to open, to lay bare." Swallow a jigger of Campari with soda on ice; its unabashed bitteeness may cause you to shake your head dubiously over what has been proclaimed a prime libational pleasure. But soon waves of hunger sweep over you, and you can hardly wait for the antipasto tray. Thoughts of the anticipated anchovy fillets, cracked black olives, prosciutto, roasted-pepper salad and wafer-thin slices of Genoa salami are almost overpowering.

The apértif's ancient origins are a reminder that the world's first great wines were sharp potations. In 400 B.C., Hippocrates stopped prescribing medicines long enough to conjure up a lusty elixir of wine, resin and bitter almonds. Pliny, an anti-apéritif man, called the consumption of such concoctions before meals "an outlandish fashion recommended by doctors who are always trying to advertise themselves by some newfangled ideas." Undaunted, adventurous Romans began to create preprandial potations not only from the grape but from turnips, radishes, asparagus, parsley, thyme, mint, hyssop and almost anything else that sprang up around the villa. Even seawater was added for tang. Often, grapevines were surrounded by other plants placed close enough to the roots so that their insinuating essences would seep through the soil into the fruit before it was plucked. If, now and then, a decidedly toxic plant like wormwood worked its way into a wine, pleasure-seeking Romans didn't hesitate to drink it anyway—as long as it didn't offend their aesthetic sensibilities.

Modern apéritifs, happily, are admixtures of wine, spirits and as many as 40 different kinds of harmless but equally exotic spices, roots, barks, herbs, buds and flowers from every corner of the earth. The family is a surprisingly large one with several distinct branches: the wine-based apértifs (such as Byrrh, Dubonnet and Punt e Mes), the vermouths (sweet and dry), the distilled apéritifs (Amer Picon, Pernod, pastis and the like) and such stomach-settling bitters as Dutch Boonekamp.

In American frontier days, plainsmen mixed a pint of water with two tablespoons of buffalo gall for a "wholesome and exhilarating drink." Some years later, Kansans refined the formula, combining a mere ounce of wahoo (bark of the winged elm tree, also used for making string and rope) with a quart of whiskey. Somewhat more sophisticated American traditions are observed, along with the European, in the following roster of contemporary wines and liquors used as aperitifs.

Amer Picon A bittersweet French apéritif liqueur of quinine, orange and gentian, sometimes mixed with ice, soda and grenadine, served as an apéritif punch in an 8-oz. glass.

Boonekamp bitters Dutch-style bitters taken neat before a meal as a stomachic.

Byrrh (pronounced *beer)* A French proprietary apéritif wine with a tangy aftertaste.

Campari An Italian *aperitivo,* 48 proof, taken with soda and often with a twist of orange peel. Mixed half-and-half with Italian sweet vermouth, you get an americano; with Italian sweet vermouth and gin, a negroni.

Chambery One of the lightest and most delicately flavored of all French dry vermouths with a hint of wild strawberries.

Crème de cassis Made from black currants, it's actually a liqueur because of its sweetness. In the best-known version, it's combined with vermouth, ice and soda as a vermouth cassis or with white wine as a *vin blanc cassis.*

Dubonnet A quinine-flavored apéritif wine originally imported from France, now made in the U.S., in both red and white types. One or two parts Dubonnet to one part gin is a Dubonnet cocktail.

Fernet Branca Of Italian origin, now made in the U.S., it combines compatibly with gin or cognac and vermouth as a preprandial cocktail.

Lillet This French red or white apéritif wine has a subtle orange flavor with a subdued bitterness.

Ouzo A Middle Eastern high-proof anise liqueur taken before or after dinner.

Pastis An anise-flavored apéritif liqueur that, like ouzo, turns milky white when mixed with water. It's a favorite of Marseilles fishermen and Riviera jet-setters.

Pernod A 90-proof French anise-flavored apéritif liqueur, reminiscent of absinthe, which is now illegal. When used in place of vodka in a screwdriver, it's called the tiger's tail.

Pikina A rose-colored French proprietary wine with special appeal for those who like a light, dry apéritif.

Port wine In its white version, this consummate Portuguese product—with its full-bodied flavor and bouquet—is immensely popular in France and Belgium as a sundown apéritif.

Positano   A semidry apéritif vermouth with pleasant, decisive aftertaste.

Punt e Mes   A deep, dark Italian apéritif wine known for its provocative bitterness.

Raki   A brandy-based high-proof anise-flavored apéritif liqueur from the Middle East.

St.-Raphaël   A proprietary French apéritif wine noted for its full body and clean flavor.

Sherry, fino   Bone-dry Spanish sherry, served as an apéritif with or without ice. Even medium-dry sherries are now appearing as appetite sharpeners.

Vermouth   An herb-flavored wine, fortified with brandy, containing 16 to 19 percent alcohol. May be either red or white. At one time, French vermouth was light, dry, almost white; Italian vermouth, sweet, heavy, red. Nowadays, both types are produced in Italy, France, South America and the U.S. For mixing purposes, dry vermouth should be light in color with subtle overtones; sweet vermouth, round in flavor, sweet but not cloying. But both should be able to stand in their own right as straight iced drinks, trenchant, tantalizing, never tiresome.

It should be obvious even from this basic list that the choice of appetite arousers is as diverse as it is diverting. Sipped straight from the bottle or elaborately combined, any of these lively potations will turn on your taste buds with delightful dispatch.

13

LIQUEURS—CORDIALLY SPEAKING

From the hippest of the hip to the squarest of the square, all classes of tipplers seem to derive equal pleasure from liqueurs. A chick who doesn't have the faintest idea of what ingredients go into pastis or prunelle will nevertheless receive the same luxurious wavelengths from either of these drinks. Liqueurs are infusions, percolations or distillations made from fantastically complex formulas containing—besides brandy or spirits and sugar—fruits, flowers, herbs, seeds, spices, roots, bark and kernels gathered from every corner of the world. Infusion is the same as making tea: Fresh apricots or other fruits are steeped in a tank with brandy till both fruit and brandy are intimately united. Percolation is like making coffee: Sloes, for example, are placed in a basket, and spirits from the bottom of the percolator are pumped over them to make sloe gin (which isn't a gin at all but a liqueur). Finally, some liqueurs are distillations through a flavor head containing, in the case of curaçao, say, sweet and bitter orange peels. Some liqueurs, like brown crème de cacao, are made by all three forms of legerdemain; white crème de cacao is made by distillation alone.

Although there seem to be as many different kinds of liqueurs as there are people who sip them, concocted from tender rose petals to flakes of 20-carat gold, each liqueur is an individual chef d'oeuvre and should be treated lovingly or, at the very least, thoughtfully. Free-lance hosts who dust off the old bottle of crème de cacao just because it happens to have lingered on the shelf for too many years should be told that liqueur isn't something you palm off like a box of leftover bonbons. It needs an occasion. Of course, the mere sight of the liqueur bottle—the deep-blue curaçao, the outlandishly tall bottle of Galliano or the squat crown of Oriental green-tea liqueur—will often create the occasion. A simple pony of suave Benedictine will make a routine dinner memorable. And long after the coffee has been poured, the jug of crème de café will keep the postprandial session alive and glowing. In cooking, too, you'll remember the flaming Grand Marnier dancing around the crepes long after you've forgotten the *poulet* that preceded it.

There are still muleheaded drinking men around who think that liqueurs, because they're sweet, should be served only when a light of love is present. In 1601, John Rudolph Glauber in his *Description of New Philosophical Furnaces* pointed out that his "Cordial Extract," among other things, "refreshes the spirits and corroborates the brains and other parts of the body." Any man whose parts may be in need of corroboration should drink a moderate quantity of green Chartreuse (110 proof) to find out just how virile a liqueur can be. And if you think that sweetness alone makes a liqueur, try tart, semidry Cherry Heering poured over the rocks.

Serious liqueur drinkers know that the old proprietary liqueurs with their complex flavor blends, some with over a hundred ingredients, are much less likely to become tiresome than some of the simple fruit flavors such as peach or blackberry. But even many of the seemingly simple liqueurs often reveal a mystic kind of fragrance or unidentifiable flavor that is found under one label and not another. One need only compare the Kahlúa coffee liqueur from Mexico to the Expresso coffee liqueur from Italy to see the vast gulf between liqueurs derived from a similar source.

Men shopping for liqueurs are often bewildered by the nomenclature on the bottles. In the first place, let it be understood that the words *liqueur* and *cordial* mean exactly the same thing. For many generations, both English and American puritans shunned the word *liqueur,* thinking it would identify them too closely with the hard-liquor set; if a drink was called

"A Clove Cordial" or "A Conserve of Cowslips Good Against Melancholie," it was considered perfectly respectable. Early liqueur drinkers in Europe used both words together, *liqueurs cordialis,* meaning "liqueurs of the heart," to describe the mellifluent compounds invented by monks and dispensed in monasteries for all whose spiritual comfort was miraculously braced by a small potion of bodily comfort. To add to the word scatterment, some French liqueurs, in France, are still called *digestifs.* Besides the words *liqueur* and *cordial, fruit-flavored brandy* appears on many American products these days. This term also refers to a sweet type of after-dinner drink but with this basic difference: Fruit-flavored brandy must be made with a brandy base, while other liqueurs can be made with a base of any distilled spirits. Also, fruit-flavored brandies are generally somewhat less sweet than liqueurs and crèmes and somewhat higher in proof. The word *crème* normally means a liqueur of special smoothness and of a flavor with pronounced body. The word *liqueur* is all-inclusive, taking in the crèmes, the fruit-flavored brandies and the cordials. Outstanding cognacs, rums and Scotches sometimes bear the word *liqueur* on their labels, but don't be misled. It's a boast of excellence rather than a literal description of the contents, which have no resemblance to a true sweet liqueur. Finally, one more semantic misdemeanor: In the New York–New Jersey area, local liquor regulations forbid selling hard liquor in half-pint bottles. To fill the needs of drinkers on the run, whiskeys, gins, vodkas and such are slightly sweetened and bottled in half-pints, ready for the coat or hip pocket; they're sometimes called dry liqueurs. However silly the term may sound, it simply means a spirit with as little sweetness as possible that still stays within the federal definition of a liqueur.

In the thirties, right after Prohibition, many of the domestic liqueurs offered were only a shade better than Uncle Judd's peach pits aged in a jug on the back porch; the comparison between domestic and European liqueurs was too painful to describe. But a change gradually set in, and by World War Two, when European supplies were cut off, American liqueurs had passed their awkward adolescence and had grown to mature adulthood. Today American distilleries produce some of the smoothest liqueurs made anywhere. Famous original U.S. proprietary brands such as Southern Comfort and Forbidden Fruit are renowned throughout the world. Old World names such as Bols, De Kuyper and Garnier are now represented by liqueurs produced in the States under the same names. In many cases European liqueur specialists have simply transferred their operations to the New World, using the Old World formulas, and in some cases the Old World essences on which the liqueurs were originally based, while liberating the liqueur user from the import duty. Nine-tenths of all liqueurs sold in the States are now made here.

Nowadays many men prefer their liqueur libations biting cold; frequently they're drizzled over rocks or over crushed ice as frappés. An easy way to avoid dilution is simply to place both bottles and glasses in the refrigerator for several hours before serving. If a tray of assorted liqueurs is passed with the cheese and crackers, pint-size bottles or tenths are more easily handled than fifths. For men who don't have the shelf room to store a wide assortment of liqueurs, the compartmented bottle containing from two to four assorted liqueurs is a convenient asset.

What makes all liqueurs such effective tools in the hands of skillful barmen is the fact that, for mixing purposes, liqueurs are composite masterpieces to start with. When you crack open a bottle of whiskey, you know that it's made from grain; rum comes from sugar; wine, from grapes. But even as presumably simple a liqueur as the blackberry-flavored brandy made in this country by Leroux contains no fewer than seven different kinds of blackberries; each must be balanced from crop to crop each year and from batch to batch. And to make the final blend even more deliciously fruity, a small stream of fresh raspberries, with their soft, silken flavor, or rich-scented loganberries may be added as artful overtones. All of this, in substance, means that when you concoct a drink such as a tall blackberry collins, you're starting out with compound rather than simple interest from the very first ounce you draw out of the bottle.

In recent years liqueur cocktails, icy mixtures of liqueurs, fruit juices and in many cases sweet cream, have all but supplanted the heavier, more conventional desserts at many party tables. They're easy, exciting, and the number of creative combinations add up to what Milton called "a wilderness of sweets."

Here now, from abisante to zitronen, is our lexicon of the principal liqueurs available in the U.S.

Abisante   One of the modern replacements for the now-outlawed absinthe. The pale-green anise-flavored liqueur turns opalescent when allowed to drip slowly over ice.

Abricots, crème d'   French cream of apricot liqueur. It's luscious when drizzled over cracked ice in a champagne glass.

Absinthe   This anise-flavored liqueur was originally 136 proof and made with wormwood, and it was hard to tell whether the proof or the poison was more shattering. It is now illegal in most countries. The firm of Pernod, which originally made absinthe in France, still turns out a luscious 90-proof liqueur in its own name.

Advocaat   An eggnog liqueur, originally from Holland and now concocted in the U.S. This 40-proof mixture of grain neutral spirits, egg yolks and sugar usually goes into holiday tipple, accented with rum or brandy.

Allasch   A sweeter version of kümmel, it takes its name from the Latvian estate where kümmel liqueur was once made. Expropriated by other kümmelists, the name means little now.

Almond, crème d'   A pink liqueur flavored with almonds and fruit stones; similar to creme de noyaux.

Amaretto   A liqueur of apricot pits.

Amer Picon   A bitter French apéritif liqueur of quinine, oranges and gentian. It always appears in mixed drinks before the meal rather than as a postprandial liqueur.

Anise; Anisette; Anesone   Liqueurs flavored with anise seeds, reminiscent of licorice; they're usually white but may be colored red. Although anise is the principal feature of the flavor profile, other spices are used by individual bottlers. Proofs range from the 60s to 100; anesone is usually higher in proof and less sweet than anise.

Apricot liqueur; apry   Other names for crème d'abricots.

Banana liqueur; bananes, crème de   Cream of banana liqueur, known for its fidelity to the original fruit flavor. Usually quite sweet, it's delicious in a banana daiquiri.

Benai   An American liqueur of the Benedictine type.

Benedictine   One of the greatest of the monastery liqueurs, made of herbs, roots and sugar, with a cognac base. It started reviving tired monks in 1510. Now a proprietary liqueur, the letters *D.O.M.* on the label stand for *Deo Optimo Maximo,* "to God, most good, most great." The B & B is brandy and Benedictine, one of the most urbane of after-dinner potions.

Blackberry liqueur; blackberry-flavored brandy   The latter is less sweet than the liqueur. It makes a superb blackberry sour. Not to be confused with the completely dry Hungarian blackberry brandy.

Cacao, crème de   Liqueur with a base of cacao (chocolate) and vanilla beans. It is available in both brown and white versions, the latter always used in grasshopper cocktails, the former in alexanders.

Cacao Mit Nuss   Crème de cacao with a hazelnut flavor.

Café, crème de   A coffee liqueur.

Casanova   An Italian liqueur with a brandy base and scented with orange and herbs.

Cassis, crème de   A low-proof liqueur made from French black currants. Although sweet, it's used as an apéritif in vermouth cassis or white-wine cassis.

Cerise, crème de   French name for cherry liqueur.

Chartreuse   Green 110 proof or yellow 86 proof, it has been made by the Carthusian monks since 1605. The green, most eminent of all liqueurs, contains 130 herbs. The Carthusian order, twice expelled from France, took the secret formula with them to Spain but couldn't find the precise herbs, and Chartreuse in exile never came up to the one produced on native soil. A few bottles of pre-expulsion Chartreuse, made before 1903, were sold recently at $125 per bottle.

Cheri-Suisse   A liqueur flavored with chocolate and cherries, extremely well balanced.

Cherry liqueur   It appears also as cherry-flavored brandy, Cherry Heering in Denmark and Cherry Karise in the U.S. Made of cherries and pits, it's noted for a tart fruit accent. It's equally good on the rocks or over shaved ice, sipped through a straw.

Chocla Menthe   An American liqueur of crème de menthe and chocolate.

Chococo   Coconut and chocolate are blended in this liqueur.

Chokalu   Mexican chocolate liqueur in the crème de cacao family.

Ciao   A relatively new liqueur from Italy with a mellow, fruity aftertaste, made, as most liqueurs are, from a hush-hush recipe.

Claristine   Spicy liqueur with herbs, now a proprietary brand, once made by the Clarist nuns of Belgium, whose convent was destroyed in World War One. It tests the capabilities of both sexes.

Coffee liqueur   It comes under many names, including Kahlúa from Mexico, Tia Maria from Jamaica, Expresso from dark-roasted Italian coffee, crème de café, Brazilia, Pasha from Turkey, etc. Any of the large galaxy is delightful ice-cold with heavy sweet cream floating on top.

Cointreau   A liqueur of the orange family, cousin to triple sec, curaçao and Grand Marnier.

Cordial Médoc   A French liqueur made from a blend of oranges, cherries, brandy and crème de cacao.

Curaçao   A liqueur made of the dried peel of small green oranges grown in the Dutch West Indies, plus spices and sometimes port wine and rum. It may be white, blue or green, although it is normally orange in color from the maceration of bitter orange peels.

Curaçao and Cognac   Orange liqueur and top-quality cognac.

Czasakorte   Pear liqueur from Hungary.

Drambuie   Originally from a recipe presented to the Mackinnon family, present guardians of its formula, by Bonnie Prince Charlie, this liqueur, made from Scotch whisky at least ten years old, heather honey and herbs, gets its name from the Gaelic phrase *an dram buidheach,* or "the drink that satisfies."

Fior di alpi; fiore d'alpe; flora di alpi; flora alpina   All four spellings refer to an Italian liqueur of herbs and spices. The bottle contains a twig covered with crystallized sugar.

Fleur de Mocha   A liqueur of Colombian and Javanese coffees.

Forbidden Fruit   A proprietary American liqueur of West Indian grapefruit and brandy.

Fraises, crème de; fraisette   This strawberry liqueur of either cultivated or wild strawberries is magnificent in white-wine cups or parfaits.

Framboise, crème de   This raspberry liqueur—not to be confused with framboise, a white, unsweetened raspberry brandy—makes a refreshing summer highball with lemon juice, soda water and ice. It also takes the place of Melba sauce in peach Melba.

Frappémint   A proprietary American crème de menthe noted for its enduring flavor.

Galliano Liquore   A spicy but extremely smooth liqueur from Livorno, Italy, with flavor overtones of anise and vanilla.

Gebirgs Enzian   A liqueur with the flavor of gentian root.

Ginger-flavored brandy A U.S. and English infusion of fresh ginger root and brandy; perfect for hot grog.

Glayva A Scotch liqueur made with honey, herbs and anise.

Goldwasser, Danziger An aromatic liqueur made since 1598 with flavors of orange, coriander and caraway, and containing specks of gold leaf of at least 22 carats. Harmless and delicious, it is beloved by Indian princes who once sprinkled gold on puddings. Silberwasser (silver water), in the same genre, has disappeared in a world where the gold standard predominates.

Grand Marnier A distinguished French orange liqueur with a cognac base.

Grasshopper A chocolate-mint liqueur usually shaken with ice and cream to make a grasshopper cocktail.

Herbsaint Another substitute for absinthe, without harmful wormwood.

Honey punch; honey liqueur Close your eyes and the first sip will remind you of easily flowing honey. It's a natural mixer in brandy milk punch, eggnog, etc.

Irish Mist Irish whiskey and honey make this mellifluent liqueur a delightful after-dinner drink either taken straight or in Irish coffee.

Izarra Similar to Chartreuse, this French liqueur is offered in both yellow and green types.

Kirsch, crème de A sweet, white cherry liqueur—not to be confused with the completely dry kirsch white brandy.

Kümmel A caraway-flavored liqueur, usually colorless, varying considerably in sweetness, depending on brands.

Likier Smaku Ozynowego Polish-style blackberry-flavored brandy.

Liqueur d'or A French liqueur, like Goldwasser, made of orange, herbs and spices, with tiny flecks of gold in accordance with an ancient tradition that held that gold was the key to health and immortality.

Lochan Ora This is one of the newest Scotch-based liqueurs sweetened with honey and flavored with herbs.

Mandarines, crème de   A French liqueur with a tangerine flavor.

Maraschino   A white liqueur of small, black marasca cherries and pits; used mostly as a mixer.

Mastic; mastikha; mastika   A Middle Eastern liqueur made of the mastic shrub. It is extremely pleasant, high proof, on the dry side, and lacks the resin flavor found in Greek wine.

Menthe, crème de   This liqueur of mint leaves may be white, green, pink or gold. The small amount of menthol in fresh mint leaves gives it its refreshing coolness.

Moka, crème de   A coffee liqueur.

Noyaux, crème de   A pink liqueur made with the stones of such fruits as plums, cherries, peaches and apricots, producing a predominantly almond flavor.

O-Cha   Japanese green-tea liqueur with a bitter aftertaste; the perfect finale for an oriental dinner.

Ojen   A colorless anise-flavored Spanish liqueur. There are some high-proof bottlings in both sweet and dry varieties.

Ouzo   This most famous of all Greek apéritif liqueurs, normally mixed four parts water to one ouzo, is usually above 90 proof.

Parfait amour   Although the words *parfait amour* mean "perfect love," liqueurmen have never agreed on the same formula for perfection. One kind is made of lemon, citron and coriander; another of anisette, vanilla and orange; a third is produced from flowers, including violets. The only constant is its purple color.

Pastis; pastis de Marseille   A licorice-flavored French liqueur used as both an apéritif and a thirst quencher. It makes an immensely refreshing on-the-rocks drink.

Peach liqueur   Made from an infusion of whole fruit, sometimes fresh, or fresh and dried mixed, with brandy or neutral spirits as a base. It is an essential, though small, ingredient in fish-house punch.

Peppermint schnapps   Crème de menthe with less sugar and more alcohol; usually taken straight.

Pimento Dram   A Jamaican rum liqueur with peppery overtones.

Pineapple liqueur; licor de piña   Liqueur from the Carribean or Hawaii with the pleasant tartness of fresh fruit.

Ponche Real   Spanish orange liqueur with a brandy base.

Pousse-café   A liqueur of cacao, anisette and curaçao. Not to be confused with a mixed drink of the same name.

Prunella; prunelle, crème de   Liqueur with the predominant flavor of small tart plums, sometimes blended with prunes and sometimes with figs and vanilla.

Raki   A high-proof anise-flavored liqueur from the Middle East.

Reishu   Melon liqueur from the Far East.

Rock and rum   The same as rock and rye, except with a rum base; superb in milk punch.

Rock and rye   Rye whiskey, rock-candy syrup and fruit juices, with slices of fruit in the bottle. Another type contains crystallized sugar and no fruit. This old-fashioned winter solacer is a natural for hot drinks in mugs as well as for mixed-fruit drinks.

Roiano   An amber Italian liqueur with the flavor of anise and vanilla.

Rose, crème de   A liqueur of vanilla, spices and the aroma of rose petals. An enchanting end for a shish-kebab party.

Rosémint   A pink-hued mint liqueur used in the firefly cocktail.

Rosolio   Similar to crème de rose.

Rumona   One of the newest liqueurs from Jamaica, with flavors faintly reminiscent of vanilla, chocolate and coffee.

Sabra   A chocolate-orange combination from Israel.

Sambuca   A proprietary Italian liqueur made from the sambuca plant. Like anise in flavor but more subtle, it's usually served with a few roasted coffee beans for munching.

Sloe gin   This red liqueur, made from the sloe plums of the blackthorn bush, is not a gin at all, though juniper berries are sometimes used in its manufacture. It is probably called gin after the European holiday drinks made of gin, crushed sloe and sugar. Some types, as indicated on the label, will produce a creamy head when shaken with ice.

Southern Comfort   A famed American liqueur of whiskey base and peaches, it's excellent as a mixer in tall and short drinks. Its 100 proof adds to its comforting qualities.

Strega   This pale-yellow Italian liqueur is to Italy what Chartreuse is to France, a monument to the subtle blending of unidentifiable flavors of herbs and fruits.

Swedish punch   A Swedish liqueur of arak (East Indian aromatic rum), tea, spices and citrus flavor; also known as arrack punsch or caloric punsch.

Tangerine   A liqueur of tangerines with a mild flavor of spices.

Tea Breeze   French tea-flavored liqueur.

Tia Maria   A Jamaican proprietary coffee liqueur made from noted Blue Mountain coffee and spices.

Triple Sec   A colorless orange-flavored liqueur in the same family as curaçao, Cointreau, etc. It is also flavored with orange-flower water, orris root and other fragrances. Excellent in sidecars of equal parts brandy, Triple Sec and lemon juice.

Tuaca   An Italian milk brandy, with orange flavor, reminiscent of coconut.

Van Der Hum   Literally, "What's his name?" An African liqueur flavored with native tangerine peel and spices.

Van der Mint   A rich chocolate-mint liqueur from Holland.

Vanille, crème de   A once-delightful mixing liqueur, made with vanilla beans, now almost extinct.

Vieille Curé   A French herb-flavored monastery liqueur with a brandy base.

Violette, crème de   Liqueur of violet petals and vanilla.

Visnoka   Wild-cherry liqueur from eastern Europe.

Wishniak; wisniowka   A Polish cherry-flavored liqueur, also made in the U.S., sometimes flavored with other fruits in addition to cherries.

Yvette, crème   U.S. proprietary liqueur similar to crème de violette.

Zitronen Eis   Lemon liqueur.

14

BRANDY— THE EAU DE VIE

"Claret is the liquor for boys, port for men; but he who aspires to be a hero must drink brandy." Either Samuel Johnson's classic 18th Century dictum no longer applies or the fact that U.S. cognac consumption has tripled in recent years suggests that heroes have proliferated of late at an unparalleled rate. In any case, Dr. Johnson was on the right track to this extent: Brandy taken neat is in itself heroic. There is something about brandy's finesse that caresses the senses and even the palm of your warming hand. Frenchmen call it *largeur,* a spreading glow that suffuses the whole body. Whatever your brandy persuasion, discount the myth that it's necessary to sate your palate with a formal 12-course dinner before a great brandy can make its presence truly felt. Though it outshines almost any flavor or aroma that has gone before it, it's an impressive finale for even the most informal casserole dinner or buffet supper.

It's a quality achieved simply by distilling wine. Those who passed Chem I may recall that alcohol has a lower boiling point than water and that when wine is heated in a still, the vapors rise—leaving the water behind—and then later condense to become the *eau de vie.* The first raw spirits trickling out of medieval European alembics were properly used for treating battle wounds rather than drinking. How they evolved into what we now know as brandy is explained in a number of well-aged, well-blended myths.

One story concerns a Dutch sea captain who had been shipping wine from France to Holland and was rowing in the Charente River near the area which now produces cognac. He dropped his hat into the water, fished it out and noticed that it was twice as heavy. As he wrung it out, he reasoned: Why not extract the water from his vinous cargo, save a fortune in shipping costs and then later restore the water to the wine? He arranged to have the wine distilled, only to discover, upon tasting it, a new kind of Dutch courage so stunning that he couldn't possibly think of restoring the water to his *brandewijn* (Dutch for "burnt wine").

Or perhaps you prefer this legend: In England during the 16th Century, importers often received wine from the same area of France. It didn't travel well and was frequently spoiled upon arrival at the English docks. To salvage their investment, they distilled the wine into brandywine, a product which Chaucer had long before identified as the "water of immortality." It was a reasonable name because the powerful distillate, stored in wooden kegs, seemed, unlike wine, to live on and on for years without spoiling.

Italian specialists in drinking mythology easily explain how brandy came to be aged in wood. The way they tell it, an alchemist in the 15th Century stored his aqua vitae in a cellar barrel. To keep it out of the hands of mercenary soldiers about to plunder his village, he buried the barrel of raw brandy. He died, however, before he could retrieve his trove. Years later, someone discovered the hidden barrel of grappa, half-empty from evaporation, its raw white liquid now infused with a golden color and an indescribably noble flavor.

COGNAC

However accidental its beginnings, the method of making and aging brandy has evolved over the centuries into an art of the highest order—an art that achieves its supreme expression in the creation of cognac. Finest of the brandies, cognac is as unique as its old home, the countryside astride the Charente and Gironde Rivers of which the sleepy town of Cognac is the center.

Sixty-four thousand grapegrowers, each with his little plot of
land, toil in a land saturated with more sun than any other grape
region in France. An odd freak of nature makes the otherwise
unfriendly soil—a dour mixture of chalk and pebbles—just about
perfect for growing the tart grapes that turn into greenish wine
and eventually into aged brandy. Pot stills, kept under
government lock and key when the distilling season is over, are
identical with those used three centuries ago. Just as important
as the grapes and stills is the wood, from the nearby Limousin
forest, in which the cognac is put to sleep. So heady are the
vapors around the ancient brandy casks that workmen wear
safety belts to keep them from tumbling into the vats. No
railroad has ever been permitted to go into the Cognac region.
The old distillers fear that a spark might accidentally cause the
whole countryside to go up in flames, for during its long
hibernation, enough brandy is released as fumes into the air each
day to provide cognac for all France.

When buying cognac it's well to be familiar with the
inscriptions and annotations printed on the labels. The phrase
fine champagne cognac, for example, has no allusion whatever
to the bubbly wine produced in an altogether different section of
France. The word *champagne* also means "an open stretch of
land," and on a cognac label, it's the tip-off that the grapes used
came mainly from two of the finest open sections in the heart of
the Cognac region, identified on the map as Grande Champagne
and Petite Champagne. (There are five other sections of Cognac,
but these are of less importance.) To be labeled *fine champagne,*
cognac must contain grapes of which at least 60 percent came
from the Grande Champagne. To be labeled *grande fine
champagne,* the cognac must have been made from grapes 100
percent of which came from the Grande Champagne heartland.

Stars on cognac labels, and other brandy labels as well, don't
offer any really meaningful information to the buyer. You can,
for instance, buy a bottle of French brandy with no fewer than
five stars on the label for less than four dollars; it's a good
mixing brandy for sidecars and brandy sours, but it's not from
the Cognac region and it's completely out of the major-league
class. For those interested in myth and mystique, a single star
was once used by vintners to mean a good vintage after a poor
year. Two stars meant the bottle represented a succession of two
good years, and so on. According to one old cognac tale, the
good year was 1811, the Year of the Comet, which was
succeeded by two more wonderful years. Some cognac houses
themselves take credit for having originated the three stars, since
stars, like pearls, were symbols of the gems of cognacland. From
a practical standpoint, stars are only the cognac maker's way of
giving a subjective nod to what *he* considers a better than
average quality. You're not likely to come across a well-known
label with less than three stars. Recently, however, such
distinguished firms as Hennessy have dropped the stars entirely

from their cognac labels, since they consider them meaningless.

A somewhat more meaningful method of coding employs initials. The most common are V.O. (very old) and V.S.O.P. (very superior old pale or particular). The most interesting thing about these initials is that they represent English rather than French designations, obviously coined for the export trade. As with stars, they can't always be taken as a strict code of quality, but bottles marked V.S.O.P. by a particular brandy shipper are usually finer spirits than a bottling from the same shipper's cognac without these initials. The V.S.O.P. signet is usually an assurance that the brandy thus marked is largely composed of 20- to 25-year-old stock. V.V.S.O.P. (very, very superior old pale) signifies stock about 40 years old. X.O. (extra old), *cordon bleu* and *La Reine* are also designates of old cognacs of the finest quality. Sometimes these are called liqueur cognacs, though they have no relation to sweet liqueurs or cordials.

Interestingly, in a blind tasting of cognac by professional cognac tasters, a cognac marked with three stars was given a higher rating than the cognac marked V.S.O.P. by the same distinguished shipper. A great Scotch such as Chivas Regal doesn't need the myth or mystique of stars or initials to tell its story; cognac makers are beginning to come around to the same sensible viewpoint.

The whole question of age is disposed of very simply by American import laws. *No* age is permitted to be printed on a bottle of cognac, except a very insignificant amount of vintage cognacs made from grapes of a specific year. The quantity of these vintage cognacs is so small, and their quality so dubious, that they seldom become a significant item even in a cognac collector's library. The American ruling is reasonable since the greatest cognacs are blends of different vineyards, different distilleries and different years. In mixing their artful blends, the cognacmasters choose one for mellowness, another for virility, another for finesse.

Naturally, a superb cognac contains more liquid age than youth. One sagacious brandyman, when asked for the perfect age of a cognac, said it was the same as that for a woman —somewhere between 25 and 40. Brandy connoisseurs all agree that waters of immortality beyond the age of 50 begin to slip in quality. Stories about the excellence of a dusty bottle taken from Napoleon's foot locker are so much romantic nonsense. In the cellars of the old cognac houses, there may be a cask here and there containing cognac a hundred years old, but these are museum pieces from which most of the glory has gone with the years. And remember that cognac ages only in the wood, never in the bottle; when you buy it, therefore, the best advice is, use it. It will never attain a greater quality. And once opened, don't keep it around too long. Frequent uncorking eventually will cause it to lose its original glow.

You may confidently forget all about stars, initials and other identification tags when you buy cognac bearing the labels of the eminent old brandy shippers. Generally speaking, price is one of the better yardsticks. Two others are equally dependable—your nose and mouth. In the last analysis, cognac can be properly assessed only as it trickles down your throat. You should find yourself not only drinking it but drinking to it.

NON-COGNAC GRAPE BRANDIES

The only other French brandy one can talk about in the same breath with cognac is armagnac. Though it's distilled from the same type of grapes grown in the Cognac region, the earth of its home, Gascony, is unlike that of the Cognac area, and the black oak used in making Gascon casks results in a different marriage of wood and spirits. The taste is somewhat harder and more pungent than cognac, but the brandy of Armagnac is still in the pantheon of great spirits and has immense appeal to the brandy-faithful everywhere.

Marc, a common brandy in France, is distilled from the stems and skins of grapes and has a woody, rustic flavor. Although you aren't likely to find it at your corner liquor store, you'll meet it in many French bistros. Other French grape brandies exported to this country are light-tasting and excellent for mixing purposes.

German brandies from the valley of the Rhine are superb distillates with a faintly sweet perfume, due to the fact that the Rhenish grapes are left on the vine longer than the French. While the best-known ambassadors of Spain and Portugal are sherry and port, both countries produce brandies as fortifiers for their wines. Each has its own bouquet and, to many brandy noses, is reminiscent of the national wine. Metaxa, from Greece, the richest-tasting of all brandies, is made from the sweet muscat grape and is a semiliqueur. Greek ouzo, with its pronounced anise flavor, is called a brandy in some quarters but, because of its sweetness, a liqueur in others. (See page 72.)

Pisco is a nearly clear 90-proof Peruvian brandy distilled from the muscat or mission grapes of Chile and Peru. It is aged briefly in paraffin-lined containers to keep the brandy from acquiring the color or flavor of the wood. The youthful, high-proof spirit gives you a sensation somewhat akin to a slight earthquake. It usually finds its way into the Peruvian pisco sour, a brandy sour made from pisco with a small amount of egg white and a few drops of bitters.

It's not surprising to find many of the best metropolitan bars using California brandy as a mixer. It never aspires to the subtleties of a cognac, but its easygoing personality seems to

make it just right for stingers, sidecars and other brandy
concoctions.

WHITE FRUIT BRANDIES

Great brandies aren't all derived from the meat within a
grapeskin. Superb distillations are extracted from other fruits and
are generally white, fiery and unaged in order to preserve their
straight fruity essence. Usually not a trace of sugar is apparent.
The most noted of these is kirsch (or kirschwasser), a white
brandy made of cherries and cherry pits. Crushed plums are
used to make quetsch or mirabelle in France and slivovitz in
central Europe. The latter is an exception to the no-aging rule and
develops a light golden aura after six or eight years in the wood.
The lush flavor of red raspberries is drawn into framboise in
France and Himbeergeist in Germany. Perhaps the most
spectacular of the white fruit brandies is Switzerland's pear
brandy, which comes with a large whole pear in the bottle.
When the pear on the tree is still in its infancy, it is slipped
through the neck of the bottle. The bottle is attached to the tree,
and the pear blooms and eventually grows to natural size. Later,
both bottle and pear are detached from the tree, and the bottle is
filled with white pear brandy which, incidentally, seems to have
more of the pear fragrance than the fresh pear itself.

APPLE BRANDY

Long before George Washington wrote to Samuel Laird
asking for his apple-brandy recipe, Americans were distilling
what we now call applejack. Currently used as a cocktail mixer,
it is famed particularly for its role in the jack-rose cocktail. Its
French counterpart, calvados, is a suave postprandial potation.
Applejack, although aged, keeps a vivid perfume of the apple.
Calvados retains a subtler hint of the fruit, perhaps because of its
longer aging. Vets of World War Two who remember the
Normandy invasion shouldn't confuse the white lightning
surreptitiously made in the cellars of French applegrowers with
the present-day extremely suave ten-year-old calvados.

The newest form of liquid apple made in the U.S., called
blended apple brandy, is a union of aged apple brandy and
neutral grain spirits. It's lighter and more satiny than straight
apple brandy, and as a mixer in drinks like the jack rose or
applejack and ginger ale dances rings around its older version.

15
WINE—
IN VINO
FELICITAS

The witchery of wine is that it constantly changes. The grapes on the vine vary from day to day and from year to year. Wine changes in the fermenting vats, in the cellar and even in the bottle. It changes when it's transported over the ocean and finally in the wineglass as its perfume slowly rises in the air. Because wine is a living thing, it has the fascination of anything that is born and matures. The Frenchman regards it as a thing of beauty—a changing beauty but not an irresolute one. And to describe the incredible finesse of this beauty, he can find only one simile in his language. His wine, he says, is like a woman.

One can drink a glass of fino sherry as an apéritif or enjoy a glass of *vin rosé* during the afternoon, but for the most part, wine belongs on the festive board. Like bread, it can be served from the beginning to the end of a meal. But, unlike bread, it's not mere

ballast. It's the coaxer, the instigator, the thrust and parry. The
natural dryness of wine, like mellow but caustic humor, makes it
the perfect counterpoint for food. It's the magic that makes the
plump oysters tangier, the hot onion soup friendlier, the duck
richer, the veal cutlet more succulent and the melon more exotic.

To learn about wines and their differences, one need only
taste several at the same sitting. It works something like this: If
you were suddenly asked to describe the tastes of four different
kinds of apples, you might be stumped. But if you were to sit
down and carefully taste a McIntosh, a Winesap, a Jonathan and
a Delicious, you'd detect almost unbelievable variations in
flavor, texture and aroma. In a few moments you'd be an apple
connoisseur, talking about sweetness, dryness, mellowness,
liveliness, aroma and all sorts of qualities that you had never
tagged before. In wine drinking, something of the same skill
develops after you've sampled several different wines arrayed
alongside each other. Normally, of course, a wine drinker doesn't
order three different kinds of Burgundy with his mutton chop.
But a wine-tasting party (see page 335) is fun in itself and an
educational lark. The important thing is to compare wines that
are indeed comparable; don't open a bottle of Spanish Rioja, one
of French Chablis and a bottle of New York State Niagara. If
possible, compare wines from the same grape, like three
California Cabernet Sauvignons or two California Cabernet
Sauvignons with two French red Bordeaux. Provide plenty of
glasses and provide one or two hard cheeses and some water
crackers or breadsticks to clear the palate between sippings.

When you first drink wine, it may be with a gulp. You may
not pause to hold the glass between thumb and forefinger, slowly
twirling it to admire the bright-purple liquid while waiting for
its bouquet to rise in the glass until it reaches your nostrils. But
after you've enjoyed several wines, you'll want to wait for what
winemen call the first taste—the wine's fragrance. The second
taste occurs when you drink the wine slowly and your taste buds
savor the body, the soft flow of the grape itself. Finally, you'll
experience the third sensation, the mature delight of the
lingering aftertaste. In time you'll come to look upon these three
phases as distinct flavor experiences, just as when you eat a hot
Welsh rabbit, you experience first the aroma of the bubbling
cheese, then the eating thereof and finally the slow tang of the
aftertaste.

But wine drinking involves more than just tasting. To enjoy
the whole experience most fully, you should, therefore, become
familiar with such refinements as:

Corksmanship Before drawing the cork from a bottle of table
wine, carefully remove the outer foil covering and wipe the
bottletop to remove any dust. Then use any of the corkscrews
pictured on the color pages in this volume. When the cork is out,

the bottletop should again be carefully wiped with a clean towel to remove any loose cork or foreign matter around the rim. Smell the cork. If the bottle has been lying properly on its side, it should smell of wine. On very rare occasions the wine is corky; that is, it smells of a spoiled cork, like rotten wood, giving the wine an off-flavor—so far off, in fact, that the wine must be discarded. It happens so rarely, however, that the possibility needn't concern you. Very rarely a bottle of wine will have turned sharp and sour, actually vinegary, losing the natural dryness of a fine table wine. But again, the chance of opening a really defective bottle these days is extremely rare.

Decanting   Very old red table wines will sometimes show a sediment in the bottle. Vintage port, unless it's been rebottled before being shipped, will throw off a crust. You can check sediment by holding the bottle in front of a light bulb at eye level. When removing a very old bottle from its prone position the bin, lift it very slowly and carefully into an upright position, since the sediment, if present, will be on the side of the bottle. Let it sift to the bottom; if there's an unusually large amount of sediment—a half inch or more—the wine should be decanted: Stand the bottle upright for several hours; then pour very slowly into a decanter in one steady motion. Do not tilt the bottle back and forth during decanting—and stop pouring before the sediment is reached, using a light bulb again, if necessary, to check the level.

Serving Wine   Chill white table wines about two hours in the refrigerator before serving, or about a half hour in a champagne bucket with ice. Bring your reds to the serving room at least an hour before they're to be used, so that they can reach room temperature, ideally between 60° and 70° F. (Rich Burgundies are sometimes preferred at a cellar temperature—between 50° and 60° F.—but if you don't have a cool cellar, and if your dining room isn't subject to a blazing Sahara sun, you'll undoubtedly settle for your air-conditioned comfort, which most red wines find very compatible.) Draw the cork from a bottle of red wine when it's brought out, to allow the wine to breathe, i.e., to allow its bouquet to begin expanding for later enjoyment.

The practice of wrapping a napkin around a bottle of wine before pouring is now looked upon as an affectation; besides, guests like to look at a label. Certainly, if a wine is impressively delicious, they want to know its name and shipper, just as they like to talk about a new car or suit of clothes. Bottles which have been chilled in cracked ice may drip water when they're poured, but even in this case it's better to pour the wine while holding the bottle off the table than to use a napkin.

Before serving, pour a bit of wine into your own glass and sample it; then, if you're satisfied—and again, the chances are about one in a thousand that you won't be—fill the glasses of your guests no more than one-third to one-half full—assuming they're the large tulip-shaped glasses of 9 to 11 ounces or big-bellied Burgundy glasses. Finally, fill your own and propose a toast.

The wine basket now in common use may have been intended originally as a substitute for decanting, i.e., to keep the bottle on its side with the sediment undisturbed. It doesn't serve that purpose, nor is it any longer the intention. The basket, however, does make it easy to slide the wine down the table, and the pouring is somewhat easier than from the upright bottle.

The day of the 14-course dinner, each "progress" with its special wine, is over. The usual practice calls for one or two wines with each meal. If it's one, it makes good sense to observe the old rule concerning red wine with red meats or white wine with poultry of fish—for the simple reason that they go best together. A hearty roast beef, for example, would clobber the delicate flavor of a white Burgundy, whereas a red Burgundy would survive and complement the meat. Conversely, the red would overwhelm a delicate pompano *en papillote.* If you are serving more than one wine, it's a good notion to progress from dry to sweet, from light to heavy, from young to old—not because it's a rule but because experience suggests this is the road to greater enjoyment of both food and drink.

Winology In Europe a year may be great, good, fair or poor for most vineyards, and, naturally, the great or good years will be proudly proclaimed as vintage years, commanding vintage prices. In the U.S. wine-growing areas, the steadier weather conditions make vintages much less important. But there are all sorts of other factors that can make the vintage charts doubtful and sometimes even downright silly. A great Burgundy uncorked after it's lain in the cellar only three years may actually have required six to ten years to reach its peak of maturity. If you're a wine collector, well and good. But if you're buying a bottle or two of this "great" vintage year for tonight's dinner party, you're buying a wine that should have remained in a cellar gathering cobwebs rather than be presented for enjoyment here and now. A white wine, by the same token, with an optimum bottle life of five years will be way past its prime in eight years. It's also possible for a vineyard on one side of the hill to have luscious grapes during a particular year while the vintner on the other side has a mediocre yield—or for one vineyard to come up with a delightful wine in an otherwise "poor" year. The answer to all such dilemmas is to choose a reputable wine merchant, who can provide you with a vintage chart showing the gradings of a variety of wines by vintages and who can guide you in the same way a decorator can guide you in choosing furniture. Remember, of course, that no vintage chart and no wine merchant, however experienced, can be a substitute for tasting.

If for every seven bottles of table wine that Americans drink, only one is now imported, the exporters—particularly the French—have their nomenclature rather than the taxman largely to thank. Trying to decipher wine labels can be just as tiresome and confusing as attempting to make sense out of vintages, and the average young guy can go quietly nuts trying to figure out what's what. The hundreds of châteaux and the meaning of château bottling, estate bottling, *clos, cru, grand cru, premier grand cru,* etc.; the confusion arising from such facts as that Château Margaux—a claret, which does not mean the French word *clairet*—which comes from Médoc, is a Bordeaux; that it may be marked *Appelation contrôlée* or *Appellation Margaux contrôlée*—all tend to discourage the man who has even a few other interests to occupy his mind. To avoid possible boredom or frustration, it's easiest—and perfectly adequate—to remember this: The best French reds and whites are deemed by most connoisseurs to be the best in the world; German whites from the Rhine and Moselle districts have an unsurpassed fruity fragrance; Italian wines tend to be hearty and earthy; Spain is famed for its sherry and Portugal for its port. U.S. wines, while not challenging the very greatest of France or Germany, are now challenging, and in many cases surpassing, the *good* wines of those countries. Let's take a look at each of them in turn.

WINES OF FRANCE

There are many areas in France that produce illustrious wines: The Champagne section, the Rhone valley with its Hermitage and famed Châteauneuf-du-Pape, and the Alsace with its flowery, spicy German-type wines. But the most noted are the wines of Bordeaux and Burgundy, favorites of *viveurs* all over the world for many generations.

Bordeaux, in the southwest corner of France, is noted for five famous sections—the Médoc, the Graves, the Sauternes, the St.-Emilion and the Pomerol. (In England the reds from Bordeaux are known as clarets.) The best of the Bordeaux wines come from a specific château or property. There are hundreds of châteaux originally classified into so-called growths in 1855. Additional classifications were made in 1953 and 1955, and, naturally, the owners of many wines classified in the fourth growth of Médoc now argue heatedly that they should be reclassified in the second or first growths. Just as naturally, those in the first growth never argue that they should be classified second or third. But over the years most French winemen, when they can be objective, agree that the classifications are generally fair as guides to quality.

Bordeaux reds are known for their tangy fruitiness, their fine balance and the gracefulness with which they age to long life.

Those from the Médoc section, most of which are reds, are known for their virile flavor and include such famous château names as Margaux, Haut-Brion and Mouton-Rothschild and such noted Communes as St.-Julien and St.-Estèphe. The area of Bordeaux known as the Graves (from the gravelly, pebbly texture of its soil) produces both red and white wines, although the whites are best known in this country. From the Sauternes section come the stunningly beautiful sweet wines of France, of which the greatest is Château d'Yquem, a wine celebrated in poems and novels for generations. Finally there are the St.-Emilion and Pomerol wines often called the Burgundies of Bordeaux because of their virile body and rich color.

Most of the Burgundy region is known as the Côte d'Or, or "slope of gold," which consists of two main divisions: the Côte de Nuits and the Côte de Beaune. Three other wine areas in Burgundy—the Mâconnais, Beaujolais and Chablis—are almost as eminent in the wine world. Unlike the Bordeaux vineyards, each of which is owned by a private family or corporation, the Burgundy vineyards may have as many as 40 owners each. So valuable is the chalky soil that in one vineyard, Clos de Vougeot, the workmen are instructed to shake the dirt from their shoes before they leave the estate, in order not to lose any of the incomparable earth.

Many of the Burgundy wines are known by the vineyard, as in the case of the Clos de Vougeot. In other cases, the wine bears the name of the commune. Sometimes the names of the village and the wine will be joined, as with the Vosne-Romanée or the Gevrey-Chambertin. Actually, the wine sold as Gevrey-Chambertin, although a fine Burgundy red, is basking in the light of the illustrious name Chambertin, which—when it appears alone on a label—refers to the magnificent red Burgundy which was once Napoleon's favorite. Most renowned of the red Burgundies is Romanée-Conti, famous for its full velvety flavor and longevity; most illustrious of the whites is Montrachet. Chablis is, however, the most reasonably priced all-purpose white wine in Burgundy. Like its red counterpart, Beaujolais, it can be served with anything from shrimp to sweetbreads.

France is not only one of the world's greatest exporters of wine but also one of its greatest importers. A huge river of wine flows from Algeria to France, and in this kind of situation, hanky-panky is inevitable. In recent years the French government has taken active steps to assure the genuineness of the labels on French wines. Laws known as the *Appellations d'Origine* have placed strict regulation on the use of château names. The legend *Appellation contrôlée* on a bottle insures the geographical location of the wine. It means that the region, district or vineyard designated is guaranteed; it is, of course, no guarantee of quality. *Mise en bouteille au château* or *à la propriété* is an assurance that the wine was bottled on the property indicated on the label. *Cru,* when applied to wine, refers to growth or classification, such as *grand cru, premier cru,* etc.

WINES OF GERMANY

No wines in the world are more spontaneously accepted with the very first sip than the great white wines from the valleys of the Rhine and Moselle rivers. Experienced and inexperienced students of Bacchus seem to react alike to their soft, rich and fruity flavors. Most German wines are drunk in their youth, and after five years tend to go downhill, although a few—made from overripe grapes touched by what the French call the "noble rot" and the Germans call the *Edelfäule*—have the luscious sweetness of French sauternes and may enjoy a greater longevity. While German red wines are insignificant, the whites are natural partners with fish and poultry, and many of them are magnificent all-purpose wines, going as easily with a rich game stew as with brook trout. In England, German white wine is known as hock and in the summer serves as a classical thirst quencher mixed with cold club soda.

Liebfraumilch, which originally identified a wine from a specific vineyard near the Church of Our Beloved Lady, in Worms, has become over the years a catchall term for almost any German white wine, fair or good—although the more expensive Liebfraumilchs are delightful and well worth the investment. *Moselblümchen,* meaning "little flower of the Moselle," is another general term for wine from the Moselle region. Many of the Rhine wines bear the name of a town, as does Niersteiner, from the town of Nierstein. Others are labeled *Schloss,* which literally means "castle" but is actually the designation of a particular vineyard, like a French château wine or estate-bottled wine. The terminology on German wine labels is often mystifying to non-Teutonic wine drinkers. Here are a few translations:

Natur   A natural wine, unsugared.

Wachstum   Growth of a single vineyard, usually followed by the name of the vineyard or owner.

Kabinett   The best wine of a specific vineyard.

Fass or Fuder   The cask in which a distinguished wine was matured; often the cask number will be indicated.

Original Abfüllung   Original bottling by the grower; same as a château-bottled wine.

Spätlese   Wine from a picking of late, ripe grapes.

Auslese   Special selection of ripe grape bunches.

Beerenauslese   Literally, "berry selection"; wine pressed from selected single ripe grapes.

Trockenbeerenauslese   Wine pressed from selected grapes so ripe they are almost raisins.

WINES OF ITALY

As a nation, Italians are undoubtedly the least self-conscious wine drinkers in the world. Accustomed to downing it in great drafts, they would no more think of debating the merits of last night's wine than they'd chatter about last night's pasta. According to them, wine is something for which the whole body thirsts; you accept it eagerly, enjoy it enormously, and then quietly forget about it till the next meal. Now and then, of course, an Italian businessman might slip out of his office for a small glass of Campari or a quick glass of apéritif wine and some salted almonds. But at mealtime he wants his full bottle of *vino* on the table, and if it's not there, it's as though someone had snatched away his roast, his bread or his salad.

Though there are some good and very distinquished Italian wines, none can challenge the greatest of the French Bordeaux or Burgundies. But this situation gives the Italian not the slightest sense of inferiority. Those exceedingly rare wines and their rare vintages, after all, are seldom enjoyed by Frenchmen. They go to only a few select places, mostly London and New York, where wine pundits can afford the esoteric hobby of discussing one year versus another, and one grape versus another. Besides, who would want to be running around in a Rolls-Royce all day, every day? There are times—most of the time, in fact—when the Fiat is more natural and more easy fun.

Although the billion-gallon river of Italian wine runs mostly red each year, there are some excellent bibulous specimens among the whites as well. Starting at the top of the Italian boot, Piedmont is the home of Italy's greatest red, Barolo—a wine whose praises were sung by Julius Caesar and which ages beautifully. From the same area come Barbaresco and Barbera (the latter now a flourishing California red), as well as the noted sparkling white wine, Asti Spumante—which, though not as dry as champagne, is a wonderfully festive wine. Americans should realize that Asti Spumante comes under many labels and that each differs considerably in body; so taste testing is important if you're choosing one for a large party. From Venetia, to the east,

are two sturdy and eminent reds, Bardolino and Valpolicella.
And from the town of Veneto, near Verona, comes the kind of
wine that might very well have inspired Romeo's declamations
—a white whose finesse clearly entitles it to its name: Soave.
Tuscany, farther down the boot, is the home of Chianti, certainly
the best-known Italian wine name in the U.S. Like *Liebfraumilch*
in Germany, the word *Chianti* has been used and misused for
almost any red wine in a straw-covered bottle. Actually, the
genuine Chianti, called Chianti Classico, some of it in an
ordinary bottle without straw, comes from a delimited Chianti
zone and can be identified by the black rooster on the label. The
best Chianti mellows richly with age. Orvieto, a white wine
named after its place of origin in Umbria, comes in two forms: a
wine of medium dryness and a lighter, sweeter version. Like
Chianti, it always arrives in the U.S. in the straw-covered *fiaschi*.
The wine called Lachryma Christi is pressed from grapes grown
on the slopes of Mt. Vesuvius. The name means "the tears of
Christ," and legend has it that they were shed because the lovely
Neapolitan area was inhabited by creatures considerably more
fiendish than human; where the tears fell, the vines grew.
Fittingly, it is the most pleasant and softest of the wines grown
in this area. Beyond the tip of the Italian boot is the strange and
passionate island of Sicily, which is known for, among other
things, its Marsala, a sweet, fortified dessert wine best served
bitingly cold and best used for gracing a cheese platter and bowl
of fresh fruit rather than a sweet chocolate soufflé.

SHERRY, PORT AND MADEIRA

That port is the exclusive indulgence of doddering London
clubmen and that sherry is designed mainly for elderly distaff tea
parties are stubborn sterotypes that should be laid to rest. White
ports are now among the most popular of all apéritifs sipped at
sundown in Parisian and Belgian cafés. There are watering spots
where ice-cold fino sherry has supplanted the martini, and still
others where it's used in place of vermouth in the martini
pitcher. Even the semisweet and sweet sherries flow over the
rocks regularly at the cocktail hour.

The most important thing on the labels of both sherry and
port is the shipper's name, and when you look at a bottle of
either one, you'll find less pretentious terminology than on
almost any other bottling of fine wine. The great sherries are all
blends, as are all ports—outside of vintage ports—and the
blending arts in Spain and Portugal are the accumulated
knowledge of centuries of training and skill. Consequently, when

you see names like Sandeman, Harvey's, Gonzalez Byass, Cockburn, Robertson Bros., Pedro Domecq, Williams and Humbert, Duff Gordon and others, you can invariably count upon wines that are amazingly consistent in spite of snowstorms, withering heat, hail, and good, bad and indifferent years.

Both sherry and port are fortified—that is, wines whose fermentation has been arrested at a desired point by adding brandy to them. Years ago both suffered from cloudiness, the result of sedimentation in the bottle. A new process called supercooling, wherein the wines are held at low but not below-zero temperatures just before bottling, eliminates this annoying problem.

Bottles of port and sherry, unlike table wines, may be opened, recorked and then left in your liquor cabinet without any fear of spoiling. But both are at their best shortly after they're opened the first time. In Spain, for instance, a host wouldn't think of pouring from the bottle opened yesterday. Instead, he'll open a new one—perhaps a bone-dry fino sherry—to start his party and then continue serving it through soup and fish courses like any other table wine. If there's any left over, it's used for cooking.

Sherries run the spectrum from the palest of finos or manzanillas, usually served as apéritifs, to the medium-dry amontillados, all the way to the deep olorosos or cream sherries, which are magnificent dessert wines. Spanish sherries are developed, aged and blended in the solera system, whereby young wines are gradually moved into casks containing older wines. The younger wines thus take on the rich flavor, deep color and full-bodied maturity of the senior sherries much sooner than if they had remained alone, leading the indeterminate asocial life followed by most table wines in their own casks.

In contrast to sherries, which darken with age, ports lose color as they get older. All young ones, outside of white ports, are a deep, intense purple. As they ripen, they turn ruby, indicating a fine port which is mature but not terribly old. In time, they become tawny, with brown overtones and still deeper flavor. Most of the ports sent to this country from Portugal are either ruby or tawny, and both are complicated blends which somehow remain remarkably consistent in quality over the years.

Vintage ports are those of a particularly good year, kept in casks for two years and then bottled; names like Da Silva, Rochas and Hooper represent the finest of these. During their long bottle life, they throw off a crust, and most of them until recently required decanting. A few vintage ports, those of the war years, have been decanted in Portugal and shipped in new bottles, thus eliminating a formerly tedious job. If you make a hobby of vintage ports, recent vintages selected for bottling include '27s, '34s, '35s, '42s, '43s, '45s, '47s, '50s, '55s, '58s and

'60s. Although one can still buy 1890 and early-1900 ports, most collectors nowadays seem to prefer vintages not quite as ancient as in other generations. For the young bachelor who doesn't have the space to lay down bottles for future years—or the patience to wait for them—there are bottlings of vintage reserve ports, blends of old ports of different vintage years, which needn't be decanted and which are great for after-coffee sipping. White ports from Portugal (not the California variety) are apéritif wines with a lively bouquet but very little sugar—a welcome change-of-pace drink for those who want to be stimulated, not stunned, at the cocktail hour.

The Portuguese island of Madeira became famous as a source of American wines during colonial days. But in cookbooks even today, particularly in France, Madeira is often the wine called for rather than sherry, which it resembles in color, flavor and the solera system in which it's made. Though only a small amount is imported to America, all the Madeiras (from Sercial, the lightest, to Verdelho or Bual, of medium sweetness, to the rich, dark Malmsey) are pleasant and warming wines to be sipped on a lazy winter afternoon in the States.

WINES OF THE UNITED STATES

Once upon a time vinophiles looked upon the U.S. as a great place in which to live, but you wouldn't want to drink its wines. Wines for winos? Of course. And wines for cooking? OK. But wines to talk about in the same breath with the prestige products of France and Germany? You're kidding. That, however, was once upon a time. Wine drinking is the most steadfast of pleasures, but wine making is the most fluid of arts (no pun intended).

Looking for equals in European and U.S. wines is like trying to find identical rivers. Each breathes its own prevailing atmosphere, is hugged by its own soil and flows along its own course. Juice crushed from the grapes on one hill is quite different from the product of the very same variety grown on another hill. When a specific grape, such as the Pinot Chardonnay, is transplanted from the Côte d'Or in Burgundy to the Sonoma Valley in California, it's destined to yield an entirely different cup of cheer—not necessarily better or worse, but definitely different. Long before former-President Johnson ordered our embassies abroad to eschew the foreign grape in favor of American wines, the vintages of the two continents were being judged side by side. Thomas Jefferson, after serving two bottles of U.S. wine sent to him as a gift, wrote to the donor saying that his guests could not tell the difference between them and "the far-famed Burgundy named Chambertin." In a series of wine-tasting sessions a while ago at Harvard, Columbia and Williams, the oenological undergrads preferred American wines over their Continental counterparts two to one. And during a recent six-year California comparative wine-tasting program in which 2500 fanciers offered their sober and civilized opinions, U.S. wines took 214 first places as against 198 for foreign wines. As you might expect, some French wine exporters sneered that the barbaric Americans couldn't be depended upon to tell good from bad. But not all Frenchmen are so condescending. Pierre Lamalle, one of the top inspectors of the prestigious *Guide Michelin,* took a gastronomic tour of this country a few years ago and tasted an American wine from a rare bottling that he said could honorably compete with any of the top wines of France of the same variety. Many U.S. wine makers now turn out a small amount of such opulent growths, usually babied in small casks until they reach their moment of perfection, that critical point of time when a great wine must be bottled lest it begin to go downhill. Some of these rare wines, like the noble bottlings of Europe, never leave the vineyard, but a few may be sent to a handful of rare-wine shops in big cities and may command five or six dollars a bottle.

American wines have so overtaken their Continental counterparts, particularly in the medium to good grades, that the dedicated vinophile no longer need store only a few popular domestic vintages for his kitchen. Indeed, a really useful cellar, once the exclusive province of European wines, may now start with its foundation deep in native soil. But when ordering domestic wines for your own cellar, don't be a victim of the name game. An American wine is known either by a generic name, such as rosé, or by the name of the grape, such as Pinot noir. Our advice is to buy generically only champagne, rosé, sherry and port. In all other cases, you'll be better off going by the name of the grape.

Names such as Chablis and burgundy on American wines would best be forgotten, if only it were possible. But since many of these European names still appear on U.S. bottlings, the resulting confusion can be unriddled by the following list of generic wine names, coupled with the grapes from which they're made:

Bordeaux—Cabernet Sauvignon
Sauternes (spelled without the added *s* in the
   U.S.)—Sauvignon Blanc and Semillon
Red Burgundy—Pinot Noir and Gamay
Chablis or white Burgundy—Pinot Chardonnay, Pinot Blanc
   and Chenin Blanc
Rhine and Alsatian wines—Johannisberg Riesling,

Emerald Riesling, Grey Riesling, Sylvaner, Traminer and
Gewurtztraminer.

These grapes are the first families of California wines. They
belong to the *Vitis vinifera,* the "wine-bearing" species whose
ancestral domain was in Europe but which now finds a home in
the counties around San Francisco. So cordial are the California
sun and soil to these grapes that one giant vineyard is planted
with 1,300,000 vines of 19 varieties of grapes. It's a versatility
unknown in Europe, where most vineyards grow only one or two
varieties.

In spite of their size, the best California wineries still mature
their table wines in small oak casks. Since California never has
to put up with the grim cold and heat that often bedevil
European vineyards, vintages don't count for much; no year can
be a disaster. There are some annual differences in the grapes,
but the quality of a wine is liable to vary more from one
vineyard to the next. When you do see a year printed on a U.S.
wine label, it usually means that it was a bottling of which the
cellarmaster was particularly proud. It also serves as a reminder
to drink the white wines, such as Sylvaner and Pinot blanc in
their youth, within two to three years of their vintage date; the
red wines retain their excellence somewhat longer, but usually
no more than four to five years with some rare exceptions.

Eastern grapes, mainly from northern Ohio and the Finger
Lakes region of New York State, are among the few fruits that
can be called really native to America. Leif Ericson marveled at
them during his explorations of the New World, which he called
Wineland the Good. The grapes used today are hybrids of those
original wild vines, and the best of the current Eastern wines are
sold by their grape names, such as the Diamond, the Delaware
and the Elvira. Smooth, clean-tasting, altogether superb, their
fruitiness recommends them to dinners of ham, wild fowl,
chicken and all dessert and cheese courses.

The biggest news in the East is the successful planting of
new French-American hybrid grapes. The amount of wine
gushing from these new vine plantings isn't large, but for the
first time, dry European-style wines are being bottled east of the
Mississippi.

CHAMPAGNE

If ever a single symbol immediately and unmistakably meant
luxurious living, it's the scintillant wine known variously as
nosetickler, gigglewater, fizz, bubbly and sometimes even as
champagne. One would not drink gin out of a lady's slipper or
christen a ship with a bottle of Scotch; occasions that call for

gaiety and celebration require a special drink, a brilliant drink, a bravura drink. But, fortunately, champagne is no longer exclusively tied to Lucullan feasts and to hidebound formal occasions. Lord Chesterfield's favorite toast is more pertinent than ever: "Give me champaign and fill it to the brim,/I'll toast in bumpers every lovely limb!" Today the pop of the cork is heard just as frequently at an *intime* table for two as in a big banquet hall. Its unparalleled flavor, tingle and *chatoyance* go equally well with beluga caviar or a platter of cheese, with breast of guinea hen or glazed Virginia ham.

Although great age doesn't mean great gigglewater (after about ten years the bubbly loses its zest), great price usually does. With few exceptions, you pay for what you get in champagne, and the more it costs, the better it usually is. There are a few important clues to excellence the knowing champagne taster will seek. One of the first is the champagne's vinosity. It's simply the essential and natural flavor of the grape; call it "grapiness" if you will, keeping in mind that it's not the flavor of the raw grape but the finished flavor of the fermented juice. Time and again a taster sampling a poor champagne will say that it tastes like water, meaning it lacks the deep, straight, unmistakable flavor of the fruit—the flavor that fills your mouth and stays there after your glass is empty. It's just like a man eating a tender steak complaining that it's less "beefy" than it should be. Dryness is often a valuable clue, too, since sugar is often, but not always, used to mask poor champagne. Aroma is important, and as in tasting wine, the best way to train both nose and palate is to taste three or four champagnes slowly, one after another. Such qualities as finesse and mellowness are learned only through long and happy practice. The effervescence of a fine champagne is shown in small steady bubbles, sometimes so small they're barely visible.

The whole *sec, brut,* extra-dry scene is a puzzler, probably because although *sec* is the French word for "dry," champagne labeled with that word is actually semisweet. Compounding the confusion, extra dry is not the driest. Here's the way it goes: *Brut* is the driest of all champagne and may taste almost sour to a virgin palate; extra dry is not quite as dry as that; *sec* is rather sweet but not cloying. You may also run across *doux,* which is very sweet.

Little American champagne bears a vintage year, but that which does is usually an estimable bottling. When French champagne carries a vintage year, it simply means that in that particular year grapes were produced that gave the champagne a unique flavor. The salient fact to remember is that most old French firms use the same fine wines for their nonvintage as for their vintage champagnes. They keep their quality uniformly high by an elaborate and artful system of blending wines from different vineyards and different years.

If you're wondering when champagne should be served, stop wondering. It can be served any time. It has been called a dessert wine, and indeed it is wizard at meal's end, but it's also the only potation that can be tippled before dinner as a cocktail and during dinner as an accompaniment to every course as well. It flatters all food and is indispensable with caviar. Some say it is grand stuff on certain mornings, too, as a specific against the horrors.

How to serve? There's no mystery. Prior to pouring it should, of course, be thoroughly chilled—but not frozen to death. The best serving temperature is between 40° and 50° F.; to achieve it, place the bottle in the refrigerator for an hour or two—as far from the freezing section as possible—or for about a half hour in the ice of a champagne bucket. Don't jostle the bottle unnecessarily before opening it or the contents will fizzle out as soon as the cork is pulled. Old hands at removing champagne corks follow this ritual: Twist off the wire muzzle. Hold the cork in your left hand, and grasp the bottom of the bottle with your right. Keep the bottle inclined slightly, but don't aim it at your guests. Be sure your grip on the cork is firm; you want it to stay in your hand, not take off like an unguided missile. Turn the bottle with your right hand, holding the cork until it pops. Make sure the cork smells of wine and has no off-odor; then wipe the rim of the bottle with a napkin.

The best glass for savoring both flavor and bouquet is the eight-ounce tulip-shaped glass. Fill it no more than one-third to one-half full. Opinions appear to coincide in regard to the saucer-shaped champagne glass with the solid stem: Although it is almost universally used for champagne cocktails and other mixed champagne drinks, it dissipates the bubbles too quickly. The best glass for showing off the sparkle is the hollow-stemmed champagne glass, although many experts claim that it, too, tends to debubble the bubbly. Ladies in the upper stratum of Continental society have discovered a trick for "storing" champagne bubbles. They scratch the inside bottom of the glass with a diamond ring, and while the tiny scratches can't be seen, they provide a kind of cache for the bubbles, and the drink's sparkle lasts longer—or at least it seems that way to ladies with sparkles on their fingers. While we're on the subject of effervescence, it's worth noting that some of the cheaper champagnes which show a great surge of froth actually have less bite than greater champagnes whose fine bubbles are literally imprisoned in the wry smile of the liquid.

All of a wine's sparkle that isn't soda water results from the fact that the chosen wine was bottled before fermentation was complete. The continuing, or second, fermentation in the bottle, as the sugar continues to change to alcohol, gives it its giggle. Besides champagne, there are all kinds of red, white and pink sparkling wines from both continents.

Frenchmen naturally take umbrage when non-French wine makers label their product champagne, and they sometimes take legal action, with varying results. *Champagne,* after all, *is* a French word, and it means a flat body of land like the wide stretch of plain country east of Paris whence all French champagne comes. In this country the word champagne can be used legally provided the section of the U.S. in which it was produced is named, such as New York State champagne or California champagne. Most other countries keep clear of the word, but just the same produce a large variety of bubbly wines. Since the import duty on all sparkling wines is a large part of the price squeeze, few foreign bottlings are imported to the U.S., but among those that are, here are some corking examples of the best:

Sparkling red Burgundy   Made in France from a quality of grapes not normally used in the still red Burgundies; on the soft, sweet side.

Sparkling Saumur   A sparkling white wine from the Loire with rather good body.

Sparkling Vouvray   Perhaps the best of the French nonchampagnes; at bottling time, extra sugar is added, which means extra bubbles as the sugar changes to alcohol.

Sparkling rosé   Imported from France; also produced in the U.S.; it's often called "pink" champagne.

Crackling rosé   A well-known import from Portugal having the quality which the French call *pétillant,* that is, with a very subdued sparkle.

Sekt   German sparkling white wine; like the German still wines, it conveys the same soft but vivid flavors of the grape.

Asti Spumante   Most of it's on the sweet side, but alluring when served cold with Gorgonzola cheese and bowl of ripe fruit.

THE LANGUAGE OF WINE

Old winemen know that carbon dioxide is not the only product that arises from the processing of grapes. There is another form of vapor, never mentioned in the chemistry texts, which is more persistent than simple CO_2. It's the poetic verbiage, the elaborate hocus-pocus of certain self-appointed knights of the wine table. Listen to these flannelmouths as they tell how one wine is "hospitable" while another one is "modest." They aren't content to enjoy a wine for its sheer liquid goodness. They must ascribe all kinds of human qualities to it. One savant tells how his wine "curtsied prettily" when he lifted it to his lips. Another detects in a certain vintage the taste of Russia leather—not just ordinary leather, mind you, but Russia leather specifically. While one of the connoisseurs raves about the cedarwood taste of a Burgundy, another describes the savor of an old St.-Emilion with its "perfume of dead leaves and taste of autumn mushrooms."

All this doesn't mean that there are no describable distinctions among good, bad and indifferent wines. The *vignerons* who work in the noted wine estates of France and elsewhere are artists with a magnificent background of experience, and they have a professional jargon which appears in long wine tomes and short essays, is heard in wineshops and in wine cellars as well as in the ordinary conversation of people who believe that wine is one of the purest forms of liquid pleasure. While their phraseology is more meaningful than that of the dillentante, it's often equally incomprehensible to the uninitiated; hence the following glossary of the most frequently used terms in the wineman's vocabulary, which should help enhance not only your expertise but also your appreciation of the fermented grape:

Acidity   The pleasant bite and natural tartness of fruit, not to be confused with sourness; without it wines would be insipid.

Amabile   An Italian term used to describe a wine which is very pleasing, often sweet.

Aroma   The smell of a wine when it's young that reveals its grape but is not a duplicate of the fresh grape flavor; as wine ages, it develops its bouquet (see below).

Astringency   A quality produced by tannin, particularly in red wines; as wines mature, tannin tends to mellow out. In all dry reds, a reasonable amount of tannin and, therefore, astringency is on the plus side.

Balance   To understand balance in wine, one should think of a common fruit such as an orange. At its best, it's both sweet and tart in such proportions that both qualities complement each other; the pungent aroma that rises when you peel it is both sharp and pleasant, and its flesh is firmly pliant, neither pulpy as an orange will sometimes be nor so soft that it's spoiling. So, too, with wine; it may be tart or very sweet, but its body, bouquet, smoothness and all other salient qualities must combine and counterbalance so that the total effect is like a scale in balance—tip one quality too much one way or the other and the wine will be out of balance.

Body Intensity rather than quality of flavor; good body is the opposite of wateriness.

Bouquet As wine ages, its original aroma changes with maturity; the finished fragrance of wine in the glass is its bouquet.

Breed A wine whose original type was great and whose present quality reflects the superior type of which it is the progeny.

Character A wine with character need not be great, but it must be one whose qualities are so definite and vivid as to be unmistakable; a rosé with its own color and fresh fruity flavor has rosé character, even though you wouldn't talk about it in the same breath with one of the great Bordeaux.

Clean Leaving an uncluttered and distinct flavor in the mouth.

Coarse A lot of flavor but not necessarily good flavor; a wine with no finesse—one to accompany a salami-and-onion sandwich.

Corky or corked When you draw a cork from a bottle of wine, the cork should smell of wine. Very rarely the cork will have spoiled, giving off an almost rotten aroma, spoiling the wine. It's an extremely rare defect.

Delicate Subtle, smooth, not very assertive but not devoid of flavor; true of many German wines.

Doux The French term for "sweet," but not used with most naturally sweet wines such as sauternes. It is sometimes applied to champagnes that have been given a heavy dosage of sweet syrup.

Dry The opposite of sweet. The greatest champagnes are dry; most notable table wines are on the dry side.

Earthy A solid flavor, reminiscent of freshly turned earth, in a complimentary sense.

Finesse Just as a delicious consommé is consummate with modest but not overbearing flavor accents, a wine with finesse has great distinction and subtlety.

Flinty A wine reminding one of something hard but not harsh.

Flowery Evocative of fragrant flower blossoms, but not perfumy in the artificial sense. A flowery wine is easy and delicate on the nostrils.

Foxy A term which describes the flavor of wines made from indigenous American grapes that Leif Ericson found in Wineland the Good. The fact that the finished wines taste so much like the original grapes makes them anathema to European wine drinkers. California wines from European rootstocks do not have this foxy flavor. That the flavor is loved by millions of Americans in the eastern half of the country only goes to prove the adage that wine is good if it tastes good.

Fresh There are wines famed for the patina of great age; others—like the Beaujolais, the rosés and many of the whites—are treasured for their fresh young flavor. Thus, millions of gallons of native Italian wines are eagerly gulped down within months of their pressing; like fresh asparagus or warm bread, they're enjoyed as fresh food in the form of drink.

Growth The word *growth* in connection with French wines is the English word for *cru.* It refers to a classification by quality—usually a high quality—and not a state in growing. To Americans it can be a misleading word, but it's been used so long by Frenchmen and Englishmen that it can't be ignored.

Hard A stubborn flavor which time, in the case of many fine wines, softens; if it fails to soften, hardness becomes harshness.

Maderisé When a white wine turns brown or a rosé turns deep orange, oxygen has done its dirty work and the wine is over the hill; it may look like Madeira, a great fortified wine, but the end result in the case of table wines is most unfavorable.

Mellow The wine maker uses this word just as everyone else does; a mellow wine is soft and full, may or may not be sweet, and of course has survived a stormy adolescence.

Mousseux A French term for sparkling wines which are not champagne, such as *Bourgogne mousseux,* or "sparkling Burgundy."

Nerveux A French term meaning well balanced and vigorous.

Nose The effect of a wine on the nose; therefore, its bouquet. It's also a verb meaning to judge a wine via the olfactory sense.

Nutty   Most often used to describe sherries of medium dryness; they're somewhat reminiscent of walnuts.

Oxidize   When wine is exposed to the oxygen of the air either too much or too long, the wine may darken and the flavor becomes lazy.

Pétillant   With a very slight sparkle; wines like some of the Swiss, the Portugese crackling rosé and the German Perlwein are examples.

Rough   Unlike the term *earthy, rough* is not a compliment. The wine may lack maturity, be puckerish and, although drinkable at an outdoor fishing party, would not be the kind you'd present at a leisurely dinner.

Rounded   Like the term *balance, rounded* describes a wine whose qualities complement each other. The wine may not be illustrious, but no one quality can be said to be notoriously wrong.

Sec   French term for "dry," although *sec* when used to describe champagne means on the sweet side, if not the very sweetest.

Soft   A pleasing, harmonious wine but not an insipid one.

Spicy   Although cloves, nutmeg and cinnamon don't normally go into wine making, a wine is called spicy when its flavor is young, provocative and pleasant, characteristic of many of the young German wines.

Spritzig   German term for a wine with a small, light natural sparkle.

Tannin   The elements in a wine which make it puckerish; grapes vary in their tannin content, but the red wines which become memorable with age all contain it.

Tart   As in food, a tart wine has a pleasant acidity which is one of its main attractions.

Vitis Labrusca   Grapes indigenous to North America; see **foxy** above.

Vitis Vinifera   Grapes indigenous to Europe; cultivated and used in California wine making.

WINE CELLARS

Collecting wines is the kind of indoor hobby you can indulge in your whole life long, and it's really the best possible means of sipping your way to expertise, remembering of course that expertise isn't an end in itself but a step to pleasure. Some hobbies are lonely, but keeping a wine cellar is the most convivial of avocations. It flatters both the collector and guests of all persuasions, since wine, like music, speaks a tongue all men understand. A cellar can be a case of assorted wines resting on its side or a subterranean vault ennobled with cobwebs. Whatever your tastes and facilities, you'll find something to your liking among the following three suggested cellars—containing from 18 to 112 bottles each. Remember, they are suggestions, not dicta. We've also included two all-American cellars for men who may want to excel in the fine wines now flowing from American vineyards. Because of the wide variation in prices, costs of individual bottles are not indicated. Totals, however, are approximated for each cellar.

Use will determine the rate and kind of your replacements. For general guidance: a bottle of wine (24 ounces) serves three to four; a half bottle is enough for two. If you average one dinner party a week, two large parties a month, and you drink wine with meals, your annual needs should be well covered by ten cases.

A note about storage: It's unlikely that you live in a manor house with its own wine vaults to provide ideal conditions for the maturation and keeping of wine, but you should do the best you can to approximate these conditions. Avoid sunlight, strive for evenness of temperature (perhaps of greater importance, even, than coolness—which is highly desirable), and pick a closet or cupboard where the wine can rest quietly—away from slamming doors and stored gear to which there must be daily access. Place white wines (which are most delicate) in the coolest spot (probably closest to the floor), Burgundies above the whites, red Bordeaux on top. Never store bottles standing; lay them on their sides so that the entire cork stays wet, which will prevent its crumbling and keep the seal airtight.

The Modest Cellar (18 bottles, under $50)
2 Champagne (French)
3 Red (Burgundy or Bordeaux)
3 White (Alsatian, Rhine or Moselle)
3 Rosé (French, Italian, Portugese or U.S.)
3 California red
3 New York white
1 Sherry (Spanish)

The Superior Cellar (36 bottles, under $100)
3 Champagne (French)
3 Red Bordeaux
3 Red Burgundy
3 Red Italian
3 White Bordeaux (Graves or Sauternes)
3 White Burgundy (Chablis or Pouilly-Fuissé)
3 White (Alsatian, Rhine or Moselle)
3 Rosé (French, Italian, Portugese or U.S.)
3 California red
3 California white
3 New York white
1 Sherry (Spanish, dry)
1 Sherry (Spanish, medium or sweet)
1 Port

The Munificent Cellar (112 bottles, under $400)
6 Champagne (French)
6 Champagne (American)
4 Sparkling red Burgundy
4 Sparkling white (German or Italian)
6 Red Bordeaux (regional)
6 Red Bordeaux (château-bottled)
6 Red Burgundy (Beaujolais)
6 Red Burgundy (estate-bottled)
4 Red Italian
4 White Bordeaux (Graves)
4 White Bordeaux (Sauternes)
4 White Burgundy (Chablis or Pouilly-Fuissé)
4 White Burgundy (estate-bottled)
4 White Alsatian (Riesling or Gewurtztraminer)
4 White Moselle
4 White Rhine
4 White Italian
6 California red
6 California white
6 California rosé
6 New York white
2 Sherry (Spanish, dry)
2 Sherry (Spanish, medium or sweet)
2 Port
2 Madeira

The Modest American Cellar (24 bottles, under $65)
3 Cabernet Sauvignon
2 Pinot Noir
1 Gamay Beaujolais
2 Rosé
2 Zinfandel

1 Barbera
2 Delaware
2 Diamond
1 Sauvignon Blanc
2 Johannisberg Riesling
2 Dry Emerald Riesling
1 Champagne *blanc de blancs*
3 Champagne *brut*

The Munificent American Cellar (97 bottles, under $275)
8 Cabernet Sauvignon
4 Pinot Noir
3 Gamay Beaujolais
4 Rosé
8 Zinfandel
5 Barbera
8 Delaware
8 Diamond
5 Sauvignon Blanc
8 Johannisberg Riesling
8 Dry Emerald Riesling
5 Champagne *blanc de blancs*
8 Champagne *brut*
2 Sherry
3 Pinot Chardonnay
4 Maryland red
3 Chenin Blanc
3 Dry Semillon

16

BEER
AND ALE—
A HOPFEST

Ask some of our more
solemn pundits what
Noah took along on the
ark and nine times out of ten
they'll begin reciting names of
animals. They're right, of course,
but how many of these Biblical
experts know of the Sumerian
tablet which describes the rest of
Noah's cargo as well and reads,
". . . with beer and stronger brews,
oil and wine, I filled large jars"?
Latin scholars might well be
reminded of the fact that Julius
Caesar not only crossed the
Rubicon in 49 B.C. but climaxed
the feat by serving the drink he
admired above everything
else—beer. Surely there are no
horn-rimmed pedants who haven't
heard of Charlemagne; yet how
many know that he once
interrupted affairs of state long
enough to call all able beermasters
to his court and lecture them on
how to brew beer for the best
results? Thousands of
Shakespearean scholars have
studied the Bard's genius with
awe and perseverance, but without
discovering one of the keys to

Shakespeare's greatness: His father was the official ale taster of
Stratford-on-Avon. When Catherine the Great felt she was
beginning to lose some of her pepper, she followed the advice of
her Scottish physician, Dimsdale, and drank English-brewed
beer.

Ask students of American history why the Pilgrims landed
at Plymouth Rock on their way to Virginia. The average crammer
will answer, "Because they ran out of provisions." Give the
groggy boy a zero for vagueness. Explain to him that the
colonists on the *Mayflower* boarded a vessel that was well
stocked with beer and that they had to cut their voyage short, as
the ship's journal tells us, because of "our victuals being much
spent, especially our beere." Ask another history major what
John Alden was most noted for. Instantly he'll respond, "He won
Priscilla Mullen's hand while speaking on behalf of Captain
Miles Standish." Wrong again. A cooper by trade, Alden was
asked to join the *Mayflower* company for the extremely
important task of caring for the vessel's beer kegs.

Down through history to modern times, beer continued to
attract the brains and the pacesetters of society: Washington in
his own hand wrote a recipe for small beer, Madison among
other notables was a brewery owner, in France Pasteur wrote his
famous *Etudes sur la bière,* and the first air-conditioning unit
ever installed was in a brewery in Virginia in the latter part of
the 19th Century.

Today beer still weaves its rare and special magic. It may be
a common brand put up in millions of gallons annually. You
may drink it from a bottle or bucket, from an exquisite blue
crockery stein or from a cool pewter mug. It may be unique or
taste like many other brands of beer. And yet, though you drink
it night after night, in fraternity houses, saloons or penthouses,
the first grand gulp always revives the same singular sensation of
unexampled goodness. You can drink too much beer, but you
can hardly get tired of it. It's difficult to convey in words the
qualities that give gusto to a fine glass of brew, but the elixir of
all beer, the very soul of its flavor, is the refreshing bite which
comes from the hops and which is always damned by non–beer
drinkers because it's bitter, as though that quality were
unpalatable. Now, it's a fact that most youngsters dislike things
that are bitter. But as we grow and our taste buds become more
experienced, we begin to savor goods that may be sour,
salty—and frequently bitter. Among the many kinds of bitterness
we've welcomed in this country are the astringency of quinine
water in a gin and tonic, the soft bitterness of Italian black
olives, the sweet bitterness of the dark-chocolate fondant on an
éclair, the subtlety of bitters in an old-fashioned cocktail and the
deep bitterness of an imported stout.

When you taste beer slowly and deliberately, the earthy tang
of the hops rests on your tongue as the beer goes slowly down.

There's a mild aftertaste, too, and this is most important to recognize when you're learning to discriminate between one kind of beer and another. If it's a fine, well-balanced beer with a good body, the subtle aftertaste lingers on. If it's a watery beer, there's hardly any aftertaste at all.

This echo of the original flavor is somehow quite stimulating to the appetite, and almost automatically you find yourself reaching for the pretzels, the anchovy canapés or the Swiss cheese. When the icebox is raided and the remains of the cold roast turkey are torn apart and laid between thin slices of rye bread, only one thing is needed for perfection itself—the Pilsner glass of cold beer, sparkling and happy as hops. No man needs to be told that the only partner for a dozen cherrystone clams or a fried deviled crab is a bottle of dry, pale ale. Even such sauce dishes as Hungarian beef goulash or hot curried shrimp are best sent on their way with mugs of foamy beer. Certainly the annual alumni steak dinner would be incomplete without two or three kegs freshly tapped for the occasion.

Every beer drinker should know a few simple facts about the art of the brewmaster. Beer is made from malt, hops, yeast and water, with an alcoholic strength of about 3.5 percent by weight. The malt in beer is made by germinating barley. The actual brewing process consists of four main steps: First, the malt is boiled with water; the liquor thus produced is called wort (rhyming with *curt*). Then hops are added and boiled; as we've already noted, they give the brew its snappy, bitter flavor. In the third step, the hops are removed and yeast is added to start fermenting the brew. Finally, after the fermentation period, the beer is aged.

Most of the beer we drink in this country is lager beer, a pale, light brew introduced into the United States from Germany during the middle of the last century. Besides malt, other grains, such as corn and rice, are frequently used to make the wort for lager; they give the brew its light body. The German word *Lager* means "storehouse," and all lager beers are stored for several months before going into bottle, can or keg.

The difference between lager beer and ale is that in brewing beer, a yeast is used that settles to the bottom of the vat during fermentation, and it's fermented at a low temperature. Ale, on the other hand, is fermented at high temperatures—between 50° and 70° F.—and the yeast used to make it remains at the top of the liquid during fermentation. These differences give ale a racier and more pronounced hop flavor than beer. It's also sometimes higher in alcoholic content.

New beer drinkers often think that all beer tastes alike. And as a matter of fact, a number of American beers *are* similar in flavor to one another. Some brewers want it this way, because they feel that public taste in the United States demands a certain flavor norm, which they have attained. Nevertheless, there are many flavor differences which veteran beer drinkers quickly detect. If you're in an experimental mood some night, pour a half-dozen different brands of light beer into glasses. Take a careful swallow of each and you'll begin discerning surprising variations in flavor, dryness, sparkle and head.

DARK BEER

Velvety dark beer is intended for those who drink beer like wine, not like water. You pour it at the *gemütlich* dinner when you're serving roast tenderloin of beef, at the special board when you're carving a crown of lamb, or at the season's first feast of cold fresh Kennebec salmon. Even with fare as casual as Roquefort cheese and sourdough French bread, or with bowls of fresh crab lump and mayonnaise, it's an extremely pleasant turn of the beer tide to be able to ask your guests whether they'd prefer dark Danish Carlsberg or Oyster Stout from the Isle of Man. Understandably, beer drinkers are fiercely loyal to one kind of brew. But when four good men of different loyalties are sitting around a pinochle table, the most convivially ubiquitous balm you can dole out, after dealing the cards, is tankards of rich black beer.

There's no exact point on the beer spectrum that separates light from dark. Beers range in color from the palest American blonds to the blackest of British stouts—but even the latter aren't literally black. Hold a glass of Guinness up to the light and you'll see ruby threads among the ebony. Then there are in-between hues like the Mexican Cerveceria Moctezuma, which leans toward the dark side. What makes a beer turn from light to dark when it's brewed is largely a matter of heat. During the brewing process, the barley malt is roasted. At a low temperature, its color is light; at a higher temperature, the color is deeper brown and the resulting beer is dark. Like dark-roasted coffee, it captures that special crowd that appreciates espresso or *café noir* rather than just another cup of coffee.

In rare instances, you may encounter a phony dark beer. It's simply a light beer to which color has been added. You can spot it first by its flavor and sometimes by its head. If the bead is a deep brown and collapses quickly, a fake pigment has been introduced. If it is light brown and the flavor lingers, then the beer is the genuine dark brew worthy of Gambrinus himself. Needless to say, the foam on any great beer is creamy thick and holds itself proudly to the last drop.

Dark beers, like certain women, mature beautifully. Most light beers are at their peak of flavor about two to three weeks after they've come from the brewery; because their shelf life is so short, they should be bought at a shop with a rapid turnover. But the dust on a bottle of dark beer, like the cobwebs on bottles of rare red Burgundies, is often a badge of quality. Why? Oxidation. The small amount of air in the headspace at the top of the bottle actually helps age a dark beer to perfection, whereas it weakens its lighter liquid brethren. Britain's Guinness in bottles will handily survive 18 months—a far cry from the suds Queen Elizabeth I drank, so strong "no man durst touch," and which the good queen insisted should be matured at least seven or eight hours before she would drink it.

Once a year American and European brewers genuflect to the goat that heralds spring and the bock-beer season. Bock is a dark beer with more than usual body and is hoppier—that is, with the added pleasant bitterness that comes from hops rather than malt, a captivating prelude for a man learning to savor the brunet brews.

The darkest and boldest in flavor of imported brews are the British stouts. Mackeson's, once called milk stout because it's brewed with milk sugars, will actually float on top of certain British beers that are lighter in color. Guinness speaks the brogue of its old Dublin dynasty. You may be somewhat less than ecstatic the *first* time you sip it. Like that first sip of Italian apéritif bitters, stout's rich and insolent flavor will probably take your taste buds by storm. But then, as it slowly flames your appetite and lingers in the back of your mouth, you'll inevitably want more and more. When Guinness is finished brewing, fresh wort (beer with unspent yeast) is added just before the stout is poured into bottles or kegs. As with champagne, the fermentation is then completed in the container, giving the stout its rare ebullience.

SERVING BEER

Among enlightened bibbers, beer excites quite different reactions at different temperatures. Extremely quick cooling in the freezing section of your refrigerator will cause it to lose flavor and acquire a harsh edge in taste. Extreme heat is just as harmful. In Belgium, the champion beer-drinking country in the world, it is quaffed at about 50° F. And when professional beer tasters in our country do their thing, the brew is usually from 40° to 50° F. At these temperatures, the aromatic qualities are more easily detected. This doesn't mean you must stick a thermometer into the next mug you serve. But if you remove the cans or bottles from your refrigerator 15 to 20 minutes before you pour, your beer will probably reach a most pleasant temperature for civilized guzzling.

When pouring beer, some hosts tip the neck of the bottle or can gingerly against the side of the glass, pouring slowly so the glass is filled up with as much liquid and as little head as possible. The trouble is, when beer is poured in this manner, most of the carbon dioxide is trapped in the glass, and the head turns out to be a thin wafer instead of the snowy high collar it should be. It's true that the carbon dioxide is what gives the beer its tingle and revival power, but too much of it is stultifying. When, on the other hand, beer is poured straight to the bottom of the glass, with the bottle or can held one or two inches above the rim, it builds a rich, creamy cap and loses just enough of its carbonation to make its softness and mellowness much more evident. When poured in this manner, a superior beer will not only form a deep, dense head, but as the beer is slowly sipped, a lace of foam will cling to the sides of the glass.

Equally important in serving beer correctly are clean glasses, for the smallest trace of foreign matter will affect both the taste of the beer and the formation of the head. Wash beer glasses in very hot water with a detergent, followed by hot rinse water. But don't towel them. And just before pouring the beer, rinse them again in clear, cold water. If you belong to the ferocious fraternity that uses beer glasses for stressing points during an argument, you'll want heavy seidels or steins. If you enjoy drinking your beer in curvacious company, you'll want thin Pilsner glasses, or perhaps the large tulip-shaped goblets which show off the brilliant clarity of a superb beer. The glass bottoms on old pewter mugs were designed for the same purpose.

To set up your own beer-tasting criteria, you don't have to emulate the original ale testers in London, known there as conners. These august connoisseurs always wore leather trousers. To test a brew, they'd pour a little on a wooden bench and then sit down. If, after three minutes, their trousers stuck to the bench, the ale was deemed "good for man's body in lawful measure." A better way to explore three or four different brands of beer or ale is to pour them into large tulip-shaped glasses, just as you would wine at a wine-tasting party. All first-rank beers, particularly the dark members of the tribe, have a definite malty aroma that is part of their taste profile. Don't try to taste them immediately after a meal. Wait an hour or so, or taste them before the meal. Sip them a little at a time. Keep a pile of breadsticks or unsalted crackers (water crackers, if possible) and wedges of hard cheese nearby. Take small nibbles of each between tasting to clear the palate. You'll probably be surprised at the extent of your own flavor-consciousness. You'll notice such characteristics as hop flavor, body (that is, intensity of flavor), sweetness, mellowness, sharpness, blandness and many other qualities that you never expected to be able to identify. With plenty of beer, the hopfest can go on for hours.

A. E. Housman once proclaimed, "And malt does more than Milton can/To justify God's ways to man." To which we can only add: Let there be light, and let there be dark, and plenty of both.

Note to American Beer Drinkers Traveling in the British

Isles: Americans are often completely broken up by British beer terminology. To the Briton, the words *beer* and *ale* are now synonymous, like *car* and *automobile* in the U.S. At one time the English word *ale* meant a brew made without hops, but today ale and beer in Britain are both made with malt and hops. The British word *bitter* means a beer with a very heavy hop flavor: *mild,* darker and less strong than bitter. *Burton* refers to a strong dark beer (not black and not necessarily made at Burton on Trent). If you want American-type beer in Britain, be sure to ask for *lager,* fermented at a low temperature with a light hop flavor. It's served at a temperature that the British call *cool* and that most Americans living on the pleasures of the ice age call tepid.

PART THREE

the art of mixing drinks made
easy in over 700 recipes; plus a
plenitude of hors d'oeuvres for
all occasions

17
COCKTAILS

 The most overwhelmingly popular of all potables, the open sesame to brunch parties, lunch parties, dinner parties, midnight supper parties and the next morning's revival parties, the cocktail is undoubtedly America's most noted contribution to the world of bibulous pleasure. The stories concerning the origin of the word *cocktail* are nearly as many and varied as the mixtures themselves. Among them, the following legends have enjoyed long vintage life:

The word came from the French word *coquetel,* once used to describe a mixed drink in the Bordeaux region.

Southern army officers were once served a luscious mixed drink by a lovely Southern belle. Her name? Octelle, suh!

A distinguished American general was invited to the court of a Mexican monarch whose daughter appeared with a drink in the royal cup of gold encrusted with rubies. When the obvious question of who would drink first racked all the king's men, the daughter solved the problem very intelligently by drinking the libation herself. The stunning princess's name was, of course, Coctel.

Western horse traders whose nags weren't worth the price of their pelts, on sale day, fed their horses liquor whose effects made them cock their tails and come to life with incredible spirits.

Morning tipplers in New Amsterdam, visiting inns for a pick-me-up, would invariably run into Dutch barmaids who (you guessed it) used the tails of roosters for sweeping away last night's litter.

A young Irish lass (this one by James Fenimore Cooper) not only managed to procure and roast chickens from Tory farmers for her Revolutionary guests, but decorated their drinks with feathers from the cocks' tails.

Whether or not these stories are any truer than Bunyan's blue ox, it's clear that the cocktail goes deep into America's drinking heritage. And even today, Americans remain the foremost masters and idolaters of the cocktail.

Cocktails range from appetite-awakening bone-dry martinis to velvety dessert cocktails that correctly climax a rich feast. Men taking the lead at their own cocktail parties should weigh the counsel in chapter 7, "Barmanship." In time, as your cocktail repertoire expands, the ups and downs of the cocktail shaker will become second nature. But even the most polished perfectionists at their bars follow certain well-tested guidelines for cocktails, hence the following review of the more important considerations in drink making:

1. Inferior liquors aren't masked in cocktails. A fine gin will seem even finer in a martini. The same goes for whiskeys, rums, vodkas and vermouths.

2. Don't imitate free-pouring bartenders in public bars. Use standard measures, whether they be teaspoons, jiggers, ounces, cups or quarts. When you multiply quantities for party drinking, be mathematically accurate.

3. Ice must be hard, cold and clean—not weeping. Fresh ice at 0° F. or below will produce a much brisker drink than lazy ice turning to water.

4. Though cocktails must be icy cold (proper dilution is part of the art), they shouldn't be watery. Anyone can begin shaking cocktails. An artist knows when to stop. Normally 2 to 2$^{1}/_{2}$ ounces poured into a cocktail shaker will grow to approximately 4 ounces after proper shaking.

5. Use the proper glass for each cocktail, and be sure that it's sparkling clean and prechilled. The glass should first chill the hand and then the lips; the icy cocktail itself will take care of the rest.

6. You should, of course, use fresh ingredients in your cocktails, especially when it comes to fruit juices.

7. Cocktails with fruit juices, eggs, syrups, etc., are normally shaken; those containing only liquor and vermouth are stirred (although one of the most eminent martini men of modern times,

Somerset Maugham, insisted that his martinis be *shaken*). The stirred cocktail is clear; the shaken cloudy.

8. Make your own personal recipe changes only with the greatest care, remembering that some cocktails are dominated by a single, straight, powerful flavor—the martini by gin, for instance, or the negroni by Campari—while others are a medley of flavors: liquors, fortified wines, juices, bitters, fruits, etc. A fine cocktail of the latter type is always in delicate balance; even its aftertaste leaves a pleasant sense of the tart and the sweet, the strong and the weak. Sometimes adding or subtracting an eighth of a teaspoon will make a noticeable difference. Be creative if you will, but create slowly and deftly. A new drink is always an evolution.

The cocktails that follow are designed for a 4½-ounce cocktail glass, except in those cases where an old-fashioned or other glass is used. The parsimonious three-ounce cocktail glasses are now skeletons in most liquor closets; not only does the larger cocktail provide more sumptuous bliss for the guests, but it's a boon to the host since it means fewer refills and the coveted chance to sit down, drink and enjoy the revels.

AFTER-DINNER COCKTAILS

On a dinner or late-supper menu, the after-dinner cocktail can take the place of the dessert or supplement it. As a libation, it's frankly sweet and toothsome. It goes perfectly with a platter of cheese and crackers, a fresh fruit bowl or both. It graciously replaces the ubiquitous pie and the gooey ice cream. For the harried host who has neither the time to make, nor the energy to shop for, a fresh dessert, it's a deliverance. Freshly concocted, any of the following are an imaginative way to conclude a brunch, lunch or dinner.

BLUE ANGEL

½ oz. blue curaçao
½ oz. parfait amour
½ oz. brandy
½ oz. lemon juice
½ oz. cream

Shake well with ice. Strain into prechilled cocktail glass. Cool, incredibly smooth.

CADIZ

¾ oz. amontillado sherry
¾ oz. blackberry liqueur
½ oz. Triple Sec
½ oz. cream

Shake well with ice. Strain over rocks in prechilled old-fashioned glass.

½ oz. Galliano or
   Roiano
½ oz. passion-fruit
   syrup
2 teaspoons lemon juice
½ oz. light rum
½ egg white
⅓ cup crushed ice

CALM VOYAGE

*Put all ingredients into blender.
Blend at low speed 10–15 seconds.
Pour into prechilled deep-saucer
champagne glass. Mendelssohn is
good accompaniment on this trip.*

1 oz. coffee liqueur
1 oz. curaçao
½ oz. cream
⅓ cup crushed ice

CARA SPOSA

*Put all ingredients into blender.
Blend at low speed 10–15 seconds.
Pour into prechilled deep-saucer
champagne glass. Although any
kind of coffee liqueur may be used
in this drink, the espresso-coffee
liqueur is especially pleasant.*

1¼ ozs. light rum
¾ oz. cherry liqueur
½ oz. cream
⅓ cup crushed ice

CHERRY RUM

*Put all ingredients into blender.
Blend at low speed 10–15 seconds.
Pour into prechilled deep-saucer
champagne glass.*

1½ ozs. banana liqueur
1½ ozs. orange juice
1½ ozs. cream
¾ oz. grenadine
¾ cup crushed ice

CHIQUITA PUNCH

*Put all ingredients into blender.
Blend at high speed 10 seconds.
Pour into prechilled old-fashioned
glass. Created by Bill Nolan, head
bartender at the Los Angeles
Playboy Club.*

1 oz. light rum
½ oz. crème de cacao
½ oz. crème de menthe
½ oz. cream
1 teaspoon 151-proof
   rum

CHOCOLATE RUM

*Shake light rum, crème de cacao,
crème de menthe and cream well
with ice. Strain into prechilled
cocktail glass. Float 151-proof rum
on top.*

COFFEE GRASS-HOPPER

³/₄ oz. coffee liqueur
³/₄ oz. white crème de menthe
³/₄ oz. cream

Shake well with ice. Strain into prechilled cocktail glass.

COFFEE ROIANO

1¹/₂ ozs. Roiano
¹/₂ oz. coffee liqueur
¹/₂ oz. cream
¹/₃ cup crushed ice

Put all ingredients into blender. Blend at low speed 10–15 seconds. Pour into prechilled deep-saucer champagne glass. May be served not only at the end of a meal but at any time of the day.

DULCET

1 oz. vodka
¹/₂ oz. curaçao
¹/₂ oz. anisette
¹/₂ oz. apricot liqueur
1 teaspoon lemon juice
¹/₂ brandied apricot

Shake vodka, curaçao, anisette, apricot liqueur and lemon juice well with ice. Strain over cracked ice or rocks in prechilled old-fashioned glass. Add brandied apricot.

FROZEN BLACK CURRANT

1 oz. crème de cassis
1 oz. pineapple juice
¹/₂ oz. brandy
¹/₃ cup crushed ice
1 slice orange

Put crème de cassis, pineapple juice, brandy and crushed ice into blender. Blend at low speed 10–15 seconds. Pour into prechilled deep-saucer champagne glass. Add orange slice.

GOLD CADILLAC

³/₄ oz. crème de cacao
³/₄ oz. Galliano
³/₄ oz. cream
¹/₃ cup crushed ice

Put all ingredients into blender. Blend at low speed 10–15 seconds. Pour into prechilled deep-saucer champagne glass. For another version, omit crushed ice, shake well with ice and strain into prechilled cocktail glass.

GOLDEN FROG

¹/₂ oz. Strega
¹/₂ oz. Galliano
¹/₂ oz. vodka
¹/₂ oz. lemon juice
³/₄ cup crushed ice

Put all ingredients into blender. Blend at high speed 10 seconds. Pour into prechilled old-fashioned glass, as served in the Denver Playboy Club.

GRASSHOPPER

³/₄ oz. white or brown
  crème de cacao
³/₄ oz. green crème
  de menthe
³/₄ oz. cream

Shake well with ice. Strain into prechilled cocktail glass.

IL MAGNIFICO

³/₄ oz. Tuaca liqueur
³/₄ oz. curaçao
³/₄ oz. cream
¹/₃ cup crushed ice

Put all ingredients into blender. Blend at low speed 10–15 seconds. Pour into prechilled deep-saucer champagne glass. May be served before, with or after the espresso.

MOCHA MINT

³/₄ oz. coffee liqueur
³/₄ oz. crème de menthe
³/₄ oz. crème de cacao

Shake well with ice. Strain into prechilled sugar-and-coffee-frosted cocktail glass.

ORACABESSA

1 oz. banana liqueur
¹/₂ oz. lemon juice
¹/₂ oz. 151-proof rum
1 slice banana
1 slice lemon

Dip banana slice into lemon juice or orange juice to prevent discoloration. Shake banana liqueur, lemon juice and rum well with ice. Strain over rocks in old-fashioned glass. Add banana and lemon slices.

ORANGE COMFORT

1/2 oz. Southern Comfort
1/2 oz. anisette
3/4 oz. orange juice
1/2 oz. lemon juice
1 slice cocktail orange in
   syrup

Shake Southern Comfort, anisette, orange juice and lemon juice well with ice. Strain into prechilled cocktail glass. Garnish with cocktail-orange slice.

ORANGE FLOWER

1 oz. curaçao
1/2 oz. cherry liqueur
1/2 oz. orange juice
1 teaspoon lemon juice
1 dash orange-flower
   water
1/3 cup crushed ice

Put all ingredients into blender. Blend at low speed 10–15 seconds. Pour into prechilled deep-saucer champagne glass. Exhilarating finale for a roast-goose dinner.

PINK ALMOND

1/2 oz. crème de noyaux
1/2 oz. orgeat or orzata
1 oz. blended whiskey
1/2 oz. kirschwasser
1/2 oz. lemon juice
1 slice lemon

Shake crème de noyaux, orgeat, whiskey, kirsch and lemon juice well with ice. Strain over rocks in prechilled old-fashioned glass. Add lemon slice.

PINK SQUIRREL

1 oz. crème de noyaux
1 oz. white crème de
   cacao
3/4 oz. cream

Shake well with ice. Strain into prechilled sugar-frosted cocktail glass. Pinker and smoother than a pink lady.

RUSSIAN COFFEE

3/4 oz. coffee liqueur
3/4 oz. vodka
3/4 oz. cream
1/3 cup crushed ice

Put all ingredients into blender. Blend at low speed 10–15 seconds. Pour into prechilled deep-saucer champagne glass.

1¼ ozs. oloroso sherry
1¼ ozs. coffee liqueur
2 teaspoons cream

SHERRIED COFFEE

Shake sherry and coffee liqueur well with ice. Strain over rocks in prechilled old-fashioned glass. Float cream on top.

³/₄ oz. Galliano
³/₄ oz. brandy
1 teaspoon white crème de menthe
¹/₃ cup finely crushed ice

SNIFTER

Pour liquors into prechilled brandy snifter. Add crushed ice. Stir. May be served with or without straw. You can get it either way at the Miami Playboy Club.

1 oz. Southern Comfort
1 oz. peach liqueur
¹/₂ oz. cream
1 slice fresh or brandied peach

SOUTHERN PEACH

Shake Southern Comfort, peach liqueur and cream well with ice. Strain over rocks or coarsely cracked ice in prechilled old-fashioned glass. Add peach slice. It's peaches and cream brought up to date.

1 oz. strawberry liqueur
¹/₂ oz. kirschwasser
¹/₂ oz. light rum
¹/₂ oz. orange juice
1 teaspoon lemon juice
1 large strawberry

STRAWBERRY KISS

Shake strawberry liqueur, kirschwasser, rum, orange juice and lemon juice well with ice. Strain into prechilled sugar-frosted cocktail glass. Add strawberry.

1 oz. gin
1 oz. blackberry brandy
¹/₂ oz. banana liqueur
¹/₂ oz. heavy cream

YELLOW FINGERS

Shake well with ice. Strain into prechilled saucer champagne glass. Winner of the 1967 Bombay Gin Safari Contest, Waldorf-Astoria, New York.

AMERICANO

1¹/₄ ozs. Campari
1¹/₄ ozs. sweet vermouth
Lemon peel
Club soda (optional)

Stir Campari and sweet vermouth well with ice. Strain into a prechilled cocktail glass. Twist lemon peel above drink and drop into glass. If you prefer, a Delmonico or old-fashioned glass may be used instead—with a rock or two and a splash of soda.

APPLE BYRRH

1 oz. calvados
¹/₂ oz. Byrrh
¹/₂ oz. dry vermouth
¹/₂ teaspoon lemon juice
Lemon peel

Shake calvados, Byrrh, vermouth and lemon juice well with ice. Strain into prechilled cocktail glass. Twist lemon peel above drink and drop into glass. Then pass the deviled-ham canapés.

BITTERSWEET

1¹/₄ ozs. sweet vermouth
1¹/₄ ozs. dry vermouth
2 dashes Angostura
 bitters
1 dash orange bitters
Orange peel

Stir both kinds of vermouth and both kinds of bitters well with ice. Strain into prechilled cocktail glass. Twist orange peel above drink and drop into glass. Salted shelled pistachios go well with this taste teaser.

BUTTERFLY

³/₄ oz. dry vermouth
³/₄ oz. sweet vermouth
¹/₂ oz. Red Dubonnet
¹/₂ oz. orange juice

Shake everything well with ice. Strain over rocks in prechilled old-fashioned glass. This combination of o.j. and three fortified wines is extremely light.

BYRRH BRANDY

³/₄ oz. Byrrh
³/₄ oz. cognac
³/₄ oz. dry vermouth

Combine and stir well with ice. Strain into prechilled cocktail glass.

BYRRH CASSIS

1½ ozs. Byrrh
¼ oz. crème de cassis
½ oz. lemon juice
1 slice lemon
Iced club soda (optional)

Shake Byrrh, crème de cassis and lemon juice well with ice. Strain over rocks in prechilled old-fashioned glass. Add lemon slice—and a splash of soda if desired.

BYRRH COCKTAIL

1¼ ozs. Byrrh
1¼ ozs. gin
Lemon peel

Stir Byrrh and gin well with ice. Strain into prechilled cocktail glass or over rocks in prechilled old-fashioned glass. Twist lemon peel above drink and drop into glass.

CALIFORNIAN

1½ ozs. sweet vermouth
1 oz. blended whiskey
2 ozs. orange juice
1 teaspoon orgeat

Combine and shake well with ice. Strain over large ice cube in prechilled old-fashioned glass. Be sure the orange juice is freshly squeezed from ripe California navels or Valencias in midseason.

CANADIAN AND CAMPARI

1 oz. Canadian whisky
½ oz. Campari
1 oz. dry vermouth
Lemon peel

Stir whisky, Campari and vermouth well with ice. Strain into prechilled cocktail glass. Twist lemon peel above drink and drop into glass. A perfect drink to sip while anticipating the antipasto.

CARDINAL II

¾ oz. gin
¾ oz. Campari
¾ oz. dry vermouth
Lemon peel

Stir gin, Campari and vermouth well with ice. Strain into prechilled cocktail glass. Twist lemon peel above drink and drop into glass.

COMBO

2¹/₂ ozs. dry vermouth
¹/₂ teaspoon curaçao
¹/₄ teaspoon Angostura
  bitters
¹/₂ teaspoon sugar
1 teaspoon cognac

Shake everything well with ice. Strain over rocks in prechilled old-fashioned glass. An elusive, but not illusive, glow is created by this combination of apéritif flavors.

DIABOLO

1¹/₂ ozs. imported dry
  white port
1 oz. dry vermouth
¹/₄ teaspoon lemon juice
Lemon peel

Shake port, vermouth and lemon juice well with ice. Strain into prechilled cocktail glass. Twist lemon peel above drink and drop into glass.

DUBONNET COCKTAIL

1¹/₄ ozs. Red Dubonnet
1¹/₄ ozs. gin
Lemon peel

Stir Dubonnet and gin well with ice. Strain into prechilled cocktail glass. Twist lemon peel above drink and drop into glass.

FINO

1¹/₄ ozs. fino sherry
1¹/₂ ozs. sweet vermouth
1 slice lemon

Stir sherry and vermouth well with ice. Strain over rocks in prechilled old-fashioned glass. Garnish with lemon slice.

FLORIDIAN

1¹/₂ ozs. dry vermouth
¹/₂ oz. Forbidden Fruit
1 teaspoon Falernum
2 ozs. grapefruit juice
2 dashes orange bitters
1 slice lime

Shake vermouth, Forbidden Fruit, Falernum, grapefruit juice and bitters well with ice. Strain over large ice cube in prechilled old-fashioned glass. Garnish with lime slice.

GIN AND CAMPARI

1¹/₄ ozs. gin
1¹/₄ ozs. Campari
Orange peel

Stir gin and Campari well with ice. Strain over rocks in prechilled old-fashioned glass. Twist orange peel above drink and drop into glass. Savor it in sips.

LILLET COCKTAIL

1¹/₂ ozs. Lillet
1 oz. gin
Lemon peel

*Stir Lillet and gin well with ice.
Strain into prechilled cocktail
glass. Twist lemon peel above
drink and drop into glass.*

LILLET NOYAUX

1¹/₂ ozs. Lillet
1 oz. gin
¹/₄ teaspoon crème de
   noyaux
Orange peel

*Stir Lillet, gin and crème de
noyaux well with ice. Strain into
prechilled cocktail glass. Twist
orange peel above drink and drop
into glass. The scintillating flavor
of Lillet is even more pleasant
when this drink is poured on the
rocks.*

NEGRONI

³/₄ oz. Campari
³/₄ oz. gin
³/₄ oz. sweet vermouth

*Stir well with ice. Strain into
prechilled cocktail glass. Similar
to the cardinal II except that the
vermouth is sweet instead of dry.
May be served on the rocks with a
twist of lemon or splash of soda or
both.*

PICON ON
THE ROCKS

1¹/₂ ozs. Amer Picon
¹/₂ oz. lemon juice
Club soda
1 slice lemon

*Pour Amer Picon and lemon juice
over rocks in prechilled
old-fashioned glass. Add a splash
of soda. Stir. Garnish with lemon
slice.*

PICON PUNCH

1¹/₂ ozs. Amer Picon
¹/₄ teaspoon grenadine
Iced club soda
1 tablespoon cognac
Lemon peel

*Pour Amer Picon, grenadine and a
splash of soda over rocks in a
prechilled old-fashioned glass.
Stir. Float cognac on top of drink.
Twist lemon peel above drink and
drop into glass. Although Amer
Picon is a sweet liqueur,
Frenchmen for over a century
have sipped it avidly before
mealtime. There's just enough
bitterness to balance the sweet.*

PLUM APÉRITIF

1½ ozs. dry vermouth
½ oz. cognac
¼ oz. prunelle
1 slice lemon

Stir vermouth, cognac and prunelle well with ice. Strain over rocks in prechilled old-fashioned glass. Add lemon slice. A small jar of fresh beluga caviar will make the mise en scène *perfect.*

PUNT E MES NEGRONI

¾ oz. Punt e Mes
¾ oz. gin
¾ oz. sweet vermouth

Stir well with ice. Strain into prechilled cocktail glass. May be served on the rocks with a twist of lemon or splash of soda or both. Punt e Mes is one of those Italian apéritifs that cause you first to shudder, then instantly to ask for more.

RUM APÉRITIF

1 oz. dry vermouth
1 oz. light rum
1 teaspoon dark Jamaican rum
1 teaspoon raspberry syrup
½ oz. lemon juice
Lemon peel

Shake vermouth, both kinds of rum, raspberry syrup and lemon juice well with ice. Strain into prechilled cocktail glass. Twist lemon peel above drink and drop into glass. This apéritif could just as well be included among the rum cocktails. The effect in either case is the same: a ravenous appetite.

SANCTUARY

1 oz. Red Dubonnet
½ oz. Amer Picon
½ oz. Cointreau
½ oz. lemon juice
1 slice lemon

Shake Dubonnet, Amer Picon, Cointreau and lemon juice well with ice. Strain over rocks in prechilled old-fashioned glass. Add lemon slice. Pass hot hors d'oeuvres.

SILVER KIRSCH

1½ ozs. Positano
1 oz. kirsch
½ oz. lemon juice
½ egg white
1 teaspoon sugar
⅓ cup crushed ice

Mix all ingredients in blender for 10 seconds at high speed. Pour into prechilled old-fashioned glass.

SLOE VERMOUTH

1 oz. sloe gin (creamy cap)
1 oz. dry vermouth
½ oz. lemon juice

Shake well with ice. Strain into prechilled cocktail glass. A soft divertissement on a lazy afternoon.

SOUTHWEST ONE

¾ oz. vodka
¾ oz. orange juice
¾ oz. Campari bitters

Shake well with ice. Strain into prechilled glass. Named after the London district in which the popular drink originated.

TRIO

¾ oz. dry vermouth
¾ oz. sweet vermouth
¾ oz. gin

Stir well with ice. Strain into prechilled cocktail glass. A drink for rebels from the dry-martini crowd.

VERMOUTH CASSIS

2¼ ozs. dry vermouth
½ oz. crème de cassis
Iced club soda

Pour vermouth and crème de cassis over one or two rocks in a prechilled old-fashioned glass, a large wineglass or an 8-oz. highball glass. Stir. Add soda, which Frenchmen use to stretch the drink into a long apéritif. Americans seem to prefer the drink less diluted. A vin blanc cassis is the same drink with dry white wine used instead of vermouth. A slice of lemon may be used as a garnish if desired.

VERMOUTH MARASCHINO

2 ozs. dry vermouth

¹/₂ oz. maraschino

   liqueur

¹/₂ oz. lemon juice

2 dashes orange bitters

1 maraschino cherry

Shake vermouth, maraschino liqueur, lemon juice and bitters well with ice. Strain over large ice cube in prechilled old-fashioned glass. Garnish with cherry.

VERMOUTH TRIPLE SEC

1 oz. dry vermouth

¹/₂ oz. Triple Sec

1 oz. gin

2 dashes orange bitters

Lemon peel

Shake vermouth, Triple Sec, gin and bitters well with ice. Strain into prechilled cocktail glass. Twist lemon peel above drink and drop into glass.

ZAZA

2 ozs. Red Dubonnet

1 oz. gin

1 slice orange

Stir Dubonnet and gin well with ice. Strain over rocks in prechilled old-fashioned glass. Cut into the orange slice and place it on the rocks. Your nose should catch the aroma of the orange before your lips meet the drink. While there are many versions of this Dubonnet cocktail, these are the proportions we like best.

APPLE-BRANDY COCKTAILS

APPLE AND GINGER

1¹/₄ ozs. applejack

³/₄ oz. ginger-flavored

   brandy

¹/₂ oz. lemon juice

¹/₂ teaspoon sugar

Shake well with ice. Strain into prechilled cocktail glass. A cool alfresco drink.

APPLE BLOSSOM

1¹/₂ ozs. applejack
1 oz. apple juice
¹/₂ oz. lemon juice
1 teaspoon maple syrup
¹/₃ cup crushed ice
1 slice lemon

Put applejack, apple juice, lemon juice, maple syrup and crushed ice into blender. Blend at low speed 10-15 seconds. Pour into prechilled deep-saucer champagne glass. Add lemon slice.

APPLE DUBONNET

1 oz. calvados
1 oz. Red Dubonnet
1 slice lemon

Stir calvados and Dubonnet well with ice. Strain over rocks in prechilled old-fashioned glass. Add lemon slice.

APPLE GRAND MARNIER

1 oz. calvados
¹/₂ oz. Grand Marnier
¹/₂ oz. cognac
Lemon peel
Orange peel

Stir calvados, Grand Marnier and cognac well with ice. Strain over rocks in prechilled old-fashioned glass. Twist lemon peel and orange peel above drink and drop into glass.

APPLE LILLET

1 oz. calvados
1 oz. Lillet
1 slice orange

Stir calvados and Lillet well with ice. Strain over rocks in prechilled old-fashioned glass. Add orange slice. A perfect drink to kill time while waiting for the hot onion soup.

APPLECAR

³/₄ oz. applejack
³/₄ oz. Cointreau or
   curaçao
³/₄ oz. lemon juice

Shake well with ice. Strain into prechilled cocktail glass. The appleman's sidecar.

APPLEHAWK

1¹/₄ ozs. applejack
1¹/₄ ozs. unsweetened
   grapefruit juice
¹/₂ teaspoon sugar

Shake well with ice. Strain into prechilled cocktail glass.

APPLEJACK MANHATTAN

1³/₄ ozs. applejack
³/₄ oz. sweet vermouth
1 dash orange bitters
1 maraschino cherry

Stir applejack, vermouth and bitters well with ice. Strain into prechilled cocktail glass. Add cherry.

APPLEJACK RABBIT

1¹/₂ ozs. applejack
¹/₂ oz. lemon juice
¹/₂ oz. orange juice
1 teaspoon maple syrup

Shake well with ice. Strain into prechilled sugar-frosted cocktail glass. Salted nuts or toasted coconut chips are good companions.

APPLEJACK SOUR

2 ozs. applejack
¹/₂ oz. lemon juice
1 teaspoon sugar
¹/₂ slice lemon

Shake applejack, lemon juice and sugar well with ice. Strain into prechilled whiskey-sour glass. Add lemon slice.

BITTER APPLE

2 ozs. applejack
2 dashes Angostura
  bitters
Iced club soda
Lemon peel

Pour applejack and bitters into prechilled old-fashioned glass. Add ice slices or cubes to fill glass. Add a splash of soda. Stir well. Twist lemon peel over drink and drop into glass. Aromatic, potent and dry.

BLENHEIM

1 oz. applejack
¹/₂ oz. apricot-flavored
  brandy
³/₄ oz. lemon juice
1 teaspoon grenadine
1 dash orange bitters

Shake well with ice. Strain into prechilled sugar-frosted cocktail glass.

FROZEN APPLE

1½ ozs. applejack
½ oz. lime juice
½ egg white
1 teaspoon sugar
⅓ cup crushed ice

Put all ingredients into blender. Blend at low speed 10–15 seconds. Pour into prechilled deep-saucer champagne glass. A cocktail to pave the way for a roast suckling pig.

FROZEN APPLE AND BANANA

1½ ozs. applejack
½ oz. banana liqueur
½ oz. lime juice
⅓ cup crushed ice
1 slice banana

Put applejack, banana liqueur, lime juice and ice into blender. Blend at low speed 10–15 seconds. Pour into prechilled deep-saucer champagne glass. Add banana slice.

JACK ROSE

2 ozs. applejack
½ oz. lime juice or
  lemon juice
1 teaspoon grenadine

Shake well with ice. Strain into prechilled cocktail glass. The classic applejack, drink.

POLYNESIAN APPLE

1¼ ozs. applejack
¾ oz. pineapple juice
½ oz. California brandy
1 pineapple stick

Shake applejack, pineapple juice and brandy well with ice. Strain over rocks in prechilled old-fashioned glass. Add pineapple stick. A standby cocktail when spareribs are slowly turning on the spit over charcoal.

PUERTO APPLE

1¼ ozs. applejack
¾ oz. light rum
½ oz. lime juice
1½ teaspoons orgeat or
  orzata
1 slice lime

Shake applejack, rum, lime juice and orgeat well with ice. Strain over rocks in prechilled old-fashioned glass. Add lime slice.

RABBIT'S FOOT

³/₄ oz. applejack
³/₄ oz. light rum
¹/₂ oz. orange juice
¹/₂ oz. lemon juice
¹/₄ oz. grenadine
1 slice orange

Mix applejack, rum, orange juice, lemon juice and grenadine well with ice. Strain into prechilled old-fashioned glass. Add ice to fill glass. Garnish with orange slice. Created by Roy Devlin, head bartender at the Cincinnati Playboy Club.

BRANDY COCKTAILS

ALABAMA

1³/₄ ozs. brandy
¹/₂ oz. lemon juice
1 teaspoon curaçao
¹/₂ teaspoon sugar
Orange peel

Shake brandy, lemon juice, curaçao and sugar well with ice. Strain into prechilled sugar-frosted cocktail glass. Twist orange peel above drink and drop into glass.

BAYOU

1³/₄ ozs. brandy
¹/₄ oz. peach liqueur
¹/₂ oz. mango nectar
2 teaspoons lime juice
1 slice fresh or brandied peach

Shake brandy, peach liqueur, mango nectar and lime juice well with ice. Strain over rocks in prechilled old-fashioned glass. Garnish with peach slice.

BOMBAY

1 oz. brandy
¹/₂ oz. dry vermouth
¹/₂ oz. sweet vermouth
¹/₂ teaspoon curaçao
¹/₄ teaspoon Pernod
1 slice fresh or canned mango

Shake brandy, both kinds of vermouth, curaçao and Pernod well with ice. Strain over rocks in prechilled old-fashioned glass. Add mango slice. Serve before a curry dinner.

BRANDIED APRICOT

1¹/₂ ozs. brandy
¹/₂ oz. apricot-flavored brandy
¹/₂ oz. lemon juice
Orange peel

Shake brandy, apricot-flavored brandy and lemon juice well with ice. Strain into prechilled sugar-frosted cocktail glass. Twist orange peel above drink and drop into glass.

BRANDIED CORDIAL MÉDOC

1¹/₂ ozs. brandy
¹/₂ oz. Cordial Médoc
¹/₂ oz. lemon juice
Orange peel

Shake brandy, Cordial Médoc and lemon juice well with ice. Strain into prechilled cocktail glass. Twist orange peel above drink and drop into glass. Either California brandy or cognac may be used with good results.

BRANDIED GINGER

2 ozs. brandy
¹/₂ oz. ginger-flavored brandy
1 teaspoon lime juice
1 teaspoon orange juice
1 piece preserved ginger in syrup

Shake brandy, ginger-flavored brandy, lime juice and orange juice well with ice. Strain over rocks in prechilled old-fashioned glass. Garnish with preserved ginger.

BRANDTINI

1¹/₂ ozs. brandy
1 oz. gin
1 teaspoon dry vermouth
Lemon peel or cocktail olive

Stir brandy, gin and vermouth well with ice. Strain into prechilled cocktail glass. Twist lemon peel above drink and drop into glass, or serve with cocktail olive.

BRANDY ALEXANDER

³/₄ oz. brandy
³/₄ oz. crème de cacao
³/₄ oz. cream

Shake well with ice. Strain into prechilled cocktail glass.

BRANDY AND AMER PICON

2 ozs. cognac
¹/₂ oz. Amer Picon
Lemon peel
Orange peel

Stir cognac and Amer Picon well with ice. Strain over rocks in prechilled old-fashioned glass. Twist lemon peel and orange peel above drink and drop into glass.

BRANDY CASSIS

1³/₄ ozs. brandy
¹/₂ oz. lemon juice
2 teaspoons crème de cassis
Lemon peel

Shake brandy, lemon juice and crème de cassis well with ice. Strain into prechilled cocktail glass. Twist lemon peel above drink and drop into glass.

BRANDY CRUSTA

Peel of ¹/₂ lemon, in one spiral
2 ozs. brandy
¹/₂ oz. curaçao
2 teaspoons lemon juice
1 dash bitters
1 teaspoon maraschino liqueur

Place lemon peel and cracked ice or rocks in prechilled sugar-frosted old-fashioned glass. Shake brandy, curaçao, lemon juice, bitters and maraschino liqueur well with ice. Strain into glass.

BRANDY FINO

1¹/₂ ozs. brandy
¹/₂ oz. very dry sherry
¹/₂ oz. Drambuie
¹/₂ slice orange
Lemon peel

Shake brandy, sherry and Drambuie well with ice. Strain over rocks in prechilled old-fashioned glass. Add orange slice. Twist lemon peel above drink and drop into glass.

BRANDY GUMP

2 ozs. brandy
¹/₂ oz. lemon juice
¹/₂ teaspoon grenadine

Shake well with ice. Strain into prechilled cocktail glass. A good one to relax with after an all-day sail.

BRANDY MANHATTAN

2 ozs. brandy
¹/₂ oz. sweet vermouth
1 dash bitters (optional)
1 maraschino cherry

Stir brandy, vermouth and bitters well with ice. Strain into prechilled cocktail glass. Add cherry. For a dry brandy manhattan, use dry instead of sweet vermouth.

BRANDY MELBA

1½ ozs. brandy
¼ oz. peach liqueur
¼ oz. raspberry liqueur
½ oz. lemon juice
2 dashes orange bitters
1 slice fresh or brandied peach

Shake brandy, peach liqueur, raspberry liqueur, lemon juice and bitters well with ice. Strain into prechilled cocktail glass. Add peach slice. If raspberry liqueur isn't available, raspberry syrup may be substituted.

BRANDY SOUR

2 ozs. brandy
½ oz. lemon juice
¼ oz. orange juice
½ to 1 teaspoon sugar
½ slice lemon

Shake brandy, lemon juice, orange juice and sugar well with ice. Strain into prechilled whiskey-sour glass. Add lemon slice. Softer than a whiskey sour.

CHAMPS ÉLYSÉES

1½ ozs. cognac
½ oz. yellow Chartreuse
½ oz. lemon juice
1 dash Angostura bitters (optional)

Shake well with ice. Strain over rocks in prechilled old-fashioned glass. Bitters may be omitted for a more pronounced Chartreuse flavor.

CHERRY BLOSSOM

1¼ ozs. brandy
¾ oz. wild-cherry liqueur
2 teaspoons lemon juice
¼ teaspoon curaçao
¼ teaspoon grenadine

Shake well with ice. Strain into prechilled sugar-frosted cocktail glass. Rub rim of glass with wild-cherry liqueur before dipping into sugar.

CLASSIC

1½ ozs. brandy
½ oz. lemon juice
¼ oz. maraschino liqueur
¼ oz. curaçao

Shake well with ice. Strain into prechilled cocktail glass. More tart than earlier versions of the brandy classic.

DEAUVILLE

1 oz. brandy
½ oz. lemon juice
½ oz. apple brandy
½ oz. Triple Sec

Shake well with ice. Strain into prechilled cocktail glass.

DRY COLD DECK

1³/₄ ozs. brandy
¹/₂ oz. dry vermouth
¹/₄ oz. white crème de
  menthe

Shake well with ice. Strain into prechilled cocktail glass. A sophisticated stinger.

FEMINA

1¹/₂ ozs. brandy
¹/₂ oz. Benedictine
¹/₂ oz. orange juice
1 slice cocktail orange in
  syrup

Shake brandy, Benedictine and orange juice well with ice. Strain over rocks in prechilled old-fashioned glass. Add orange slice. Not biting in the "sour" tradition, but cool and comforting.

FOXHOUND

1¹/₂ ozs. brandy
¹/₂ oz. cranberry juice
1 teaspoon kümmel
1 teaspoon lemon juice
¹/₂ slice lemon

Shake brandy, cranberry juice, kümmel and lemon juice well with ice. Strain over rocks in prechilled old-fashioned glass. Add lemon slice. Serve before a dinner of pheasant or partridge.

FROUPE

1¹/₄ ozs. brandy
1¹/₄ ozs. sweet vermouth
1 teaspoon Benedictine

Stir well with ice. Strain into prechilled cocktail glass. Like a sunset's afterglow.

FROZEN BRANDY AND PORT

1¹/₂ ozs. brandy
1 oz. port
1 small egg
1 teaspoon powdered
  sugar
¹/₃ cup crushed ice
Grated nutmeg

Put brandy, port, egg, sugar and ice into blender. Blend 20 seconds at low speed. Pour into prechilled saucer champagne glass. Sprinkle with nutmeg. Also known as coffee flip when crushed ice is omitted and drink is shaken with ice in regular cocktail shaker.

FROZEN BRANDY AND RUM

1½ ozs. brandy
1 oz. golden rum
½ oz. lemon juice
1 egg yolk
1½ teaspoons sugar
⅓ cup crushed ice

Put all ingredients into blender. Blend 15-20 seconds at low speed. Pour into prechilled saucer champagne glass. Soothing.

HARVARD

1½ ozs. brandy
½ oz. dry vermouth
1 teaspoon grenadine
2 teaspoons lemon juice

Shake well with ice. Strain into prechilled cocktail glass. Drier than earlier versions, but still crimson.

JAPANESE

2 ozs. brandy
¼ oz. orgeat or orzata
¼ oz. lime juice
1 dash Angostura bitters
Lime peel

Shake brandy, orgeat, lime juice and bitters well with ice. Strain into prechilled cocktail glass. Twist lime peel above drink and drop into glass.

LA JOLLA

1½ ozs. brandy
½ oz. banana liqueur
2 teaspoons lemon juice
1 teaspoon orange juice

Shake well with ice. Strain into prechilled sugar-frosted cocktail glass.

McBRANDY

1½ ozs. brandy
1 oz. apple juice
1 teaspoon lemon juice
1 slice lemon

Shake brandy, apple juice and lemon juice well with ice. Strain into prechilled cocktail glass. Add lemon slice. Serve before a dinner of roast ham or duck.

PHOEBE SNOW

11/4 ozs. brandy
1¼ ozs. Red Dubonnet
¼ teaspoon Pernod

Shake well with ice. Strain into prechilled cocktail glass.

PICASSO

1¹/₂ ozs. cognac
¹/₂ oz. Red Dubonnet
¹/₂ oz. lime juice
1 teaspoon sugar
Orange peel

Shake cognac, Dubonnet, lime juice and sugar well with ice. Strain into prechilled cocktail glass. Twist orange peel above drink and drop into glass.

POLONAISE

1¹/₂ ozs. brandy
¹/₂ oz. blackberry liqueur or blackberry-flavored brandy
¹/₂ oz. very dry sherry
1 teaspoon lemon juice
2 dashes orange bitters

Shake well with ice. Strain over rocks in prechilled old-fashioned glass.

QUAKER

1¹/₂ ozs. brandy
¹/₂ oz. rum
¹/₂ oz. lemon juice
1 teaspoon raspberry syrup or grenadine
Lemon peel

Shake brandy, rum, lemon juice and raspberry syrup well with ice. Strain into prechilled cocktail glass. Twist lemon peel above drink and drop into glass. Two rounds of these and all will be Friends.

SANTA FE

1¹/₂ ozs. brandy
¹/₂ oz. grapefruit juice
¹/₂ dry vermouth
1 teaspoon lemon juice

Shake all ingredients well with ice. Strain into prechilled sugar-rimmed cocktail glass.

SARATOGA

2 ozs. brandy
¹/₂ oz. pineapple juice
1 teaspoon lemon juice
¹/₂ teaspoon maraschino liqueur
1 dash Angostura bitters

Shake well with ice. Strain into prechilled cocktail glass.

³/₄ oz. brandy
³/₄ oz. curaçao
³/₄ oz. lemon juice

SIDECAR
Shake well with ice. Strain into prechilled cocktail glass. All three ingredients may be varied to suit one's taste. For a strong brandy accent, use 1¹/₂ ozs. brandy, ¹/₂ oz. curacao and ¹/₂ oz. lemon juice. One of the most venerable of traditional cocktails.

2 ozs. brandy
¹/₂ oz. sloe gin (creamy cap)
1 teaspoon lemon juice
Lemon peel

SLOE BRANDY
Shake brandy, sloe gin and lemon juice well with ice. Strain into prechilled cocktail glass. Twist lemon peel above drink and drop into glass.

1¹/₂ ozs. brandy
¹/₂ oz. lemon juice
¹/₄ oz. crème d'ananas
¹/₄ oz. white crème de menthe
1 pineapple stick

SOUTH PACIFIC
Shake brandy, lemon juice, crème d'ananas and crème de menthe well with ice. Strain over rocks in prechilled old-fashioned glass. Garnish with pineapple stick.

1¹/₄ ozs. brandy
1¹/₄ ozs. white crème de menthe

STINGER
Shake well with ice. Strain into prechilled cocktail glass. For a dry stinger, increase brandy to 2 ozs. and reduce crème de menthe to ¹/₂ oz. May be offered before or after dinner. It is frequently served with a glass of ice water on the side.

1³/₄ ozs. brandy
³/₄ oz. Tuaca liqueur
Lemon peel

THUMPER
Stir brandy and Tuaca well with ice. Strain into prechilled old-fashioned glass. Add ice cubes or ice slices to fill glass. Stir well. Twist lemon peel above drink and drop into glass. One of Italy's oldest liqueurs shines in this drink.

VIA VENETO

1³/₄ ozs. brandy
¹/₂ oz. sambuca
¹/₂ egg white
2 teaspoons lemon juice
1 teaspoon sugar

Shake well with ice. Strain over rocks in prechilled old-fashioned glass. An engaging patio drink that's a little on the sweet side.

WATERBURY

1¹/₂ ozs. brandy
¹/₂ oz. lime juice
¹/₂ egg white
¹/₂ teaspoon grenadine
¹/₂ teaspoon powdered
  sugar

Shake well with ice. Strain into prechilled sugar-frosted cocktail glass.

CHAMPAGNE COCKTAILS

AMERICANA

1 teaspoon 100-proof
  bourbon
¹/₂ teaspoon sugar
1 dash bitters
4 ozs. iced *brut*
  champagne
1 slice fresh or brandied
  peach

Stir bourbon, sugar and bitters in prechilled champagne glass. Add champagne and peach slice.

CARIBBEAN CHAMPAGNE

¹/₂ teaspoon light rum
¹/₂ teaspoon banana
  liqueur
1 dash orange bitters
4 ozs. iced *brut*
  champagne
1 slice banana

Pour rum, banana liqueur and bitters into prechilled champagne glass. Add champagne. Stir very gently. Add banana slice.

CHAMPAGNE FRAISE

½ teaspoon strawberry
  liqueur
½ teaspoon kirschwasser
4 ozs. iced *brut*
  champagne
1 large fresh strawberry

Pour strawberry liqueur and kirsch into prechilled champagne glass. Tilt glass so that liqueurs coat bottom and sides of glass. Add champagne. Float strawberry on drink. (Measure ½ teaspoons precisely—don't overpour.)

CHAMPAGNE MANHATTAN

1 oz. Canadian whisky
¼ oz. sweet vermouth
1 dash bitters
3 ozs. iced *brut*
  champagne
1 brandied cherry

Stir whisky, vermouth and bitters well with ice. Strain into prechilled champagne glass. Add champagne and brandied cherry.

CHAMPAGNE NORMANDE

1 teaspoon calvados
½ teaspoon sugar
1 dash Angostura bitters
4 ozs. iced *brut*
  champagne

Stir calvados, sugar and bitters in prechilled champagne glass. Add champagne. Stir very gently.

CHAMPAGNE NOYAUX

½ oz. crème de noyaux
1 teaspoon lime juice
1 large toasted almond
4 ozs. iced *brut*
  champagne
1 slice lime

Stir crème de noyaux and lime juice in prechilled champagne glass. Add almond. Pour champagne into glass. Stir slightly. Float lime slice on top.

CHAMPAGNE OLD-FASHIONED

½ oz. Grand Marnier
½ oz. Forbidden Fruit
1 dash orange bitters
4 ozs. iced *brut*
  champagne
1 slice lemon

Into prechilled old-fashioned glass, pour liqueurs and bitters. Add champagne. Stir very gently. Launch with lemon slice.

CHAMPAGNE POLONAISE

1 teaspoon blackberry
  liqueur
¹/₂ teaspoon cognac
4 ozs. iced *brut*
  champagne

Pour blackberry liqueur and cognac into prechilled sugar-frosted champagne glass. Add champagne. Stir very gently.

CHARTREUSE CHAMPAGNE

¹/₂ teaspoon green
  Chartreuse
¹/₂ teaspoon cognac
4 ozs. iced *brut*
  champagne
Lemon peel

Pour Chartreuse, cognac and champagne into prechilled champagne glass. Stir very gently. Twist lemon peel above drink and drop into glass. Toast the Carthusian order.

CHERRY CHAMPAGNE

¹/₂ oz. iced Cherry
  Heering
4 ozs. iced *brut*
  champagne
¹/₂ pitted fresh cherry

Pour Cherry Heering into neck of prechilled hollow-stemmed champagne glass. Add champagne. Float cherry on drink.

CLASSIC CHAMPAGNE COCKTAIL

¹/₂ teaspoon sugar
1 dash Angostura bitters
4 ozs. iced *brut*
  champagne
Lemon peel

Stir sugar and bitters in prechilled champagne glass. Add champagne. Usually, the sparkle of the champagne will blend the ingredients, and little if any stirring is necessary. Twist lemon peel above drink and drop into glass.

MELBA CHAMPAGNE

¹/₂ oz. himbeergeist (raspberry brandy, not liqueur)
4 ozs. iced *brut* champagne
1 fresh or thawed frozen raspberry
Raspberry sherbet, hard-frozen

Pour himbeergeist into prechilled champagne glass. Add champagne and the raspberry. With a fruit-baller, scoop out a single small ball of sherbet. Float on champagne.

ORANGE CHAMPAGNE

Peel of ¹/₂ orange, in one spiral
2 teaspoons curaçao
4 ozs. iced *brut* champagne

Place orange peel in prechilled champagne glass. Add curaçao and champagne. Stir very gently.

SPARKLING GALLIANO

¹/₂ oz. Galliano
¹/₂ teaspoon lemon juice
4 ozs. iced *brut* champagne
Cucumber peel, 1¹/₂ inches long, ¹/₂ inch wide

Pour Galliano and lemon juice into prechilled champagne glass. Stir. Add champagne and cucumber peel. Drink to the stars.

GIN COCKTAILS

ALEXANDER WITH COFFEE

³/₄ oz. gin
³/₄ oz. coffee liqueur
³/₄ oz. cream

Shake well with ice. Strain into prechilled sugar-frosted cocktail glass. Moisten rim of glass with coffee liqueur before dipping into sugar. Especially good with espresso-coffee liqueur. Like all alexanders, which are really sweet cocktails, this one is both a pre- and postprandial drink.

ALEXANDER WITH GIN

³/₄ oz. gin
³/₄ oz. crème de cacao
³/₄ oz. cream

Shake well with ice. Strain into prechilled cocktail glass. (Alexanders made with a brandy base instead of gin will be found among brandy cocktails.)

ALEXANDER WITH PRUNELLE

³/₄ oz. gin
³/₄ oz. prunelle
³/₄ oz. cream
Ground cinnamon

Shake gin, prunelle and cream well with ice. Strain into prechilled cocktail glass. Sprinkle lightly with cinnamon.

ALEXANDER'S SISTER

³/₄ oz. gin
³/₄ oz. white or green
  crème de menthe
³/₄ oz. cream

Shake well with ice. Strain into prechilled cocktail glass.

BENNETT

1¹/₂ ozs. gin
¹/₂ oz. lime juice
¹/₂ teaspoon sugar
2 dashes Angostura
  bitters
Lime peel

Shake gin, lime juice, sugar and bitters well with ice. Strain into prechilled cocktail glass. Twist lime peel above drink and drop into glass.

BERLINER

1¹/₂ ozs. gin
¹/₄ oz. dry kümmel
¹/₂ oz. dry vermouth
¹/₄ oz. lemon juice

Shake well with ice. Strain into prechilled cocktail glass. Best appreciated with freshly made, well-buttered smoked-salmon canapès.

BISCAYNE

1 oz. gin
¹/₂ oz. light rum
¹/₂ oz. Forbidden Fruit
¹/₂ oz. lime juice
1 slice lime

Shake gin, rum, Forbidden Fruit and lime juice well with ice. Strain over rocks in prechilled old-fashioned glass. Add lime slice.

BLUE DEVIL

1½ ozs. gin
½ oz. blue curaçao
½ oz. lemon juice
1 slice lemon

Shake gin, curaçao and lemon juice well with ice. Strain into prechilled cocktail glass garnished with lemon slice. A gentle blues chaser.

BONNIE PRINCE

1¼ ozs. gin
½ oz. Lillet
¼ oz. Drambuie

Shake well with ice. Strain into prechilled cocktail glass. Inspired by gin drinkers with both French and Scottish blood in their veins.

BRITTANY

1½ ozs. gin
½ oz. Amer Picon
¼ oz. orange juice
¼ oz. lemon juice
Orange peel

Shake gin, Amer Picon, orange juice and lemon juice well with ice. Strain into prechilled cocktail glass. Twist orange peel above drink and drop into glass.

BRONX

1½ ozs. gin
½ oz. orange juice
¼ oz. dry vermouth
¼ oz. sweet vermouth

Shake well with ice. Strain into prechilled cocktail glass. For a drier bronx, omit sweet vermouth and increase gin to 1¾ ozs. One of the few inventions of the Prohibition era really worth retaining when made with fine gin rather than the notorious bathtub variety.

CHATHAM

1¼ ozs. gin
½ oz. ginger-flavored
   brandy
¼ oz. lemon juice
1 small piece preserved
   ginger in syrup

Shake gin, ginger-flavored brandy and lemon juice well with ice. Strain into prechilled cocktail glass. Garnish with preserved ginger.

CHERRY SLING

1½ ozs. gin
½ oz. cherry liqueur
½ oz. lime juice

Shake well with ice. Strain into prechilled cocktail glass. Use a tart cherry liqueur such as Cherry Heering or the domestic Cherry Karise for best results.

CLOISTER

1¹/₂ ozs. gin
¹/₂ oz. grapefruit juice
¹/₄ oz. lemon juice
¹/₄ oz. yellow Chartreuse

Shake well with ice. Strain into prechilled cocktail glass. A contemplative kind of drink, perfect for an autumn sundown.

CLOVER CLUB

1¹/₂ ozs. gin
³/₄ oz. lemon juice
1 teaspoon grenadine or
  raspberry syrup
¹/₂ egg white

Shake well with ice. Strain into prechilled cocktail glass.

CLOVER CLUB ROYAL

1¹/₂ ozs. gin
³/₄ oz. lemon juice
1 teaspoon grenadine or
  raspberry syrup
¹/₂ egg yolk

Shake well with ice. Strain into prechilled cocktail glass. A trifle richer than the clover club, above, this velvety cocktail is even smoother when made with ¹/₃ cup crushed ice in a blender and poured over the rocks in an old-fashioned glass.

COCONUT GIN

1¹/₂ ozs. gin
¹/₂ oz. lemon juice
¹/₄ oz. maraschino
  liqueur
¹/₄ oz. cream of coconut

Cream of coconut, from the can, should be well mixed before using. Shake all ingredients well with ice. Strain into prechilled sugar-frosted cocktail glass. Sets up a beautiful indoor tropical breeze.

COLD GIN TODDY

2 ozs. gin
¹/₂ teaspoon sugar
Lemon peel

Shake gin and sugar well with plenty of ice and strain into old-fashioned glass filled with large cubes or slices of ice. Twist lemon peel above drink and drop into glass.

COPENHAGEN

1 oz. gin
1 oz. aquavit
1/4 oz. dry vermouth
1 large stuffed olive

Stir gin, aquavit and vermouth well with ice. Strain into prechilled cocktail glass. Add olive.

CORDIAL MÉDOC

1 oz. gin
1/2 oz. Cordial Médoc
1/2 oz. dry vermouth
1/4 oz. lemon juice

Shake well with ice. Strain into prechilled cocktail glass. For a bon-voyage cocktail party before flying to Paris.

CORDIAL MÉDOC SOUR

1 1/2 ozs. gin
1/2 oz. Cordial Médoc
1/2 oz. lemon juice
1/2 slice orange

Shake gin, Cordial Médoc and lemon juice well with ice. Strain into prechilled whiskey-sour glass. Garnish with orange slice.

DUNDEE

1 oz. gin
1/2 oz. Scotch
1/2 oz. Drambuie
1/4 oz. lemon juice
Lemon peel

Shake gin, Scotch, Drambuie and lemon juice well with ice. Pour over rocks in prechilled old-fashioned glass. Twist lemon peel above drink and drop into glass.

FOGGY DAY

1 1/2 ozs. gin
1/4 oz. Pernod
1 slice lemon
Lemon peel

Shake gin and Pernod well with ice. Strain over rocks in prechilled old-fashioned glass. Rub outside of lemon peel around rim of glass and drop peel into glass. Add lemon slice. Created by Jerry Wyman, head bartender at the Phoenix Playboy Club.

GENOA

3/4 oz. gin
3/4 oz. grappa
1/2 oz. sambuca
1/2 oz. dry vermouth
1 olive

Stir gin, grappa, sambuca and vermouth well with ice. Strain into prechilled cocktail glass. Add olive.

GIMLET

2 ozs. gin
1/2 oz. Rose's lime juice

Stir extremely well with ice. Strain into prechilled cocktail glass. Long stirring is absolutely essential to present this English classic in its best light. The above formula, 4-to-1, may be made 5-to-1, if desired, by adding 1/2 oz. gin. Glass may be sugar-frosted by moistening rim with Rose's lime juice before dipping into sugar.

GIN AND LIME

1 1/2 ozs. gin
1/2 oz. fresh lime juice
1/2 oz. orange juice
1 teaspoon Rose's lime juice
Lime peel

Shake gin, fresh lime juice, orange juice and Rose's lime juice well with ice. Strain into prechilled cocktail glass. Twist lime peel above drink and drop into glass. A superb cocktail to sip with English potted shrimp or anchovy-paste canapés.

GIN AQUAVIT

1 1/2 ozs. gin
1/2 oz. aquavit
1/2 oz. lemon juice
1 teaspoon sugar
1/2 egg white
1 teaspoon cream

Shake well with ice. Strain into prechilled old-fashioned glass containing two or three ice cubes. A light, foamy drink to serve before passing a platter of Danish open sandwiches.

GIN CASSIS

1 1/2 ozs. gin
1/2 oz. lemon juice
1/2 oz. crème de cassis

Shake well with ice. Strain into prechilled cocktail glass, or into prechilled old-fashioned glass with one or two rocks.

GIN DAIQUIRI

1 1/2 ozs. gin
1/2 oz. light rum
1/2 oz. lime juice
1 teaspoon sugar

Shake well with ice. Strain into prechilled sugar-frosted cocktail glass.

GIN OLD-FASHIONED

¹/₄ teaspoon sugar
1 or 2 dashes Angostura
  bitters
1³/₄ ozs. gin
Lemon peel

Put sugar and bitters into prechilled old-fashioned glass. Stir until sugar dissolves, adding a teaspoon of water if necessary to complete the process. Add gin and two or three ice cubes or large pieces of coarsely cracked ice. Stir well. Twist lemon peel above drink and drop into glass. Old-fashioneds are frequently garnished with orange slice, lemon slice, pineapple, cherry, etc., but knowledgeable old-fashioned men shun the fruit salad.

GIN SIDECAR

³/₄ oz. high-proof English
  gin
³/₄ oz. Triple Sec
³/₄ oz. lemon juice

Shake well with ice. Strain into prechilled cocktail glass. The gin substitutes for brandy in this version of the sidecar.

GIN SOUR

1¹/₂ ozs. gin
¹/₂ oz. lemon juice
¹/₄ oz. orange juice
1 teaspoon sugar
¹/₂ slice orange
1 maraschino cherry

Shake gin, lemon juice, orange juice and sugar well with ice. Strain into prechilled whiskey-sour glass. Garnish with orange slice and cherry.

GIN SOUTHERN

1¹/₂ ozs. gin
¹/₂ oz. Southern Comfort
¹/₄ oz. grapefruit juice
¹/₄ oz. lemon juice

Shake well with ice. Strain into prechilled cocktail glass. For drinking men who appreciate verandas and magnolia blossoms.

GOLDEN HORNET

1¹/₂ ozs. gin
¹/₂ oz. amontillado
  sherry
¹/₂ oz. Scotch
Lemon peel

Stir gin and sherry well with ice. Strain over two rocks in prechilled old-fashioned glass. Float Scotch on top. Twist lemon peel over drink and drop into glass. Created by Tom Moore, head bartender at the New York Playboy Club.

GRANVILLE

1¹/₂ ozs. gin
¹/₄ oz. Grand Marnier
¹/₄ oz. calvados
¹/₄ oz. lemon juice

Shake well with ice. Strain into prechilled cocktail glass.

GREEN DEVIL

1¹/₂ ozs. gin
¹/₂ oz. lime juice
¹/₄ oz. green crème de menthe
2 sprigs mint

Shake gin, lime juice and crème de menthe well with ice. Strain over two or three rocks in prechilled old-fashioned glass. Tear several mint leaves to release aroma before adding to drink as garnish.

HUDSON BAY

1 oz. gin
¹/₂ oz. cherry liqueur
¹/₂ oz. orange juice
¹/₄ oz. lime juice
¹/₄ oz. 151-proof rum
1 slice lime

Shake gin, cherry liqueur, orange juice, lime juice and rum well with ice. Strain into prechilled cocktail glass. Add lime slice. A winter or summer cocktail with prodigious thawing powers.

JAMAICA GLOW

1¹/₂ ozs. gin
¹/₂ oz. dry red wine
¹/₂ oz. orange juice
1 teaspoon dark Jamaican rum
1 slice lime

Shake gin, wine, orange juice and rum well with ice. Strain into prechilled sugar-frosted cocktail glass. Add lime slice. This relic of plantation days is still a magnificent reviver for surf riders and scuba divers.

JOULOUVILLE

1 oz. gin
¹/₂ oz. apple brandy
¹/₂ oz. lemon juice
¹/₄ oz. sweet vermouth
¹/₄ teaspoon grenadine

Shake well with ice. Strain into prechilled cocktail glass.

KEY COCKTAIL

1¹/₂ ozs. gin
¹/₂ oz. lime juice
¹/₄ oz. dark Jamaican rum
¹/₄ oz. Falernum
1 pineapple stick

Shake gin, lime juice, rum and Falernum well with ice. Strain into prechilled cocktail glass. Garnish with pineapple stick.

MARTINI

Over the years, the martini, most famous of all cocktail-hour thoroughbreds, has evolved into a drink that is practically all gin with only the faintest hint of vermouth. This preference for drier and drier martinis (while *dry* usually means less sweet, in reference to martinis it means less vermouth) has spawned some strange equipment and a countless number of jokes. Some barmen ritualize the exacting vermouth formula with a long R_x dropper; some spray their vermouth from atomizers. The fanatical, reaching the *reductio ad absurdum,* claim they waft the vermouth bottletop over the gin or mutter the word *vermouth* under their breath while stirring their raw concoction in the mixing glass. It would be unfortunate if the use of vermouth in the martini became extinct, for its bite, however faint, is trenchant. It turns cold gin into a civilized cocktail.

Most top-flight barmen make their martinis with about ten or twelve parts gin to one part dry vermouth. The drink may be served "up," meaning in a regular stemmed cocktail glass, or on the rocks in an old-fashioned glass. You can drop a twist of lemon peel into the glass or rub the rim with the peel before adding it to the drink. The martini's most common garnish is an olive, pitted or stuffed. With a cocktail-onion garnish, it turns into a gibson.

A martini must be piercingly cold; at its best, both gin and vermouth are prechilled in the refrigerator, well stirred with ice and poured into a prechilled glass. Energetic stirring with the ice is all-important; the dilution makes the drink both smooth and palatable. Those who merely combine gin and vermouth beforehand and then refrigerate without stirring wind up serving raw slugs to guests who are quickly cargoed and who completely miss the pleasure of a well-made martini.

Although vermouth is the spirited minor ingredient, a bottle opened for pouring and left standing in the liquor cabinet for weeks will lose its bell-ringing zest. To retain as much as possible of the flavor of the aromatic herbs used in making vermouth, store the opened bottle in the refrigerator. It's a good idea for the martini man to buy his vermouth in pint bottles and make frequent replacements.

Here are several variations on the familar martini theme:

12-to-1 MARTINI
2 ozs. gin
1 teaspoon dry vermouth

8-to-1 MARTINI
2 ozs. gin
1/4 oz. dry vermouth

4-to-1 MARTINI
2 ozs. gin
1/2 oz. dry vermouth

GIBSON
As noted, any of the above martini mixtures garnished with a cocktail onion.

---

1 1/2 ozs. gin
3/4 oz. dry vermouth
1 dash Angostura bitters

BLENTON
Stir well with ice. Strain into prechilled cocktail glass. A martini variation so old that it's new. Total effect on the palate: warming and elevating.

---

1 oz. gin
1/2 oz. dry vermouth
1/2 oz. sweet vermouth
1/2 oz. strawberry liqueur
1 large strawberry

BLOODHOUND
Shake gin, both kinds of vermouth and strawberry liqueur well with ice. Strain into prechilled cocktail glass. Drop strawberry into glass. The best dry vermouth for this one is Chambery fraise.

---

2 ozs. gin
1/2 oz. fino sherry

FINO MARTINI
Stir well with ice. Strain into prechilled cocktail glass. Add olive or lemon twist. Serve with a side dish of freshly toasted, salted almonds.

---

2 ozs. gin
1/4 oz. dry vermouth
Curaçao

FLYING DUTCHMAN
Into a prechilled cocktail glass, pour enough curaçao so that when the glass is slowly twirled, it will coat the sides. Stir gin and vermouth well with ice. Strain into glass.

2 ozs. gin
Italian sweet vermouth

GIN AND IT

*Stir gin well with ice. Into a
prechilled cocktail glass, pour
enough vermouth so that when the
glass is slowly twirled, it will coat
the sides. Add the gin. The
English drink is often served at
room temperature. The It stands
for the Italian vermouth. A gin
and French is the same drink with
French dry vermouth instead.*

2 ozs. gin
$1/2$ oz. dry vermouth
$1/4$ oz. sweet vermouth

KNICKERBOCKER

*Stir well with ice. Strain into
prechilled cocktail glass. Serve
without benefit of cherry, olive or
lemon twist. This version of the
martini appeals to those who like
vermouth in both sweet and dry
forms.*

$3/4$ oz. gin
$3/4$ oz. dry vermouth
$3/4$ oz. dry Marsala
Lemon peel

MARSALA MARTINI

*Stir gin, vermouth and Marsala
well with ice. Strain into
prechilled cocktail glass. Twist
lemon peel above drink and drop
into glass.*

2 ozs. gin
$1/2$ oz. dry vermouth
$1/2$ teaspoon maraschino
liqueur
2 dashes orange bitters

MARTINEZ

*Stir well with ice. Strain into
prechilled cocktail glass. Martini
men with a strain of Spanish in
their veins go for this one. Alleged
to have been the original martini.*

2 ozs. Dutch genever gin
$1/2$ oz. dry vermouth
Lemon peel

MARTINI, HOLLAND STYLE

*Stir gin and vermouth well with
ice. Strain into prechilled cocktail
glass. Twist lemon peel above
drink and drop into glass.*

PAISLEY MARTINI

2¹/₄ ozs. gin
¹/₄ oz. dry vermouth
1 teaspoon Scotch

Stir well with ice. Strain into prechilled cocktail glass. The flavor of the Scotch in this 9-to-1 martini is just subtle enough to let the drinker know that something delightfully offbeat is in his glass.

PERFECT

1¹/₂ ozs. gin
¹/₂ oz. dry vermouth
¹/₂ oz. sweet vermouth

Stir well with ice. Strain into prechilled cocktail glass. Add olive or twist of lemon peel if desired. Modern martini men would call this an "imperfect" martini, but perfect *is its traditional name.*

PERNOD MARTINI

2 ozs. gin
¹/₂ oz. dry vermouth
¹/₈ teaspoon Pernod

Stir well with ice. Strain into prechilled cocktail glass. Very pleasant with an onion-stuffed olive. Some bartenders pour a soupçon of Pernod into the glass, swirl it around and then add the martini.

RACQUET CLUB

2 ozs. gin
¹/₂ oz. dry vermouth
2 dashes orange bitters

Shake, don't stir, with ice in silver cocktail shaker until shaker is completely frosted. Strain into cocktail glass so cold it's somewhat uncomfortable to hold.

SAKETINI

2 ozs. gin
¹/₂ oz. sake

Stir well with ice. Strain into prechilled cocktail glass. If desired, an olive or twist of lemon peel may be added. The saketini is a reminder that dry vermouth and rice wine bear an uncanny resemblance to each other.

2 ozs. gin
1/2 oz. sweet vermouth
Orange peel

SWEET MARTINI

*Stir gin and vermouth well with
ice. Strain into prechilled cocktail
glass. Twist orange peel above
drink and drop into glass. While
sweet martini sounds like a
contradiction in terms, the drink
is not only tolerable but titillating.*

1 oz. gin
1/2 oz. sambuca
1/2 egg white
1 teaspoon cream
1/2 oz. lime juice

MATINÉE

*Shake all ingredients well with
ice. Strain into prechilled cocktail
glass. A comfortable midafternoon
cocktail. May also be served as a
pick-me-up the morning after with
a spray of freshly ground nutmeg.*

1 1/2 ozs. gin
1/2 oz. lemon juice
1/2 teaspoon sugar
2 sprigs fresh mint
1 slice lemon
1/2 slice orange

MINTED GIN

*Shake gin, lemon juice and sugar
well with ice. Strain into
prechilled old-fashioned glass
with rocks. Garnish drink with
lemon and orange slices. Tear
mint leaves before placing on
rocks. A perfect drink for
unwinding after 18 holes on the
fairway.*

1 1/2 ozs. gin
1/2 oz. plum brandy
1/4 oz. orange juice
1/4 oz. lemon juice
1 brandied cherry

MOLDAU

*Shake gin, plum brandy, orange
juice and lemon juice well with
ice. Strain into prechilled
old-fashioned glass with two or
three ice cubes. Garnish with
brandied cherry.*

1 oz. gin
1/2 oz. golden rum
1/2 oz. lime juice
1/2 oz. pineapple juice
1/2 teaspoon sugar

MORRO

*Shake well with ice. Strain into
prechilled sugar-frosted glass.
Moisten rim of glass with
Falernum before dipping into
sugar. Once tasted, the marriage of
gin and rum is one of those
unions that no man in his right
drinking sense would dream of
putting asunder. Fruit juices in
this drink help fortify the nuptials.*

ORANGE BLOSSOM

1¹/₂ ozs. gin
1 oz. orange juice
¹/₂ slice orange

Shake gin and orange juice well with ice. Strain into prechilled sugar-frosted cocktail glass. Glass may be sugar-frosted by moistening rim with orange peel before dipping into sugar. Add orange slice.

ORANGE BLOSSOM FROZEN

1¹/₂ ozs. gin
2 ozs. orange juice
¹/₂ oz. curaçao
¹/₂ oz. lemon juice
2 drops orange-flower water
¹/₄ cup cracked ice
¹/₂ slice orange

Put gin, orange juice, curaçao, lemon juice, orange-flower water and ice into blender. Spin 5–8 seconds. Pour into deep-saucer champagne or old-fashioned glass. Place orange slice on top.

PINK GIN

2 ozs. gin
2 dashes Angostura bitters

In Britain, the custom is simply to stir these ingredients at room temperature in a small cocktail glass. For American tastes, it's more pleasant if the gin and bitters are well stirred with ice and then poured into a prechilled glass. This is one of the drinks that sustained Sir Francis Chichester so beautifully on his long, lonely trip round the world.

PINK LADY

1¹/₂ ozs. gin
¹/₄ oz. lime juice
1 teaspoon cream
1 teaspoon grenadine
¹/₂ egg white

Shake well with ice. Strain into prechilled cocktail glass. Glass may be sugar-frosted by moistening rim with grenadine before dipping into sugar.

PIROUETTER

1 oz. gin
1/2 oz. Grand Marnier
1 oz. orange juice
1 teaspoon lemon juice
Orange peel

Shake gin, Grand Marnier, orange juice and lemon juice well with ice. Strain into prechilled cocktail glass. Twist orange peel above drink and drop into glass.

POLISH SIDECAR

3/4 oz. gin
3/4 oz. Polish or
   Polish-style blackberry
   liqueur
3/4 oz. lemon juice

Shake well with ice. Strain into prechilled cocktail glass. A large fresh blackberry, if available, is a pleasant garnish for this drink.

POMPANO

1 oz. gin
1/2 oz. dry vermouth
1 oz. grapefruit juice
4 dashes orange bitters
1 slice orange

Shake gin, vermouth, grapefruit juice and bitters well with ice. Strain over rocks in prechilled old-fashioned glass. Garnish with orange slice. A perfect cocktail for Florida- or Caribbean-bound vacationers.

PRINCETON

1 1/4 ozs. gin
3/4 oz. dry vermouth
1/2 oz. lime juice

Shake well with ice. Strain into prechilled cocktail glass. Like the bronx (page 144), it's one of very few drinks born in Prohibition days really worth retaining. Named for the great seat of learning which, during the Noble Experiment, distinguished itself even more for its prowess in soaking up bathtub gin.

RED CLOUD

1 1/2 ozs. gin
1/2 oz. apricot liqueur
1/2 oz. lemon juice
1 teaspoon grenadine
1 dash bitters

Shake well with ice. Strain into prechilled cocktail glass.

RENAISSANCE

1¹/₂ ozs. gin
¹/₂ oz. dry sherry
¹/₂ oz. cream
Freshly grated nutmeg

Shake gin, sherry and cream well with ice. Strain into prechilled cocktail glass. Spray with nutmeg. A drink to savor after a lengthy tour of art galleries.

RENDEZVOUS

1¹/₂ ozs. gin
¹/₂ oz. kirschwasser
¹/₄ oz. Campari
Lemon peel

Shake gin, kirschwasser and Campari well with ice. Strain into prechilled cocktail glass. Twist lemon peel above drink and drop into glass. An appetite arouser best sipped while a double-thick filet is browning over the charcoals.

ROCKY DANE

1 oz. gin
¹/₂ oz. dry vermouth
¹/₂ oz. Cherry Heering
¹/₄ oz. kirsch
Lemon peel

Shake gin, vermouth, Cherry Heering and kirsch well with ice. Strain over rocks in prechilled old-fashioned glass. Twist lemon peel above drink and drop into glass.

ROSE

1 oz. gin
¹/₂ oz. apricot-flavored
  brandy
¹/₂ oz. dry vermouth
¹/₂ oz. lemon juice
1 teaspoon grenadine
Lemon peel

Shake gin, apricot-flavored brandy, vermouth, lemon juice and grenadine well with ice. Strain into prechilled cocktail glass. Twist lemon peel above drink and drop into glass.

ST.-LÔ

1¹/₂ ozs. gin
¹/₂ oz. calvados
¹/₂ oz. lemon juice
1 teaspoon sugar

Shake well with ice. Strain into prechilled cocktail glass.

1 oz. gin
¹/₄ oz. rum
¹/₂ oz. grapefruit juice
¹/₄ oz. curaçao
¹/₂ oz. lemon juice

SAN SEBASTIAN

*Shake well with ice. Strain into
prechilled cocktail glass.
Recommended for galley
bartenders after a lazy
Sunday-afternoon sail.*

1 oz. gin
¹/₂ oz. fino sherry
¹/₂ oz. orange juice
¹/₂ oz. lemon juice
¹/₂ teaspoon sugar

SEVILLE

*Shake well with ice. Strain into
prechilled sugar-rimmed glass.*

2 ozs. gin
¹/₂ oz. lemon juice
1 teaspoon sugar
2 sprigs fresh mint

SOUTH SIDE

*Shake gin, lemon juice and sugar
well with ice. Strain into
prechilled cocktail glass. Tear
several leaves of each mint sprig
before adding to drink. Although
not as well known as the mint
julep, the south side is a delightful
summery cocktail with a delicate
mint accent.*

1¹/₂ ozs. gin
¹/₂ oz. strawberry liqueur
¹/₄ oz. lime juice
1 dash orange bitters
1 slice lime

STRAWBERRY
SWIG

*Shake gin, strawberry liqueur,
lime juice and bitters well with
ice. Strain into prechilled
old-fashioned glass with several
rocks. Garnish with lime slice.*

1¹/₂ ozs. gin
¹/₂ oz. lemon juice
¹/₂ oz. Strega
1 slice lemon

STREGA SOUR

*Shake gin, lemon juice and Strega
well with ice. Strain into
prechilled sugar-frosted cocktail
glass. Moisten rim of glass with
Strega before dipping into sugar.
Garnish with lemon slice.*

TURF

1 oz. gin
1 oz. dry vermouth
1/4 oz. Pernod
1/4 oz. lemon juice
1 slice lemon

Shake gin, vermouth, Pernod and lemon juice well with ice. Strain over rocks in prechilled old-fashioned glass. Add lemon slice.

VERBOTEN

1 oz. gin
1/2 oz. Forbidden Fruit
1/2 oz. lemon juice
1/2 oz. orange juice
1 brandied cherry

Shake gin, Forbidden Fruit, lemon juice and orange juice well with ice. Strain into prechilled cocktail glass. Garnish with brandied cherry.

WHITE ROSE

1 1/4 ozs. gin
1/2 oz. orange juice
1/2 oz. lime juice
1 teaspoon sugar
1/2 egg white

Shake well with ice. Strain into prechilled cocktail glass. There are dozens of different recipes bearing the name white rose. This balmy concoction is designed for sipping in the vicinity of a glowing fireplace.

WOODSTOCK

1 1/2 ozs. gin
1 oz. lemon juice
1/4 oz. maple syrup
1 dash orange bitters

Shake well with ice. Strain into frosty cocktail glass. A drink from the ski country.

RUM COCKTAILS

ACAPULCO

1 1/2 ozs. light rum
1/2 oz. lime juice
1/4 oz. triple sec
1/2 egg white
1/2 teaspoon sugar
2 fresh mint leaves

Shake rum, lime juice, triple sec, egg white and sugar well with ice. Strain into prechilled cocktail glass. Tear each mint leaf partially and drop into glass.

APRICOT LADY

1½ ozs. light rum
1 oz. apricot-flavored
brandy
½ oz. lime juice
½ teaspoon curaçao
½ egg white
¼ cup crushed ice
½ slice orange

Put rum, apricot-flavored brandy, lime juice, curaçao, egg white and ice into blender. Blend 15 seconds at low speed. Pour into prechilled old-fashioned glass. Add ice cubes or ice slices to fill glass to rim. Place orange slice on top.

APRICOT PIE

1 oz. light rum
1 oz. sweet vermouth
½ teaspoon apricot-
flavored brandy
½ teaspoon lemon juice
¼ teaspoon grenadine
Orange peel

Shake rum, vermouth, apricot-flavored brandy, lemon juice and grenadine well with ice. Strain into prechilled cocktail glass. Twist orange peel above drink and drop into glass.

BACARDI

1½ ozs. light or golden
Bacardi rum
½ oz. lime juice
1 teaspoon grenadine

Shake well with ice. Strain into prechilled cocktail glass or over rocks in a prechilled old-fashioned glass. The proprietary name Bacardi, a rum originally distilled in Cuba but now made in Puerto Rico and other Spanish-speaking lands, has long been the title of this classic rum cocktail.

BANANA MANGO

1½ ozs. light rum
¼ oz. banana liqueur
½ oz. mango nectar
½ oz. lime juice
1 slice fresh mango

Shake rum, banana liqueur, mango nectar and lime juice well with ice. Strain over rocks in prechilled old-fashioned glass. Add mango slice.

BEACHCOMBER

1½ ozs. rum
½ oz. lime juice
½ oz. Triple Sec
¼ teaspoon maraschino
liqueur

Shake well with ice. Strain into prechilled sugar-rimmed cocktail glass.

BEACHCOMBER'S GOLD

1¹/₂ ozs. light rum
¹/₂ oz. dry vermouth
¹/₂ oz. sweet vermouth

Stir well with ice. Strain into prechilled deep-saucer champagne glass. Add cracked ice or ice slices to fill glass. The same mixture of rum and both kinds of vermouth is also known as the rum perfect, usually served in a regular cocktail glass without added ice. Either way, it's delightful.

BEE'S KNEES

1¹/₂ ozs. light rum
³/₄ oz. orange juice
¹/₂ oz. lime juice
1 teaspoon sugar
2 dashes orange bitters
Orange peel

Shake rum, orange juice, lime juice, sugar and bitters well with ice. Strain into prechilled cocktail glass. Twist orange peel above drink and drop into glass. A speakeasy heirloom whose orange accent is most mellow.

BETWEEN THE SHEETS

³/₄ oz. light rum
³/₄ oz. California brandy
³/₄ oz. Cointreau
¹/₂ oz. lemon juice

Shake well with ice. Strain into prechilled cocktail glass. An exhilarating variation on the rum sidecar.

BLACK DEVIL

2 ozs. light rum
¹/₂ oz. dry vermouth
1 black olive

Stir rum and vermouth well with ice. Strain into prechilled cocktail glass. Add black olive.

BOLERO

1¹/₂ ozs. light rum
³/₄ oz. apple brandy
¹/₄ teaspoon sweet
  vermouth
Lemon peel

Stir rum, apple brandy and vermouth well with ice. Strain into prechilled sugar-frosted cocktail glass. Twist lemon peel above drink and drop into glass.

1½ ozs. light rum
½ oz. lemon juice
½ oz. orange juice
½ teaspoon sugar
½ slice lemon

BOLO
*Shake rum, lemon juice, orange
juice and sugar well with ice.
Strain into prechilled cocktail
glass or prechilled whiskey-sour
glass. Garnish with lemon slice.*

1½ ozs. light rum
½ oz. passion-fruit
  syrup
¾ oz. lime juice
½ oz. orange juice
1 teaspoon 151-proof
  rum
½ cup crushed ice

BORINQUEN
*Put all ingredients into blender.
Blend at low speed 10 seconds.
Pour into prechilled double
old-fashioned glass. Add ice cubes
or cracked ice to fill glass. Garnish
with gardenia if available.*

---

1 oz. light rum
1 oz. Red Dubonnet
2 dashes Angostura
  bitters
Lemon peel

BUSHRANGER
*Shake rum, Dubonnet and bitters
well with ice. Strain into
prechilled cocktail glass. Twist
lemon peel above drink and drop
into glass.*

---

2 ozs. light rum
¼ oz. orzata
1 teaspoon grenadine
¼ oz. Triple Sec
1 oz. lime juice
1 slice lime

CARDINAL
COCKTAIL I
*Shake rum, orzata, grenadine,
Triple Sec and lime juice well
with ice. Strain into prechilled
old-fashioned glass. Add ice cubes
to bring liquid to rim. Garnish
with lime slice.*

---

1 oz. light rum
1 oz. gin
½ oz. lime juice
1 teaspoon sugar
1 slice orange

CARIB
*Shake rum, gin, lime juice and
sugar well with ice. Strain over
rocks in prechilled old-fashioned
glass. Garnish with orange slice.*

CASA BLANCA

2 ozs. golden rum
1 dash Angostura bitters
1 teaspoon lime juice
¹/₄ teaspoon curaçao
¹/₄ teaspoon maraschino
  liqueur

Shake well with ice. Strain into prechilled cocktail glass.

CHERRY DAIQUIRI

1¹/₂ ozs. light rum
¹/₂ oz. lime juice
¹/₂ oz. tart cherry liqueur
¹/₄ teaspoon kirschwasser
Lime peel

Shake rum, lime juice, cherry liqueur and kirsch well with ice. Strain into prechilled cocktail glass. Twist lime peel above drink and drop into glass.

CHINA

2 ozs. golden rum
¹/₄ teaspoon grenadine
¹/₄ teaspoon passion-fruit
  syrup
1 teaspoon curaçao
1 dash Angostura bitters

Shake well with ice. Pour into prechilled cocktail glass. A sweet drink, but not a dessert cocktail; one to set the mood for a roast-duck dinner.

COLUMBIA

1¹/₂ ozs. light rum
¹/₂ oz. raspberry syrup
¹/₂ oz. lemon juice
1 teaspoon kirschwasser

Shake well with ice. Strain into prechilled sugar-frosted cocktail glass. The kirschwasser, though small in proportion, comes through vividly.

CONCH SHELL

4 ozs. light rum
¹/₂ oz. lime juice

Shake well with ice. Strain over rocks in prechilled double old-fashioned glass. Allow at least an hour for polishing this one off.

CONTINENTAL

1³/₄ ozs. light rum
¹/₂ oz. lime juice
¹/₂ teaspoon sugar
¹/₂ teaspoon green crème
  de menthe

Shake well with ice. Strain into prechilled cocktail glass. A light bracer before a seafood dinner.

CORKSCREW

1½ ozs. light rum
½ oz. dry vermouth
½ oz. peach liqueur
1 slice lime

Shake rum, vermouth and peach liqueur well with ice. Strain into prechilled cocktail glass. Add lime slice.

CREOLE

1½ ozs. light rum
1 dash Tabasco sauce
1 teaspoon lemon juice
Iced beef bouillon or
　consommé (undiluted)
Salt and pepper

Put two large ice cubes into prechilled old-fashioned glass. Add rum, Tabasco and lemon juice. Stir well. Fill glass with beef bouillon. Sprinkle with salt and pepper. Stir again. A pleasant pick-me-up or prebrunch cocktail.

CUBA LIBRE COCKTAIL

1 oz. light rum
½ oz. 151-proof rum
½ oz. cola drink
½ oz. lime juice
½ teaspoon sugar
Lime peel

Shake both kinds of rum, cola drink, lime juice and sugar well with ice. Strain into prechilled cocktail glass. Twist lime peel above drink and drop into glass. Not to be confused with cuba libre, a tall rum-cola drink that's somewhat slower in its liberating effects.

CULROSS

1½ ozs. golden rum
½ oz. Lillet
1 teaspoon apricot-
　flavored brandy
1 teaspoon lime juice

Shake well with ice. Strain into prechilled cocktail glass as a straight-up drink or over the rocks in a prechilled old-fashioned glass. Equally good either way.

DAIQUIRI

2 ozs. light rum
½ oz. lime juice
½ teaspoon sugar

Shake well with ice. Pour into prechilled sugar-frosted cocktail glass or over the rocks in an old-fashioned glass. Sugar may be increased if a sweeter daiquiri is desired.

DERBY DAIQUIRI

1½ ozs. light rum
½ oz. lime juice
1 oz. orange juice
½ oz. simple syrup
⅓ cup crushed ice

Put all ingredients into blender. Blend 10–15 seconds at low speed. Pour into prechilled oversize cocktail glass or deep-saucer champagne glass.

DEVIL'S TAIL

1½ ozs. golden rum
1 oz. vodka
½ oz. lime juice
¼ oz. grenadine
¼ oz. apricot liqueur
⅓ cup crushed ice
Lime peel

Put rum, vodka, lime juice, grenadine, apricot liqueur and ice into blender. Blend at low speed 10–15 seconds. Pour into prechilled deep-saucer champagne glass. Twist lime peel above drink and drop into glass. Powerful, but pleasant rather than pugnacious.

EL PRESIDENTE

1½ ozs. golden rum
½ oz. dry vermouth
1 teaspoon dark
   Jamaican rum
1 teaspoon curaçao
2 teaspoons lime juice
¼ teaspoon grenadine

Shake well with ice. Strain into prechilled cocktail glass. Hail to the chief.

FERN GULLY

1 oz. dark Jamaican rum
1 oz. light rum
½ oz. cream of coconut
½ oz. lime juice
2 teaspoons orange juice
1 teaspoon orzata
⅓ cup crushed ice

Put all ingredients into blender. Blend 10–15 seconds at low speed. Pour into prechilled deep-saucer champagne glass. More rummy than the usual frozen daiquiri, but delicious.

FORT LAUDERDALE

1½ ozs. golden rum
½ oz. sweet vermouth
¼ oz. orange juice
¼ oz. lime juice
1 slice cocktail orange in
   syrup

Shake rum, vermouth, orange juice and lime juice well with ice. Strain over rocks in prechilled old-fashioned glass. Add orange slice.

FROSTY DAWN
COCKTAIL

1½ ozs. light rum
1 oz. orange juice
½ oz. Falernum
¼ oz. maraschino
   liqueur

Shake well with ice. Strain over rocks in prechilled old-fashioned glass.

FROZEN APPLE
DAIQUIRI

1½ ozs. light rum
½ oz. apple juice
½ oz. lemon juice
⅓ cup crushed ice
1 teaspoon sugar
1 wedge apple, with skin

Put rum, apple juice, lemon juice, crushed ice and sugar into blender. Blend 10–15 seconds at low speed. Pour into prechilled deep-saucer champagne glass. Add apple wedge.

FROZEN BERKELEY

1½ ozs. light rum
½ oz. California brandy
½ oz. passion-fruit
   syrup
½ oz. lemon juice
⅓ cup crushed ice

Put all ingredients into blender. Blend 10–15 seconds at low speed. Pour into prechilled deep-saucer champagne glass.

FROZEN DAIQUIRI

1½ to 2 ozs. light rum
½ oz. lime juice
½ to 1 teaspoon sugar
½ cup crushed ice

Put all ingredients into blender. Blend at low speed 10–15 seconds. Pour into prechilled deep-saucer champagne glass. May be served with a small straw. The drink may be made rummier by floating a teaspoon of 151-proof rum on top of the daiquiri in the glass, or the drink may be made with golden rum or any of the heavier-bodied rums such as Jamaican, Barbados or Martinique.

FROZEN GUAVA DAIQUIRI

1¹/₂ ozs. light rum
1 oz. guava nectar (not syrup)
¹/₂ oz. lime juice
1 teaspoon banana liqueur
¹/₃ cup crushed ice

Put all ingredients into blender. Blend 10–15 seconds at low speed. Pour into prechilled deep-saucer champagne glass.

FROZEN GUAVA-ORANGE DAIQUIRI

1¹/₂ ozs. light rum
³/₄ oz. guava syrup
¹/₂ oz. lime juice
¹/₂ oz. orange juice
¹/₃ cup crushed ice

Put all ingredients into blender. Blend 10–15 seconds at low speed. Pour into prechilled deep-saucer champagne glass.

FROZEN MINT DAIQUIRI

2 ozs. light rum
¹/₂ oz. lime juice
6 large mint leaves
1 teaspoon sugar
¹/₂ cup crushed ice

Put all ingredients into blender. Blend 20 seconds at low speed. Pour into prechilled deep-saucer champagne glass. Perfect prelude to a lamb-chop dinner.

FROZEN PASSION-FRUIT DAIQUIRI

1¹/₂ ozs. light rum
¹/₂ oz. passion-fruit syrup
¹/₂ oz. lime juice
¹/₂ oz. orange juice
¹/₄ oz. lemon juice
¹/₃ cup crushed ice

Put all ingredients into blender. Blend at low speed 10–15 seconds. Pour into prechilled deep-saucer champagne glass.

FROZEN PEACH DAIQUIRI

1¹/₂ ozs. light rum
¹/₂ oz. lime juice
¹/₄ cup frozen sliced
    peaches, thawed
¹/₂ oz. syrup from frozen
    peaches
¹/₃ cup crushed ice

Put all ingredients into blender. Blend at low speed 10–15 seconds. Pour into prechilled deep-saucer champagne glass. You'll find the rich flavor of the frozen peaches and their syrup peachier than the fresh fruit for this drink.

FROZEN PINEAPPLE DAIQUIRI

1¹/₂ ozs. light rum
¹/₂ oz. lime juice
¹/₂ teaspoon sugar
4 canned pineapple
    chunks, drained
¹/₃ cup crushed ice

Put all ingredients into blender. Blend 10–15 seconds at low speed. Pour into prechilled deep-saucer champagne glass. The canned pineapple is actually better than the fresh for this fruity cocktail.

FROZEN SESAME DAIQUIRI

1¹/₂ ozs. rum
¹/₂ oz. sesame-seed syrup
    (*ajonjoli*)
¹/₂ oz. lime juice
¹/₂ oz. dry vermouth
¹/₂ oz. orange juice
¹/₃ cup crushed ice

Put all ingredients into blender. Blend at low speed 10–15 seconds. Pour into prechilled deep-saucer champagne glass.

FROZEN SOURSOP DAIQUIRI

1¹/₂ ozs. light rum
¹/₄ oz. dark Jamaican
    rum
1 oz. guanabana
    (soursop) nectar
¹/₄ oz. lime juice
¹/₄ cup sliced banana
¹/₃ cup crushed ice

Put all ingredients into blender. Blend 10–15 seconds at low speed. Pour into prechilled deep-saucer champagne glass. The delicious soursop is now shipped to the States as a canned nectar.

GAUGUIN

2 ozs. light rum
¹/₂ oz. passion-fruit
  syrup
¹/₂ oz. lemon juice
¹/₄ oz. lime juice
¹/₃ cup crushed ice
1 maraschino cherry

Put rum, passion-fruit syrup, lemon juice, lime juice and ice into blender. Blend at low speed 10–15 seconds. Pour into prechilled deep-saucer champagne glass. Add cherry.

GOLDEN GATE

³/₄ oz. light rum
³/₄ oz. gin
1 teaspoon 151-proof
  rum
¹/₂ oz. lemon juice
¹/₂ oz. crème de cacao
¹/₂ teaspoon Falernum
1 slice orange

Shake light rum, gin, 151-proof rum, lemon juice, crème de cacao and Falernum well with ice. Strain over rocks in a prechilled old-fashioned glass. Add orange slice. It leaves a rich afterglow.

GUANABANA

1¹/₂ ozs. light rum
1 oz. guanabana
  (soursop) nectar
1 teaspoon lime juice

Shake well with ice. Strain into prechilled cocktail glass. Drink must be icy cold.

HURRICANE

1 oz. light rum
1 oz. golden rum
¹/₂ oz. passion-fruit
  syrup
2 teaspoons lime juice

Shake well with ice. Strain into prechilled cocktail gluss. Quantities may be doubled and drink poured over rocks in a coconut shell or double old-fashioned glass.

ISLE OF THE BLESSED COCONUT

1¹/₂ ozs. light rum
¹/₂ oz. cream of coconut
  (canned coconut syrup)
¹/₂ oz. lime juice
¹/₄ oz. lemon juice
¹/₄ oz. orange juice
¹/₂ teaspoon sugar
¹/₃ cup crushed ice

Put all ingredients into blender. Blend at low speed 10–15 seconds. Pour into prechilled deep-saucer champagne glass. Serve with a bowl of toasted coconut slices.

JADE

1³/₄ ozs. golden rum
¹/₂ teaspoon green crème
  de menthe
¹/₂ teaspoon curaçao
1¹/₂ teaspoons lime juice
1 teaspoon sugar
1 slice lime

Shake rum, crème de menthe, curaçao, lime juice and sugar well with ice. Strain into prechilled cocktail glass. Add lime slice. Minty, but not overpowering.

LEEWARD

1¹/₂ ozs. light rum
¹/₂ oz. calvados
¹/₂ oz. sweet vermouth
Lemon peel

Shake rum, calvados and vermouth well with ice. Strain over rocks in prechilled old-fashioned glass. Twist lemon peel above drink and drop into glass. Pass anchovy canapés sprinkled with chopped hard-boiled egg.

MAI TAI

3 ozs. light rum
¹/₂ oz. lime juice
¹/₄ teaspoon triple sec
¹/₄ teaspoon orzata
¹/₂ teaspoon sugar
1 slice lime
1 sprig mint
1 pineapple stick

Shake rum, lime juice, triple sec, orzata and sugar well with ice. Strain into prechilled double old-fashioned glass. Add enough cracked ice or ice cubes to fill glass. Tear one or two mint leaves partially to release flavor. Garnish with lime slice, mint sprig and pineapple stick.

MANDEVILLE

1¹/₂ ozs. light rum
1 oz. dark Jamaican rum
³/₄ oz. lemon juice
1 teaspoon Pernod
¹/₂ oz. cola drink
¹/₄ teaspoon grenadine
1 slice orange

Shake both kinds of rum, lemon juice, Pernod, cola drink and grenadine well with ice. Strain over rocks in prechilled old-fashioned glass. Add orange slice.

MUSKMELON

1¹/₂ ozs. light rum
¹/₄ cup sliced ripe
  cantaloupe meat
¹/₃ cup crushed ice
¹/₂ teaspoon sugar
¹/₂ oz. lime juice
¹/₂ oz. orange juice
1 cube cantaloupe meat
  on cocktail spear

Put rum, sliced cantaloupe, ice, sugar, lime juice and orange juice into blender. Blend at low speed 10–15 seconds. Pour into prechilled old-fashioned glass. Add ice cubes or ice slices, if necessary, to fill glass to rim. Garnish with cantaloupe cube.

NAVY GROG

1 oz. dark Jamaican rum
¹/₂ oz. light rum
¹/₂ oz. lime juice
¹/₂ oz. orange juice
¹/₂ oz. pineapple juice
¹/₂ oz. guava nectar
¹/₄ oz. Falernum
¹/₂ cup crushed ice
4 large mint leaves

Put both kinds of rum, lime juice, orange juice, pineapple juice, guava nectar, Falernum and crushed ice into blender. Blend at low speed 15 seconds. Pour into double old-fashioned glass. Add ice to fill glass to rim. Tear mint leaves partially and float on drink. Serve with straw.

OCHO RIOS

1¹/₂ ozs. Jamaican rum
1 oz. guava nectar
¹/₂ oz. cream
¹/₂ oz. lime juice
¹/₂ teaspoon sugar
¹/₃ cup crushed ice

Put all ingredients into blender. Blend at low speed 10–15 seconds. Pour into prechilled deep-saucer champagne glass. A creamy, rummy drink recommended after a spearfishing expedition.

PAGO PAGO

1¹/₂ ozs. golden rum
¹/₂ oz. fresh lime juice
¹/₂ teaspoon green
  Chartreuse
¹/₄ teaspoon white crème
  de cacao
¹/₂ oz. pineapple juice

Shake well with ice. Strain into prechilled cocktail glass. Pineapple comes through beautifully.

PENSACOLA

1½ ozs. light rum
½ oz. guava nectar
½ oz. orange juice
½ oz. lemon juice
⅓ cup crushed ice

Put all ingredients into blender. Blend 10–15 seconds at low speed. Pour into prechilled deep-saucer champagne glass.

PINK CREOLE

1½ ozs. golden rum
½ oz. lime juice
1 teaspoon cream
1 teaspoon grenadine
1 black cherry, soaked in rum

Shake rum, lime juice, cream and grenadine well with ice. Strain into prechilled cocktail glass. Add cherry.

PINK VERANDA

1 oz. golden rum
½ oz. heavy Jamaican rum
1½ ozs. cranberry juice
½ oz. lime juice
1 teaspoon sugar
½ egg white

Shake well with ice. Strain into prechilled old-fashioned glass. Add ice slices or ice cubes, if necessary, to fill glass to rim.

POLYNESIA

1½ ozs. light rum
1 oz. passion-fruit syrup
¼ oz. lime juice
½ egg white
⅓ cup crushed ice

Put all ingredients into blender. Blend 10–15 seconds at low speed. Pour into prechilled deep-saucer champagne glass.

POLYNESIAN PARADISE

1½ ozs. golden rum
1 teaspoon brown sugar
¾ oz. lime juice
½ oz. sweet vermouth
¼ oz. Triple Sec
⅓ cup crushed ice

Put all ingredients into blender. Blend at low speed 10–15 seconds. Pour into prechilled deep-saucer champagne glass. Paradise enow.

PONCE DE LEÓN

1½ ozs. light rum
½ oz. grapefruit juice
½ oz. mango nectar
1 teaspoon lemon juice

Shake well with ice. Strain into prechilled sugar-frosted cocktail glass.

PORT ANTONIO

1 oz. golden rum
½ oz. dark Jamaican rum
½ oz. lime juice
½ oz. coffee liqueur
1 teaspoon Falernum
1 slice lime

Shake both kinds of rum, lime juice, coffee liqueur and Falernum well with ice. Strain over rocks in prechilled old-fashioned glass. Add lime slice.

PORT MARIA

1½ ozs. light rum
¾ oz. pineapple juice
½ oz. lemon juice
1 teaspoon Falernum
Grated nutmeg

Shake rum, pineapple juice, lemon juice and Falernum well with ice. Strain into prechilled cocktail glass. Sprinkle nutmeg on top.

PUERTO RICAN PINK LADY

1¾ ozs. golden rum
¾ oz. lemon juice
½ egg white
1 teaspoon grenadine
⅓ cup crushed ice

Put all ingredients into blender. Blend at low speed 10–15 seconds. Pour into prechilled sugar-rimmed deep-saucer champagne glass.

ROSE HALL

1 oz. dark Jamaican rum
1 oz. orange juice
½ oz. banana liqueur
1 teaspoon lime juice
1 slice lime

Shake rum, orange juice, banana liqueur and lime juice well with ice. Strain over rocks in prechilled old-fashioned glass. Add lime slice.

1¹/₂ ozs. light rum
³/₄ oz. sherry
1 maraschino cherry

RUM AND SHERRY

*Stir rum and sherry well with ice.
Strain into prechilled cocktail
glass. Add cherry. The felicitous
blend of rum and sherry may be
made with very dry cocktail
sherry, medium amontillado or
rich cream sherry to meet your
own choice of dryness or
sweetness. All are good.*

1¹/₂ ozs. light rum
³/₄ oz. Red Dubonnet
1 teaspoon lime juice
Lime peel

RUM DUBONNET

*Shake rum, Dubonnet and lime
juice well with ice. Strain into
prechilled cocktail glass. Twist
lime peel above drink and drop
into glass.*

¹/₂ teaspoon sugar
1 or 2 dashes Angostura
    bitters
1 teaspoon water
2 ozs. light, golden or
    dark Jamaican rum
Lime peel
1 teaspoon 151-proof
    rum

RUM
OLD-FASHIONED

*Mix sugar, bitters and water in
old-fashioned glass until sugar is
completely dissolved. Add two ice
cubes or several pieces of cracked
ice. Add 2 ozs. rum. Stir well.
Twist lime peel above drink and
drop into glass. Float 151-proof
rum on top.*

1¹/₂ ozs. light rum
3 ozs. cold fresh orange
    juice
1 slice orange

RUM
SCREWDRIVER

*Put rum and orange juice (without
ice) into blender. Blend 10–15
seconds at low speed. Pour over
rocks in old-fashioned glass.
Garnish with orange slice. A drink
sometimes known as the Aunt
Agatha, though it's the most
un–Aunt Agathaish drink we can
imagine. A perfect brunch
beginner.*

RUM SOUR

2 ozs. light or golden
  rum
1/2 oz. lemon juice
1 teaspoon orange juice
1 teaspoon rock-candy
  syrup or sugar
1/2 slice lemon

Shake rum, lemon juice, orange juice and syrup or sugar well with ice. Strain into prechilled whiskey-sour glass. Add lemon slice. A teaspoon of 151-proof rum may be floated on the drink for a more rummish accent. For a heavier-bodied but richly mellow rum sour, use dark Jamaican rum.

SAGUENAY

1 oz. light rum
1 oz. dry vermouth
1 teaspoon lemon juice
2 teaspoons crème de
  cassis

Shake well with ice. Strain over rocks in prechilled old-fashioned glass. Add a splash of club soda if desired.

ST. AUGUSTINE

1 1/2 ozs. light rum
1 oz. grapefruit juice
1 teaspoon Cointreau
Lemon peel

Shake rum, grapefruit juice and Cointreau well with ice. Strain into prechilled sugar-frosted cocktail glass. Twist lemon peel above drink and drop into glass. Perfect before a pompano dinner.

SAN JUAN

1 1/2 ozs. light rum
1 oz. grapefruit juice
1 teaspoon cream of
  coconut
2 teaspoons lime juice
1/3 cup crushed ice
2 teaspoons 151-proof
  rum

Put 1 1/2 ozs. light rum, grapefruit juice, cream of coconut, lime juice and ice into blender. Blend at low speed 10–15 seconds. Pour into prechilled deep-saucer champagne glass. Float 151-proof rum on top.

SCORPION

2 ozs. light rum
2 ozs. orange juice
1½ ozs. lemon juice
1 oz. California brandy
½ oz. orzata
⅓ cup crushed ice
1 slice orange

Put rum, orange juice, lemon juice, brandy, orzata and ice into blender. Blend at low speed 10–15 seconds. Pour into prechilled double old-fashioned glass with enough ice cubes to fill glass to rim. Add orange slice.

SEPTEMBER MORN

1½ ozs. light rum
½ oz. lime juice
1 teaspoon grenadine
½ egg white

Shake well with ice. Strain into prechilled sugar-frosted cocktail glass. Glass rim may be moistened with grenadine before dipping into sugar.

SESAME

1½ ozs. light rum
½ oz. lime juice
½ oz. sesame-seed syrup
  (*ajonjoli*)

Shake well with ice. Strain into prechilled cocktail glass. Sesame is a versatile seed. It's available in syrup form in stores featuring Caribbean products. A rummy and offbeat drink.

SHARK'S TOOTH

1½ ozs. golden rum
¼ oz. lemon juice
¼ oz. passion-fruit
  syrup
¼ oz. sweet vermouth
¼ oz. sloe gin
1 dash Angostura bitters
Orange peel
1 maraschino cherry

Shake rum, lemon juice, passion-fruit syrup, vermouth, sloe gin and bitters well with ice. Strain into prechilled sugar-frosted cocktail glass. Twist orange peel above drink and drop into glass. Add cherry.

SOUTHERN BANANA COMFORT

1 oz. golden rum
1 oz. Southern Comfort
¹/₄ cup sliced banana
¹/₂ oz. lime juice
1 teaspoon sugar
¹/₃ cup crushed ice

Put all ingredients into blender. Blend at low speed 10–15 seconds. Pour into prechilled saucer champagne glass. The best possible way to usher in a platter of fried or barbecued chicken.

STRATOSPHERE

1 oz. rum
¹/₂ oz. California brandy
¹/₄ oz. tart cherry liqueur
¹/₂ oz. lemon juice
1 teaspoon sugar

Shake well with ice. Strain into prechilled cocktail glass. Pleasant to drink around a cheese fondue.

TAHITI CLUB

2 ozs. golden rum
¹/₂ oz. lime juice
¹/₂ oz. pineapple juice
¹/₂ oz. lemon juice
1 teaspoon maraschino
    liqueur
1 slice orange

Shake rum, lime juice, pineapple juice, lemon juice and maraschino liqueur well with ice. Strain into prechilled old-fashioned glass. Add cracked ice or ice cubes to fill glass. Add orange slice.

TOBAGO

1 oz. golden rum
1 oz. gin
1 teaspoon 151-proof
    rum
2 teaspoons lime juice
1 teaspoon guava syrup
    (not nectar)
¹/₃ cup crushed ice
Lime peel

Put golden rum, gin, 151-proof rum, lime juice, guava syrup and ice into blender. Blend at low speed 10–15 seconds. Pour over rocks in prechilled old-fashioned glass. Twist lime peel above drink and drop into glass.

TORRIDORA COCKTAIL

1¹/₂ ozs. light rum
¹/₂ oz. coffee liqueur
¹/₄ oz. cream
1 teaspoon 151-proof rum

Shake light rum, coffee liqueur and cream well with ice. Strain into prechilled cocktail glass. Float 151-proof rum on top. In the Caribbean, the dinner hour commences rather late, about nine o'clock in the evening. By this time, the sweetness of the cocktail hour will have passed on, and one will be left with a rummy repose and a fine appetite.

TRADE WINDS

2 ozs. golden rum
¹/₂ oz. lime juice
¹/₂ oz. plum brandy
1¹/₂ teaspoons sugar
¹/₃ cup crushed ice

Put all ingredients into blender. Blend at low speed 10–15 seconds. Pour into prechilled deep-saucer champagne glass. Potent with plum flavor but not a scalp raiser.

UNISPHERE

1¹/₂ ozs. golden rum
1 teaspoon grenadine
¹/₂ oz. lime juice
¹/₂ teaspoon Benedictine
¹/₂ teaspoon Pernod

Shake well with ice. Strain into prechilled cocktail glass. Small amounts of liqueurs come through beautifully without overpowering flavor.

TEQUILA COCKTAILS

BLOODY MARIA

1¹/₂ ozs. tequila
2 ozs. ice-cold tomato juice
1 teaspoon lemon juice
1 dash Tabasco sauce
1 dash celery salt
1 slice lemon

Pour tequila, tomato juice, lemon juice, Tabasco and celery salt into prechilled old-fashioned glass. Add rocks or ice slices to fill glass. Stir very well. Add lemon slice. Viva Maria!

BUNNY BONANZA

1¹/₂ ozs. tequila
1 oz. apple brandy
¹/₂ oz. lemon juice
1 teaspoon sugar
¹/₂ teaspoon curaçao
1 slice lemon

Shake tequila, apple brandy, lemon juice, sugar and curaçao well with ice. Strain into prechilled old-fashioned glass. Add ice to fill glass. Garnish with lemon slice, as served in the Detroit Playboy Club.

CHAPALA

1¹/₂ ozs. tequila
¹/₂ oz. orange juice
¹/₂ oz. lemon juice
1 dash orange-flower
  water
2 teaspoons grenadine
1 slice orange

Shake tequila, orange juice, lemon juice, orange-flower water and grenadine well with ice. Strain over rocks in prechilled old-fashioned glass. Add orange slice.

COCONUT TEQUILA

1¹/₂ ozs. tequila
¹/₂ oz. cream of coconut
¹/₂ oz. lemon juice
1 teaspoon maraschino
  liqueur
¹/₂ cup crushed ice

Put all ingredients into blender. Blend 20 seconds at low speed. Pour into prechilled deep-saucer champagne glass. Perfect before a Polynesian brunch.

FROZEN BLACKBERRY TEQUILA

1¹/₂ ozs. tequila
1 oz. blackberry liqueur
¹/₂ oz. lemon juice
¹/₃ cup crushed ice
1 slice lemon

Put tequila, blackberry liqueur, lemon juice and crushed ice into blender. Blend 10–15 seconds at low speed. Pour into prechilled old-fashioned glass. Add rocks to fill glass. Add lemon slice.

1¹/₂ ozs. tequila
2 ozs. pineapple juice
¹/₂ oz. lime juice
¹/₃ cup crushed ice
1 cocktail pineapple
   stick

FROZEN MATADOR

*Put tequila, pineapple juice, lime
juice and crushed ice into blender.
Blend at low speed 10–15 seconds.
Pour into prechilled deep-saucer
champagne glass. Add pineapple
stick. Or pour over rocks in
prechilled old-fashioned glass.
Add ice cubes to fill glass. Garnish
with pineapple stick.*

1¹/₂ ozs. tequila
¹/₂ oz. Triple Sec or
   curaçao
¹/₂ oz. lemon or lime
   juice

MARGARITA

*Shake well with ice. Strain into
prechilled salt-rimmed cocktail
glass. To prepare glass, rub rim
with outside of lemon peel; then
dip into salt and shake off excess.
Although traditionally the glass
for a margarita is salt-rimmed, it
may also be sugar-rimmed. A twist
of lime or lemon peel may be
added if desired.*

1¹/₂ ozs. tequila
¹/₂ oz. lime juice
1 oz. passion-fruit syrup
¹/₃ cup crushed ice
1 slice lime

MEXICO
PACIFICO

*Put tequila, lime juice,
passion-fruit syrup and crushed
ice into blender. Blend 10–15
seconds at low speed. Pour into
prechilled deep-saucer champagne
glass. Add lime slice. Exotico!*

1¹/₂ ozs. tequila
6 large mint leaves
¹/₂ oz. lemon juice
1 teaspoon sugar
¹/₂ cup crushed ice

MINT TEQUILA

*Put all ingredients into blender.
Blend at low speed 15–20 seconds.
Pour into prechilled old-fashioned
glass. Add a rock or two to fill
glass to rim. Lively and minty.*

PRADO

1¹/₂ ozs. tequila
³/₄ oz. lime juice
¹/₂ egg white
¹/₂ oz. maraschino
  liqueur
1 teaspoon grenadine
¹/₂ slice lemon
1 maraschino cherry

Shake tequila, lime juice, egg white, maraschino liqueur and grenadine well with ice. Strain into prechilled whiskey-sour glass. Add lemon slice and cherry.

SLOE TEQUILA

1 oz. tequila
¹/₂ oz. sloe gin
¹/₂ oz. lime juice
¹/₂ cup crushed ice
Cucumber peel

Put tequila, sloe gin, lime juice and ice into blender. Blend 10–15 seconds at low speed. Pour into prechilled old-fashioned glass. Add cucumber peel and fill glass with cubed or cracked ice.

SUNSET

1¹/₂ ozs. tequila
¹/₂ oz. lime juice
¹/₂ oz. grenadine
¹/₂ cup crushed ice
1 slice lime

Put tequila, lime juice, grenadine and ice into blender. Blend at low speed 10–15 seconds. Pour into prechilled old-fashioned glass. Add ice slices or cubes to fill glass. Garnish with lime slice.

TEQUILA DUBONNET

1 oz. tequila
1 oz. Red Dubonnet
1 slice lemon

Pour tequila and Dubonnet into prechilled old-fashioned glass. Add cubed or cracked ice to fill glass. Stir. Garnish with lemon slice.

TEQUILA FRESA

1¹/₂ ozs. tequila
³/₄ oz. strawberry liqueur
¹/₂ oz. lime juice
¹/₄ teaspoon orange
  bitters
1 slice lime
1 fresh strawberry

Shake tequila, strawberry liqueur, lime juice and bitters well with ice. Strain over rocks in old-fashioned glass. Add lime slice and strawberry.

TEQUILA FROZEN SCREWDRIVER

1¹/₂ ozs. tequila
3 ozs. iced orange juice
¹/₃ cup crushed ice
1 slice orange

Put tequila, orange juice and crushed ice into blender. Blend at low speed 10–15 seconds. Pour into prechilled old-fashioned glass. Add orange slice.

TEQUILA GUAYABA

1¹/₂ ozs. tequila
¹/₂ oz. guava syrup
¹/₂ oz. orange juice
¹/₂ oz. lime juice
Orange peel

Shake tequila, guava syrup, orange juice and lime juice well with ice. Pour into prechilled old-fashioned glass. Add a rock or two to fill glass. Twist orange peel above drink and drop into glass. Pass a guacamole dip.

TEQUILA OLD-FASHIONED

¹/₂ teaspoon sugar
2 dashes Angostura bitters
1¹/₂ ozs. tequila
Iced club soda
Lemon peel
1 cocktail pineapple stick

Stir sugar, bitters and 1 teaspoon water in prechilled old-fashioned glass until sugar is dissolved. Add tequila. Add rocks or cracked ice to glass. Stir well. Add a splash of soda and stir. Twist lemon peel above drink and drop into glass. Garnish with pineapple stick.

TEQUILA SOUR

2 ozs. tequila
¹/₂ oz. lemon juice
1 teaspoon sugar
¹/₂ slice lemon
1 maraschino cherry

Shake tequila, lemon juice and sugar well with ice. Strain into prechilled whiskey-sour glass. Add lemon slice and cherry.

TEQUINI

1¹/₂ to 2 ozs. tequila
¹/₂ oz. dry vermouth
Lemon peel
1 cocktail olive (optional)

Stir tequila and vermouth well with ice. Strain into prechilled cocktail glass. Twist lemon peel above drink and drop into glass. A Mexican martini. Olive may be added for a salty accent.

VODKA COCKTAILS

AQUEDUCT

1¹/₂ ozs. vodka
¹/₄ oz. curaçao
¹/₄ oz. apricot liqueur
¹/₂ oz. lime juice
Orange peel

Shake vodka, curaçao, apricot liqueur and lime juice well with ice. Strain into prechilled cocktail glass. Twist orange peel above drink and drop into glass. Make book on this drink without any qualms.

BLACK RUSSIAN

1¹/₂ ozs. vodka
³/₄ oz. Kahlúa coffee
  liqueur

Shake well with ice. Strain over rocks in prechilled old-fashioned glass. Serve at poolside before the cocktail hour or by candlelight at the witching hour.

BLOODY MARY

1¹/₂ ozs. vodka
3 ozs. tomato juice
¹/₂ oz. lemon juice
1 teaspoon catsup
1 dash Worcestershire
  sauce
1 dash celery salt
1 dash Tabasco sauce

Shake all ingredients well with ice. Strain into tall or squat 8-oz. glass.

BUCKEYE MARTINI

2¹/₄ ozs. vodka
¹/₄ oz. dry vermouth
1 large ripe black olive

Stir vodka and vermouth well with ice. Strain into prechilled cocktail glass. Add olive.

CHERRY VODKA

1¹/₄ ozs. 100-proof vodka
¹/₂ oz. lime juice
¹/₂ oz. Cherry Heering or
  Cherry Karise

Shake well with ice until the shaker is almost too cold to hold. Strain into prechilled cocktail glass.

CHIQUITA

1½ ozs. vodka
½ oz. banana liqueur
¼ cup sliced ripe
 banana
½ oz. lime juice
1 teaspoon sugar
¼ cup finely crushed ice

*Put all ingredients into blender.
Spin at low speed for 15 seconds.
Pour into deep-saucer champagne
glass.*

FLYING GRASSHOPPER

1 oz. vodka
½ oz. green crème de
 menthe
½ oz. white crème de
 cacao

*Stir well with ice. Strain into
prechilled cocktail glass. Although
it's sweet enough to be a dessert
cocktail, people insist on drinking
the grasshopper after shopping,
after the amicable settling of an
argument or at the tea hour.*

FROZEN APPLE

1½ ozs. vodka
¼ oz. calvados or
 applejack
½ oz. lime juice
¼ cup diced fresh apple
¼ cup finely crushed ice
½ teaspoon sugar

*Put all ingredients into blender.
Spin at low speed for 15 seconds.
Pour into deep-saucer champagne
glass. A north-country version of
the frozen daiquiri.*

GYPSY

2 ozs. vodka
½ oz. Benedictine
1 teaspoon lemon juice
1 teaspoon orange juice
1 slice orange

*Shake vodka, Benedictine, lemon
juice and orange juice well with
ice. Strain over rocks in prechilled
old-fashioned glass. Add orange
slice.*

KREMLIN COLONEL

2 ozs. vodka
½ oz. lime juice
1 teaspoon sugar
2 large fresh mint leaves

*Shake vodka, lime juice and sugar
well with ice. Strain into
prechilled cocktail glass. Tear
each mint leaf in half to release
aroma and drop into glass.*

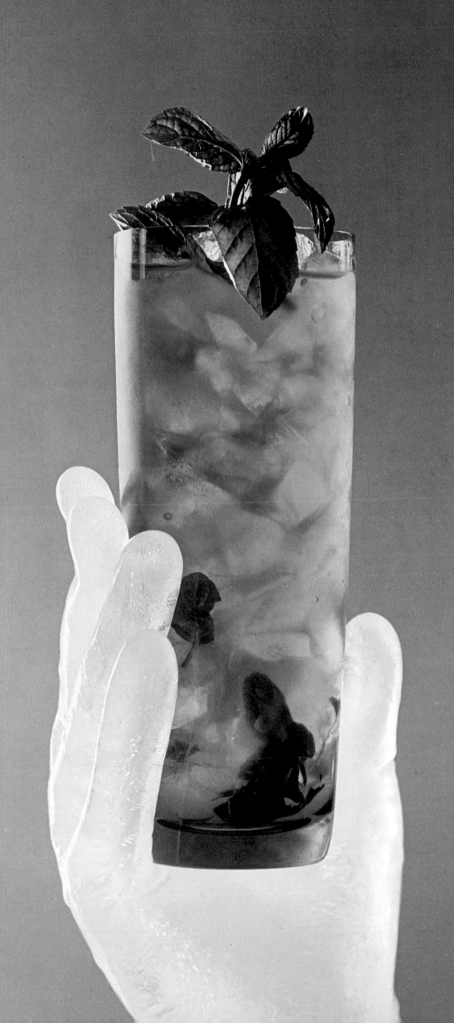

KRETCHMA

1 oz. vodka
1 oz. crème de cacao
¹/₂ oz. lemon juice
¹/₂ teaspoon grenadine

Shake well with ice. Strain into prechilled cocktail glass. Serve to girls with a deep addiction to chocolate.

LORENZO

1 oz. vodka
1 oz. Tuaca liqueur
¹/₂ oz. lime juice

Shake well with ice. Strain into prechilled sugar-frosted cocktail glass. Rim of glass may be moistened with Tuaca before dipping into sugar. One sip of this and you'll understand why Lorenzo de'Medici was called Il Magnifico.

RED APPLE

1 oz. 100-proof vodka
1 oz. apple juice
¹/₂ oz. lemon juice
¹/₂ teaspoon grenadine
1 dash orange bitters

Shake well with ice. Strain into prechilled cocktail glass. Not to be confused with a vodka and apple juice, a lowball rather than a cocktail.

RUSSIAN BEAR

1 oz. vodka
¹/₂ oz. crème de cacao
¹/₂ oz. cream

Shake well with ice. Strain into prechilled cocktail glass.

RUSSIAN ESPRESSO

1¹/₂ ozs. vodka
¹/₂ oz. espresso-coffee
   liqueur
¹/₂ teaspoon lemon juice
Lemon peel

Pour vodka, coffee liqueur and lemon juice over rocks in prechilled old-fashioned glass. Stir well. Twist lemon peel above drink and drop into glass. A coexistence cocktail.

SALTY DOG

2 ozs. vodka
¹/₂ oz. unsweetened
   grapefruit juice
1 teaspoon lemon juice
Salt

Shake vodka, grapefruit juice and lemon juice well with ice. Strain into prechilled cocktail glass. Sprinkle drink with several generous dashes of salt.

SCREWDRIVER

1½ ozs. vodka
4½ ozs. ice-cold orange
  juice, freshly squeezed
1 teaspoon lemon juice
  (optional)

Shake extremely well with ice or pour into blender and blend with ice at high speed for 5 seconds. Strain into prechilled tall or squat 10 oz. glass. Lemon juice gives the screwdriver an extra twist.

SOVIET

1½ ozs. vodka
½ oz. amontillado
  sherry
½ oz. dry vermouth
Lemon peel

Stir vodka, sherry and vermouth well with ice. Strain over rocks in prechilled old-fashioned glass. Twist lemon peel above drink and drop into glass. Liquid tranquilizer.

SVETLANA

1½ ozs. 100-proof vodka
½ oz. sweet vermouth
¼ oz. kirsch
¼ oz. orange juice
Orange peel

Shake vodka, vermouth, kirsch and orange juice well with ice. Strain into prechilled cocktail glass. Twist orange peel above drink and drop into glass. Serve biting cold. No nyets *will be heard.*

TOVARICH

1½ ozs. vodka
½ oz. kümmel
½ oz. lime juice
Lime peel

Shake vodka, kümmel and lime juice well with ice. Strain into prechilled cocktail glass. Twist lime peel above drink and drop into glass.

VODKA FRAISE

¾ oz. vodka
¾ oz. light rum
½ oz. strawberry liqueur
½ oz. lime juice
½ teaspoon grenadine
½ large fresh strawberry

Shake vodka, rum, strawberry liqueur, lime juice and grenadine well with ice. Strain into prechilled sugar-frosted cocktail glass. Float strawberry on top.

VODKA GIMLET

2 ozs. vodka
½ oz. Rose's lime juice

Stir well with ice. Strain into prechilled cocktail glass.

VODKA GRAND MARNIER

1½ ozs. vodka
½ oz. Grand Marnier
½ oz. lime juice
1 slice orange

Shake vodka, Grand Marnier and lime juice well with ice. Strain over rocks in prechilled old-fashioned glass. Garnish with orange slice.

VODKA MARTINI

2¼ ozs. vodka
¼ oz. dry vermouth

Stir well with ice. Strain into prechilled cocktail glass or serve over rocks. Garnish with twist of lemon peel or olive. Lacks the zip of the gin-based martini, but is wonderful midday solace for vodka partisans.

VODKA OLD-FASHIONED

½ teaspoon sugar
2 dashes Angostura bitters
1 teaspoon water
2 ozs. vodka
Lemon peel

Dissolve sugar with bitters and water in old-fashioned glass. Add vodka. Fill glass to rim with cubes, slices or coarsely cracked pieces of ice. Stir very well. Twist lemon peel above drink and drop into glass.

VODKA SOUR

1¾ ozs. vodka
¾ oz. lemon juice
1 teaspoon sugar
1 slice lemon
1 maraschino cherry

Shake vodka, lemon juice and sugar well with ice. Strain into prechilled whiskey-sour glass. Garnish with lemon slice and cherry.

VODKA STINGER

1½ ozs. vodka
½ ozs. white crème de menthe

Shake extremely well with ice. Pour into prechilled cocktail glass. Drink must be extremely cold. May be pre- or postprandial.

WARSAW

1½ ozs. vodka
½ oz. blackberry liqueur
½ oz. dry vermouth
1 teaspoon lemon juice
Lemon peel

Shake vodka, blackberry liqueur, vermouth and lemon juice well with ice. Strain into prechilled cocktail glass. Twist lemon peel above drink and drop into glass. The Poles are famed for their tart blackberry liqueur, and if you can get your hands on it or on the Leroux domestic blackberry liqueur called Likier Smaku, you'll really bring the warsaw to life.

WHISKEY COCKTAILS

ALLEGHENY

1 oz. bourbon
1 oz. dry vermouth
¼ oz. blackberry liqueur
¼ oz. lemon juice
1 dash Angostura bitters
Lemon peel

Shake bourbon, vermouth, blackberry liqueur, lemon juice and bitters well with ice. Strain into prechilled cocktail glass. Twist lemon peel above drink and drop into glass.

BLACK HAWK

1 oz. blended whiskey
1 oz. sloe gin (creamy cap)
½ oz. lemon juice
1 maraschino cherry (optional)

Shake whiskey, sloe gin and lemon juice well with ice. Strain into prechilled cocktail glass. Garnish with cherry.

BOURBONNAISE

1½ ozs. bourbon
½ oz. dry vermouth
¼ oz. crème de cassis
¼ oz. lemon juice

Shake well with ice. Strain over rocks in prechilled old-fashioned glass. A perfect way to introduce a French girl to American bourbon.

CANADIAN APPLE

1½ ozs. Canadian
  whisky
½ oz. calvados
¼ oz. lemon juice
1 teaspoon sugar
Ground cinnamon
1 slice lemon

Shake whisky, calvados, lemon juice, sugar and a spray of cinnamon well with ice. Strain over rocks in prechilled old-fashioned glass. Add lemon slice. A delight before a holiday dinner of roast turkey or goose.

CANADIAN CHERRY

1½ ozs. Canadian
  whisky
½ oz. Cherry Heering or
  Cherry Karise
¼ oz. lemon juice
¼ oz. orange juice

Shake well with ice. Strain into prechilled sugar-frosted cocktail glass. Glass rim may be moistened with cherry liqueur before dipping into sugar.

CANADIAN COCKTAIL

1½ ozs. Canadian
  whisky
½ oz. lemon juice
¼ oz. curaçao
1 teaspoon sugar
2 dashes bitters

Shake well with ice. Strain into prechilled cocktail glass or over rocks in old-fashioned glass.

CANADIAN OLD-FASHIONED

1½ ozs. Canadian
  whisky
2 dashes Angostura
  bitters
½ teaspoon curaçao
½ teaspoon lemon juice
Lemon peel
Orange peel

Pour whisky, bitters, curaçao and lemon juice into prechilled old-fashioned glass. Add rocks. Stir. Twist lemon peel and orange peel above drink and drop into glass. More suave than the conventional old-fashioned made with U.S. blended whiskey.

CANADIAN PINEAPPLE

1½ ozs. Canadian
   whisky
½ oz. pineapple juice
½ oz. lemon juice
½ teaspoon maraschino
   liqueur
1 cocktail pineapple
   stick

Shake whisky, pineapple juice, lemon juice and maraschino liqueur well with ice. Strain over rocks in prechilled old-fashioned glass. Add pineapple stick.

CHAPEL HILL

1½ ozs. blended whiskey
½ oz. curaçao
½ oz. lemon juice
1 slice cocktail orange in
   syrup

Shake whiskey, curaçao and lemon juice well with ice. Strain over rocks in prechilled old-fashioned glass. Garnish with orange slice. Pass freshly toasted, salted pecans.

COMMODORE

1¾ ozs. blended whiskey
2 teaspoons lime juice
1 teaspoon orange juice
1 teaspoon strawberry
   liqueur
1 dash orange bitters

Shake well with ice. Strain into prechilled cocktail glass. A subtle blend of whiskey and fruit flavors that's appreciated at the end of a lazy Sunday sail.

COMMONWEALTH

1¾ ozs. Canadian
   whisky
¼ oz. lemon juice
½ oz. Van der Hum
   liqueur
Tangerine peel or orange
   peel

Shake whisky, lemon juice and Van der Hum well with ice. Strain into prechilled sugar-frosted cocktail glass. Twist tangerine peel above drink and drop into glass. Serve before a dinner of grilled lobster tails.

CROTON

1¾ ozs. bourbon or
   blended whiskey
¼ oz. cocktail sherry
Lemon peel

Stir whiskey and sherry well with ice. Strain into prechilled cocktail glass. Twist lemon peel above drink and drop into glass. A patio or terrace cocktail to be served with a bowl of fresh iced shrimp and a tangy cocktail sauce.

CURRIER

1½ ozs. blended whiskey
½ oz. kümmel
¼ oz. fresh lime juice
¼ oz. Rose's lime juice
1 slice lime

Shake whiskey, kümmel and both kinds of lime juice well with ice. Strain into prechilled cocktail glass. Add lime slice. A cocktail to savor between the fox hunt and breakfast.

DELTA

1½ ozs. blended whiskey
½ oz. Southern Comfort
½ oz. lime juice
½ teaspoon sugar
½ slice orange
1 slice fresh peach

Shake whiskey, Southern Comfort, lime juice and sugar well with ice. Strain over rocks in prechilled old-fashioned glass. Garnish with orange and peach slices. A drink to accompany Gershwin on the hi-fi.

GLASGOW

1½ ozs. Scotch
¾ oz. lemon juice
¼ oz. dry vermouth
¼ oz. orzata

Shake well with ice. Strain into prechilled cocktail glass. Serve with thin slices of Nova Scotia salmon on hot buttered toast.

HABITANT COCKTAIL

1½ ozs. blended
  Canadian whisky
1 oz. lemon juice
1 teaspoon maple-sugar
  syrup
1 slice orange
1 maraschino cherry

Shake whisky, lemon juice and syrup well with ice. Strain over rocks in prechilled old-fashioned glass. Garnish with orange slice and cherry, as served in the Montreal Playboy Club.

INDIAN RIVER

1½ ozs. blended whiskey
½ oz. unsweetened
  grapefruit juice
¼ oz. raspberry liqueur
¼ oz. sweet vermouth

Shake well with ice. Strain over rocks in prechilled old-fashioned glass.

KENTUCKY

1½ ozs. 86-proof
   bourbon
½ oz. lemon juice
½ oz. pineapple juice
1 teaspoon maraschino
   liqueur

Shake well with ice. Strain into prechilled sugar-frosted cocktail glass.

LAWHILL

1¼ ozs. blended whiskey
¾ oz. dry vermouth
¼ teaspoon Pernod
¼ teaspoon maraschino
   liqueur
½ oz. orange juice
1 dash Angostura bitters

Shake well with ice. Strain into prechilled cocktail glass. A superb cocktail to mix beforehand, strain into a thermos and tote along on a picnic.

MANHASSET

1½ ozs. blended whiskey
½ oz. lemon juice
¼ oz. dry vermouth
¼ oz. sweet vermouth
Lemon peel

Shake whiskey, lemon juice and both kinds of vermouth well with ice. Strain into prechilled cocktail glass. Twist lemon peel above drink and drop into glass.

MANHATTAN

In the national drink derby, two or three cocktail generations ago, the manhattan and the martini always wound up in a dead heat. At the present time, the manhattan occupies the second spot. Manhattanites, though less demanding than martini fans, have nevertheless stirred up many spirited variations on the whiskey-vermouth theme. In public pouring houses, the usual manhattan is made with 1½ ounces of whiskey. At private bars, a more generous allowance of whiskey is likely. Here's what most manhattanites expect:

MANHATTAN

1½ to 2 ozs. blended
   whiskey
½ oz. sweet vermouth
1 dash bitters (optional)
1 maraschino cherry

Stir whiskey, vermouth and bitters well with ice. Strain into prechilled coctail glass. Add cherry.

Dry Manhattan: Use dry instead of sweet vermouth; a twist of lemon peel or an olive may be substituted for the cherry.

Bourbon Manhattan: Use 86- or 100-proof bourbon instead of blended whiskey; if 100-proof bourbon is used, a little extra stirring is in order.

Canadian Manhattan: Use Canadian instead of U.S. blended whiskey; don't overstir or the delicate flavor of the Canadian spirits will become pallid.

MAY COCKTAIL

1½ ozs. blended whiskey
¼ oz. kirschwasser
¼ oz. strawberry liqueur
Chilled May wine
1 slice lemon

Shake whiskey, kirschwasser and strawberry liqueur well with ice. Strain into prechilled old-fashioned glass with a large ice cube. Fill glass with May wine. Stir. Garnish with lemon slice.

NEVINS

1½ ozs. bourbon
½ oz. grapefruit juice
¼ oz. apricot liqueur
¼ oz. lemon juice
1 dash Angostura bitters

Shake well with ice. Strain into prechilled sugar-frosted cocktail glass.

NEW WORLD

1¾ ozs. blended whiskey
½ oz. lime juice
1 teaspoon grenadine
Lime peel

Shake whiskey, lime juice and grenadine well with ice. Strain into prechilled cocktail glass. Twist lime peel above drink and drop into glass. Drink this one while listening to Dvorak before a midnight supper.

NEW YORK SOUR

2 ozs. blended whiskey
½ oz. lemon juice
1 teaspoon sugar
Chilled dry red wine
½ slice lemon

Shake whiskey, lemon juice and sugar well with ice. Strain into prechilled 6-oz. sour glass. Fill glass with dry red wine. Stir. Garnish with lemon slice. A miniature punch in a sour glass.

1¹/₂ ozs. blended whiskey
¹/₂ oz. lime juice
1 teaspoon sugar
¹/₄ teaspoon grenadine
Lemon peel
Orange peel

NEW YORKER

*Shake whiskey, lime juice, sugar
and grenadine well with ice.
Strain into prechilled
sugar-frosted cocktail glass. Twist
lemon peel and orange peel above
drink and drop into glass. A fruity
terrace cocktail appreciated
equally under sun or stars.*

1¹/₂ ozs. bourbon
¹/₂ oz. sweet vermouth
¹/₂ oz. orange juice
¹/₄ teaspoon yellow
   Chartreuse
¹/₂ slice orange
¹/₂ slice lemon

NIGHT SHADE

*Shake bourbon, vermouth, orange
juice and Chartreuse well with ice.
Strain over rocks in prechilled
old-fashioned glass. Add orange
and lemon slices. Pass freshly
fried, generously salted shrimp
chips.*

¹/₂ teaspoon sugar
1 or 2 dashes Angostura
   bitters
1 teaspoon water
1¹/₂ to 2 ozs. blended
   whiskey
Lemon peel

OLD-FASHIONED

*Stir sugar, bitters and water in
prechilled old-fashioned glass
until sugar dissolves. Fill glass
with ice cubes or large pieces of
cracked ice. Add whiskey. Stir
well. Twist lemon peel above
drink and drop into glass. An
old-fashioned may be made with
U.S. blended whiskey, Canadian,
Irish or Scotch. In smart men's
clubs, the words* garnish *and*
garbage *were once synonymous;
orange and lemon slices, cherries,
cocktail sticks, etc., were
considered female diversions for
filling a glass with fruit instead of
the cocktail itself. Over the years,
this attitude has been somewhat
mitigated. Generally, however,
most men and women appreciate
the old-fashioned unencumbered
with superfluous fruit.*

PRINCE EDWARD

1³/₄ ozs. Scotch
¹/₂ oz. Lillet
¹/₄ oz. Drambuie
1 slice cocktail orange in
syrup

*Shake Scotch, Lillet and Drambuie
well with ice. Strain over rocks in
prechilled old-fashioned glass.
Garnish with orange slice.*

QUEBEC

1¹/₂ ozs. Canadian
whisky
¹/₄ oz. Amer Picon
¹/₄ oz. maraschino
liqueur
¹/₂ oz. dry vermouth

*Shake well with ice. Strain into
prechilled sugar-frosted cocktail
glass.*

ROB ROY

1¹/₂ to 2 ozs. Scotch
¹/₂ oz. sweet vermouth
1 dash orange bitters
(optional)

*Stir well with ice. Strain into
prechilled cocktail glass. The rob
roy is, of course, simply a Scotch
manhattan, and variations in
whisky and vermouth proportions
may be made to your own
drinking taste. A light rather than
a smoky Scotch is preferred by
most people. A brandied cherry
may be added for a special
flourish. For a dry rob roy, use dry
vermouth; add a twist of lemon if
desired.*

ROB ROY, HOLIDAY STYLE

¹/₂ teaspoon Drambuie
2 ozs. Scotch
¹/₄ oz. dry vermouth
¹/₄ oz. sweet vermouth
1 maraschino or
brandied cherry

*Pour Drambuie into a prechilled
cocktail glass and swirl it around
to coat bottom and sides of glass.
Stir Scotch and both kinds of
vermouth well with ice. Strain
into glass. Add cherry.*

RUSTY NAIL

³/₄ oz. Scotch
³/₄ oz. Drambuie

*Pour over rocks in prechilled
old-fashioned glass. Stir.*

SAZERAC

¹/₄ teaspoon abisante,
    anesone or any other
    absinthe substitute
¹/₂ teaspoon sugar
¹/₄ teaspoon bitters
    (Peychaud's, if
    possible)
2 ozs. blended whiskey
    or bourbon
Lemon peel

*Swirl abisante around in
prechilled old-fashioned glass
until inside is completely coated.
Add sugar, bitters and 1
tablespoon water. Stir until sugar
is dissolved. Add a large ice cube
and whiskey. Stir well. Twist
lemon peel above drink and drop
into glass. A New Orleans
specialty and a magnificent
prebrunch drink.*

SAZERAC À LA PLAYBOY

¹/₄ teaspoon Pernod
1 small sugar cube
2 dashes Peychaud's
    bitters
1 dash Angostura bitters
1¹/₂ ozs. straight rye
Lemon peel

*Pour Pernod into prechilled
old-fashioned glass and roll glass
until inside is entirely coated.
Add sugar, both kinds of bitters
and enough cold water to barely
cover sugar. Muddle until sugar is
completely dissolved. Add
whiskey and a large ice cube. Stir
well. Twist lemon peel above
drink and drop into glass. Created
by George Crouchette, head
bartender at the New Orleans
Playboy Club.*

SCOTCH HOLIDAY SOUR

2 ozs. light Scotch
1 oz. cherry liqueur
¹/₂ oz. sweet vermouth
1 oz. lemon juice
¹/₂ egg white
1 slice lemon

*Shake Scotch, cherry liqueur,
vermouth, lemon juice and egg
white well with ice. Strain into
prechilled oversize sour glass or
into prechilled old-fashioned glass
with a large rock. Garnish with
lemon slice.*

SEABOARD

1 oz. blended whiskey
1 oz. gin
¹/₂ oz. lemon juice
1 teaspoon sugar
2 sprigs mint

*Shake whiskey, gin, lemon juice
and sugar well with ice. Strain
over rocks in prechilled
old-fashioned glass. Tear several
leaves of each mint sprig before
dropping into drink.*

THE SHOOT

1 oz. Scotch
1 oz. dry sherry
1 teaspoon lemon juice
1 teaspoon orange juice
1/2 teaspoon sugar

Shake well with ice. Strain into prechilled cocktail glass. Serve before a dinner of roast pheasant or partridge.

SINGAPORE

1½ ozs. Canadian
   whisky
1/4 oz. sloe gin
1/4 oz. Rose's lime juice
1/2 oz. lemon juice
Cucumber peel

Shake whisky, sloe gin, Rose's lime juice and lemon juice well with ice. Strain over rocks in prechilled old-fashioned glass. Add cucumber peel.

SOUTHERN GINGER

1½ ozs. 100-proof
   bourbon
1 oz. ginger ale
1/4 oz. lemon juice
1/2 teaspoon ginger-
   flavored brandy
Lemon peel

Shake bourbon, ginger ale, lemon juice and ginger brandy well with ice. Strain into prechilled cocktail glass. Twist lemon peel above drink and drop into glass.

STONYBROOK

1½ ozs. blended whiskey
1/2 oz. triple sec
1/4 teaspoon orzata
1/2 egg white
Lemon peel
Orange peel

Shake whiskey, Triple Sec, orzata and egg white well with ice. Strain into prechilled cocktail glass. Twist lemon peel and orange peel above drink and drop into glass. A drink to accompany barquettes of hot deviled crab meat.

TROIS RIVIÈRES

1½ ozs. Canadian
   whisky
1/2 oz. Red Dubonnet
1/4 oz. Cointreau
Orange peel

Shake whisky, Dubonnet and Cointreau well with ice. Strain into prechilled cocktail glass. Twist orange peel above drink and drop into glass. Perfect before a midnight collation.

2 ozs. blended whiskey
1/4 oz. lemon juice
1/4 oz. lime juice
2 teaspoons Benedictine
1 teaspoon sugar
1/2 slice lemon
1/2 slice lime

TWIN HILLS
Shake whiskey, lemon juice, lime juice, Benedictine and sugar well with ice. Strain into prechilled whiskey-sour glass. Garnish with lemon and lime slices. Offbeat but a very superior sour.

2 ozs. blended U.S.
   whiskey or Canadian
   whisky
1/2 oz. lemon juice
1 teaspoon sugar
1/2 teaspoon grenadine
1 slice lemon

WARD EIGHT
Shake whiskey, lemon juice, sugar and grenadine well with ice. Strain into tall 8-oz. glass. Add cracked ice or ice slices to fill glass. Stir. Garnish with lemon slice. A pleasant tall cocktail that survived Prohibition.

2 ozs. blended whiskey
3/4 oz. lemon juice
1 teaspoon sugar
1/2 slice lemon
1 maraschino cherry
   (optional)

WHISKEY SOUR
Shake whiskey, lemon juice and sugar well with ice. Strain into prechilled whiskey-sour glass. Garnish with lemon slice and cherry, if desired. For a more tart drink, reduce amount of sugar. For a more mellow whiskey sour, use 1/2 oz. lemon juice and 1/4 oz. orange juice. Sours made with Canadian or Scotch whiskies are pleasing variants, the former having a strong appeal for the distaff side.

1/2 teaspoon sugar
2 teaspoons water
2 ozs. bourbon or
   blended whiskey
Lemon peel (optional)

WHISKEY TODDY, COLD
Put sugar and water into prechilled old-fashioned glass. Stir until sugar dissolves. Fill glass with ice cubes or large pieces of cracked ice. Add whiskey. Stir well. Twist lemon peel above drink and drop into glass. Must be stinging cold.

MISCELLANEOUS COCKTAILS

ANDALUSIA

1¹/₂ ozs. very dry sherry
¹/₂ oz. cognac
¹/₂ oz. light rum
1 dash Angostura bitters

Stir well with ice. Strain into prechilled cocktail glass.

BRANDIED MADEIRA

1 oz. Madeira
1 oz. brandy
¹/₂ oz. dry vermouth
Lemon peel

Stir Madiera, brandy and vermouth well with ice. Pour over rocks in prechilled old-fashioned glass. Twist lemon peel above drink and drop into glass.

BRANDIED PORT

1 oz. tawny port
1 oz. brandy
¹/₂ oz. lemon juice
1 teaspoon maraschino liqueur
1 slice orange

Shake port, brandy, lemon juice and maraschino liqueur well with ice. Strain over rocks in prechilled old-fashioned glass. Add orange slice.

CLARET COCKTAIL

1 oz. dry red wine
1 oz. brandy
¹/₄ oz. curaçao
¹/₄ oz. lemon juice
¹/₂ teaspoon anisette
Orange peel

Shake wine, brandy, curaçao, lemon juice and anisette well with ice. Strain into prechilled cocktail glass. Twist orange peel above drink and drop into glass.

CREAMY ORANGE

1 oz. orange juice
1 oz. cream sherry
¹/₂ oz. cream
2 teaspoons brandy

Shake well with ice. Strain into prechilled cocktail glass. A gentle introduction to a brunch omelette.

FIORD

1 oz. brandy
$^1/_2$ oz. aquavit
$^1/_2$ oz. orange juice
$^1/_2$ oz. lime juice
1 teaspoon grenadine

*Shake well with ice. Strain into
prechilled cocktail glass.*

FLORIDA

$1^1/_4$ ozs. orange juice
$^1/_2$ oz. gin
$^1/_4$ oz. kirschwasser
$^1/_4$ oz. triple sec
1 teaspoon lemon juice

*Shake well with ice. Strain into
prechilled sugar-frosted cocktail
glass. A drink with less hard
liquor than citrus juice, but one
which always clears up the fog.*

FROZEN AQUAVIT

$1^1/_2$ ozs. aquavit
$^1/_2$ oz. lime juice
$^1/_2$ egg white
$^1/_2$ cup crushed ice
1 teaspoon sugar
1 teaspoon kirschwasser

*Put all ingredients into blender.
Blend at low speed 10–15 seconds.
Pour into prechilled deep-saucer
champagne glass.*

GENEVER COCKTAIL

$1^1/_2$ ozs. Dutch genever
   gin
$^1/_2$ oz. lime juice
$^1/_2$ oz. orange juice
1 teaspoon sugar
1 dash Angostura bitters

*Shake well with ice. Strain over
rocks in prechilled old-fashioned
glass. Odd but very obliging.*

GRAPPA STREGA

1 oz. grappa
1 oz. Strega
$^1/_4$ oz. lemon juice
$^1/_4$ oz. orange juice
Lemon peel

*Shake grappa, Strega, lemon juice
and orange juice well with ice.
Strain into prechilled cocktail
glass. Twist lemon peel above
drink and drop into glass.*

KIR

3¹/₂ ozs. ice-cold dry
   white wine
¹/₂ oz. ice-cold crème de
   cassis

*Pour into prechilled 7- or 8-oz.
wide-bellied wineglass.
Add an ice cube or two if desired.
Proportions may be varied, but the
7-to-1* vin blanc–cassis *ratio above
(actually a variation of the
vermouth cassis) is the most
commonly accepted version.*

MIDNIGHT SUN

1¹/₂ ozs. aquavit
¹/₂ oz. unsweetened
   grapefruit juice
¹/₂ oz. lemon juice
1 teaspoon sugar
¹/₂ teaspoon grenadine
¹/₂ slice orange

*Shake aquavit, grapefruit juice,
lemon juice, sugar and grenadine
well with ice. Strain into
prechilled whiskey-sour glass.
Add orange slice. Keep herring
tidbits within reach.*

PERNOD DRIP

1¹/₂ ozs. Pernod
1 cube sugar

*The first requirement for this drink
is an absinthe drip glass. If you
don't own a drip glass, you can
use a tea strainer over an
old-fashioned glass as a substitute.
First pour the Pernod into the
glass. Place the strainer on the
glass. Put the sugar over the drip
section on top of the glass. Pack a
mound of crushed or finely
cracked ice atop the sugar. When
the ice has melted, the drip is
ready. Strictly for curio seekers in
the spirit world.*

PISCO SOUR

1¹/₂ ozs. pisco brandy
¹/₂ oz. lemon juice
1 tablespoon sugar
1 tablespoon egg white
Angostura bitters

*Shake pisco, lemon juice, sugar
and egg white well with ice. Strain
into prechilled cocktail glass with
sugar-frosted rim. Float a few
drops bitters on top. May also be
poured into small punch cups.*

1 oz. gin
³/₄ oz. green Chartreuse
³/₄ oz. cognac

ROCKY GREEN DRAGON

Shake extremely well with ice. Strain over rocks in prechilled old-fashioned glass. A potent dragon to be slowly sipped, not gulped.

1¹/₂ ozs. Pernod
¹/₂ oz. anisette
¹/₄ oz. cream
¹/₂ egg white

SUISSESSE

Shake well with ice. Pour into prechilled cocktail glass. Perfect midnight cocktail that's really more Mediterranean than Swiss.

1¹/₂ ozs. quetsch,
   mirabelle or slivovitz
¹/₂ oz. lemon juice
¹/₂ oz. orange juice
1 teaspoon maraschino
   liqueur
1 teaspoon sugar

YELLOW PLUM

Shake well with ice. Strain into prechilled cocktail glass. Tart, triumphant, titillating.

18

HIGH SPIRITS— MEDIUM-TALL AND KING-SIZE POTABLES

If the word *highball* is heard less and less frequently these days, the drink itself is called for more and more often. Drinkers everywhere now ask for Scotch and soda, bourbon and water, applejack and ginger ale and other happy mixtures suited to their own thirst specifications. Although the highball is the easiest drink in the world to define—a small amount of something strong with a larger amount of something weak in a tall glass with ice—it's the one potable for which you seldom see a recipe. As a matter of fact, a host who, in the intimacy of his own digs, strictly follows a highball recipe is inhospitable. It's the one drink guests themselves expect to mix to their own tastes, in the same way that they salt and pepper their food. No two-finger measurements are alike and no two guests will ever say "when" at the same point on the stopwatch. Even at commuter stand-up bars, where whiskey is carefully measured in a standard jigger, the bubbly water usually remains in the hands of the highballer pouring his soda, Seven-Up or tonic water to his own level.

But the highball is only one of countless potables in tall glasses. A tall drink at the end of a long, tiring day can do things no short drink can ever hope to do. A wilted worthy need only look at a lofty drink clinking with ice, and miraculous changes take place within him. His collar seems to cling less tenaciously. He begins to talk in more relaxed, civilized tones. And then, as the first sip of a tall drink passes over his tongue and throat, like springwater gurgling into a hot arroyo, he feels the unparalleled pleasure of a long-delayed thrill.

One of the obvious virtues of tall mixed drinks is that they never seem to get in the way of food or vice versa. A man may hesitate to eat a trout *au bleu* while drinking a manhattan, but he won't hesitate to drink a tall spritzer of Rhine wine and soda before, during or after the trout. Although Europophilian wine pundits will be horrified at the thought, many a tall cooler at many a fine feast supplants *both* the cocktail and the wine. Ounce for ounce, a tall cooler with club soda is actually no stronger than wine. But in the final analysis, tall drinks are made not for debating but for happy guzzling.

In preparing tall drinks, whether they be 8, 12 or 20 ounces, the host should follow this modern code for presenting them:

Use a fine liquor. The flavor of a poor liquor is actually intensified in a tall drink; you have time to scrutinize it more carefully than when you down it in one gulp. This doesn't mean that you must buy a 16-year-old bonded whiskey the next time you serve a round of whiskey collinses. But you should seek one of the eminent brands of liquor that are mellow, smooth and pleasing whether taken straight or in a tall drink.

Be meticulous about the quality of the iced club soda or the ginger ale. For a small number of highballers, serve splits of soda or ginger ale. Larger bottles of carbonated waters, except for a party, just stand around going quietly flat unless you and your guests are unusually speedy drinkers.

Add bubblewater just before drinks are delivered. For optimum sparkle and so that it retains its fizz as long as possible, pour it against the inside of the tilted glass. Be sure the effervescent water is ice-cold.

Plain tap water, if used, must be clear and clean, without evidence of rust, lime, iron, chlorination or other urban evils. Use bottled springwater, if necessary, when your guests decline bubbles.

Use enough liquor in a tall drink, at least 1½ ounces in an 8-ounce glass and up to 2 ounces or more in 12- to 20-ounce glasses.

Use thin glassware with heavy bottoms to avoid the well-known sliding drink.

The gin and tonic has not only joined the tall-drink derby, but in many circles is way out in front both in summer and winter. Bitter lemon and bitter orange have joined the same fraternity. As the British Empire becomes more and more liquidated, the British-inspired bubblies seem to become more and more popular.

Among simple highballs, the whiskey highball is the best known. But there's no dogma that interdicts the use of any liquor in a highball, from aquavit to zubrovka. One of the best contemporary highballs is light, dry rum and iced club soda or iced tonic water.

So-called lowballs are actually served in glasses which hold as much as their taller cousins but which are squat in shape rather than long; old-fashioned-type glasses ranging from 7 to 11 ounces are considered lowballs.

BUCKS

Bucks are medium-long drinks—served in tall eight-ounce glasses—that always contain ginger ale and fresh lemon or lime juice. Traditionally the fruit was squeezed and dropped into the glass. You'll find you get better bucks if the lemon or lime juice is measured into the glass and the drink then garnished with a slice of fruit as its crowning touch.

APPLE BUCK

1½ ozs. applejack
1 teaspoon ginger-
   flavored brandy
½ oz. lemon juice
Iced ginger ale
1 chunk preserved ginger
   in syrup

Shake applejack, ginger brandy and lemon juice well with ice. Strain into 8-oz. glass half-filled with ice. Add ginger ale. Stir. Add preserved ginger.

BRANDY BUCK

1½ ozs. brandy
1 teaspoon crème de
   menthe
½ oz. lemon juice
Iced ginger ale
Fresh grapes

Shake brandy, crème de menthe and lemon juice well with ice. Strain into 8-oz. glass half-filled with ice. Add ginger ale. Stir. Add three or four seedless grapes or two large pitted black grapes cut in half.

GIN BUCK

1¹/₂ ozs. gin
¹/₂ oz. lemon juice
Iced ginger ale
1 slice lemon

*Shake gin and lemon juice well
with ice. Strain into 8-oz. glass
half-filled with ice. Add ginger
ale. Stir. Add lemon slice.*

GREEK BUCK

1¹/₂ ozs. Metaxa brandy
¹/₂ oz. lemon juice
Iced ginger ale
1 teaspoon ouzo
1 slice lemon

*Shake Metaxa and lemon juice
well with ice. Strain into 8-oz.
glass half-filled with ice. Add
ginger ale. Stir. Float ouzo on top
of drink. Add lemon slice.*

NEW ORLEANS BUCK

1¹/₂ ozs. light rum
¹/₂ oz. lime juice
¹/₂ oz. orange juice
2 dashes Peychaud's
  bitters
Iced ginger ale
1 slice lime

*Shake rum, lime juice, orange
juice and bitters well with ice.
Strain into 8-oz. glass half-filled
with ice. Add ginger ale. Stir. Add
lime slice.*

ORANGE BUCK

1¹/₂ ozs. gin
1 oz. orange juice
¹/₂ oz. lemon juice
Iced ginger ale
1 slice cocktail orange in
  syrup

*Shake gin, orange juice and lemon
juice well with ice. Strain into
8-oz. glass half-filled with ice.
Add ginger ale. Stir. Add orange
slice.*

PEACH BUCK

1¹/₄ ozs. vodka
2 teaspoons peach-
  flavored brandy
¹/₂ oz. lemon juice
Iced ginger ale
1 slice lemon
1 slice fresh or brandied
  peach

*Shake vodka, peach-flavored
brandy and lemon juice well with
ice. Strain into 8-oz. glass
half-filled with ice. Add ginger
ale. Stir. Garnish with lemon and
peach slices.*

RUM BUCK

1½ ozs. light rum
½ oz. lime juice
Iced ginger ale
1 slice lime
Toasted slivered
   almonds

Shake rum and lime juice well with ice. Strain into 8-oz. glass half-filled with ice. Add ginger ale. Stir. Add lime slice and about a teaspoon of almonds.

COBBLERS

Like a fix (see page 239), of which it is a larger version, a cobbler is concocted in the glass and drunk without club soda, quinine water or any other sparkling diluents. Though the recipes that follow are designed to fill a 12-ounce glass—including the cracked ice that forms the base of each—they can be extended or abbreviated to fit your own glassware. The cracked ice in a filled glass will usually collapse somewhat when stirred with liquor; an ice refill is then necessary.

BRANDY COBBLER

1½ ozs. brandy
½ oz. curaçao
½ oz. lemon juice
1 teaspoon sugar
1 teaspoon kirschwasser
1 cocktail pineapple
   stick

Fill a 12-oz. glass with finely cracked ice. Add brandy, curaçao, lemon juice, sugar and kirschwasser. Stir well until sugar is dissolved. Add more ice to fill glass to rim. Stir. Garnish with pineapple stick.

CHERRY COBBLER

1½ ozs. gin
½ oz. Cherry Heering or
   Cherry Karise
½ oz. crème de cassis
1 teaspoon sugar
½ oz. lemon juice
1 slice lemon
1 maraschino cherry

Fill a 12-oz. glass with finely cracked ice. Add gin, Cherry Heering, crème de cassis, sugar and lemon juice. Stir well until sugar dissolves. Add more ice to fill glass to rim. Stir. Add lemon slice and cherry.

CLARET COBBLER

4 ozs. dry red wine
$1/2$ oz. lemon juice
$1/2$ oz. orange juice
$1/2$ oz. maraschino
  liqueur
$1/2$ slice orange
$1/2$ slice lime

*Fill a 12-oz. glass with finely
cracked ice. Add wine, lemon
juice, orange juice and
maraschino liqueur. Stir well. Add
more ice to fill glass to rim. Stir.
Garnish with orange and lime
slices.*

PORT COBBLER

4 ozs. tawny port
$3/4$ oz. brandy
$1/2$ teaspoon sugar
Lemon peel
Orange peel
2 large mint leaves

*Fill a 12-oz. glass with finely
cracked ice. Add port, brandy and
sugar. Stir well. Add more ice to
fill glass to rim. Stir. Twist lemon
peel and orange peel above drink
and drop into glass. Tear mint
leaves partially and drop into
glass.*

SHERRY COBBLER

$2^1/2$ ozs. sherry
1 oz. brandy
$1/2$ oz. orange juice
$1/2$ teaspoon sugar
1 slice cocktail orange in
  syrup

*Fill a 12-oz. glass with finely
cracked ice. Add sherry, brandy,
orange juice and sugar. Stir well
until sugar dissolves. Add more
ice to fill glass to rim. Stir.
Garnish with orange slice.*

WHISKEY COBBLER

$2^1/2$ ozs. blended whiskey
$3/4$ oz. lemon juice
$1/2$ oz. grapefruit juice
$1^1/2$ teaspoons orgeat or
  orzata
$1/2$ slice orange
1 slice fresh or brandied
  peach

*Fill a 12-oz. glass with finely
cracked ice. Add whiskey, lemon
juice, grapefruit juice and orgeat.
Stir well. Add more ice to fill glass
to rim. Stir. Garnish with orange
and peach slices.*

COLLINSES

Among the oldest and best-known tall summer drinks, collinses always start with liquor, lemon juice and soda and bear a striking resemblance to fizzes (page 242). A tom collins and a gin fizz are for all practical purposes the same drink. A lemon slice is an accepted garnish. Some bartenders dress up the collins with orange slices, cherries and other bits of fruit, although this practice is frowned upon by veteran benders at the bar.

APPLEJACK COLLINS

2 ozs. applejack
1 teaspoon sugar
1 oz. lemon juice
2 dashes orange bitters
Iced club soda
1 slice lemon

Shake applejack, sugar, lemon juice and bitters well with ice. Strain into tall 14-oz. glass half-filled with ice. Add soda. Stir. Add lemon slice.

B & B COLLINS

2 ozs. cognac
1/2 oz. lemon juice
1 teaspoon sugar
Iced club soda
1/2 oz. Benedictine
1 slice lemon

Shake cognac, lemon juice and sugar well with ice. Strain into tall 14-oz. glass half-filled with ice. Add soda. Stir. Float Benedictine on drink. Add lemon slice.

BOURBON COLLINS

2 ozs. 100-proof bourbon
2 dashes Peychaud's bitters
1/2 oz. lemon juice
1 teaspoon sugar
Iced club soda
1 slice lemon

Shake bourbon, bitters, lemon juice and sugar well with ice. Strain into tall 14-oz. glass half-filled with ice. Add soda. Stir. Add lemon slice.

BRANDIED BANANA COLLINS

1¹/₂ ozs. brandy
1 oz. banana liqueur
¹/₂ oz. lemon juice
Iced club soda
1 slice lemon
1 slice banana

Shake brandy, banana liqueur and lemon juice well with ice. Strain into tall 14-oz. glass half-filled with ice. Add soda. Stir. Add lemon and banana slices.

COEXISTENCE COLLINS

2 ozs. vodka
¹/₂ oz. lemon juice
1 teaspoon sugar
1 teaspoon kümmel
Iced club soda
Cucumber peel, 2 inches
  long, ¹/₂ inch wide
Lemon peel

Shake vodka, lemon juice, sugar and kümmel well with ice. Strain into tall 14-oz. glass half-filled with ice. Add soda. Stir. Add cucumber peel. Twist lemon peel above drink and drop into glass.

MINT COLLINS

2 ozs. gin
4 large mint leaves
¹/₂ oz. lemon juice
1 teaspoon sugar
¹/₂ cup crushed ice
Iced club soda
1 slice lemon

Put gin, mint leaves, lemon juice, sugar and crushed ice into blender. Blend at high speed 15 seconds or until mint leaves are finely chopped. Pour into tall 14-oz. glass. Add soda to fill glass. Stir. Add lemon slice.

TOM COLLINS

2 to 2¹/₂ ozs. gin
1 to 2 teaspoons sugar
¹/₂ to 1 oz. lemon juice
Iced club soda
1 slice lemon (optional)
1 slice orange (optional)
1 maraschino cherry
  (optional)

Shake gin, sugar and lemon juice well with ice. Strain into tall 14-oz. glass half-filled with ice. Add soda. Stir. Add lemon slice and/or orange slice and/or cherry.

JOHN COLLINS

Same drink as tom collins except made with Dutch genever gin.

COOLERS—MISCELLANEOUS TALL DRINKS

For every taste, for every mood, for every summer day, the following potpourri of coolers and icy tall drinks will be as welcome as the trade winds to becalmed vessels on a sweltering sea.

AMER PICON COOLER

1½ ozs. Amer Picon
1 oz. gin
½ oz. cherry liqueur
½ oz. lemon juice
1 teaspoon sugar
Iced club soda

Shake Amer Picon, gin, cherry liqueur, lemon juice and sugar well with ice. Strain into tall 14-oz. glass half-filled with ice. Add soda. Stir.

APPLE BRANDY COOLER

2 ozs. brandy
1 oz. light rum
3 ozs. apple juice
½ oz. lime juice
1 teaspoon dark
   Jamaican rum
1 slice lime

Shake brandy, light rum, apple juice and lime juice well with ice. Strain into tall 14-oz. glass. Add ice to fill glass. Stir. Float dark rum on drink. Add lime slice.

APPLE KNOCKER

2½ ozs. applejack
½ oz. sweet vermouth
3 ozs. orange juice
½ oz. lemon juice
1½ teaspoons sugar
½ cup crushed ice

Put all ingredients into blender. Blend at high speed 15–20 seconds. Pour into tall 14-oz. glass. Let drink settle a moment. Add ice to fill glass. Stir.

1¹/₂ ozs. ice-cold
   100-proof vodka
Ice-cold beer or ale
2 dashes Tabasco sauce

BEER BUSTER

Pour vodka, beer and Tabasco sauce into prechilled tall 14-oz. glass or beer mug. Stir lightly. A drink for those who like to key up with beer rather than with cocktails before dinner, for football fans hoarse from cheering, for men who like a long, cold drink with their bubbling-hot Welsh rabbit and for cheese connoisseurs with a thirst.

1¹/₂ ozs. light rum
¹/₄ cup sliced banana
¹/₄ cup pineapple juice
¹/₂ oz. lime juice
2 dashes Peychaud's
   bitters
¹/₂ cup crushed ice
Iced bitter-lemon soda

BITTER BANANA COOLER

Put rum, sliced banana, pineapple juice, lime juice, bitters and crushed ice into blender. Blend 10–15 seconds at high speed. Pour into tall 14-oz. glass. Let foamy cap of drink settle somewhat. Add two ice cubes. Fill glass with bitter-lemon soda. A tall drink in the frozen-daiquiri tradition.

2 ozs. bourbon
1 oz. lemon juice
¹/₂ oz. lime juice
1 teaspoon grenadine
1 teaspoon sugar
Iced bitter-lemon soda
1 slice lemon

BITTER BOURBON LEMONADE

Shake bourbon, lemon juice, lime juice, grenadine and sugar well with ice. Strain into tall 14-oz. glass. Add two ice cubes. Fill glass with bitter-lemon soda. Garnish with lemon slice. A bittersweet pleasure.

1 oz. brandy
1 oz. oloroso (cream)
   sherry
¹/₂ oz. cherry liqueur
1 teaspoon lemon juice
Iced bitter-lemon soda
1 slice lemon

BITTER BRANDY AND SHERRY

Shake brandy, sherry, cherry liqueur and lemon juice well with ice. Strain into tall 14-oz. glass with two large ice cubes. Add soda. Stir. Add lemon slice.

BITTER-LEMON COOLER

1½ ozs. dry vermouth
1 oz. gin
1 teaspoon raspberry
   syrup
1 teaspoon lemon juice
Iced bitter-lemon soda
Lemon peel

Shake vermouth, gin, raspberry
syrup and lemon juice well with
ice. Strain into tall 14-oz. glass
containing two large ice cubes.
Add bitter-lemon soda. Stir. Twist
lemon peel above drink and drop
into glass.

BITTER-ORANGE COOLER

2½ ozs. orange juice
3 ozs. sweet vermouth
½ oz. lemon juice
½ oz. cherry liqueur
Iced bitter-orange soda
1 slice orange

Shake orange juice, vermouth,
lemon juice and cherry liqueur
well with ice. Pour into tall 14-oz.
glass with two large ice cubes.
Add soda. Stir. Garnish with
orange slice.

BLENDED COMFORT

2 ozs. blended whiskey
½ oz. Southern Comfort
¼ cup thawed frozen
   peaches
½ oz. dry vermouth
1½ ozs. lemon juice
1 oz. orange juice
½ cup crushed ice
1 slice lemon
1 slice cocktail orange in
   syrup

Put whiskey, Southern Comfort,
peaches, vermouth, lemon juice,
orange juice and crushed ice into
blender. Blend 10–15 seconds.
Pour into tall 14-oz. glass. Add ice
to fill glass. Garnish with lemon
and orange slices.

BRANDIED PEACH SLING

1¾ ozs. brandy
½ oz. peach-flavored
   brandy
¾ oz. lemon juice
1 teaspoon sugar
Iced club soda
1 slice brandied or
   thawed frozen peach
Lemon peel

Shake brandy, peach-flavored
brandy, lemon juice and sugar
well with ice. Strain into tall
14-oz. glass half-filled with ice.
Add soda. Stir. Add peach slice.
Twist lemon peel above drink and
drop into glass.

BRIGHTON PUNCH

1 oz. bourbon
1 oz. cognac
¾ oz. Benedictine
1 oz. orange juice
½ oz. lemon juice
1 oz. iced club soda
½ slice orange
1 slice lemon

Shake bourbon, cognac, Benedictine, orange juice and lemon juice well with ice. Strain into tall 14-oz. glass. Add soda and enough ice to fill glass. Stir. Garnish with orange and lemon slices. An individual punch brewed outside a punch bowl.

BUNNY MOTHER

1¼ ozs. vodka
1 oz. orange juice
1 oz. lemon juice
1 teaspoon sugar
¼ oz. grenadine
¼ oz. Cointreau
½ slice orange
1 maraschino cherry

Shake vodka, orange juice, lemon juice, sugar and grenadine well with ice. Strain into prechilled 12-oz. mug. Add coarsely cracked ice to fill mug to ½ inch from top. Float Cointreau on top. Garnish with orange slice and cherry, as served at the San Francisco Playboy Club.

BYRRH CASSIS COOLER

2 ozs. Byrrh
½ oz. crème de cassis
Iced club soda
1 slice lemon

Put ice cubes up to the rim in a tall 14-oz. glass. Add Byrrh and crème de cassis. Add soda. Stir. Garnish with lemon slice. Quickens the appetite even though slightly sweet. Nice to hold in your hands when the blanquette de veau *is simmering in the kitchen.*

CALYPSO COOLER

2½ ozs. light rum
1 oz. frozen concentrated
   pineapple juice,
   thawed but not diluted
½ oz. lime juice
1 teaspoon sugar
Iced club soda
1 thin slice fresh
   pineapple
1 slice lime

Shake rum, pineapple juice, lime juice and sugar well with ice. Strain into tall 14-oz. glass. Add a splash of soda and ice to fill glass. Garnish with pineapple and lime slices.

CARTHUSIAN COOLER

1 oz. yellow Chartreuse
1 oz. bourbon
Iced club soda

Put three large ice cubes into a tall 14-oz. glass. Add Chartreuse and bourbon. Fill glass with soda. Stir.

CHABLIS COOLER

1/2 oz. grenadine
1/2 oz. lemon juice
1/4 teaspoon vanilla
extract
1 oz. vodka
Iced chablis

Sugar-frost a tall 14-oz. glass. Pour grenadine, lemon juice, vanilla extract and vodka into glass. Stir well. Add three large ice cubes. Fill glass to rim with chablis. Stir.

CHARTREUSE COOLER

1 oz. yellow Chartreuse
3 ozs. orange juice
1 oz. lemon juice
Iced bitter-lemon soda
1 slice orange

Shake Chartreuse, orange juice and lemon juice well with ice. Strain into tall 14-oz. glass half-filled with ice. Fill glass with bitter-lemon soda. Add orange slice.

CLARET COOLER

4 ozs. chilled dry red
wine
1/2 oz. brandy
1 oz. orange juice
1/2 oz. lemon juice
3 ozs. iced club soda
Orange rind, 3 inches
long, 1/2 inch wide
1 slice lemon

Pour wine, brandy, orange juice, lemon juice and soda into tall 14-oz. glass. Add ice cubes or cracked ice to fill glass. Stir. Place orange rind in drink. Float lemon slice on top.

CLARET RUM COOLER

3 ozs. chilled dry red
  wine
1 oz. light rum
1/2 oz. kirschwasser
1/2 oz. Falernum
3 ozs. iced club soda
1 slice orange
1 large fresh strawberry

*Pour wine, rum, kirschwasser,
Falernum and soda into tall 14-oz.
glass. Add ice cubes or cracked
ice to fill glass. Stir. Garnish with
orange slice and strawberry.*

COCONUT COOLER IN SHELL

1 coconut
1/2 cup crushed ice
1 oz. canned cream of
  coconut
1 1/2 ozs. light rum
1 oz. cream

*Remove end of coconut opposite
coconut eyes. The best procedure
is to hold the base of the coconut
firmly in the left hand. With a
very heavy French knife or
cleaver, chop top off by striking
coconut glancing blows
diagonally. Several whacks may
be necessary. Avoid spilling
coconut juice if possible. Pour out
coconut juice and save it. Into
blender, pour 1/4 cup coconut
juice, ice, cream of coconut, rum
and cream. Blend at high speed 10
seconds. Pour into coconut shell.
Place coconut shell in large dish
surrounded with finely crushed
ice. There will usually be enough
juice from one coconut for three or
four drinks. Reserve drinks may be
made up beforehand, poured into
a pitcher and stored in the
refrigerator. Coconut shells may
then be refilled when necessary.
Byron once said nothing calmed
the spirit as much as rum and true
religion. The balmy beneficence of
the preceding recipe will bear out
that astute poet to the fullest.*

COFFEE COOLER

4 ozs. cold coffee
1½ ozs. vodka
1 oz. cream
1 oz. coffee liqueur
1 teaspoon sugar
1 small dip coffee ice
   cream

Shake coffee, vodka, cream, coffee liqueur and sugar well with ice. Strain into tall 14-oz. glass. Add ice cream. A sweet cooler that serves as both iced coffee and dessert in one glass.

COFFEE EGGNOG

1½ ozs. Canadian
   whisky
1 oz. coffee liqueur
1 small egg
4 ozs. milk
½ oz. cream
1 teaspoon sugar
½ teaspoon instant
   coffee
Ground coriander seed

Shake whisky, coffee liqueur, egg, milk, cream, sugar and instant coffee with ice extremely well—about twice the usual mixing time. Strain into tall 14-oz. glass. Sprinkle with coriander.

COLD IRISH

1½ ozs. Irish whiskey
2 teaspoons Irish Mist
   liqueur
Iced coffee soda
Sweetened whipped
   cream
Crème de cacao

Pour whiskey and Irish Mist into tall 14-oz. glass. Add one large ice cube. Fill glass to within 1 inch of top with soda. Stir. Flavor whipped cream with crème de cacao, using ½ oz. crème de cacao for each ½ cup heavy cream used for whipping. Add a large dollop of whipped-cream topping to each drink.

COOL COLONEL

1½ ozs. bourbon
1 oz. Southern Comfort
3 ozs. chilled strong
   black tea
2 teaspoons lemon juice
2 teaspoons sugar
Iced club soda

Pour bourbon, Southern Comfort, tea, lemon juice and sugar into tall 14-oz. glass. Stir until sugar dissolves. Add two large ice cubes and a splash of soda. Stir. Breathe deeply. Tilt head. Bend elbow.

CORDIAL MÉDOC CUP

1 oz. Cordial Médoc
¹/₂ oz. cognac
1 oz. lemon juice
¹/₂ teaspoon sugar
Iced *brut* champagne
1 slice orange

Shake Cordial Médoc, cognac, lemon juice and sugar well with ice. Strain into 10-oz. glass with two large ice cubes. Fill glass with champagne. Stir very slightly. Add orange slice. A tall drink for toasting.

CUBA LIBRE

2 ozs. golden rum
¹/₂ lime
Iced cola drink

Half fill a tall 14-oz. glass with coarsely chopped ice or ice cubes. Add rum. Squeeze lime above drink and drop into glass. Fill with cola. Stir well. Heavier rums such as Jamaican or Martinique may be used in place of golden rum or may be mixed half-and-half with it. A teaspoon of 151-proof rum may be floated on top of drink for a rummy bite.

CUCUMBER CHAMPAGNE

Cucumber peel
1 oz. Benedictine
¹/₂ oz. lemon juice
8 ozs. iced *brut*
   champagne

Prechill a 10-oz. Pilsner glass. Wash cucumber, rubbing with a vegetable brush or towel if necessary to remove any waxy coating. Cut a long strip of peel, about ¹/₂ inch wide, the entire length of the cucumber. Place in glass. Pour Benedictine and lemon juice into glass. Slowly add champagne. Stir very slightly. Let drink set a few minutes for flavors to ripen.

CURAÇAO COOLER

1 oz. blue curaçao
1 oz. vodka
¹/₂ oz. lime juice
¹/₂ oz. lemon juice
Iced orange juice
Lemon peel
Lime peel
Orange peel

Shake curaçao, vodka, lime juice and lemon juice well with ice. Strain into tall 14-oz. glass. Add two large ice cubes. Fill glass with orange juice. Stir well. Twist each of the peels above the drink and drop into glass. Cool as the blue-green Caribbean itself.

CREAMY SCREWDRIVER

6 ozs. orange juice
1 small egg yolk or
  1/2 large yolk, slightly
  beaten
2 ozs. vodka
3/4 cup finely cracked ice
1 teaspoon sugar

Put all ingredients into well of blender. Blend about 20 seconds. Pour over two or three ice cubes in tall 14-oz. glass. Add more ice cubes if necessary to fill glass. A prebrunch potation.

DOUBLE DERBY

2 1/2 ozs. bourbon
2 ozs. cold strong black
  tea
2 ozs. claret
1 oz. red-currant syrup
1 oz. orange juice
1/2 oz. lemon juice
1 slice cocktail orange in
  syrup

Pour bourbon, tea, claret, red-currant syrup, orange juice and lemon juice into double old-fashioned glass. Add ice cubes to fill to brim. Stir well. Add orange slice. If red-currant syrup is not available, red-currant jelly to which a teaspoon of hot water has been added may be heated over a low flame and stirred constantly until jelly is liquid.

DRY-MANHATTAN COOLER

2 ozs. blended whiskey
1 oz. dry vermouth
2 ozs. orange juice
1/2 oz. lemon juice
1/2 oz. orgeat or orzata
Iced club soda
1 maraschino cherry

Shake whiskey, vermouth, orange juice, lemon juice and orgeat well with ice. Strain into tall 14-oz. glass. Add a splash of soda and ice to fill glass. Stir. Add cherry.

ENGLISH MULE

3 ozs. ice-cold
  green-ginger wine
1 1/2 ozs. gin
2 1/2 ozs. ice-cold orange
  juice
Iced club soda
1 piece preserved ginger
  in syrup

Put three ice cubes into tall 14-oz. glass. Pour wine, gin and orange juice into glass. Stir well. Fill glass with soda. Stir slightly. Fasten preserved ginger, well drained, onto cocktail spear. Fit spear into straw in glass.

FRENCH FOAM

1 teaspoon sugar
1 dash Angostura bitters
1 teaspoon brandy
1 teaspoon kirschwasser
1 split ice-cold *brut*
  champagne
Lemon sherbet

Put sugar, bitters, brandy and kirschwasser into 10-oz. Pilsner glass. Stir with a tall stirring rod until sugar dissolves. Fill glass three-quarters full with champagne. Float a small scoop of sherbet on top. The scoop should contain no more than 2 liquid ounces (a parfait scoop). If such a scoop is not available, use a tablespoon to add the small amount of sherbet.

FRENCH 75

1¹/₂ ozs. cognac
1 oz. lemon juice
1 teaspoon sugar
Iced *brut* champagne

Shake cognac, lemon juice and sugar well with cracked ice. Strain into 10-oz. glass with two large ice cubes. Fill to rim with champagne. Stir very slightly. Gin is sometimes substituted for cognac, making a champagne collins out of this tall classic.

GEORGIA RUM COOLER

2¹/₂ ozs. light rum
1 teaspoon salted
  peanuts
¹/₂ oz. lemon juice
1 teaspoon grenadine
1 teaspoon Falernum
¹/₂ cup crushed ice
Iced club soda
Ground cinnamon

Put rum, peanuts, lemon juice, grenadine, Falernum and crushed ice into blender. Blend at high speed 30 seconds. Pour into tall 14-oz. glass. Let froth on drink settle. Add two ice cubes and a splash of soda. Stir. Sprinkle lightly with cinnamon. Pass a platter of cold country ham sliced paper-thin.

GIN SWIZZLE

2 ozs. gin
¹/₂ teaspoon Angostura
  bitters
¹/₂ oz. lime juice
1 teaspoon sugar
Iced club soda

Shake gin, bitters, lime juice and sugar well with ice. Strain into tall 14-oz. glass half-filled with ice. Add soda. Stir. A patriarchal drink invented when swizzle sticks were smart. Toothsome tipple now best handled in cocktail shaker and tall glass.

GRANADA

1 oz. very dry (fino)
   sherry
1 oz. brandy
1/2 oz. curaçao
Iced tonic water
1 slice orange

Shake sherry, brandy and curaçao well with ice. Pour into tall 14-oz. glass. Add two large ice cubes. Add tonic water. Stir. Add orange slice.

GRAPEFRUIT COOLER

2 ozs. blended whiskey
4 ozs. unsweetened
   grapefruit juice
1/2 oz. red-currant syrup
1 teaspoon lemon juice
1/2 slice orange
1/2 slice lemon

Shake whiskey, grapefruit juice, red-currant syrup and lemon juice well with ice. Strain into tall 14-oz. glass. Add ice to fill glass. Stir. Garnish with orange and lemon slices.

GRAPEFRUIT NOG

1/2 cup unsweetened
   grapefruit juice
1 oz. lemon juice
1 tablespoon honey
1 1/2 ozs. brandy
1 small egg
1/2 cup crushed ice

Put all ingredients into blender. Blend 20 seconds. Pour into double old-fashioned glass or tall 14-oz. glass. Add ice cubes to fill glass.

GUAVA COOLER

1 1/2 ozs. rum
1 1/2 ozs. guava nectar
1/2 teaspoon sugar
1/2 oz. maraschino
   liqueur
1/2 oz. lemon juice
1/2 oz. pineapple juice
Iced club soda
1 canned guava shell
1/2 slice lemon

Shake rum, guava nectar, sugar, maraschino liqueur, lemon juice and pineapple juice well with ice. Strain into tall 14-oz. glass half-filled with ice. Add soda. Stir. Garnish with guava shell and lemon slice. Wonderful cooler before or with a jambalaya feast.

HONEYDEW
COOLER

¹/₃ cup diced ripe
 honeydew melon
1¹/₂ ozs. gin
¹/₄ teaspoon Pernod
1 tablespoon cream
³/₄ oz. lemon juice
¹/₂ teaspoon sugar
¹/₂ cup crushed ice
Iced club soda

*Put honeydew, gin, Pernod, cream,
lemon juice, sugar and crushed ice
into blender. Blend at low speed
15-20 seconds. Pour into tall
14-oz. glass. When foam settles,
add a splash of soda and ice to
fill glass to rim, if necessary.*

HORSE'S NECK
WITH GIN

Peel of whole lemon
2 ozs. gin
¹/₂ oz. lemon juice
Iced ginger ale

*To peel lemon, start at stem end,
using a sharp paring knife, and
cut peel about ¹/₂ inch wide in a
continuous strip until lemon is
completely peeled. Place peel in a
14-oz. highball glass so that the
top of peel overlaps rim of glass,
with the rest spiraling down into
glass. Fill glass with coarsely
cracked ice. Pour gin and lemon
juice into glass. Fill with ginger
ale. Stir.*

ICED RUM
COFFEE

1¹/₂ ozs. light rum
1 teaspoon dark
 Jamaican rum
6 ozs. iced
 double-strength coffee
Sugar
2 tablespoons sweetened
 whipped cream

*Pour rums and coffee into tall
14-oz. glass. Add ice to fill glass.
Add sugar to taste. Top with
whipped cream.*

ICED RUM TEA

1½ ozs. light rum
½ oz. 151-proof rum
6 ozs. iced strong black
 tea
1 teaspoon sugar
1 teaspoon Falernum
1 teaspoon lemon juice
1 slice lemon
2 large mint leaves

Pour rums, tea, sugar, Falernum and lemon juice into tall 14-oz. glass. Add ice to fill glass. Stir. Garnish with lemon slice and mint leaves partially torn. To prevent tea clouding, let it cool to room temperature before combining with ice.

INDEPENDENCE SWIZZLE

2 ozs. dark Jamaican
 rum
3 dashes Angostura
 bitters
1 teaspoon honey
1 teaspoon sugar
½ oz. lime juice
1 slice lime

In tall 14-oz. glass, stir rum, bitters, honey, sugar and lime juice until honey is blended with other ingredients. Add finely cracked ice to fill glass. Twirl with a swizzle stick if you have one, or stir and churn with a barspoon or iced-tea spoon. As drink is stirred, ice will melt. Add more ice as necessary to fill glass to rim, swizzling or stirring until ice and liquids reach top of glass. Add lime slice. A drink used to celebrate the independence of Trinidad and Tobago.

JAMAICA ELEGANCE

1½ ozs. golden Jamaican
 rum
½ oz. brandy
½ oz. pineapple juice
1 oz. lime juice
1 teaspoon simple syrup
 or rock-candy syrup
1 slice lime

Shake rum, brandy, pineapple juice, lime juice and syrup well with ice. Strain into prechilled tall 14-oz. glass. Add ice to fill glass. Add lime slice. Created by C. Scott, head bartender at the Jamaica Playboy Club.

1½ ozs. light rum
½ oz. dark Jamaican
rum
½ oz. 151-proof rum
½ oz. Falernum
½ oz. lime juice
Iced ginger beer
½ slice pineapple in
crème de menthe
1 cube preserved ginger
in syrup

JAMAICA GINGER

*Shake the three kinds of rum,
Falernum and lime juice well with
ice. Strain into tall 14-oz. glass
half-filled with ice. Fill glass with
ginger beer. Stir. Garnish with
pineapple and ginger.*

2½ ozs. bourbon
½ oz. green crème de
menthe
6 mint leaves
1 teaspoon sugar
1 oz. lime juice
Iced club soda
3 tall mint sprigs

JOCOSE JULEP

*Put into blender, without ice,
bourbon, crème de menthe, 6 mint
leaves, sugar and lime juice.
Blend 10-15 seconds or until mint
is very finely chopped. Pour into
tall 14-oz. glass half-filled with
ice. Add soda. Stir. Insert mint
sprigs. Serve to nearest belle.*

2 ozs. Irish whiskey
1½ ozs. Madeira or
sherry
1 oz. orgeat
1 oz. lemon juice
Iced club soda
1 slice lemon

KERRY COOLER

*Into tall 14-oz. glass, pour
whiskey, Madeira, orgeat and
lemon juice. Stir well. Add three
large ice cubes. Fill glass with
soda. Stir. Float lemon slice on
top.*

1½ ozs. kirschwasser
½ lime
Iced cola drink

KIRSCH CUBA LIBRE

*Put three large ice cubes into a
tall 14-oz. glass. Add
kirschwasser. Squeeze lime above
drink and drop into glass. Fill
with cola. Stir.*

LEMON RUM COOLER

2 ozs. light rum
1 teaspoon 151-proof
rum
2 ozs. pineapple juice
1/2 oz. lemon juice
1/2 oz. Falernum
Iced bitter-lemon soda
1 slice lemon

Shake both kinds of rum, pineapple juice, lemon juice and Falernum well with ice. Strain into tall 14-oz. glass. Add two ice cubes. Fill glass with bitter-lemon soda. Add lemon slice.

MANGO COOLER

3 ozs. ice-cold mango
nectar
1 1/2 ozs. vodka
1/2 oz. ice-cold lemon
juice
1 1/2 ozs. ice-cold orange
juice
1/2 oz. Cointreau
1 slice orange
1 slice mango, if in
season

Into tall 14-oz. glass, pour mango nectar, vodka, lemon juice, orange juice and Cointreau. Add ice to fill glass. Garnish with orange and mango slices. A fruity libation to serve before an oriental or Polynesian menu.

MINT JULEP

12 mint leaves on stem
1 teaspoon sugar
2 teaspoons water
2 1/2 ozs. 86- or 100-proof
bourbon
6 mint leaves on stem

Tear the 12 mint leaves partially while leaving them on stem. Place in tall 12-oz. glass or silver julep mug with sugar and water. Muddle or stir until sugar is completely dissolved. Fill glass with finely cracked ice. Add bourbon. Stir. Ice will dissolve partially. Add more ice to fill glass to rim, again stirring. Tear the 6 mint leaves partially to release aroma and insert into ice with leaves on top. Serve with or without straw.

MINT JULEP, DRY, PARTY STYLE

1 quart bourbon
1 pint finely chopped
  mint leaves
8 sprigs mint

(Serves 8)
Steep mint leaves in bourbon for 1 hour at room temperature. Fill eight tall 14-oz. glasses with finely cracked ice. Strain bourbon and pour into glasses, allowing 4 ozs. minted bourbon per glass. Stir. Add more ice to fill glass to rim. Tear a few leaves of each of the mint sprigs and fit a sprig into each glass. If your party is late getting started, store prepared juleps in freezer. A few sips of this unsweetened julep should turn the longest of hot summer days into the coolest.

MOBILE MULE

2 ozs. light rum
$1/2$ lime
Iced ginger beer

Pour rum into tall 12- or 14-oz. glass or copper mug with ice cubes or cracked ice. Squeeze lime above drink and drop into glass. Fill with ginger beer. Stir. A switch on the vodka-inspired moscow mule.

MOSCOW MULE

$1^{1}/_{2}$ to 2 ozs. vodka
$1/2$ lime
Iced ginger beer

Pour vodka into tall 12- or 14-oz. glass or copper mug with ice cubes or cracked ice. Squeeze lime above drink and drop into glass. Fill with ginger beer. Stir. A variation on the moscow mule includes a long spiral of lemon peel in the mug.

NECTARINE COOLER

2 ozs. vodka
3 ozs. iced orange juice
1/4 cup cold sliced ripe
   nectarine
1 teaspoon sugar
1/3 cup crushed ice
Iced club soda
1 slice fresh nectarine
1 slice lemon

Put vodka, orange juice, nectarine, sugar and crushed ice into blender. Blend at low speed 15–20 seconds. Pour into tall 14-oz. glass. Add a splash of soda and ice to fill glass. Stir. Garnish with nectarine and lemon slices.

ORANGE COOLER IN SHELL

1 extra-large California
   orange
1 oz. 151-proof rum
1/2 oz. curaçao
1/2 oz. lime juice
1 teaspoon sugar
1 slice cocktail orange in
   syrup

Cut a cap off top of orange about 1/2 inch from top. With a sharp grapefruit knife, gouge out the meat, leaving orange shell intact. Squeeze enough juice from meat to make 1 1/2 ozs. Shake orange juice, rum, curaçao, lime juice and sugar well with ice. Strain into orange shell. Place orange shell in a bowl or soup dish about 7 inches in diameter. Pack finely crushed ice around orange. Fasten orange slice onto cocktail spear and place across orange cup. Serve with a short colored straw. A show-off concoction for drink hobbyists and rum specialists.

ORANGE OASIS

4 ozs. ice-cold fresh
   orange juice
1 1/2 ozs. gin
1/2 oz. cherry liqueur
Iced ginger ale
1 slice orange

Pour orange juice, gin and cherry liqueur into tall 14-oz. glass. Add ice cubes or ice slices to rim of glass. Add ginger ale. Stir. Garnish with orange slice.

2 ozs. iced Rhine wine
2 ozs. iced very dry
sherry
1 oz. orange juice
1 teaspoon lime juice
½ oz. maraschino
liqueur
1 dash Angostura bitters
1 oz. iced club soda
1 slice lemon

PANAMA COOLER
Shake Rhine wine, sherry, orange juice, lime juice, maraschino liqueur and bitters well with ice. Strain into tall 14-oz. glass. Add soda. Fill glass with ice. Stir. Add lemon slice.

4 ozs. passion-fruit
nectar (not syrup)
1½ ozs. light rum
1 oz. gin
½ oz. lemon juice
1 oz. orange juice
2 sprigs mint

PASSION-FRUIT COOLER
Shake passion-fruit nectar, rum, gin, lemon juice and orange juice well with ice. Strain into tall 14-oz. glass. Add enough coarsely cracked ice or ice cubes to fill glass. Decorate with mint after partially tearing several leaves to release fragrance.

1½ ozs. Pimm's No. 1
Cup
Iced Seven-Up or lemon
soda
1 slice lemon
Cucumber peel

PIMM'S CUP
Pour Pimm's Cup into 8- or 10-oz. glass or Pimm's glass tankard with ice. Fill with Seven-Up. Add lemon slice and cucumber peel. Stir. The old English gin sling is bottled as Pimm's No. 1 Cup, made with a gin base and fruit flavors. Other prepared Pimm's Cups are bottled with other liquor bases, but the No. 1 is the best known in the U.S.

2 ozs. gin
½ oz. white crème de
menthe
3 ozs. pineapple juice
1 oz. lemon juice
Iced club soda
1 cocktail pineapple
stick
1 green cocktail cherry

PINEAPPLE MINT COOLER
Shake gin, crème de menthe, pineapple juice and lemon juice well with ice. Strain into tall 14-oz. glass. Add a splash of soda and ice to fill glass. Stir. Garnish with pineapple stick and cherry.

PINK LEMONADE À LA PLAYBOY

5 ozs. chilled rosé wine
2 ozs. chilled lemon juice
2 ozs. chilled orange
  juice
1/2 oz. kirschwasser
2 teaspoons sugar
1 slice lemon
1 maraschino cherry

Into tall 14-oz. glass, pour wine, lemon juice, orange juice, kirschwasser and sugar. Stir well until sugar dissolves. Add two large ice cubes and enough ice-cold water (not club soda) to fill glass. Stir. Garnish with lemon slice and cherry.

PINK RUM AND TONIC

2 1/2 ozs. light rum
1/2 oz. lime juice
1 teaspoon grenadine
Iced tonic water
1 slice lime

Shake rum, lime juice and grenadine well with ice. Strain into tall 14-oz. glass half-filled with ice. Add tonic water. Stir. Add lime slice. Curiously refreshing yo-ho-ho.

PLAYBOY COOLER

1 1/4 ozs. golden Jamaican
  rum
1 1/4 ozs. Jamaican coffee
  liqueur
3 ozs. pineapple juice
2 teaspoons lemon juice
Cola drink
1 slice pineapple

Shake rum, coffee liqueur, pineapple juice and lemon juice well with ice. Strain into prechilled tall 14-oz. glass. Add ice to fill glass to 1 inch from top. Add cola. Garnish with pineapple slice. Serve with long straw, as at the London Playboy Club.

1 large chilled pineapple
1/2 cup pineapple sherbet
6 ozs. light rum
3 ozs. orange juice
1 1/2 ozs. lime juice
1/2 oz. maraschino
   liqueur

QUADRUPLE PINEAPPLE

*(4 single or 2 double drinks)
The pineapple should measure at
least 7 inches from base to top of
fruit, not including stem. Cut a
cap off pineapple about 1/2 inch
from top. To remove meat from
pineapple, cut a deep circle
around edge of pineapple about 1/2
inch from rim, leaving a large
cylinder of fruit which must then
be gouged out. A very sharp
boning knife is a good instrument
for the job. Cut wedges of fruit
loose by slicing diagonally toward
rim of fruit. Use a grapefruit knife
or large parisienne-potato cutter to
remove small pieces of fruit. Do
not pierce shell of fruit or it will
not hold liquid. The cavity of the
pineapple should be large enough
to hold 2 measuring cups of
liquid. Test it for size. Cut hard
core of fruit away and discard it.
Cut enough tender pineapple meat
to make 1/2 cup fruit in small dice.
Into well of blender, put the 1/2
cup diced pineapple, sherbet, rum,
orange juice, lime juice and
maraschino liqueur. Blend 5
seconds. Pour into pineapple.
Place pineapple in deep dish or
bowl surrounded with finely
crushed ice. Place two or four
colored straws in drink, allowing
for two or four pineapple sippers.
An elaborate production, beloved
by rum barons. A second round
may be prepared beforehand from
the same pineapple and blended
just before refilling pineapple.*

RASPBERRY CLARET CUP

4 ozs. dry red wine
1 oz. brandy
1 oz. Himbeergeist (dry white raspberry brandy)
³/₄ oz. raspberry syrup
1 oz. lemon juice
Iced club soda
2 or 3 fresh or frozen whole raspberries

Be sure wine and brandies are ice-cold before mixing drink. Put three ice cubes into tall 14-oz. collins glass. Pour wine, brandy, Himbeergeist, raspberry syrup and lemon juice into glass. Stir until all ingredients are very well blended. Fill glass with soda. Stir slightly. Float raspberries on top.

ROCK-AND-RYE COOLER

1¹/₂ ozs. vodka
1 oz. rock and rye
¹/₂ oz. lime juice
Iced bitter-lemon soda
1 slice lime

Shake vodka, rock and rye and lime juice well with ice. Strain into tall 14-oz. glass half-filled with ice. Add bitter-lemon soda. Stir. Add lime slice.

ROMAN COOLER

1¹/₂ ozs. gin
¹/₂ oz. Punt e Mes
¹/₂ oz. lemon juice
1 teaspoon sugar
Iced club soda
Lemon peel

Shake gin, Punt e Mes, lemon juice and sugar well with ice. Strain into tall 14-oz. glass. Add soda and ice to fill glass. Twist lemon peel above drink and drop into glass.

ROMAN FRULLATI

3 ozs. gin
¹/₄ cup diced Delicious apple, with skin
¹/₄ cup diced ripe pear, with skin
¹/₄ cup frozen sliced peaches, thawed
1 oz. maraschino liqueur
1 oz. orzata or orgeat
¹/₂ cup crushed ice

Put all ingredients into blender. Blend at high speed 20 seconds. Pour into tall 14-oz. glass. Add ice, if necessary, to fill glass to rim.

RUM AND COCONUT COOLER

2¹/₂ ozs. light rum
1 oz. cream of coconut
¹/₂ oz. lemon juice
Iced club soda
1 slice lemon
1 maraschino cherry

Shake rum, cream of coconut and lemon juice well with ice. Strain into tall 14-oz. glass half-filled with ice. Add a splash of soda. Garnish with lemon slice and cherry.

RUM AND PINEAPPLE COOLER

2¹/₂ ozs. light rum
2 ozs. pineapple juice
¹/₂ oz. lemon juice
1 teaspoon 151-proof
    rum
1 teaspoon sugar
1 dash Angostura bitters
Iced club soda
1 pineapple chunk
1 papaya chunk in syrup

Shake rum, pineapple juice, lemon juice, 151-proof rum, sugar and bitters well with ice. Strain into tall 14-oz. glass. Add a splash of soda and ice to fill glass. Garnish with pineapple and papaya chunks fastened onto a cocktail spear.

RUM CITRUS COOLER

2 ozs. light rum
1 oz. orange juice
¹/₂ oz. lime juice
¹/₂ oz. Cointreau
1 teaspoon sugar
Iced Seven-Up
1 slice lime
¹/₂ slice lemon

Shake rum, orange juice, lime juice, Cointreau and sugar well with ice. Strain into tall 14-oz. glass half-filled with ice. Add Seven-Up. Stir. Garnish with lime and lemon slices. Solace or celebration after 18 holes on the fairway.

RUM CURAÇAO COOLER

1 oz. dark Jamaican rum
1 oz. curaçao
¹/₂ oz. lime juice
Iced club soda
1 slice lime
¹/₂ slice orange

Shake rum, curaçao and lime juice well with ice. Strain into tall 14-oz. glass. Add a splash of soda and ice to fill glass. Garnish with lime and orange slices.

RUM ROYALE

1 oz. light rum
2 ozs. sauternes
1¹/₂ ozs. lemon juice
2 ozs. pineapple juice
1 teaspoon sugar
1 dash Peychaud's bitters
1 cube pineapple
1 maraschino cherry

Shake rum, sauternes, lemon juice, pineapple juice, sugar and bitters well with ice. Strain into prechilled tall 14-oz. glass. Add ice to fill glass. Affix pineapple cube and cherry to cocktail spear and rest on rim of glass. Created by Al Hawn, head bartender at the Kansas City Playboy Club.

ST.-CROIX COOLER

Peel of ¹/₂ large orange
2 ozs. light rum
¹/₂ oz. dark Jamaican
   rum
1 oz. brandy
1 tablespoon brown
   sugar
2¹/₂ ozs. orange juice
1¹/₂ ozs. lemon juice
1 dash orange-flower
   water
Iced club soda

Cut orange peel from stem end in one continuing spiral about ¹/₂ inch wide. Place peel in tall 14-oz. glass, permitting one end to overhang rim. Shake both kinds of rum, brandy, brown sugar, orange juice, lemon juice, and orange-flower water well with ice. Strain into glass. Fill glass to rim with coarsely cracked ice or ice cubes. Add a splash of soda. Stir. A rich tropical cooler that will easily outlast two ordinary cocktails.

SAN JUAN SLING

³/₄ oz. light rum
³/₄ oz. cherry liqueur
³/₄ oz. Benedictine
¹/₂ oz. lime juice
Iced club soda
Lime peel

Shake rum, cherry liqueur, Benedictine and lime juice well with ice. Strain into tall 14-oz. glass half-filled with ice. Add soda. Twist lime peel above drink and drop into glass.

SCOTCH HORSE'S NECK

Peel of whole lemon in
   one spiral
3 ozs. Scotch
¹/₂ oz. sweet vermouth
¹/₂ oz. dry vermouth

Place lemon peel in tall 14-oz. glass with one end of peel overhanging rim of glass. Add Scotch and both kinds of vermouth. Fill glass with cracked ice. Stir. Add more ice, if necessary, to fill glass. Every horse's neck is improved if it ages about 10 minutes before sipping.

SCOTCH SOLACE

2¹/₂ ozs. Scotch
¹/₂ oz. honey
¹/₂ oz. triple sec
4 ozs. milk
1 oz. cream
¹/₈ teaspoon freshly
grated orange rind

*Pour Scotch, honey and Triple Sec
into 14-oz. glass. Stir until honey
is thoroughly blended. Add milk,
cream and orange rind. Add ice
cubes to fill glass to brim. Stir
well. Cold, creamy and soothing.*

SCREWDRIVER WITH SHERRY

¹/₂ cup orange juice
2 ozs. oloroso sherry
1 oz. vodka
¹/₂ cup crushed ice

*Put all ingredients into blender.
Blend 20 seconds. Pour into
double old-fashioned or tall 14-oz.
glass. Add ice cubes to fill glass.
An outsize screwdriver especially
suited for the brunchboard.*

SINGAPORE GIN SLING

1¹/₂ ozs. gin
1 oz. cherry-flavored
brandy
1 oz. lime juice
Iced club soda
1 slice lime

*Shake gin, cherry-flavored brandy
and lime juice well with ice.
Strain into tall 14-oz. glass
half-filled with ice cubes. Fill
glass with soda. Add lime slice.*

SLOE CRANBERRY COOLER

2¹/₂ ozs. ice-cold sloe gin
6 ozs. ice-cold cranberry
juice
1¹/₄ ozs. lemon juice
1 slice lemon

*Pour sloe gin, cranberry juice and
lemon juice into tall 14-oz. glass.
Add ice cubes to fill glass. Stir
well. Add lemon slice.*

STEEPLEJACK

2 ozs. apple brandy
2¹/₂ ozs. iced apple juice
2¹/₂ ozs. iced club soda
1 teaspoon lime juice
1 slice lime

*Pour apple brandy, apple juice,
soda and lime juice into tall
14-oz. glass. Add ice to fill glass.
Stir. Add lime slice.*

STRAWBERRY BLONDE

3 fresh strawberries
1 oz. strawberry liqueur
6 ozs. well-chilled Rhine
  wine
1/2 oz. kirschwasser
Iced club soda
1 slice lime

Marinate strawberries in strawberry liqueur for 1 hour. Fasten strawberries onto cocktail spear. Pour Rhine wine, strawberry liqueur and kirschwasser into tall 14-oz. glass. Add a splash of soda and ice to fill glass. Stir. Add lime slice. Place speared strawberries over rim of glass.

STRAWBERRY CREAM COOLER

1 1/2 ozs. gin
1/4 cup frozen sliced
  strawberries (fruit and
  syrup), thawed
1 oz. lemon juice
2 tablespoons cream
1 teaspoon sugar
Iced club soda

Put gin, strawberries, lemon juice, cream and sugar into blender. Blend 10–15 seconds at high speed. Pour into tall 14-oz. glass. Add a splash of soda and ice to fill glass. Stir.

STRAWBERRY VER-MOUTH COOLER

2 1/2 ozs. dry vermouth
1/4 cup fresh
  strawberries, hulled
  and sliced
1 oz. gin
2 teaspoons red-currant
  syrup
1/2 cup crushed ice
Iced club soda
1 slice lemon

Put vermouth, strawberries, gin, red-currant syrup and ice into blender. Blend 10–15 seconds at low speed. Pour into tall 14-oz. glass containing two ice cubes. Add a splash of soda. Stir. Garnish with lemon slice.

TALL DUTCH EGGNOG

1 1/2 ozs. advocaat liqueur
1 1/2 ozs. light rum
1/2 oz. 151-proof rum
1 oz. orange juice
6 ozs. milk
1 teaspoon sugar
1/2 cup finely cracked ice
Ground cinnamon

Put advocaat, both kinds of rum, orange juice, milk, sugar and ice into blender. Blend at high speed 10 seconds. Pour into tall 14-oz. glass. Sprinkle with cinnamon. The Dutch way of getting the new year to roll as merrily as possible.

TALL ISLANDER

2 ozs. light rum
3 ozs. pineapple juice
1 oz. lime juice
1 teaspoon dark
   Jamaican rum
1 teaspoon sugar syrup
Iced club soda
1 slice lime

Shake light rum, pineapple juice, lime juice, dark rum and syrup well with ice. Strain into tall 14-oz. glass. Add a splash of soda and ice to fill glass. Stir. Add lime slice. Bound to make natives unrestless; equally at home in a high-rise or down among the sheltering palms.

TEQUILA SUNRISE

2 ozs. tequila
$1/2$ oz. lime juice
$1/2$ oz. curaçao
1 teaspoon crème de
   cassis
Iced club soda
1 slice lime

Shake tequila, lime juice, curaçao and crème de cassis well with ice. Strain into tall 14-oz. glass half-filled with ice. Fill glass with soda. Stir. Garnish with lime slice. One to contemplate while waiting for the hot chili.

TIGER TAIL

4 ozs. ice-cold fresh
   orange juice
1 oz. Pernod
1 slice lime

Pour orange juice and Pernod into tall 12- or 14-oz. glass. Add cracked ice to fill glass. Stir. Add lime slice. Magnificent breakfast first course.

VERMOUTH COOLER

2 ozs. sweet vermouth
1 oz. vodka
$1/2$ oz. lemon juice
1 teaspoon sugar
Iced club soda
1 slice lemon

Shake vermouth, vodka, lemon juice and sugar well with ice. Strain into tall 14-oz. glass half-filled with ice. Add soda. Stir. Add lemon slice.

WATERMELON CASSIS

2 ozs. gin
$^1/_2$ cup diced
   watermelon, seeds
   removed
$^1/_2$ oz. crème de cassis
$^3/_4$ oz. lemon juice
$^1/_2$ cup crushed ice
Iced club soda
1 slice lemon

Put gin, watermelon, crème de cassis, lemon juice and crushed ice into blender. Blend at low speed 10–15 seconds. Pour into tall 14-oz. glass. Let drink settle for a few moments. Add two ice cubes and a splash of soda. Add lemon slice.

WATERMELON COOLER

$^1/_2$ cup diced
   watermelon, sans seeds
$2^1/_4$ ozs. light rum
$^1/_2$ oz. lime juice
$^1/_4$ oz. maraschino
   liqueur
1 teaspoon sugar
$^1/_2$ cup crushed ice
1 slice lime

Put watermelon, rum, lime juice, maraschino liqueur, sugar and ice into blender. Blend 10–15 seconds at low speed. Pour into tall 14-oz. glass. When foam subsides, add ice to fill glass. Stir. Add lime slice.

WHITE-WINE COOLER

6 ozs. chilled dry white
   wine
$^1/_2$ oz. brandy
2 dashes orange bitters
1 teaspoon kümmel
2 teaspoons sugar
$^1/_2$ oz. lemon juice
Iced club soda
Cucumber peel, 2 inches
   long, $^1/_2$ inch wide

Put wine, brandy, bitters, kümmel, sugar and lemon juice into tall 14-oz. glass. Stir until sugar dissolves. Add a splash of soda and ice to fill glass. Stir. Add cucumber peel.

DAISIES

The daisy, which originated in the mauve decade, is a medium-tall drink served if possible in knob glassware, a silver mug or any vessel that conveys a feeling of sumptuousness. An amalgam of spirits and fruit juice, it is invariably sweetened with a red agent such as grenadine or raspberry syrup and usually topped with a float of some compatible liqueur—a last-minute touch which adds to its subtlety and good humor.

APPLEJACK DAISY

1¹/₂ ozs. applejack
¹/₂ oz. lime juice
1 teaspoon raspberry
   syrup
Iced club soda
1 teaspoon ginger-
   flavored brandy
1 slice lime

Shake applejack, lime juice and raspberry syrup well with ice. Strain into tall 8-oz. glass half-filled with ice. Add soda. Stir. Float ginger-flavored brandy on drink. Add lime slice.

BOURBON DAISY

1¹/₂ ozs. bourbon
¹/₂ oz. lemon juice
1 teaspoon grenadine
Iced club soda
1 teaspoon Southern
   Comfort
¹/₂ slice orange
1 cocktail pineapple
   stick

Shake bourbon, lemon juice and grenadine well with ice. Strain into tall 8-oz. glass half-filled with ice. Add soda. Stir. Float Southern Comfort on drink. Garnish with orange slice and pineapple stick.

CANADIAN DAISY

1¹/₂ ozs. Canadian
   whisky
¹/₂ oz. lemon juice
1 teaspoon raspberry
   syrup
Iced club soda
1 teaspoon Metaxa
   brandy
2 fresh or thawed frozen
   raspberries

Shake whisky, lemon juice and raspberry syrup well with ice. Strain into tall 8-oz. glass half-filled with ice. Add soda. Stir. Float Metaxa on drink. Add raspberries.

GIN DAISY

1½ ozs. gin
½ oz. lemon juice
1½ teaspoons raspberry
 syrup
Iced club soda
1 slice lemon
2 sprigs mint

*Shake gin, lemon juice and
raspberry syrup well with ice.
Strain into tall 8-oz. glass
half-filled with ice. Add soda.
Garnish with lemon slice and mint
sprigs.*

HAWAIIAN DAISY

1½ ozs. light rum
½ oz. pineapple juice
1 teaspoon lime juice
1 teaspoon grenadine
Iced club soda
1 teaspoon 151-proof
 rum
1 papaya chunk in syrup

*Shake light rum, pineapple juice,
lime juice and grenadine well with
ice. Strain into tall 8-oz. glass
half-filled with ice. Add soda. Stir.
Float 151-proof rum on drink. Add
papaya chunk.*

WHISKEY DAISY

1½ ozs. blended whiskey
1 teaspoon red-currant
 syrup
½ oz. lemon juice
Iced club soda
1 teaspoon yellow
 Chartreuse
1 slice lemon

*Shake whiskey, red-currant syrup
and lemon juice well with ice.
Strain into tall 8-oz. glass
half-filled with ice. Add club soda.
Stir. Float Chartreuse on drink.
Add lemon slice.*

FIXES

Fixes are medium-tall drinks in which the ingredients are
"fixed" in the glass itself, which is packed with crushed or
finely cracked ice. As with the cobbler, no club soda or other
extender is added, and shaking or straining is unnecessary. The
simple fix of liquor, sugar, ice and a slice of lemon is an
heirloom from Victorian drinking days. Modern variations make
gloriously refreshing summer libations.

APPLE GINGER FIX

½ teaspoon sugar
1 oz. applejack
1 oz. ginger-flavored
brandy
½ oz. lemon juice
1 slice lemon

Dissolve sugar in a teaspoon of water in an 8-oz. glass. Add applejack, ginger-flavored brandy and lemon juice. Fill glass with crushed ice. Stir well. Add more ice to fill glass to rim. Stir. Garnish with lemon slice.

BOURBON SLOE GIN FIX

½ teaspoon sugar
1½ ozs. bourbon
½ oz. sloe gin
½ oz. lemon juice
1 slice lemon
1 slice fresh or brandied
peach

Dissolve sugar in a teaspoon of water in an 8-oz. glass. Add bourbon, sloe gin and lemon juice. Fill glass with crushed ice. Stir well. Add more ice to fill glass to rim. Stir. Garnish with lemon and peach slice.

BRANDY BERRY FIX

1 teaspoon sugar
2 ozs. brandy
1 teaspoon strawberry
liqueur
½ oz. lemon juice
1 slice lemon
1 large strawberry

Dissolve sugar in 2 teaspoons of water in an 8-oz. glass. Add brandy, strawberry liqueur and lemon juice. Fill glass with crushed ice. Stir well. Add more ice to fill glass to rim. Stir. Garnish with lemon slice and strawberry.

CANADIAN BLACKBERRY FIX

½ teaspoon sugar
1½ ozs. Canadian
whisky
½ oz. blackberry liqueur
½ oz. lemon juice
1 slice lemon
1 fresh blackberry, if
available

Dissolve sugar in a teaspoon of water in an 8-oz. glass. Add whisky, blackberry liqueur and lemon juice. Fill glass with crushed ice. Stir well. Add more ice to fill glass to rim. Stir. Garnish with lemon slice and blackberry.

CHERRY RUM FIX

1 teaspoon sugar
1¹/₂ ozs. vodka
¹/₂ oz. Cherry Heering or
  Cherry Karise
¹/₂ oz. lemon juice
1 slice lemon
1 brandied cherry

Dissolve sugar in 2 teaspoons of water in an 8-oz. glass. Add vodka, Cherry Heering and lemon juice. Fill glass with crushed ice. Stir well. Add more ice to fill glass to rim. Stir. Garnish with lemon slice and cherry.

DERBY RUM FIX

1 teaspoon sugar
2 ozs. light rum
¹/₂ oz. lime juice
1 oz. orange juice
1 slice cocktail orange in
  syrup
1 maraschino cherry

Dissolve sugar in 2 teaspoons of water in an 8-oz. glass. Add rum, lime juice and orange juice. Fill glass with crushed ice. Stir well. Add more ice to fill glass to rim. Stir. Garnish with orange slice and cherry.

GIN MINT FIX

1 teaspoon sugar
2 ozs. gin
¹/₂ oz. lemon juice
1 teaspoon white crème
  de menthe
2 large mint leaves

Dissolve sugar in 2 teaspoons of water in an 8-oz. glass. Add gin, lemon juice and crème de menthe. Fill glass with crushed ice. Stir well. Add more ice to fill glass to rim. Stir. Tear mint leaves slightly and float on drink.

IRISH FIX

1 teaspoon sugar
2 ozs. Irish whiskey
¹/₂ oz. lemon juice
¹/₂ slice orange
¹/₂ slice lemon
2 teaspoons Irish Mist

Dissolve sugar in 2 teaspoons of water in an 8-oz. glass. Add whiskey and lemon juice. Fill glass with crushed ice. Stir well. Add more ice to fill glass to rim. Stir. Garnish with orange and lemon slices. Float Irish Mist on top.

SCOTCH ORANGE FIX

1 teaspoon sugar
1 3-inch piece orange
  peel, in one spiral
2 ozs. Scotch
¹/₂ oz. lemon juice
1 teaspoon curaçao

Dissolve sugar in 2 teaspoons of water in an 8-oz. glass. Place orange peel in glass. Add Scotch and lemon juice. Fill glass with crushed ice. Stir well. Add more ice to fill glass to rim. Stir. Float curaçao on drink.

WHISKEY OUZO FIX

1 teaspoon sugar
2 ozs. blended whiskey
1/2 oz. lemon juice
1 teaspoon ouzo
Lemon peel

Dissolve sugar in 2 teaspoons of water in an 8-oz. glass. Add whiskey and lemon juice. Fill glass with crushed ice. Stir well. Add more ice to fill glass to rim. Stir. Float ouzo on top of drink. Twist lemon peel above drink and drop into glass.

FIZZES

Fizzes are effervescent cooling agents all built on lemon or lime juice and iced club soda. They're designed here for tall 14-ounce glasses, but they can easily be stretched into 16-, 18- or 20-ounce portions for further appeasement of parched throats.

APRICOT ANISE FIZZ

1³/₄ ozs. gin
1/2 oz. apricot-flavored brandy
1/4 oz. anisette
1/2 oz. lemon juice
Iced club soda
1/2 brandied or fresh apricot
Lemon peel

Shake gin, apricot-flavored brandy, anisette and lemon juice well with ice. Strain into tall 14-oz. glass half-filled with ice. Fill glass with soda. Stir. Add brandied apricot. Twist lemon peel above drink and drop into glass.

AQUAVIT FIZZ

2¹/₂ ozs. aquavit
1/2 oz. lemon juice
1 teaspoon sugar
1/2 egg white
1 teaspoon Cherry Heering or Cherry Karise
Iced club soda
Lemon peel
1 brandied cherry

Shake aquavit, lemon juice, sugar, egg white and Cherry Heering well with ice. Strain into tall 14-oz. glass half-filled with ice. Fill glass with soda. Stir. Twist lemon peel above drink and drop into glass. Add brandied cherry.

BAYARD FIZZ

2 ozs. gin
1/2 oz. lemon juice
2 teaspoons maraschino
  liqueur
1 teaspoon raspberry
  syrup
Iced club soda
1 slice lemon
2 fresh or thawed frozen
  raspberries

Shake gin, lemon juice, maraschino liqueur and raspberry syrup well with ice. Strain into tall 14-oz. glass half-filled with ice. Fill glass with soda. Stir. Add lemon slice and raspberries.

BLUEBERRY RUM FIZZ

2 1/2 ozs. light rum
1 teaspoon triple sec
1/2 oz. blueberry syrup
3/4 oz. lemon juice
Iced club soda
1 slice lemon
3 large fresh blueberries

Shake rum, triple sec, blueberry syrup and lemon juice well with ice. Strain into tall 14-oz. glass half-filled with ice. Fill glass with soda. Stir. Add lemon slice and blueberries.

BRANDIED PEACH FIZZ

2 ozs. brandy
1/2 oz. peach-flavored
  brandy
1/2 oz. lemon juice
1 teaspoon sugar
1 teaspoon banana
  liqueur
Iced club soda
1 slice fresh or brandied
  peach

Shake brandy, peach-flavored brandy, lemon juice, sugar and banana liqueur well with ice. Strain into tall 14-oz. glass half-filled with ice. Fill glass with soda. Stir. Garnish with peach slice.

BRANDY MINT FIZZ

2 ozs. brandy
2 teaspoons white crème
  de menthe
1 teaspoon crème de
  cacao
1/2 oz. lemon juice
1/2 teaspoon sugar
Iced club soda
2 large fresh mint leaves

Shake brandy, crème de menthe, crème de cacao, lemon juice and sugar well with ice. Strain into tall 14-oz. glass half-filled with ice. Fill glass with soda. Stir. Tear mint leaves partially and place on top of drink.

CALVADOS FIZZ

2 ozs. calvados
¹/₂ oz. lemon juice
1 teaspoon sugar
¹/₂ egg white
1 teaspoon cream
Iced club soda
1 slice lime
1 maraschino cherry

*Shake calvados, lemon juice,
sugar, egg white and cream well
with ice. Strain into tall 14-oz.
glass half-filled with ice. Fill glass
with soda. Stir. Add lime slice
and cherry. A fine wintertime fizz
while waiting for the roast
suckling pig.*

DANISH GIN FIZZ

1¹/₂ ozs. gin
¹/₂ oz. Cherry Heering or
   Cherry Karise
¹/₄ oz. kirschwasser
¹/₂ oz. lime juice
1 teaspoon sugar
Iced club soda
1 slice lime
1 maraschino cherry

*Shake gin, Cherry Heering,
kirschwasser, lime juice and sugar
well with ice. Strain into tall
14-oz. glass half-filled with ice.
Fill glass with soda. Stir. Add
lime slice and cherry. A single
round will pave the way for a
Danish open-sandwich party.*

DUBONNET FIZZ

1 oz. Red Dubonnet
1 oz. cherry-flavored
   brandy
1 oz. orange juice
¹/₂ oz. lemon juice
1 teaspoon kirschwasser
Iced club soda
1 slice lemon
1 fresh or canned pitted
   black cherry

*Shake Dubonnet, cherry-flavored
brandy, orange juice, lemon juice
and kirschwasser well with ice.
Strain into tall 14-oz. glass
half-filled with ice. Fill glass with
soda. Stir. Add lemon slice and
cherry.*

FERN GULLY
FIZZ

1 oz. dark Jamaican rum
1 oz. light rum
1 oz. pineapple juice
³/₄ oz. lime juice
1 teaspoon sugar
Iced club soda
1 slice or chunk fresh
   pineapple
1 slice lime

*Shake both kinds of rum,
pineapple juice, lime juice and
sugar well with ice. Strain into tall
14-oz. glass half-filled with ice.
Fill glass with soda. Stir. Garnish
with pineapple and lime slices.*

FRAISE FIZZ

1¹/₂ ozs. gin
1 oz. Chambery fraise
¹/₂ oz. lemon juice
1 teaspoon sugar
Iced club soda
Lemon peel
1 large strawberry, sliced
  in half

Shake gin, Chambery fraise, lemon juice and sugar well with ice. Strain into tall 14-oz. glass half-filled with ice. Fill glass with soda. Stir. Twist lemon peel above drink and drop into glass. Add strawberry. Perfect as an apéritif.

GIN FIZZ

2 ozs. gin
¹/₂ oz. lemon juice
1 teaspoon sugar
Iced club soda
1 slice lemon

Shake gin, lemon juice and sugar well with ice. Strain into tall 14-oz. glass half-filled with ice. Fill glass with soda. Stir. Add lemon slice. Brandy, whiskey, rum or vodka may be used in place of the gin. A 10- or 12-oz. glass may be used instead of the 14-oz., but any diminution in its size only shortens the pleasure of the long, lazy drink implied by a fizz.

GOLDEN GIN FIZZ

2¹/₄ ozs. gin
1 oz. lemon juice
1 egg yolk
2 teaspoons sugar
Iced club soda
1 slice lemon
Freshly ground nutmeg
  (optional)

Shake gin, lemon juice, egg yolk and sugar well with ice. Strain into tall 14-oz. glass half-filled with ice. Fill glass with soda. Stir. Add lemon slice. Sprinkle with nutmeg if desired.

JAPANESE FIZZ

2¹/₄ ozs. blended whiskey
³/₄ oz. port
¹/₂ oz. lemon juice
1 teaspoon sugar
Iced club soda
Orange peel
1 cocktail pineapple
  stick

Shake whiskey, port, lemon juice and sugar well with ice. Strain into tall 14-oz. glass half-filled with ice. Fill glass with soda. Stir. Twist orange peel above drink and drop into glass. Add pineapple stick.

MORNING-GLORY FIZZ

2 ozs. Scotch
1 teaspoon Pernod
$^1/_2$ oz. lemon juice
1 teaspoon sugar
$^1/_2$ egg white
1 dash Peychaud's bitters
Iced club soda
1 slice lemon

Shake Scotch, Pernod, lemon juice, sugar, egg white and bitters well with ice. Strain into tall 14-oz. glass half-filled with ice. Fill glass with soda. Stir. Add lemon slice. A drink for the elite of the fizz fraternity.

NEW ORLEANS GIN FIZZ

$2^1/_2$ ozs. gin
1 oz. lemon juice
$^1/_2$ egg white
1 teaspoon cream
$^1/_4$ teaspoon orange-
flower water
2 teaspoons sugar
Iced club soda
1 slice lemon

Shake gin, lemon juice, egg white, cream, orange-flower water and sugar well with ice. Strain into tall 14-oz. glass half-filled with ice. Fill glass with soda. Stir. Garnish with lemon slice. A variation of the Ramos gin fizz (page 247).

ORANGE FIZZ

2 ozs. gin
$1^1/_2$ ozs. orange juice
$^1/_2$ oz. lemon juice
2 teaspoons triple sec
1 teaspoon sugar
2 dashes orange bitters
Iced club soda
1 slice orange

Shake gin, orange juice, lemon juice, triple sec, sugar and bitters well with ice. Strain into tall 14-oz. glass half-filled with ice. Fill glass with soda. Stir. Add orange slice.

OSTEND FIZZ

$1^1/_2$ ozs. kirschwasser
$^1/_2$ oz. crème de cassis
$^1/_2$ oz. lemon juice
1 teaspoon sugar
Iced club soda
1 slice lemon

Shake kirschwasser, crème de cassis, lemon juice and sugar well with ice. Strain into tall 14-oz. glass half-filled with ice. Fill glass with soda. Stir. Add lemon slice. Splendid with a summer smorgasbord.

PEACHBLOW FIZZ

2 ozs. gin
1/2 oz. strawberry liqueur
1/2 oz. lemon juice
1/2 teaspoon sugar
1 teaspoon cream
Iced club soda
1 slice lemon
1 large fresh strawberry

Shake gin, strawberry liqueur, lemon juice, sugar and cream well with ice. Strain into tall 14-oz. glass half-filled with ice. Fill glass with soda. Stir. Garnish with lemon slice and strawberry. A classic old fizz—and a semantic mystery, since there's no peach in the recipe—but a joy for parched throats.

RAMOS GIN FIZZ

2 ozs. gin
1 egg white
1/2 oz. cream
2 teaspoons sugar
1/2 oz. lemon juice
1/4 oz. lime juice
1/2 teaspoon orange-
   flower water
1 cup crushed ice
Iced club soda

Put gin, egg white, cream, sugar, lemon juice, lime juice, orange-flower water and crushed ice into blender. Blend at high speed 5 seconds. Pour into tall 14-oz. glass. Add enough club soda to fill glass. Stir. In the old days, no New Orleans bartender would think of serving a Ramos gin fizz if the drink hadn't been shaken at least 5 minutes. The electric blender does a better job in 5 seconds.

ROYAL GIN FIZZ

2¹/₄ ozs. gin
1 oz. lemon juice
1 whole egg
2 teaspoons sugar
Iced club soda
1 slice lemon

Shake gin, lemon juice, egg and sugar well with ice. Strain into tall 14-oz. glass half-filled with ice. Fill glass with soda. Stir. Add lemon slice.

RUM COCONUT FIZZ

2¹/₄ ozs. light rum
1/2 oz. cream of coconut
1/2 oz. lime juice
Iced club soda
1 slice lime

Shake rum, cream of coconut and lime juice well with ice. Strain into tall 14-oz. glass half-filled with ice. Fill glass with soda. Stir. Add lime slice. Sip while the teriyaki is browning over the charcoal.

RUM PINEAPPLE FIZZ

2 ozs. golden rum
1/2 oz. 151-proof rum
1/3 cup fresh pineapple,
   small dice
1/2 egg white
1 teaspoon sugar
1/2 oz. lemon juice
1/2 oz. lime juice
1/2 cup crushed ice
Iced club soda
1 slice lime

Put both kinds of rum, pineapple, egg white, sugar, lemon juice, lime juice and ice into blender. Blend at low speed 10–15 seconds. Pour into tall 14-oz. glass. Add ice cubes to almost fill glass. Add a splash of soda and lime slice.

SLOE GIN FIZZ

1 oz. sloe gin (creamy
   cap)
1 oz. gin
3/4 oz. lemon juice
Iced club soda
1 slice lemon

Shake sloe gin, gin and lemon juice well with ice. Strain into tall 14-oz. glass half-filled with ice. Fill glass with soda. Stir. Add lemon slice.

TEQUILA FIZZ

2 ozs. tequila
1 1/2 ozs. lemon juice
2 teaspoons sugar
2 dashes Angostura
   bitters
1 small egg
Iced club soda
Salt

Shake tequila, lemon juice, sugar, bitters and egg well with ice. Strain into tall 14-oz. glass half-filled with ice. Fill glass with soda. Stir. Sprinkle very lightly with salt.

WHISKEY CURAÇAO FIZZ

2 ozs. blended whiskey
1/2 oz. curaçao
1 teaspoon sugar
1 oz. lemon juice
Iced club soda
1/2 slice orange

Shake whiskey, curaçao, sugar and lemon juice well with ice. Strain into tall 14-oz. glass half-filled with ice. Fill glass with soda. Stir. Add orange slice.

RICKEYS

The first time you try a rickey, your reaction may be the same kind of shudder you get with the first taste of Campari or Greek olives. But the instant shock of pleasure to a heat-weary body will draw you back until you're happily addicted.

The word *rickey* evokes an immediate association with gin. But the gin rickey—though it's a justifiably renowned classic among warm-weather coolers—is only one among a multitude of these refreshingly effervescent lime libations. Other rickeys can be made by substituting other liquors for gin. Bourbon, blended whiskey, Canadian whisky, Scotch, apple brandy, vodka and rum all make interesting and refreshing rickeys. But more imaginative rickeys may be created, too, as witnessed by these tried and tested formulas.

APPLE RUM RICKEY

3/4 oz. applejack
3/4 oz. light rum
1/4 large lime
Iced club soda
Orange peel

Put three ice cubes into 8-oz. glass. Add applejack and rum. Squeeze lime above drink and drop into glass. Add soda. Stir. Twist orange peel above drink and drop into glass.

AQUAVIT RICKEY

1 1/2 ozs. aquavit
1 teaspoon extra-dry
  kümmel
1/4 large lime
Iced club soda

Put three ice cubes into 8-oz. glass. Add aquavit and kümmel. Squeeze lime above drink and drop into glass. Add soda. Stir.

FINO RICKEY

3/4 oz. very dry (fino)
  sherry
3/4 oz. gin
1/4 large lime
Iced club soda

Put three ice cubes into 8-oz. glass. Add sherry and gin. Squeeze lime above drink and drop into glass. Add soda. Stir. Serve with something salty—such as a bowl of assorted stuffed olives or anchovy canapés.

GIN RICKEY

1½ ozs. gin
¼ large lime
Iced club soda

*Put three ice cubes into 8-oz.
glass. Add gin. Squeeze lime
above drink and drop into glass.
Add soda. Stir.*

KIRSCH RICKEY

1½ ozs. kirschwasser
¼ large lime
Iced club soda
2 large fresh or canned
    pitted black cherries

*Put three ice cubes into 8-oz.
glass. Add kirschwasser. Squeeze
lime above drink and drop into
glass. Add soda. Stir. Cut fresh
cherries in half, remove pits and
fasten halves to cocktail spear; or
fasten canned cherries to spear.
Place spear across glass.*

OUZO COGNAC RICKEY

1 oz. ouzo
1 oz. cognac
¼ large lime
Iced club soda

*Put three ice cubes into 8-oz.
glass. Add ouzo and cognac.
Squeeze lime above drink and
drop into glass. Add soda. Stir.
Ouzo has a delightful but forceful
flavor, and cognac is one of the
few liquors that can stand up to it
and live compatibly with it in the
same drinking glass. A plate of
freshly toasted, salted almonds on
the side really brings the
ouzo-cognac combination into
proper perspective.*

PEAR RICKEY

1½ ozs. dry pear brandy
    (birnebrande)
¼ large lime
Iced club soda
2 wedge slices fresh ripe
    pear

*Put three ice cubes into 8-oz.
glass. Add pear brandy. Squeeze
lime above drink and drop into
glass. Add soda. Stir. Fasten the
pear slices to a cocktail spear and
place across rim of glass. Munch
pear piecemeal while you drink.*

PLUM RICKEY

1½ ozs. plum brandy
(quetsch, mirabelle or
slivovitz)
¼ large lime
Iced club soda
3 wedge slices fresh ripe
plum

*Put three ice cubes into 8-oz.
glass. Add plum brandy. Squeeze
lime above drink and drop into
glass. Add soda. Stir. Fasten the
plum slices to a cocktail spear
and place across rim of glass.*

RASPBERRY RICKEY

1½ ozs. himbeergeist
¼ large lime
Iced club soda
3 fresh or thawed frozen
raspberries

*Put three ice cubes into 8-oz.
glass. Add himbeergeist. Squeeze
lime above drink and drop into
glass. Add soda. Stir. Float frozen
raspberries on drink or fasten
fresh raspberries to cocktail spear
as garnish.*

TEQUILA RICKEY

1½ ozs. tequila
¼ large lime
Iced club soda
Salt
1 slice cocktail orange in
syrup

*Put three ice cubes into 8-oz.
glass. Add tequila. Squeeze lime
above drink and drop into glass.
Add soda. Stir. Sprinkle lightly
with salt. Fasten orange slice to
cocktail spear. Munch it before or
after each swallow.*

SANGAREES

Sangarees are slightly sweet lowball drinks on the rocks.
Unlike an old-fashioned, the sangaree contains no bitters. Each
drink receives a benediction of freshly grated nutmeg and should
be very well stirred for proper dilution.

APPLE GINGER SANGAREE

1½ ozs. apple brandy
½ oz. green-ginger wine
1 slice lemon
Freshly grated nutmeg

*Pour apple brandy and ginger
wine over rocks in old-fashioned
glass. Stir. Add lemon slice.
Sprinkle lightly with nutmeg.*

BRANDY SANGAREE

½ teaspoon sugar
Iced club soda
2 ozs. brandy
1 teaspoon Madeira
Orange peel
Freshly grated nutmeg

Stir sugar and 1 tablespoon soda in prechilled old-fashioned glass until sugar dissolves. Add brandy and Madeira. Add ice to rim of glass. Stir. Add a splash of soda. Stir. Twist orange peel above drink and drop into glass. Sprinkle lightly with nutmeg.

IRISH CANADIAN SANGAREE

1¼ ozs. Canadian
   whisky
½ oz. Irish Mist liqueur
1 teaspoon orange juice
1 teaspoon lemon juice
Freshly grated nutmeg

Pour whisky, Irish Mist, orange juice and lemon juice into prechilled old-fashioned glass. Stir. Add ice to rim of glass. Stir. Sprinkle lightly with nutmeg.

SANGAREE COMFORT

1 oz. bourbon
1 oz. Southern Comfort
1 teaspoon lemon juice
1 teaspoon peach-
   flavored brandy
½ teaspoon sugar
Iced club soda
Freshly grated nutmeg

Stir bourbon, Southern Comfort, lemon juice, peach-flavored brandy and sugar in prechilled old-fashioned glass. Add ice to rim of glass. Add splash of soda. Stir. Sprinkle lightly with nutmeg.

SCOTCH SANGAREE

½ teaspoon honey
Iced club soda
2 ozs. Scotch
Lemon peel
Freshly grated nutmeg

Stir honey, 1 tablespoon soda and Scotch in prechilled old-fashioned glass until honey dissolves. Add ice to rim of glass. Add a splash of soda. Stir. Twist lemon peel above drink and drop into glass. Sprinkle lightly with nutmeg.

19

ODDBALLS

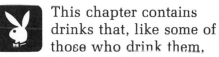 This chapter contains drinks that, like some of those who drink them, refuse to be classified in conventional categories. But each of the offbeat offerings that follows has a special appeal that sets it apart as a perfect potation to please that special someone or to make a fête more festive: the creamy smoothness of a sherry flip sipped next to a blazing fire, the reviving effects of an eye-opening pick-me-up the moanin' after a long night, the unparalleled pleasure of the sight and taste of a superbly created pousse-café, the crowning touch that a mist or frappé adds to any dinner. The only thing these drinks have in common—with those we've already discussed as well as with one another—is their excellence as libations for discriminating drinkers.

FLIPS

Flips, like pousse-cafés and frappés, prove that good liquids often come in small glasses. A flip is simply a liquor or wine with egg and sugar, shaken to a gay froth. Flips are rich; too much egg makes them overrich, in fact. For each drink it's best to use a small pullet-size egg or one large egg for two flips. A classic brandy flip, for instance, is made like this: 2 ounces brandy, 1 small egg and 1 teaspoon sugar are shaken with plenty of ice and then strained into a Delmonico glass. The flip is then lightly topped with freshly grated nutmeg. Following the same pattern, standard flips are made by substituting whiskey, gin, rum, applejack, port, sherry or Madeira for the brandy.

The following snug comforts are for winter holidays, mornings after and long, carefree brunches near a glowing fireplace.

BRANDIED APRICOT FLIP

1 oz. brandy
1 oz. apricot-flavored
  brandy
1 small egg
1 teaspoon sugar
Grated nutmeg

Shake brandy, apricot-flavored brandy, egg and sugar well with ice. Strain into prechilled Delmonico glass. Sprinkle with nutmeg.

COFFEE FLIP

1 oz. cognac
1 oz. tawny port
1 small egg
1 teaspoon sugar
Grated nutmeg

Shake cognac, port, egg and sugar well with ice. Strain into prechilled Delmonico glass. Sprinkle with nutmeg.

MADEIRA MINT FLIP

1¹/₂ ozs. Madeira
1 oz. chocolate-mint
  liqueur
1 small egg
1 teaspoon sugar
Grated nutmeg

Shake Madeira, chocolate-mint liqueur, egg and sugar well with ice. Strain into prechilled Delmonico glass. Sprinkle with nutmeg.

PERNOD FLIP

1 oz. Pernod
1/2 oz. Cointreau
2 teaspoons lemon juice
1 small egg
1 teaspoon sugar
Grated nutmeg

Shake Pernod, Cointreau, lemon juice, egg and sugar well with ice. Strain into prechilled Delmonico glass. Sprinkle with nutmeg.

STRAWBERRY RUM FLIP

1 oz. strawberry liqueur
1 oz. light rum
1 teaspoon lemon juice
1 small egg
1 teaspoon sugar
Grated nutmeg

Shake strawberry liqueur, rum, lemon juice, egg and sugar well with ice. Strain into prechilled Delmonico glass. Sprinkle with nutmeg.

STREGA FLIP

1 oz. Strega
1 oz. brandy
1/2 oz. orange juice
1 teaspoon lemon juice
1 small egg
1 teaspoon sugar
Grated nutmeg

Shake Strega, brandy, orange juice, lemon juice, egg and sugar well with ice. Strain into prechilled Delmonico glass. Sprinkle with nutmeg.

TOKAY FLIP

2 1/2 ozs. imported Tokay wine (Tokaji Aszu)
1 teaspoon sugar
1 small egg
Grated nutmeg

Shake Tokay, sugar and egg well with ice. Strain into prechilled Delmonico glass. Sprinkle with nutmeg. It may cause another Hungarian revolution to suggest that the magnificent imported Tokay be turned into a flip. Actually the wine turns into sweet bliss.

FRAPPÉS

Frappés and their close cousins, mists, are even more pleasing than ice cream and cake as a finale for a feast. Cool, clean and rich, they're a mixture of liqueurs poured over finely crushed ice. You can serve them freshly made, but we prefer to swizzle them up beforehand and store them in the freezer until the drinking lamp is lit. When you take them out, you'll find that an ice cap has formed on top of each drink. But the cap will loosen after a minute or two and the drink can be sipped from the rim with or without a short straw.

ALL-WHITE FRAPPÉ

¹/₂ oz. anisette
¹/₄ oz. white crème de menthe
¹/₂ oz. white crème de cacao
1 teaspoon lemon juice

Stir without ice. Pour over crushed ice in deep-saucer champagne glass.

BANANA RUM FRAPPÉ

¹/₂ oz. banana liqueur
¹/₂ oz. light rum
¹/₂ oz. orange juice

Stir without ice. Pour over crushed ice in deep-saucer champagne glass. Cool postscript for an oriental dinner.

BRANDY APRICOT FRAPPÉ

³/₄ oz. California brandy
¹/₂ oz. apricot-flavored brandy
¹/₄ oz. crème de noyaux

Stir without ice. Pour over crushed ice in deep-saucer champagne glass.

CHARTREUSE COGNAC FRAPPÉ

³/₄ oz. yellow Chartreuse
³/₄ oz. cognac

Stir without ice. Pour over crushed ice in deep-saucer champagne glass.

CHERRY GINGER FRAPPÉ

1 oz. cherry liqueur
1/4 oz. kirschwasser
1/4 oz. ginger-flavored
   brandy
1 brandied cherry
1 piece preserved ginger
   in syrup

Stir cherry liqueur, kirschwasser and ginger-flavored brandy without ice. Pour over crushed ice in deep-saucer champagne glass. Pierce brandied cherry and preserved ginger with cocktail spear and place over rim of glass.

CHOCOLATE ORANGE FRAPPÉ

3/4 oz. white crème de
   cacao
3/4 oz. orange juice
1 teaspoon Galliano or
   Roiano

Stir without ice. Pour over crushed ice in deep-saucer champagne glass.

COFFEE GRAND MARNIER

1/2 oz. coffee liqueur
1/2 oz. Grand Marnier
1/2 oz. orange juice
1 slice orange

Stir coffee liqueur, Grand Marnier and orange juice without ice. Pour over crushed ice in deep-saucer champagne glass. Add orange slice.

COGNAC MENTHE FRAPPÉ

1 oz. green crème de
   menthe
1/2 oz. cognac
2 large mint leaves

Stir crème de menthe and cognac without ice. Pour over crushed ice in deep-saucer champagne glass. Tear each mint leaf partially and place on drink.

GRAND MARNIER QUETSCH

1 oz. Grand Marnier
¹/₄ oz. quetsch
¹/₄ oz. orange juice
1 slice lemon

Stir Grand Marnier, quetsch and orange juice without ice. Pour over crushed ice in deep-saucer champagne glass. Add lemon slice. Mirabelle or slivovitz may be used in place of quetsch, since all are plum brandies.

KÜMMEL BLACKBERRY FRAPPÉ

¹/₂ oz. kümmel
¹/₂ oz. blackberry liqueur or blackberry-flavored brandy
1 teaspoon lemon juice

Stir without ice. Pour over crushed ice in deep-saucer champagne glass.

MIXED MOCHA FRAPPÉ

³/₄ oz. coffee liqueur
¹/₄ oz. white crème de menthe
¹/₄ oz. crème de cacao
¹/₄ oz. triple sec

Sugar-frost rim of deep-saucer champagne glass. Fill with crushed ice. Stir liqueurs without ice and pour over ice in glass.

PERNOD CURAÇAO FRAPPÉ

¹/₂ oz. Pernod
¹/₂ oz. curaçao
1 teaspoon lemon juice
2 teaspoons orange juice
1 thin slice orange

Stir Pernod, curaçao, lemon juice and orange juice without ice. Pour over crushed ice in deep-saucer champagne glass. Add orange slice.

SAMBUCA COFFEE FRAPPÉ

1 oz. sambuca
$^1/_2$ oz. coffee liqueur
Roasted coffee beans

Stir the sambuca and coffee liqueur without ice. Pour over crushed ice in deep-saucer champagne glass. Place the glass on a saucer along with about a half-dozen coffee beans to munch while sipping. It's an Italian custom; the more distinguished the guest, the more coffee beans placed alongside his sambuca.

SHERRIED CORDIAL MÉDOC FRAPPÉ

1 oz. Cordial Médoc
$^1/_2$ oz. amontillado
   sherry

Stir without ice. Pour over crushed ice in deep-saucer champagne glass.

SLOE LIME FRAPPÉ

1oz. sloe gin
$^1/_2$ oz. light rum
1 slice lime

Stir sloe gin and light rum without ice. Pour over crushed ice in deep-saucer champagne glass. Add lime slice. Sip without straw.

SOUTHERN COMFORT STRAWBERRY FRAPPÉ

$^3/_4$ oz. Southern Comfort
$^3/_4$ oz. strawberry liqueur
Orange peel
1 slice lemon

Stir Southern Comfort and strawberry liqueur without ice. Pour over crushed ice in deep-saucer champagne glass. Twist orange peel above drink and drop into glass. Add lemon slice. Sip on a summer evening under the stars.

MISTS

A mist is simply straight liquor poured over crushed ice. The normal proportions are 1½ ounces of liquor poured into an eight-ounce old-fashioned glass filled with crushed ice. Sometimes a twist of lemon is added. Mists are cousins of frappés, which are sweet liqueurs poured over crushed ice. Actually, the large amount of fine ice in a mist doesn't befog the liquor's intrinsic flavor; the quality of a fine whiskey in a mist will seem more vivid than the same shot bolted straight down. We now draw the veil from ten of the best-known mists.

Brandy Mist The triumphant flavor of cognac makes the noncognac brandies seem pallid by comparison (in mixed drinks the story may be different). Metaxa, the Greek semisweet brandy, creates a velvety, tremulous mist.

Scotch Mist Best when made with a full-bodied 12-year-old Highland dew. When it comes to mists, some of the lighter Scotches turn into ordinary fog.

Vodka Mist Ice and vodka emerge as just ice and vodka, nothing more; but an added dram of dry vermouth (a mere teaspoon or so) and a twist of lemon turn the mist into an instant vodka martini. Zubrovka vodka makes a subtle mist.

Kirschwasser Mist A happy, silvery mist with a hauntingly dry aftertaste of cherries.

Bourbon Mist Either 86 or 100 proof is fine, but more important than proof is a quality aged bourbon with a smooth, ripe flavor. Half bourbon and half Southern Comfort create a heavenly mist.

Rye Mist One of the best ways of appreciating genuine straight rye.

Blended U.S. Whiskey Mist As in bourbon, smoothness shows up in the very first sip. A slice of lemon is a pleasant garnish.

Canadian Mist Use top Canadian whisky, but increase portion to 1¾ ounces to keep the cool north-country flavor from dissipating too soon.

Gin Mist It's surprising how close a gin mist is to the modern martini. Add a tiny splash of dry vermouth for a martini mist. A good way to introduce Dutch genever gin to someone who's never tasted it is via the mist.

Rum Mist   The potent flavors of Martinique and Jamaican rums emerge beautifully in mists. Light rum is extremely pleasant with a slice of lime or a small gardenia as garnish. For a more rummy accent, float a teaspoon of 151-proof rum on a light-rum mist.

PICK-ME-UPS

The ancient Egyptians thought that boiled cabbage would prevent a big head after an all-night drinking session. A ground swallow's beak blended with myrrh was recommended by the Assyrians. In South America the Warau Indian women took care of their overindulgent males by deftly tying them like mummies in hammocks until their hangovers passed. In this country the "hair of the dog"—the very thing that caused you to see double—may be the shot in the arm that will straighten your sight. For generations, experienced barmen, especially in men's clubs, where hangover victims can be observed and treated at close range, have vouched for the hair-of-the-dog therapy. Naturally, the danger of taking a swig of liquor the morning after is that the stimulus and relief it brings may provide just enough narcosis to set you right back on the rocky road to ruin. Nevertheless, the effect of a small amount of liquor, especially if combined with citrus juice or tomato juice, seems in many cases to have an extremely salutary effect. The following are from PLAYBOY's repertory of classic and modern pick-me-ups.

CANADIAN STAVE

2 ozs. Canadian whisky
1 oz. Red Dubonnet
1/2 egg white
1/4 teaspoon Angostura bitters
2 teaspoons lemon juice
2 dashes Tabasco sauce

Shake all ingredients well with ice. Strain into prechilled old-fashioned glass. Add ice cubes to fill glass. Stir well.

CLAM-JUICE COCKTAIL

4 ozs. clam juice
1/2 oz. catsup
1/4 oz. lemon juice
1 dash Worcestershire sauce
Salt and pepper
Celery salt

Shake clam juice, catsup, lemon juice, Worcestershire sauce, salt and pepper well with ice. Strain into prechilled Delmonico glass. Sprinkle with celery salt. Nonalcoholic but a wonderful bracer.

COGNAC COUPLING

2 ozs. cognac
1 oz. tawny port
¹/₂ oz. Pernod
1 teaspoon lemon juice
¹/₂ teaspoon Peychaud's
   bitters

*Shake well with ice. Strain into
prechilled old-fashioned glass.
Add ice cubes to fill glass. Stir
well.*

GIN BRACER

2 ozs. gin
¹/₂ oz. catsup
¹/₂ oz. lemon juice
1 dash Tabasco sauce
1 dash celery salt
¹/₄ teaspoon Worcester-
   shire sauce
1 cup crushed ice

*Put all ingredients into blender.
Blend at low speed 15–20 seconds.
Pour into tall 10-oz. glass. Add ice
cubes to fill glass.*

MORNING FIZZ

2 ozs. blended whiskey
¹/₂ egg white
¹/₂ oz. lemon juice
1 teaspoon sugar
¹/₂ teaspoon Pernod
Iced club soda

*Shake whiskey, egg white, lemon
juice, sugar and Pernod well with
ice. Strain into tall 8-oz. glass.
Add a splash of soda and ice to
fill glass. Stir.*

POLYNESIAN PICK-ME-UP

¹/₂ cup pineapple juice
1¹/₂ ozs. vodka
¹/₂ teaspoon curry
   powder
¹/₂ teaspoon lemon juice
1 tablespoon cream
2 dashes Tabasco sauce
¹/₂ cup crushed ice
Cayenne pepper

*Put pineapple juice, vodka, curry
powder, lemon juice, cream,
Tabasco sauce and crushed ice
into blender. Blend 10 seconds at
high speed. Pour into prechilled
old-fashioned glass. Dust very
lightly with cayenne.*

PRAIRIE OYSTER

1¹/₂ ozs. cognac
2 teaspoons cider
vinegar
¹/₂ oz. Worcestershire
sauce
1 teaspoon catsup
¹/₂ teaspoon Angostura
bitters
1 egg yolk
Cayenne pepper

Shake cognac, vinegar, Worcestershire sauce, catsup and bitters well with ice. Strain into prechilled old-fashioned glass. Add an ice cube or two to fill glass almost to rim. Place egg yolk on top of drink without breaking it. Sprinkle yolk lightly with cayenne. This oldest and most stunning of all morning-after drinks should be swallowed in one long, determined gulp. Grit your teeth. Then open your eyes very slowly.

RUDDY MARY

1¹/₂ ozs. aquavit
¹/₂ cup tomato juice
1 tablespoon cream
1 dash Tabasco
¹/₂ egg yolk
¹/₄ oz. lemon juice
¹/₄ oz. catsup
¹/₂ cup crushed ice

Put all ingredients into blender. Blend at high speed 20 seconds. Pour into old-fashioned glass. When foam settles, add ice to fill glass to rim.

POUSSE-CAFÉ

This showy little drink is one of the oldest bits of nonsense known to bartenders—and, needless to say, the number of drinkers who never stop loving nonsense is greater than ever. The pousse-café is a series of liqueurs poured into a small, straight-sided pousse-café glass so that each forms a layer. Since the liqueurs are of different weights or densities, the heaviest stays on the bottom, the next heaviest directly above it, and so on. The main problem that bedevils the pousse-café specialist is that the densities of liqueurs of the same flavor often vary from one brand to the next. One man's menthe may not rise above another man's parfait amour. Since the density of a liqueur is not indicated on the bottle's label, a certain amount of trial and error may be necessary in building a pousse-café. As a general guide, remember that frequently the higher a liqueur's alcoholic content, the lower its density. This doesn't apply in all cases, but it's something of a help. The so-called *demi-sec* liqueurs are lighter than the sweet crèmes, and U.S. fruit-flavored brandies are lighter than liqueurs. If you're in doubt about a recipe, make an experimental pousse-café before the guests arrive, and when you find a formula that works, stick to it as long as you're using the same brands of liqueurs.

To keep the ingredients from mingling, pour them slowly over the back of a teaspoon, with the tip of the spoon held against the inside of the glass. Pour slowly and steadily, keeping your eye on the liquid as it flows. If you follow this procedure carefully, the layers should stay separate; you may find, in fact, that a liqueur poured in the wrong order will seep down or rise up to its proper level and stay there intact. For a party, you can make a large number of pousse-cafés beforehand, and if you place them carefully in the refrigerator, each small rainbow will remain undisturbed until you need it.

A pousse-café may be of three, four or five layers. Each layer needn't be equal, but each should be of a distinctly different color when held at eye level. Nonalcoholic liquids such as syrups and cream may be poured along with the liqueurs or other spirits. Here are 12 pousse-café combinations, with the heaviest liquid listed first and the lighter ones in ascending order. To both create and divert conversation, make an assortment with several combinations on the same tray.

White crème de cacao, cherry liqueur, kümmel and a dab of whipped cream.

Green crème de menthe, Galliano, blackberry liqueur and kirschwasser.

Banana liqueur, Cherry Heering or Cherry Karise and cognac.

Peach liqueur, kirsch liqueur (not kirschwasser) and Pernod.

Orzata or orgeat, crème de noyaux, curaçao and sweet cream mixed with enough crème de noyaux to make cream pink.

Passion-fruit syrup, green crème de menthe, strawberry liqueur and ouzo.

Grenadine, crème de cacao, Drambuie and sweet cream flavored with crème de menthe.

Crème de noyaux, anisette, Tuaca and a dab of whipped cream.

Grenadine, crème de cacao, triple sec and Forbidden Fruit.

Crème de cacao, maraschino liqueur, Rosémint, yellow Chartreuse and cognac.

Parfait amour, cherry liqueur, anisette and sweet cream flavored with a small amount of parfait amour.

20

THE
BRIMMING
BOWL

In the world of entertaining, there is no more delightfully flexible potable than a good punch. This protean party favorite can assume any festive task to which it's put. Made with light Moselle or Rhenish wines, it can beguile your guests with a light, delicate flavor that rests easily on the tongue. Switch to the heavier-duty brandies and rums and it can singlehandedly catalyze jolly high spirits and flowing conversation.

Nevertheless, for some time the punch bowl was trotted out only at the year-end saturnalia, when it was filled with a hot wassail or a rich whiskey eggnog, emptied a few times and then stashed away in dry storage for the next 12 months. But today, more and more hosts are reviving the reigns of the four Georges of England, when men like David Garrick and Samuel Johnson vied with each other all year round to invent newer and stronger punch recipes as they ladled their way through clubs and taverns all over England, and when punch bowls in numerous shapes and sizes sparkled invitingly and were the center of conviviality at celebrations of everything from weddings to military triumphs.

Now, as then, there are a few punch recipes in which fruit has to be marinated in liquors for a day or two, but—happily—those are the exceptions. Generally, an hour or so is all you need for ripening the strong and the weak, the tart and the sweet into a really superior punch. And yet, for all its simplicity, the punch bowl, with its gleaming island of ice in a sea of liquor, turns any casual affair into a gala occasion. The mere sight of the brimming bowl seems an irresistible enticement to drinkers of all persuasions, be they light, moderate or heavy.

Punch is made cold in two ways—by prechilling all the ingredients from the brandy to the bitters, and by placing a floating island of ice in the bowl itself to both cool and properly dilute the liquid—though a few cold punches, such as some of the champagne varieties, aren't diluted with ice but instead are sometimes ice-girt in a surrounding vessel of crushed ice. These days, when the iceman no longer cometh, it's sometimes difficult to buy a really good-sized chunk. However, in our age of the cube, this is no particular problem; in fact, cubes are faster in their chilling effect than a block. But to serious punch makers, they are puny craft alongside the traditional icy blockbuster in the punch bowl. You can make your own by simply freezing water in a metal or plastic container, a deep saucepan or metal mixing bowl. For each gallon of punch, you'll normally need a chunk of ice made with two quarts of water. After freezing, dip the sides of the bowl in warm water for a few seconds and the ice will slide free. The top may form a slight peak and reveal a crack or two, but the inverted iceberg will be smooth and should float serenely.

The punch recipes that follow each make approximately a gallon of potables, enough for eight bibulous guests at three rounds apiece.

APPLE GINGER PUNCH

24 ozs. apple brandy, either calvados or applejack
2 ozs. maraschino liqueur
2 ozs. kirsch
1 quart pineapple-grapefruit juice
24 ozs. green-ginger wine
1 quart plus 1 pint ginger beer
2 red apples
2 yellow apples

Chill all ingredients. Pour all liquids except ginger beer over large block of ice in punch bowl. Stir well. Let mixture ripen 1 hour in refrigerator. Cut unpeeled apples into wedgelike slices, discarding core. Just before serving, pour ginger beer into bowl. Float apple slices on top.

ARTILLERYMEN'S PUNCH

1 quart 86-proof bourbon
9 ozs. light rum
4 ozs. dark Jamaican rum
6 ozs. apricot-flavored brandy
12 ozs. lemon juice
24 ozs. orange juice
1 quart strong black tea
1/4 cup sugar

Pour all ingredients over a large block of ice in punch bowl. Stir well to dissolve sugar. Let mixture ripen 1 hour in refrigerator before serving.

BARBADOS BOWL

8 medium-size ripe bananas
1 cup lime juice
1 cup sugar
1 fifth light rum
8 ozs. 151-proof rum
1 quart plus 12 ozs. pineapple juice
12 ozs. mango nectar
2 limes, sliced

Chill all ingredients except bananas. Cut 6 bananas into thin slices and place in electric blender with lime juice and sugar. Blend until smooth. Pour over block of ice in punch bowl. Add both kinds of rum, pineapple juice and mango nectar. Stir well. Let mixture ripen in refrigerator 1 hour before serving. Cut remaining 2 bananas into thin slices. Float banana and lime slices on punch.

3 tablespoons jasmine
   tea
3 cups boiling water
1 fifth bourbon
8 ozs. Madeira
8 ozs. lemon juice
1½ ozs. Pernod
4 ozs. Falernum
1 quart plus 1 pint
   ginger ale
3 lemons, thinly sliced

BERMUDA
BOURBON PUNCH

*Pour boiling water over tea leaves.
Steep for 5 minutes; strain, cool to
room temperature and chill in
refrigerator. Over large block of ice
in punch bowl pour tea, bourbon,
Madeira, lemon juice, Pernod and
Falernum. Stir well. Let mixture
ripen 1 hour in refrigerator. Add
ginger ale and sliced lemons. Add
several spiced walnuts (recipe
below) to each drink after pouring
it into punch cup.*

1 egg white
2 teaspoons cold water
½ lb. shelled walnuts,
   halves
1 cup sugar
1 tablespoon ground
   cinnamon
¼ teaspoon ground
   cloves
⅛ teaspoon ground
   nutmeg

SPICED WALNUTS

*Beat egg white until slightly foamy
but not stiff. Add water and mix
well. Combine egg white and
walnuts in a bowl; stir to coat
nuts; drain thoroughly in colander
to remove excess egg white. In
another bowl, combine sugar,
cinnamon, cloves and nutmeg.
Preheat oven to 325° F. Dip
walnuts, a few pieces at a time,
into sugar mixture (they should be
coated thoroughly but should not
have thick gobs of sugar adhering
to them), place them on a greased
baking sheet and bake 20 minutes,
or until medium brown. Remove
from baking sheet with spatula,
separating them from sugar
coating on pan. Cool to room
temperature.*

BLACK-CHERRY
RUM PUNCH

1 fifth light rum
4 ozs. 151-proof rum
4 ozs. dark Jamaican
  rum
2 17-oz. cans pitted
  black cherries in heavy
  syrup
8 ozs. fresh lemon juice
4 ozs. fresh orange juice
4 ozs. fresh lime juice
8 ozs. Cherry Heering
8 ozs. crème de cassis
2 limes, thinly sliced
1 quart club soda

*Put all ingredients except soda
into punch bowl. Add block of ice.
Stir well. Refrigerate 1 hour. Add
soda. Stir well.*

BRANDY
EGGNOG BOWL

12 eggs
$^1/_2$ cup sugar
1 fifth cognac or
  noncognac brandy
4 ozs. Jamaican rum
3 quarts milk
8 ozs. cream
Grated nutmeg

*Carefully separate egg yolks from
whites. In punch bowl, combine
egg yolks and sugar. Beat well
with a wire whisk. Gradually add
cognac, rum, milk and cream.
Beat well. Taste. Add more sugar
if desired. Place the bowl in the
refrigerator for at least 2 hours.
Just before serving, beat egg whites
in a separate bowl or in mixer, in
two batches if necessary, until
stiff. Fold whites into punch; that
is, do not mix them with a
round-the-bowl movement but use
the wire whisk in a down-over-up
stroke until whites are thoroughly
blended. Ladle into cups. Sprinkle
with nutmeg.*

2 quarts plus 6 ozs.
  cranberry juice
1 quart 100-proof vodka
6 ozs. cherry liqueur
1 tablespoon orange-
  flower water
24 ozs. orange juice
1 teaspoon ground
  cinnamon
1/2 teaspoon ground
  allspice
1/4 teaspoon ground
  nutmeg
2 limes, thinly sliced

CAPE COD
CRANBERRY PUNCH

*Chill all liquid ingredients. Mix
cinnamon, allspice and nutmeg
with a small amount of vodka
until a smooth, lump-free paste is
formed. Pour the paste and all
other liquids over large block of
ice in punch bowl. Stir well.
Refrigerate 1 hour before serving.
Float lime slices on top of punch.*

1 fifth blue curaçao
8 ozs. lemon juice
4 fifths dry champagne
Peel of 2 lemons

CHAMPAGNE BLUES

*Chill all ingredients. Cut lemon
peel into strips 1 1/2 to 2 inches
long and 1/4 inch wide. Pour
curaçao and lemon juice into glass
punch bowl. Stir well. Add
champagne and stir slightly. Float
lemon peel, yellow side up, in
bowl. Do not use ice in bowl. It
may be surrounded by cracked
ice, if desired, by placing glass
bowl in vessel of larger diameter.*

4 fifths iced *brut*
  champagne
5 ozs. iced kirsch liqueur
  (not dry kirschwasser)
5 ozs. iced oloroso
  (cream) sherry
4 ozs. iced lemon juice
16 ozs. iced orange juice

CHAMPAGNE PUNCH
WITH KIRSCH

*Pour all ingredients into
prechilled punch bowl. Stir
lightly. Bowl may be surrounded
by ice in larger bowl, or punch
may be made in pitchers
surrounded by ice.*

CHAMPAGNE PUNCH WITH MARASCHINO

6 ozs. maraschino
  liqueur
6 ozs. cognac
1 teaspoon orange bitters
2 oranges, thinly sliced
1 lemon, thinly sliced
4 fifths iced *brut*
  champagne

Put maraschino, cognac, orange bitters and sliced fruit into punch bowl. Let mixture brew about 1 hour in refrigerator. Place large chunk of ice in bowl. Pour champagne over ice. Stir slightly.

CHAMPAGNE SHERBET PUNCH

2 quarts lemon sherbet
  or lemon ice, frozen
  very hard
5 fifths iced *brut*
  champagne
1 1/2 teaspoons Angostura
  bitters

Be sure lemon sherbet has been in freezing section of refrigerator set at the coldest point for at least 1 day. Place lemon sherbet in prechilled punch bowl. Pour champagne over sherbet. Add bitters. Stir. Let mixture ripen in refrigerator for about 15–20 minutes before serving.

FISH HOUSE PUNCH I

1 1/2 cups sugar
1 quart cold water (not
  carbonated water)
1 fifth cognac
1 fifth golden rum
1 fifth Jamaican rum
24 ozs. lemon juice
6 ozs. peach-flavored
  brandy

Put sugar into punch bowl. Add about 1 cup of the water and stir until sugar is dissolved. Add all other ingredients, including balance of water. Let mixture ripen in refrigerator about 1 hour. Place large chunk of ice in bowl. Ladle punch over ice. Add more cold water if a weaker mixture is desired.

2 12-oz. pkgs. frozen
  sliced peaches, thawed
1 quart golden rum
1 fifth cognac
1 pint lemon juice
1 cup sugar
1 quart ice water

FISH HOUSE PUNCH II

*Put peaches into blender. Blend 1
minute at high speed. Pour over
large block of ice in punch bowl.
Add rum, cognac, lemon juice,
sugar and water. Stir well to
dissolve sugar. Let punch ripen in
refrigerator for about 1 hour before
serving. A modern version of the
colonial recipe fish house punch I.*

2 21-oz. bottles
  coffee-cream Marsala
  wine
2 24-oz. bottles Italian
  rosé wine
1 fifth plus 8 ozs. brandy
4 ozs. lemon juice
2 oranges

FLORENTINE PUNCH

*Chill all ingredients. Pour both
kinds of wine, brandy and lemon
juice over large block of ice in
punch bowl. Stir well. Refrigerate
1 hour. Cut oranges into thin
slices. Cut slices crosswise and
float atop punch.*

1 fifth light dry red wine
1 whole orange
1 ripe Elberta peach,
  peeled and sliced
6 slices lemon
1½ ozs. cognac
1 oz. triple sec
1 oz. maraschino
1 tablespoon or more
  sugar to taste
6 ozs. iced club soda

SANGRIA

*Cut entire peel of orange in a
single strip, beginning at stem end
and continuing until spiral
reaches bottom of fruit. White part
should be cut along with outer
peel, so that orange fruit is
exposed. Leave peel attached to
orange bottom, so that fruit may
be suspended in pitcher. Pour
wine into glass pitcher. Add
peach, lemon, cognac, triple sec,
maraschino and sugar. Stir to
dissolve sugar. Carefully place
orange in pitcher, fastening top
end of peel over rim. Let mixture
marinate at room temperature at
least 1 hour. Add soda and 1 tray
of ice cubes to pitcher. Stir.
Six 6–8 oz. drinks.*

WHITE SANGRIA

1 fifth dry white wine
1 whole orange
2 slices lemon
2 slices lime
1 oz. cognac
2 tablespoons sugar
1 piece stick cinnamon
8 large strawberries,
   stems removed, halved
6 ozs. iced club soda

Cut entire peel of orange, following procedure in preceeding recipe. Pour wine into glass pitcher. Add lemon, lime, cognac, sugar, cinnamon and strawberries. Stir to dissolve sugar. Carefully place orange in pitcher, fastening top end of peel over rim. Let mixture marinate at room temperature at least 1 hour. Add soda and 1 tray of ice cubes to pitcher. Stir.
Six 6-8 oz. drinks.

MOSELLE BOWL

1 very ripe medium-size
   pineapple
1/2 cup sugar
12 ozs. Grand Marnier
16 ozs. brandy
4 24-oz. bottles Moselle
   wine
1 quart large ripe
   strawberries

Cut ends off pineapple, remove shell and all "eyes" and cut lengthwise into 4 pieces. Cut away hard core from each piece; then cut crosswise into thin pieces. Place pineapple, sugar, Grand Marnier and brandy in salad bowl or mixing bowl. Marinate, covered, in refrigerator at least 24 hours— 48 hours if possible. Pour well-chilled wine into punch bowl with large block of ice. Add pineapple mixture and stir well. Let mixture ripen in bowl 1/2 hour before serving. Cut stems off strawberries. Cut lengthwise in half and float on punch.

ORANGE ALMOND BOWL

6 ozs. slivered almonds
2 tablespoons melted butter
Salt
18 ozs. blended whiskey
12 ozs. Danish aquavit
1 quart plus 8 ozs. orange juice
8 ozs. sweet vermouth
1 teaspoon orange bitters
Peel of 2 large California oranges
1½ quarts quinine water

Preheat oven to 375° F. Place almonds in shallow pan or pie plate. Pour butter over almonds, mixing well. Place pan in oven and bake until almonds are medium brown, about 8 to 10 minutes, stirring once during baking. Avoid scorching. Sprinkle with salt. Chill almonds and all other ingredients. Pour whiskey, aquavit, orange juice, vermouth and bitters over large block of ice in punch bowl. Refrigerate mixture for 1 hour. Cut orange peel into narrow strips about 2 inches long. Pour quinine water into bowl. Stir. Float orange peel and almonds on punch.

PHI BETA BLUEBERRY

1 fifth 100-proof vodka
16 ozs. Metaxa brandy
16 ozs. bottled blueberry syrup
12 ozs. lemon juice
2 quarts club soda
2 lemons, thinly sliced
1 pint cultivated blueberries

Chill all ingredients. Pour vodka, Metaxa, blueberry syrup and lemon juice over large block of ice in punch bowl. Let mixture ripen in refrigerator 1 hour before serving. Pour club soda into bowl and stir. Float lemon slices and blueberries on punch.

WHISKEY PUNCH

3 cups orange juice
1 cup lemon juice
1 cup sugar
2 lemons, thinly sliced
2 quarts blended whiskey
1 quart iced club soda

Put fruit juices and sugar into punch bowl. Stir until sugar dissolves. Add lemon slices. Place a large chunk of ice in bowl. Add whiskey. Refrigerate 1 hour. Add club soda. Stir. Additional club soda may be added if desired.

21

HOT CHEER

When hot drinks had to wait on icy weather, the ideal accompaniments for a hot-toddy party were a raging blizzard and a roaring fireplace. They're still picturesque backdrops, but nowadays any cool evening in the fall or winter is reason enough for filling the cups to the brim with grogs and nogs—and not just at the hearthside. Almost any casual brisk-weather get-together—a tail-gate party at a football or soccer field, a caravan to the ski country—is perfect for tapping the cordial pleasures of the thermos. And a demitasse cup filled with a blend of warm blackberry liqueur, cognac and lemon is the most tranquil joy we can imagine before sinking into an unbroken night's sleep.

Hot drinks should be just warm enough so that the flavors seem to float like the soft clouds on an old silk painting—but not so hot that they burn the lips. Heat them in a saucepan or chafing dish to just short of the boiling point; then turn off the flame and let them cool somewhat before pouring.

One of the oldest bar tools for making drinks hot was the loggerhead—a long iron tool with a cup or ball at one end. In colonial days the cup was used, among other purposes, for melting pitch to be poured upon the crews of attacking naval vessels; those were the days when men at loggerheads weren't kidding. It's now remembered as a fireplace device for the much more advanced purpose of heating rum flips. In time the loggerhead was succeeded by the poker, which serves just as well for those who feel like indulging in a bit of showmanship. Find one that's ash-free—old pokers with the soot of ages upon them aren't nearly as practical as clean ones that have never seen a fireplace—and heat it glowing hot in a normal gas flame. For reviving drinks that have become coolish from standing too long, keep the poker in the flame for at least three minutes before plunging it into the waiting mug.

The recipes that follow require no such fiery baptism (though it may win applause, it won't improve the drinks); nor are they intended to be enjoyed only at a bibbing party. Just as they can be served day or night, indoors or out, in fair weather or foul, they'll be the best of drinking companions with a colorful variety of meals: a warm Danish toddy of aquavit and Cherry Heering before a smorgasbord or smorrebrod, a buttered bourbon and ginger before a chafing dish of creamed chicken hash, a blackberry demitasse after an urban luau.

Several of the recipes in this chapter depart from the usual one-drink formula. The reason: For some hot potations the nature of the ingredients makes the preparation of a single drink impractical. The blue blazer, for example, should be prepared for two in order to create a decent blaze. The taste of the gin and jerry becomes unpleasantly eggy unless two are made with each egg. The average *café brûlot* set serves eight, so the *café diable* recipe is for that number. And so on; wherever a recipe makes more than a single drink, it's because careful party and taste testing have shown that the number specified is the minimum for best results. But whichever recipes you try, and for however many people, you'll find that all create warm contentment.

APRICOT TOM AND JERRY

1 egg, white and yolk
   separated
Salt
$1/8$ teaspoon ground
   allspice
$1/8$ teaspoon ground
   cinnamon
$1^1/2$ teaspoons sugar
1 oz. apricot-flavored
   brandy
1 oz. blended whiskey
1 oz. milk
1 oz. cream
Freshly grated nutmeg

Beat egg yolk until light. Add a pinch of salt and the allspice, cinnamon and sugar, blending well. Beat white separately in a small, narrow bowl until stiff. Slowly fold yolk into white. Put egg mixture into a 10-oz. tom-and-jerry mug. Heat apricot-flavored brandy, whiskey, milk and cream until bubbles appear around edge of pan. Do not boil. Pour into mug slowly, stirring as liquid mixture is added. Sprinkle with nutmeg.

BLACKBERRY DEMITASSE

1 oz. blackberry liqueur
   or blackberry-flavored
   brandy
1 tablespoon blackberry
   jelly
$1/2$ oz. cognac
$1/2$ oz. water
$1/2$ teaspoon lemon juice
$1/4$ thin slice lemon

Heat blackberry liqueur, jelly, cognac, water and lemon juice without boiling. Stir well until jelly is completely dissolved. Pour into demitasse cup. Add lemon slice.

BLUE BLAZER

6 ozs. Irish whiskey or
   Scotch
2 tablespoons honey
$1/4$ cup boiling water
Lemon peel

(Serves 2)
Both nightcap and toast, the blue blazer should be served steaming hot and sipped slowly. (And to create a decent blaze, it should always be made for two.) For mixing it you need two heavy and rather deep mugs, about 12-oz. capacity. Rinse them with hot or boiling water before mixing the drink. Then pour honey and boiling water into one mug and stir until honey is dissolved. Heat whiskey in a saucepan until it's hot but not boiling. Pour into second mug. Light it. Pour the

whiskey—carefully—back and forth between the mugs. The flowing blue-flaming stream will be best appreciated in a dimly lit room. Since a few drams of the blazing whiskey may spill, it's best to pour it over a large silver or china platter. When flames subside, pour the blazer into two thick cut-glass goblets. Twist the lemon peel over the blazer and drop it into the drink. Some bartenders wear asbestos gloves when making a blue blazer.

BUTTERED APPLE GROG

1 oz. apple brandy
1 oz. dry vermouth
2 ozs. apple juice
2 whole cloves
1/4 baked apple, fresh or
    canned
1 teaspoon sweet butter
1 slice lemon
Sugar

Heat apple brandy, vermouth, apple juice and cloves until hot but not boiling. Into an old-fashioned glass or coffee cup put baked apple, butter and lemon slice. Pour apple-brandy mixture into the glass. Add 1 teaspoon syrup if canned baked apple is used, or add sugar to taste. Stir until butter dissolves.

BUTTERED BOURBON AND GINGER

1 1/2 ozs. bourbon
1 oz. ginger-flavored
    brandy
1 teaspoon sweet butter
1 cinnamon stick
6 ozs. apple juice
Freshly grated nutmeg

Into a 10-oz. mug or silver tankard pour bourbon and ginger-flavored brandy. Add butter and cinnamon stick to mug. Heat apple juice up to boiling point, but do not boil. Pour into mug. Stir until butter dissolves. Sprinkle with nutmeg.

CAFÉ DIABLE

(8 demitasse cups)

2¹/₂ measuring cups
  extra-strong fresh
  black coffee
2 cinnamon sticks,
  broken in half
8 whole allspice
4 whole cardamom
  seeds, removed from
  shell
Grated rind of ¹/₂ orange
5 ozs. cognac
3 ozs. Grand Marnier
2 ozs. sambuca
  (anise-flavored Italian
  liqueur)
2 tablespoons sugar

In a deep chafing dish or café
brûlot *set, simmer ¹/₂ cup coffee,
cinnamon sticks, allspice,
cardamom seeds and orange rind
about 2 or 3 minutes to release
spice flavors, stirring constantly.
Add cognac, Grand Marnier and
sambuca. When liquors are hot,
set ablaze. Stir with a
long-handled ladle or spoon until
flames subside. Add balance of
coffee and sugar. When* café diable
*is hot, ladle or spoon it into
demitasse cups. A delightful
postprandial drink—but you'd
best rehearse it before debuting for
guests. Once learned, it's an
amiably engaging routine.*

CRÈME DE CACAO NIGHTCAP

(Serves 4)

¹/₄ cup cream
2 teaspoons sugar
1 tablespoon crème de
  cacao
10 ozs. milk
4 ozs. crème de cacao
2 ozs. California brandy
3 tablespoons sugar
Cocoa

*Beat cream in small, narrow bowl
until whipped. Stir 2 teaspoons
sugar and 1 tablespoon crème de
cacao into whipped cream. Store
in refrigerator until needed. Heat
milk, 4 ozs. crème de cacao,
brandy and 3 tablespoons sugar
until hot but not boiling. Pour hot
milk mixture into four footed
whiskey-sour glasses or small
goblets. Spoon whipped cream on
top. Put a small quantity of cocoa
into a small fine wire strainer.
Shake strainer above each drink,
sprinkling lightly with cocoa.
Place glass on saucer for serving.*

2 whole cloves
2 whole allspice
1 cinnamon stick
1 slice orange
2 ozs. Cherry Heering or
  domestic Cherry Karise
1 oz. aquavit
1/2 oz. kümmel
5 ozs. cranberry juice

DANISH TODDY

*Put cloves, allspice, cinnamon
stick and orange slice into a 10-oz.
mug. Heat Cherry Heering,
aquavit, kümmel and cranberry
juice until hot but not boiling.
Pour into mug.*

4 ozs. gin
1 oz. yellow Chartreuse
3 ozs. orange juice
1 teaspoon sugar
1 egg
Ground cinnamon

GIN AND JERRY
(Serves 2)

*Pour gin, Chartreuse, orange juice
and sugar into saucepan. Heat
almost to boiling point, but don't
boil. Beat egg in narrow bowl with
rotary beater until egg is very light
and foamy. Slowly, while stirring
constantly, pour hot liquid into
bowl. Pour into preheated
tom-and-jerry mugs or punch
cups. Sprinkle lightly with
cinnamon.*

2 whole cloves
2 whole allspice
1 inch stick cinnamon
1 teaspoon sugar
1 1/2 ozs. hot light rum
1/2 oz. hot dark Jamaican
  rum
Boiling water
1 teaspoon sweet butter

HOT BUTTERED RUM

*Put the cloves, allspice, stick
cinnamon and sugar into a mug
with a tablespoon or two of
boiling water. Let the mixture
stand 5 minutes. Add the hot rum
(both kinds), 2 ozs. boiling water
and butter. Stir until butter
dissolves. Add more sugar if
desired.*

2 ozs. dark Jamaican
  rum
1/2 teaspoon maraschino
  liqueur
1 oz. lemon juice
1 teaspoon sugar
1 pat butter, equal to 2
  teaspoons
Boiling water
1 slice lemon
Freshly grated nutmeg

PLAYBOY'S HOT
BUTTERED RUM

*Pour rum, maraschino liqueur and
lemon juice into 12-oz. mug. Add
sugar and butter. Fill with boiling
water. Stir to dissolve butter and
sugar. Add lemon slice. Grate
nutmeg on top. As served at the
Lake Geneva Playboy Club-Hotel.*

HOT DRAMBUIE TODDY

2 ozs. Drambuie
1/2 oz. lemon juice
1 slice lemon
1 slice orange
4 ozs. boiling water
1 piece stick cinnamon

Pour Drambuie and lemon juice into preheated mug or punch cup. (To preheat mug, fill with boiling water for about a minute; then discard water.) Add lemon slice, orange slice and 4 ozs. boiling water. Stir with cinnamon stick—and leave it in the mug.

HOT EGGNOG

1 egg
Salt
1 tablespoon sugar
3/4 cup (6 ozs.) hot milk
2 ozs. hot cognac
1 teaspoon dark
   Jamaican rum
Ground nutmeg

Put whole egg and dash of salt into mixing bowl. Beat egg until it is very thick and lemon yellow in color. Add sugar and beat until sugar is blended in. Add hot milk, cognac and rum. Stir well. Pour into mug. Sprinkle lightly with a dash of ground nutmeg.

HOT PORT FLIP

3 ozs. port wine
1 oz. cognac
1 teaspoon sugar
1/4 teaspoon instant
   coffee
1 small egg
1 tablespoon cream
Freshly grated nutmeg

Pour wine and cognac into saucepan. Add sugar. Stir well. Heat but don't boil. Stir in instant coffee. In a narrow bowl, beat egg with rotary beater until egg is very foamy. Stir in cream. Very slowly, while stirring constantly, pour hot liquid into egg mixture. Pour into preheated mug. Sprinkle with nutmeg.

HOT TODDY

1 teaspoon sugar
3 whole cloves
1 inch stick cinnamon
1 thin slice lemon
1 oz. boiling water
2 ozs. hot bourbon
2 ozs. boiling water
Ground nutmeg

Into a heavy mug put the sugar, cloves, stick cinnamon and slice of lemon. Add 1 oz. boiling water. Stir well. Let the mixture stand about 5 minutes. Add the hot bourbon and the 2 ozs. boiling water. Stir. Sprinkle lightly with nutmeg.

5 to 6 ozs. fresh, hot
   black coffee
1¹/₂ ozs. Irish whiskey
1 teaspoon sugar
Sweetened whipped
   cream

IRISH COFFEE
*Warm an 8-oz. goblet or
Irish-coffee glass by rinsing it in
very hot or boiling water. Pour
coffee and whiskey into goblet.
Add sugar. Stir until sugar is
dissolved. Add a generous dab of
whipped cream.*

1 oz. Kahlúa coffee
   liqueur
4 ozs. fresh, hot black
   coffee
Ground cinnamon
Sweetened whipped
   cream

MEXICAN COFFEE
*Pour liqueur and coffee into
Irish-coffee glass. Sprinkle with
cinnamon. Stir. Top with whipped
cream. As served in the Chicago
Playboy Club.*

1 cup boiling water
¹/₂ cup sugar
1 lemon, sliced
1 orange, sliced
12 whole allspice
12 whole cloves
4 inches stick cinnamon
1 fifth dry red wine

MULLED CLARET
(6 to 8 drinks)
*In large saucepan combine the
boiling water, sugar, sliced lemon,
sliced orange, allspice, cloves and
stick cinnamon. Bring to a boil.
Reduce flame and simmer 5
minutes. Add the wine. Bring up
to the boiling point. Do not boil,
but simmer 10 minutes. Pour the
hot mulled wine into thick glasses
or mugs. Place a slice of lemon, a
slice of orange and a few whole
spices in each glass.*

MULLED MADEIRA AND BOURBON

2¹/₂ ozs. Madeira
1 oz. bourbon
1 oz. Lillet
¹/₄ teaspoon orange bitters
4 ozs. water
1 tablespoon brown
  sugar
1 cinnamon stick
2 whole cloves
¹/₂ slice lemon
Orange peel

Heat Madeira, bourbon, Lillet, orange bitters, water and brown sugar until hot but not boiling. Put cinnamon stick, cloves and lemon slice into 10-oz. mug or metal tankard. Fill mug with Madeira mixture. Twist orange peel above drink and drop into mug.

MULLED SCOTCH

2 ozs. hot Scotch
1 oz. hot Drambuie
2 dashes bitters
1 oz. boiling water
1 maraschino cherry
Lemon peel

Into an old-fashioned glass, pour the Scotch, Drambuie, bitters and boiling water. Stir. Add the cherry. Twist lemon peel over the drink; then discard the peel.

ROCK-AND-RYE TODDY

2 ozs. rock and rye
2 dashes Angostura
  bitters
1 slice lemon
3 ozs. boiling water
1 cinnamon stick
Grated nutmeg

Pour rock and rye and bitters into old-fashioned glass. Add lemon slice. Add boiling water and cinnamon stick. Stir. Sprinkle with grated nutmeg.

SOUTHERN BLAZER
(Serves 2)

1½ ozs. Southern
  Comfort
1½ ozs. coffee liqueur
2 dashes Angostura
  bitters
3 ozs. boiling water
2 pieces lemon peel
2 pieces orange peel

Heat Southern Comfort, coffee liqueur and bitters until hot but not boiling. Pour into one 10-oz. mug. Pour boiling water into a second mug. Set mug with liquors ablaze. Pour into mug with boiling water, and immediately pour liquids back and forth between two mugs until the blazing stream subsides. Divide mixture between the two mugs. Twist a piece of lemon peel and a piece of orange peel above each drink and drop into mugs.

SWEDISH GLÖGG
(Serves 6 to 8)

1 fifth dry red wine
½ cup sugar
16 whole cloves
8 2-inch pieces stick
  cinnamon
1 cup brandy
Raisins
Peeled unsalted almonds

In a large saucepan combine the wine, sugar, cloves and stick cinnamon. Bring to the boiling point. Reduce flame and simmer 5 to 8 minutes. Stir in the brandy. Put a few raisins and almonds into each mug or glass. Add the glögg and serve.

TOM AND JERRY
(Serves 8)

2 large eggs
¼ cup sugar
2 ozs. dark Jamaican
  rum
½ teaspoon ground
  cinnamon
¼ teaspoon ground
  cloves
1 pint hot blended
  whiskey or hot
  bourbon
1 quart hot milk

Most tom-and-jerry recipes call for separating the egg yolks from the whites and beating each separately. If you have an electric beater, however, you can beat the whole eggs and get a fine foamy mixture. You can get the same results if you have a good manual egg beater and enough muscle power. In any case, beat the whole eggs very well; then slowly add the sugar. Continue beating until the mixture is very stiff and light lemon yellow in color. Add the rum, cinnamon and cloves. Beat a moment more to blend spices. Spoon the batter into tom-and-jerry mugs. Add 2 ozs. of blended whiskey or bourbon to each mug. Fill the mug with hot milk and serve.

22

HORS D'OEUVRES

Martinis are martinis, but martinis in the vicinity of a *terrine* of *pâté de foie gras* are a feast. Sydney Smith, 18th Century English wit, said, "My idea of heaven is eating *pâté de foie gras* to the sound of trumpets." A trumpet may be all right as a garnish, but the best modern orchestration for such luxury items is the soft rattle of a martini pitcher or the rhythm of a cocktail shaker—for one of the best things about drinking is eating. Liquor allows people to unwind; hors d'oeuvres *and* liquor make them soar. Although the word *hors d'oeuvre* is French, meaning literally "apart from the works," the prestigious art of amassing and presenting luscious appetizers reaches its pinnacle in the Scandinavian countries of the midnight sun, where the appetizing board is often in fact the *whole* works. In this country, also—no longer a nation of mere nibblers—the cocktail and the appetizer have become partners in equal standing.

The number of magnificent

imported and domestic hors d'oeuvres in cans, jars, bottles and
vacuum packs has reached Croesuslike proportions, as a brief
trip to your nearest gourmet shop will show you. But a tray of
four items—such as tiny cocktail mushrooms, caviar,
Westphalian ham, and Roquefort cheese in brandy—will
normally provide sufficient appetizers for eight to ten people.

Cold hors d'oeuvres must be cold, and in furtherance of
reaching this end you must be a monomaniac. The serving
platter or bowl, the plates and every ingredient in the appetizer
must be thoroughly prechilled. Cold appetizer salads are best
when served surrounded by crushed ice in a large shrimp server
or caviar server designed for that purpose. Hot hors d'oeuvres in
a sauce should be offered in a chafing dish, a fondue dish or
casserole over a spirit lamp. Small, dry hot hors d'oeuvres
should be placed on a platter lined with a linen napkin or paper
doily, or on an electric hot tray—provided they're in a single
layer in contact with the heat. If hot hors d'oeuvres are to be
placed under the broiler or in the oven at the last moment, be
sure the broiler is preheated, and keep it going for later use. But
remember that a preheated broiler works fast; avoid scorching
small filled tartlets and *bouchées.*

Both freshly made and prepared spreads should be placed
on cocktail crackers or canapé bases with a bland flavor. Be wary
of crackers accented with bacon or barbecue seasonings which
sometimes overpower delicate seafood flavors. All crackers or
cocktail biscuits should be tasted for freshness even when the
box is freshly opened. If in doubt, replace them. If in semidoubt,
place them in a warm oven for revival. Bread, too, should be
almost oven-fresh, merely firm enough to spread without tearing.

Perhaps the easiest and most impressive of all hors
d'oeuvres for intimate parties is the whole article of food, such
as a large, well-aged Gouda cheese, a smoked turkey or a smoked
Smithfield ham. You can buy the latter completely cooked and
glazed. Such centers of attention should be placed on a large
carving board flanked with appropriate carving knife, meat fork
or cheese scoop, as well as a large basket with thin slices of
French bread, salt rye bread or cocktail-size pumpernickel
rounds.

At a small cocktail party, frequently one hot and one cold
hors d'oeuvre are all the variety you need. Don't be the host with
too much too soon, particularly when drinking *intime.* At larger
revels, of course, hors d'oeuvres may be expanded to take in the
astronomical and still-expanding world of gourmandise.

When, in his *Canterbury Tales,* Chaucer speaks of "the hors
that hadde winges for to flee," he refers, of course, to "The
Pegasee." But try the following hors, and see if they don't have
the wings it takes to get your party off the ground.

Portions indicated below are hors d'oeuvre size.

Caviar can be neatly divided into two classes—the roe of the sturgeon and the roe of all other fish. Actually, the top of the sturgeon hierarchy is the beluga (Russian for the white color of the fish). It's called black caviar but, at its best, is actually gray. There's hardly a trace of saltiness in it, and although each tiny egg is intact, its texture is almost semiliquid in the mouth. There are excellent caviars of other sturgeons, such as the sevruga, in fresh forms and in sealed jars. So-called pressed caviar, made from the roe of several sturgeons, is always useful for emergency entertainment. Connoisseurs quite justly resent the fact that the word *caviar* can be used to describe the roe of the salmon, the whitefish and the lumpfish—spreads which are nevertheless widely used for canapés. The price of fresh beluga caviar is hardly extortionate when you consider that a beluga sturgeon doesn't produce eggs until it's about 20 years old, that only the most sensitive fingers can force the eggs through the sieve that separates the large eggs from the small, that caviar must be aged three months at 30° F. and that it must be kept refrigerated like fresh crab lump or any other fresh food until the moment it's devoured. For entirely too many generations, caviar was the symbol of conspicuous gourmandizing, enjoyed only by the top carriage trade. Now foodshops and gourmet stalls everywhere have taken it out of the dowager's class and turned it over to men who simply dig good eating. At the cocktail table, its jar should rest atop crushed ice held in a commodious bowl. To keep the eggs intact, an ivory or glass spoon is used. Garnishes for caviar should be kept to simple chopped egg, chopped onion or sour cream.

Caviar may be served on fresh toast fingers, canapé biscuits, tiny tartlet shells or tiny patty shells, but the most famed of all caviar vehicles are blini.

BLINI FOR CAVIAR

(Makes 25 to 30)

3 tablespoons salad oil
3 eggs
1/2 cup milk
3/4 cup water
3/4 cup whole-wheat flour
1/2 cup white flour
2 teaspoons baking powder
1/2 teaspoon salt

Blini are tiny pancakes, each about the size of a silver dollar, used as canapé bases. Originally made by a slow yeast process, this modernized version is easier and actually more toothsome.

Pour oil, eggs, milk and water into well of blender. Add whole-wheat flour, white flour (sifted before measuring), baking powder and salt. Blend until

(continued on following page)

batter is smooth. Stop blender and scrape sides when necessary to blend dry ingredients. Preheat electric skillet to 390° F. Grease lightly with salad oil. Wipe off excess oil with paper toweling. Drop batter into skillet by tablespoonfuls. When the edges of the blini are dry-looking and bubbles begin to appear in the center, turn and brown on the other side. Grease skillet lightly again before cooking second batch. Serve on white napkin. At cocktail table, spoon sour cream onto each blini. Add a dollop of caviar.

SHRIMP BEIGNETS

1 7-oz. pkg. frozen cleaned and peeled shrimps
1 cup water
2 tablespoons butter
³/₄ teaspoon salt
¹/₈ teaspoon celery salt
¹/₈ teaspoon white pepper
1 cup all-purpose flour
4 eggs
1 small onion
Deep fat for frying

(Makes about 4 dozen)
Cook shrimps, following directions on package. Drain and put through meat grinder, using fine blade. Bring water to a boil in a heavy saucepan. Add butter, salt, celery salt and pepper. When butter melts, add flour all at once. Stir well. Remove from flame. Stir until no dry flour is visible; batter will be very stiff. Transfer batter to electric mixer. Gradually add unbeaten eggs, one at a time, mixing well after each addition. Grate onion into batter. Add ground shrimps and mix well. Keep batter covered in refrigerator until very cold—at least 2 hours. Heat deep fat to 370° F. or until it shows the first wisp of smoke; or heat 1 inch of fat in electric skillet preheated to 370° F. Drop batter by heaping teaspoonfuls into fat. Turn once to brown on both sides. Drain on absorbent paper. Sprinkle with salt and serve with Chinese-style mustard.

PÂTE DE FOIÉ GRAS

Foie gras means "fat liver." *Pâté de foie gras* is the seasoned liver of a force-fed goose. The labor of stuffing grain or noodles down a goose's gullet every three hours, day and night, is rewarded with livers that sometimes weigh over two pounds apiece. The best quality of goose liver, from Strasbourg, is creamy rose in color. Although *foie gras* is available fresh in France and is sometimes airmailed to the States, we usually buy it here in tins or *terrines.* Each *pâté de foie gras* is overlaid with a rich stratum of goose or pork fat to keep the *pâté* moist and fresh-tasting. For hors d'oeuvres, *pâté de foie gras* should be biting cold. A sharp knife dipped into hot water helps to liberate thin, uniform slices.

ANCHOVY PIROSHKI

1 small onion, finely minced
2 tablespoons butter
²/₃ cup mashed potatoes made without milk
10 anchovy fillets, finely minced
Salt and pepper
2 prepared unbaked 9-inch pie shells
1 egg, beaten
2 tablespoons milk

(Makes 14)
Preheat oven to 425° F. Sauté onion in butter until onion turns yellow. Combine onion, potatoes and anchovies, and season to taste. Place pie shells on floured board and cut each into seven round pieces, using standard old-fashioned glass, 3 inches in diameter across top, for cutting. On each piece of dough, place about 2 teaspoons potato mixture. Lift one end of dough over potato mixture to make crescent-shaped turnovers. Press edges of dough with fingers, sealing tightly. Press again with tines of fork. Trim off any ragged edges. Combine egg and milk, mixing well. Brush each turnover with egg mixture and place on lightly greased cookie sheet or shallow pan. Bake 20 minutes, or until well browned. Serve warm.

FONDUE WITH PROSCIUTTO

French bread
½ lb. prosciutto ham, sliced paper-thin
½ lb. Swiss Emmentaler cheese
½ lb. natural Gruyère cheese
4 tablespoons flour
1½ cups dry white wine
2 cloves garlic
4 tablespoons kirschwasser
Salt and pepper
Freshly grated nutmeg

(Serves 8)

Cut bread into chunks about 1 inch thick, taking care that each chunk of bread includes crust. Cut ham slices in half. Roll up each half cornucopia fashion. Pile bread into breadbasket. Arrange ham slices on platter. Shred cheese by forcing it through large holes of square metal grater. Put cheese and flour into mixing bowl, tossing until cheese is coated with flour. Heat wine in top part of double boiler over direct flame until bubbles appear around edge of pan. Do not boil. Place over simmering water in bottom section of double boiler. Add cheese by handfuls to wine, stirring well. When each handful of cheese is melted, add another, stirring well, until all cheese is used. Squeeze garlic through garlic press over fondue. Stir in kirschwasser. Add salt and pepper to taste. Pour fondue into chafing dish or caquelon *and sprinkle with nutmeg before bringing it to cocktail table. Keep fondue hot over spirit lamp. Guests spear bread or ham, and dip.*

HOT GRUYÈRE AND ANCHOVY CANAPÉS

4 slices white bread
Sweet butter, at room temperature
4 ozs. Gruyère cheese, shredded
8 flat anchovy fillets, finely minced
½ cup mayonnaise
4 tablespoons grated Parmesan cheese
Paprika

(Makes 24)

Preheat oven to 450° F. Toast bread under broiler on one side only. Spread untoasted side with butter. Mix Gruyère cheese with minced anchovy fillets, mayonnaise and Parmesan cheese. Spread cheese mixture evenly on untoasted sides of bread. Sprinkle with paprika. Place bread, cheese side up, on a baking sheet or the back of an inverted baking pan. Bake 5 minutes. Cut each slice into six pieces. Serve very hot.

HOT MOZZARELLA AND ANCHOVY APPETIZERS

(Makes 32)

2 eggs, well beaten
1/2 cup heavy cream
1/8 teaspoon salt
8 ozs. mozzarella cheese, thinly sliced
8 square slices white bread
1 2-oz. can flat anchovy fillets, drained
1 3-oz. can sliced mushrooms, drained
Olive oil

Combine eggs, cream and salt, and beat well. Place cheese on four slices of bread. Place anchovies and mushrooms on cheese and top with remaining bread to make sandwiches. In large, heavy frying pan, heat 1/8 inch of oil. Holding sandwiches with both hands to keep intact, dip into egg mixture, as in making French toast. Fry sandwiches until golden brown on both sides and cut each one into eighths before serving.

EGGPLANT CAVIAR

(Serves 8)

1 large eggplant
2 medium-size fresh tomatoes
1/4 cup salad oil
2 medium-size onions, very small dice
1 small clove garlic, finely minced
1/2 green pepper, very small dice
1 tablespoon lemon juice
2 tablespoons finely minced fresh dill
Salt and pepper

Place eggplant in shallow pan in oven preheated to 450° F. Bake 45 minutes, turning once to bake evenly. Remove from pan and cut in half lengthwise. With sharp paring knife or grapefruit knife, remove pulp from eggplant shell; avoid tearing shell. Cut pulp into very small dice and set aside. Set the eggplant shells aside. Lower tomatoes into a pot of rapidly boiling water for 20–30 seconds; then hold them under cold running water for a few seconds, peel off the skin and remove stem ends. Press tomatoes to squeeze out excess liquid; then cut them into very small dice. In a shallow saucepan, heat oil. Add onions, garlic, green pepper, eggplant and tomatoes. Sauté slowly, stirring frequently, for 10 minutes, or until all vegetables are tender. Add lemon juice, dill, and salt and pepper to taste. Spoon cooked mixture into eggplant shells. Chill in refrigerator until ice-cold. Serve with sesame crackers.

BAGNA CAUDA

1 medium-size bunch
  celery
1 large cucumber
2 green peppers
2 sweet red peppers
1/4 lb. Belgian endive
1 bunch thin scallions
1 pkg. small breadsticks
1/4 lb. sweet butter
4 large garlic cloves,
  partly crushed
2 tablespoons anchovy
  paste
1/2 pint heavy cream
1 1-oz. can white
  truffles, finely minced
Ground white pepper

(Serves 6 to 8)
Trim leaves from celery. Cut off root end and separate bunch into pieces. Run a vegetable peeler along outside of celery pieces to remove tough strings. Cut celery into pieces aproximately 4 inches long and 1/2 inch wide. Peel and cut cucumber into pieces the same size as the celery. Cut peppers in half through stem ends. Discard seeds and stem ends of peppers. Cut peppers lengthwise into 1/2-inch pieces. Separate endive into pieces for dipping. Cut root end off scallions allowing about 1 inch of green part to remain. Place vegetables on top of ice in a large salad bowl. Place breadsticks near chafing dish. In the chafing dish, over a low flame, melt butter. Add garlic. Sauté only until garlic begins to brown. Remove garlic and discard. Add anchovy paste. Mix well. Add cream and truffles. Add a generous dash of pepper. Let liquid simmer about 5 minutes before guests dip vegetables and breadsticks into bagna cauda (Italian for "hot dip").

ROQUEFORT AND WINE CANAPÉS

4 ozs. Roquefort cheese
2 tablespoons dry white
  wine
1 tablespoon cognac
16 small canapé-type
  crackers
Butter, at room
  temperature
Cayenne pepper
2 tablespoons very finely
  chopped chives

(Makes 16)
Break cheese into small lumps. Force cheese through colander or wire sieve. Mix cheese with wine and cognac until very well blended. If cheese seems too soft for spreading, place in refrigerator until it's firmer. Spread crackers generously with butter. Spread with cheese uniformly to edge of crackers. Sprinkle very lightly with cayenne, then with chives. Store in refrigerator until serving time.

BAKED OYSTERS
WITH MUSHROOMS

(Makes 24)

24 large oysters on half
  shell, deep side
1 cup or less clam broth
1/4 cup light cream
1/4 lb. fresh mushrooms
3 tablespoons butter
3 tablespoons flour
2 tablespoons brandy
1 teaspoon Pernod
Salt and pepper
1/4 cup butter
3/4 cup bread crumbs
1 tablespoon finely
  minced chives

Preheat oven to 400° F. Remove oysters from shells, reserving liquid. Measure and add enough clam broth to total 1 cup. Combine with cream in saucepan and heat to boiling point, but do not boil. Set aside. Slice mushrooms, caps and stems, very thin and sauté in 3 tablespoons butter until just tender. Stir in flour, mixing well. Slowly add clam-broth mixture, stirring constantly with wire whisk. Bring sauce to a boil. Reduce flame and simmer very slowly, stirring frequently, for about 10 minutes. Add brandy and Pernod. Add salt and pepper to taste. Remove from flame and divide half the mixture among the 24 shells. Place an oyster in each shell. Spoon balance of mushroom mixture on top of oysters. Melt 1/4 cup butter in saucepan. Remove from flame and stir in bread crumbs and chives, mixing well. Place bread-crumb mixture on top of oysters, smoothing tops with spoon or spatula. Place oysters on a 1/2 inch bed of rock salt in shallow pan or casserole. (The rock salt isn't absolutely necessary, but it keeps oysters in an upright position so that as little juice as possible escapes.) Bake 15 to 20 minutes.

FRIED CHICKEN LIVERS, APPLE BRANDY SAUCE

6 ozs. chicken livers
1/2 cup apple jelly
1/4 cup apple brandy,
either calvados or
applejack
2 tablespoons orange
juice
1/4 cup pineapple juice
1 teaspoon lemon juice
1 teaspoon Dijon
mustard
1 teaspoon grated lemon
rind
2 teaspoons cornstarch
1 teaspoon butter
1/2 cup sifted flour
1/2 teaspoon baking
powder
2 egg whites, beaten stiff
Salad oil
Salt, pepper and onion
powder

(Serves 8)
*Put chicken livers into a saucepan
and cover with cold water. Bring
to a boil. Simmer 1 minute. Drain
livers. Cut livers in half—or into
three or four pieces if they're extra
large. Chill. In a saucepan, heat
apple jelly, apple brandy, orange
juice, pineapple juice, lemon
juice, mustard and lemon rind.
Stir well to blend mustard with
other ingredients. When sauce
boils, dissolve cornstarch in 2
tablespoons cold water. Slowly stir
into sauce. Simmer 2 minutes.
Remove from flame. Stir in butter.
Add salt and pepper to taste. Set
aside. Sift flour, 1/2 teaspoon salt
and baking powder. Add 1/4 cup
cold water, mixing well. Fold in
beaten egg whites until blended.
Small lumps in batter are
permissible. Heat 1/2 inch salad oil
in electric skillet preheated to
370° F. Sprinkle chicken livers
with salt, pepper and onion
powder. Dip into batter. Fry until
medium brown on both sides.
Serve with warm apple-brandy
sauce (reheated if necessary) as a
dip. Fasten cocktail spears to
chicken livers for easy handling.*

GORGONZOLA CREAM

12 ozs. Gorgonzola
cheese
6 tablespoons sweet
butter, at room
temperature
Grated Parmesan cheese
Finely minced fresh
chives

(Serves 6 to 8)
*Crumble cheese. Force it through a
wire strainer or colander. Add
butter. Mix well. Shape into round
or oval cake, 3/4 inch thick. Place
on serving plate. Sprinkle with
Parmesan cheese and chives.
Wipe rim of plate. Spread on
cocktail crackers.*

STURGEON AND AQUAVIT CANAPÉS

4 slices light
    pumpernickel bread
Aquavit
Sweet butter, at room
    temperature
4 scallions, white part
    and 1 inch of green,
    thinly sliced
1/4 lb. sturgeon, thinly
    sliced
2 tablespoons finely
    minced fresh dill
1 canned pimiento

(Makes 16)
*Sprinkle bread on one side with
aquavit. The aquavit should just
barely penetrate the opposite side
of the bread; take care that the
bread doesn't become too soggy to
handle. Turn bread over. Spread
generously with butter. Sprinkle
with scallions. Cover with one
layer of sturgeon. Bread should be
completely covered with sturgeon,
but sturgeon should not overlap
bread. Sprinkle two of the four
pieces with dill. If dill is wet from
washing, squeeze it dry in a clean
towel. Cut the four slices of bread
into four finger-shaped pieces. Cut
pimiento into eight long, thin
strips. Place a strip on each piece
of sturgeon not sprinkled with dill.
Arrange pieces alternately on
platter. Serve ice-cold.*

For *smoked salmon and aquavit canapés*—use thinly
sliced Nova Scotia salmon instead of sturgeon.

For *anchovy and aquavit canapés*—cover bread with flat
anchovy fillets. Sprinkle two slices with finely chopped
hard-boiled egg instead of dill.

For *caviar and aquavit canapés*—cover two slices of bread
with black caviar and two slices with red caviar rather than
with sturgeon. Sprinkle red caviar with dill. Place pimiento
strips on black caviar.

MELON, PROSCIUTTO AND CREAM DIP

1/2 large ripe Cranshaw
    or honeydew melon
1/2 lb. prosciutto ham,
    sliced paper-thin
1/4 cup heavy sweet
    cream
1 cup sour cream
3 tablespoons Cherry
    Heering
2 teaspoons lemon juice
2 teaspoons sugar

(Serves 8)
*Cut melon into long wedges about
1 inch wide. Cut skin off. Cut
crosswise into slices about 1 inch
thick. Wrap each piece with
prosciutto. (Large slices of
prosciutto may be cut in half if
necessary.) Place melon on large
serving platter. Keep in
refrigerator until serving time.
Beat sweet cream in cold narrow*

bowl with rotary egg beater until cream is whipped. Fold whipped cream into sour cream, using a down-over-up stroke with mixing spoon. Gradually fold in Cherry Heering, lemon juice and sugar. Serve cream as a dip for melon. Cocktail spears may be inserted in melon pieces for easy handling.

CLAM AND STOUT CANAPÉS AU GRATIN

1 8-oz. can minced clams
1/3 cup stout
2 tablespoons butter
1 medium onion, finely minced
1 medium clove garlic, finely minced
2 tablespoons finely minced green pepper
1 tablespoon finely minced parsley
1/2 teaspoon chervil
2 tablespoons flour
1/4 teaspoon Worcestershire sauce
1/4 cup bread crumbs
Salt, pepper and cayenne pepper
4 square slices white bread
Grated Parmesan cheese
Paprika
Salad oil

(Makes 16)

Drain clams, reserving juice. Add stout to juice. Set aside. Melt butter in saucepan over low flame. Add onion, garlic, green pepper, parsley and chervil. Sauté slowly, stirring frequently, until onion turns yellow. Remove from flame. Stir in flour, mixing until no lumps are visible. Heat clam broth up to boiling point. Slowly add to onion mixture, stirring well. Return to moderate flame. Simmer 10 minutes, stirring frequently. Add clams, Worcestershire sauce, bread crumbs, salt and pepper to taste and a dash of cayenne. Chill mixture in refrigerator. Preheat broiler. Toast bread under broiler flame on one side only. On untoasted side, spread clam mixture to edge of each slice. Sprinkle generously with Parmesan cheese, lightly with paprika and oil. Place under broiler flame. Broil until cheese browns lightly. Cut each slice of bread into four triangles.

PROSCIUTTO AND PROVOLONE ROLLS

6 ozs. provolone cheese,
  thinly sliced
6 ozs. prosciutto ham,
  sliced paper-thin
1/4 cup olive oil
1/4 cup dry vermouth
3 large cloves garlic
1 tablespoon finely
  minced parsley

(Serves 8)

Cut provolone cheese into strips about 3/4 inch wide and 2 inches long. Fold lengthwise. Cut pieces of prosciutto about 1 inch wide and 3 inches long. Roll prosciutto around cheese. Fasten rolls with toothpicks. Smash cloves of garlic with flat side of heavy French knife. Into a small shallow casserole or baking dish, put olive oil, vermouth, garlic and parsley. Mix well. Place rolls in casserole. Marinate rolls 3 to 4 hours in refrigerator, turning to marinate evenly. Place rolls on thin bread or cocktail crackers for serving, after removing toothpicks.

MUSHROOM SOUR-CREAM CANAPÉS

6 ozs. fresh button
  mushrooms
2 tablespoons butter
1 cup sour cream
1 tablespoon kümmel
1 tablespoon brandy
2 teaspoons dry sherry
1 teaspoon lemon juice
1/8 teaspoon Tabasco
  sauce
1 scallion, white and
  green part, very finely
  minced
Salt and pepper
French dressing
Cocktail crackers or
  Melba-toast rounds

(Serves 8)

Separate mushroom stems from caps. Set aside four of the caps for later use. Cut balance of mushrooms into extremely small dice. Sauté in butter until no liquid remains in pan. Cool mushrooms. Combine with sour cream, kümmel, brandy, sherry, lemon juice, Tabasco sauce and scallion. Season generously with salt and pepper. Chill in refrigerator at least 3 hours. Cut raw mushroom caps in thinnest possible slices. Marinate in French dressing in refrigerator. Place spread on cocktail crackers or Melba-toast rounds. Drain mushroom slices. Place one on top of each canapé.

DEVILED MUSHROOMS

1 lb. button mushrooms
  with very short stems
4 tablespoons butter, at
  room temperature
2 tablespoons salad oil
1 12-oz. can chicken
  broth with rice
2 tablespoons flour
1 teaspoon prepared
  mustard
1/2 teaspoon dry mustard
2 tablespoons dry sherry
1 tablespoon brandy
1 tablespoon white-wine
  vinegar
Brown gravy color
Salt and pepper

(Serves 8)
Cut stems off mushrooms. Melt 2 tablespoons butter with oil. Sauté mushroom caps and stems until tender. Remove stems from pan; let caps remain in pan. Put chicken broth and mushroom stems into blender. Blend until smooth. Pour into pan with mushroom caps. Bring to a boil. Combine remaining 2 tablespoons butter with flour, mixing to a smooth paste. Add to pan. While simmering, stir until sauce is thick and smooth. Add prepared mustard, dry mustard, sherry, brandy, vinegar and enough color to make sauce medium brown. Add salt and pepper to taste. Serve from chafing dish with cocktail spears. Mushrooms may be placed in tiny tartlet shells if desired.

HOT PIMIENTO CANAPÉS WITH BOURBON

1 small onion, finely
  minced
1 medium clove garlic,
  extremely finely
  minced
Butter
1 cup bread crumbs
  (freshly made if
  possible)
3 tablespoons bourbon
Salt, pepper and paprika
4 square slices white
  bread
1 4-oz. can pimientos,
  drained
Parmesan cheese

(Makes 16)
Sauté onion and garlic in 1/3 cup butter over very low flame. As soon as onion begins to turn light yellow, remove from flame. Combine with bread crumbs and bourbon, mixing well. Season with salt and pepper. Toast bread lightly. Spread generously with butter. Cut pimientos in half and divide among the four slices of toast. If pimientos do not cover bread, they may be cut into strips and divided among the four slices. Cover evenly with bread-crumb mixture. Sprinkle with Parmesan cheese and paprika. Preheat broiler flame. Broil until cheese browns lightly. Cut each slice into four triangles or squares.

CANNIBAL CANAPÉS BURGUNDY

1/4 cup red Burgundy
2 tablespoons bread
    crumbs
2 tablespoons melted
    butter
1 lb. freshly ground
    prime boneless shell
    steak
1 1/2 teaspoons salt
1/4 teaspoon freshly
    ground pepper
1/2 teaspoon Dijon
    mustard
1 tablespoon catsup
4 dashes cayenne pepper
1 small onion, extremely
    finely minced
2 egg yolks
1/2 oz. lemon juice
2 tablespoons drained
    capers
Rye Melba-toast rounds
4 sour gherkins, thinly
    sliced
2 tablespoons finely
    minced parsley

(Serves 8)
Combine Burgundy, bread crumbs and melted butter. Mix well. Add to meat in bowl. Add salt, pepper, mustard, catsup, cayenne, onion, egg yolks, lemon juice and capers. Mix very well. Spread carefully and evenly on Melba toast. Place a slice of gherkin on each canapé. Sprinkle with parsley. Arrange on platter. Store in refrigerator until serving time. A good way to introduce steak tartare to those who've never tasted raw beef.

HOT PARMESAN AND MOZZARELLA CANAPÉS

2 ozs. prosciutto ham,
    sliced paper-thin
2 ozs. mozzarella cheese
Grated Parmesan cheese
1 cup mayonnaise
1 tablespoon brandy
1 tablespoon dry white
    wine
4 square slices white
    bread
Butter at room
    temperature
Paprika

(Makes 16)
Cut prosciutto into 1/4-inch dice. Put mozzarella cheese through the large holes of a square metal grater. Combine ham, mozzarella, 1/3 cup Parmesan, mayonnaise, brandy and white wine. Mix well. Toast bread lightly. Spread with butter. Cover bread uniformly to edge with mayonnaise mixture. Sprinkle lightly with paprika and Parmesan cheese. Place under preheated broiler flame until golden brown. Cut each slice into quarters.

CHICKEN BOUCHÉES WITH TRUFFLES

(Makes 24)

1 whole breast of chicken
3 tablespoons finely minced shallots
2 medium mushrooms, extremely small dice
3 tablespoons butter
2 tablespoons brandy
2 tablespoons dry white wine
2 tablespoons flour
1 packet instant chicken bouillon
1/2 cup heavy cream
1 7/8-oz. can black truffles, finely minced
1 teaspoon yellow Chartreuse
1/2 teaspoon Worcestershire sauce
Salt and freshly ground pepper
24 hors d'oeuvre–size patty shells or *barquettes*

Boil chicken in salted water until tender, 30 to 40 minutes. Remove skin and bone from chicken. Cut into cubes 1/4 inch or less. Set chicken broth aside. Sauté shallots and mushrooms in butter until mushrooms are tender. Add brandy and white wine. Set it aflame. When flames subside, remove pan from fire and stir in flour, mixing well. Combine 3/4 cup chicken broth with instant chicken bouillon in another saucepan. Add cream. Bring up to boiling point. Slowly add to pan containing mushrooms, mixing well. Return to a moderate flame. Add chicken. Simmer, stirring frequently, for 5 minutes. Add truffles, Chartreuse and Worcestershire sauce. Add salt and pepper to taste. With small, sharp knife, hollow out centers of patty shells, if necessary, to hold chicken. Fill patty shells with chicken. Serve immediately or set aside and warm in preheated oven just before serving.

CURRIED-EGG DIP

(Serves 8)

2 hard-boiled eggs, shelled
1 1/2 cups sour cream
1/4 cup mayonnaise
2 teaspoons curry powder
1 teaspoon grated onion
2 tablespoons celery, very finely minced
2 tablespoons green pepper, very finely minced
1 tablespoon fresh dill, very finely minced
Salt and pepper

Cut eggs into large dice. Force through a fine wire strainer into mixing bowl. Add sour cream, mayonnaise, curry powder, onion, celery, green pepper and dill. Mix very well. Add salt and pepper to taste. Chill thoroughly. Serve, if possible, with freshly fried shrimp chips or freshly fried pappadums.

CAMEMBERT TOAST MALAGA

1/4 cup large raisins
1/4 cup cognac
1 8-oz. pkg. soft ripe
　Camembert cheese
8 slices French bread,
　about 3 inches in
　diameter
1/4 cup sweet butter, at
　room temperature

(Makes 16)

Put raisins into small saucepan. Cover with cold water. Slowly bring to a boil. Simmer a minute. Drain. Put raisins into cup or glass and cover with cognac. Marinate overnight. Camembert cheese should be removed from refrigerator about an hour before preparation. Cut cheese into wedges and force cheese, including rind, through a colander. Toast bread. Drain raisins, saving cognac. Sprinkle one side of each slice with reserved cognac. Don't douse bread so liberally that it falls apart when handled. Turn bread on opposite side. Spread with butter. Spread evenly with Camembert cheese. Cut each slice in half. Place raisins on top of cheese, pressing slightly to keep in place. Arrange slices in rows on serving platter.

CHEDDAR AND ONION CANAPÉS

4 square slices white
　bread
1 tablespoon salad oil
2 tablespoons butter
2 cups very thinly sliced
　onion
2 medium cloves garlic,
　finely minced
3/4 cup dry red wine
1 teaspoon beef extract
Salt and pepper
4 slices sharp Cheddar
　cheese, large enough to
　cover bread
Paprika

(Makes 16)

Preheat broiler. Under broiler flame, toast bread on one side only. Heat oil and butter in saucepan until butter just melts. Add onion and garlic. Sauté over low flame, stirring frequently, until onion is soft and yellow, not brown. Add wine and beef extract. Simmer until wine has almost completely evaporated. Season onions with salt and pepper. Preheat oven to 350° F. Divide onions, spreading them on untoasted side of bread. Place cheese on onions. Sprinkle with paprika. Place bread on baking sheet or on bottom of inverted baking pan. Bake only until cheese is soft. Do not use broiler flame for heating cheese. Cut each slice into four triangles or squares. Serve immediately.

DEVILED LOBSTER BOUCHÉES

24 very small hors
d'oeuvre–size patty
shells
1 9-oz. pkg. frozen
lobster tails
3 tablespoons instantized
flour
1 cup cold milk
2 tablespoons butter
2 teaspoons sherry
1 teaspoon brandy
1/2 teaspoon lemon juice
1/8 teaspoon anchovy
paste
1 teaspoon prepared
mustard
Salt, pepper and cayenne

(Makes 24)
*If necessary, remove insides of
patty shells with small, sharp
knife in order to create cavities for
the lobster. Cook lobster, following
directions on package. Drain.
Remove meat from lobster shells.
Cut into very small dice. Put flour
and milk into saucepan. Stir until
flour is dissolved. Add butter.
Simmer until sauce is thick and
no floury taste remains. Add
lobster, sherry, brandy, lemon
juice, anchovy paste, mustard,
and salt and pepper to taste. Add
a dash of cayenne. Mix very well.
Fill patty shells with lobster
mixture. Serve at once. If not
served immediately, place on
baking sheet. At serving time,
place baking sheet in preheated
moderate oven (375° F.) for 5 to 8
minutes, or until heated through.*

SOUR-CREAM MEDLEY

1 pint sour cream
1 tablespoon fresh
chives, finely minced
1 teaspoon fresh parsley,
finely minced
1/4 teaspoon fresh basil,
finely minced
1/4 teaspoon fresh
tarragon, finely minced
2 teaspoons horseradish
1 8-oz. can water
chestnuts, drained
2 2-oz. cans button
mushrooms, drained
12 small red radishes or
6 large radishes cut in
half
1 large green pepper, cut
into 1/2-inch squares
Salt and pepper

(Serves 6 to 8)
*Mix sour cream with chives,
parsley, basil, tarragon and
horseradish, stirring thoroughly
until well blended. In fondue dish
or casserole, combine sour-cream
mixture with water chestnuts,
mushrooms, radishes and green
pepper, tossing thoroughly. Chill
in refrigerator at least 2 hours.
Season generously with salt and
pepper. (If fresh basil and tarragon
are unavailable, don't substitute
dried herbs; simply increase
parsley by 1/2 teaspoon.) Let guests
serve themselves with long fondue
forks. Serve with small squares of
freshly buttered black bread.*

CHICKEN MOUSSE
(Serves 8)

1 whole chicken breast, boiled till tender
1 envelope plain gelatin
¼ cup cold chicken broth
1 cup hot chicken broth
4 tablespoons melted sweet butter
2 tablespoons brandy
1 teaspoon lemon juice
1 teaspoon prepared horseradish
1 tablespoon diced onion
4 dashes Tabasco sauce
Salt and white pepper

Remove skin and bones from chicken. Cut chicken into dice. Soften gelatin in cold chicken broth. Dissolve in hot chicken broth. Put diced chicken, chicken broth, butter, brandy, lemon juice, horseradish, onion and Tabasco into blender. Blend at low speed for 2 minutes, or until chicken is thoroughly puréed. Season generously with salt and pepper. Turn into bowl or small mold. Chill in refrigerator until mixture is completely jelled and very cold. Run a knife around edge of mousse. Dip bowl into warm water for a moment or two and unmold onto serving dish. Serve with thin, crisp crackers (chicken-flavored if possible) or Melba toast.

FRESH SALMON AND PEPPER SPREAD
(Serves 8)

1 lb. fresh salmon, boiled
¾ cup mayonnaise
¼ cup green pepper, diced
2 tablespoons canned pimiento, diced
2 teaspoons lemon juice
1 teaspoon tarragon vinegar
1 teaspoon prepared horseradish
1 tablespoon fresh dill, minced
Salt and pepper

Remove skin and bones from salmon. Chop salmon with heavy French knife until finely minced. Put mayonnaise, green pepper and pimiento into blender. Blend at low speed about 30 seconds, or until no solid pieces of pepper or pimiento are visible. Turn into mixing bowl. Add salmon, lemon juice, vinegar, horseradish and dill. Mix very well, adding salt and pepper to taste. Chill thoroughly in refrigerator. Serve with party rye bread or rye Melba toast.

3 lbs. shrimps (12 to 16
  per lb.)
1/2 cup catsup
2 teaspoons Pernod
2 teaspoons paprika
1/2 cup sour cream
2 tablespoons chives or
  scallions, minced
Juice of 1/2 lemon
Light cream
Salt and pepper
1/2 cup mayonnaise
2 teaspoons curry
  powder
1/8 teaspoon Tabasco
  sauce
1 clove garlic
1 7-oz. bottle sauce
  diable

FANTAIL SHRIMP COCKTAIL

(Serves 10)

*Boil shrimps in salted water.
Shrimps of this large size will
require 5 to 7 minutes boiling
time. Cool and chill in refrigerator
in own cooking liquid. Balance of
ingredients are used for four
separate cocktail sauces. All must
be icy cold for serving. Mix catsup
and Pernod. Chill in refrigerator.
In small mixing bowl, dissolve
paprika in 3 tablespoons hot
water. Add sour cream, chives and
lemon juice, mixing well.
Gradually add light cream, in very
small quantities, until sauce flows
very slowly. Sauce must be thick
enough to adhere to shrimps and
not be "soupy." Add salt and
pepper to taste. Chill in
refrigerator. In another mixing
bowl, combine mayonnaise, curry
powder and Tabasco. Force garlic
through garlic press into curry
sauce. Again, add light cream in
very small quantities until sauce
has lost its stiffness. Chill in
refrigerator. Chill sauce diable in
small bowl in refrigerator. If sauce
diable is not available, substitute
any thick bottled savory sauce for
meat or fish. Remove shells from
shrimps, leaving bottom segments
and tails intact. Remove back
veins and, with small, sharp knife,
cut shrimps from head to tail. Do
not, however, separate them into
halves. Hold each shrimp open,
book fashion, in one piece—facing
you. Turn tail end and force it
through back of shrimp until tail
stands between the two cut sides
of shrimp. It may be necessary to
cut a little slit to permit tail to go
through completely. Avoid making
a large hole or shrimp will
separate into halves. Press cut
sides of shrimps so that they can
rest flat on platter. Drain, using
paper toweling if necessary to pat*

*dry. Divide shrimps into four
equal lots. Coat one fourth with
catsup mixture, dipping shrimps
into sauce or spreading sauce with
a spoon. All the flesh of shrimps,
top and bottom, must be
thoroughly covered. Coat the
second fourth with the sour-cream
mixture, the third fourth with the
curry mixture and the balance
with the sauce diable. Arrange the
shrimps on a large silver or china
platter. Keep cold in refrigerator
until serving time.*

SMOKED-OYSTER DIP

1 3²/₃-oz. can smoked
  oysters
1 pint sour cream
1 teaspoon onion, grated
1 teaspoon fresh chives,
  minced
2 teaspoons lemon juice
4 dashes Tabasco sauce
Salt and pepper

(Serves 8)
*Drain oysters very well, discarding
oil. Put all ingredients into
blender. Blend at high speed
about 30 seconds, or until oysters
are thoroughly puréed.*

DEVILED-EGG DIP

4 hard-boiled eggs,
  shelled
1 tablespoon Dijon or
  Dijon-style mustard
1 teaspoon dry mustard
4 tablespoons sweet
  butter, at room
  temperature
1 cup sour cream
2 teaspoons anchovy
  paste
1 tablespoon fresh
  chives, minced
2 teaspoons fresh
  parsley, minced
Salt, pepper and cayenne

(Serves 8)
*Cut eggs into large dice. Force
through fine wire strainer into
mixing bowl. Add both kinds of
mustard, butter, sour cream,
anchovy paste, chives and
parsley. Mix very well. Season
generously with salt and pepper.
Add a dash of cayenne.*

PART FOUR
multiple excuses for genteel
carousings and imbibings

23

PARTY BRIEFINGS

Parties share several characteristics with rivers: They're of all lengths, and each flows on a different course. Some parties dry up at a comparatively early hour; others keep rolling along. A party can be anything from an hour's breathing spell on an apartment terrace to a year-end bacchanal. There are brunch parties where food rather than liquor becomes the feast of reason and the flow of the soul, and drinks are limited to a round or two of eye-openers. On the other hand, each day when the evening sun goes down, cocktail parties throughout the length and breadth of the land revolve almost completely around potables while food plays only a small supporting role. And, for the ambitious host, there are full-dress dinner parties where drinks begin with the preprandial cocktails and stretch on through the amontillado with the soup, the Rhine wine with the seafood, the Burgundy with the roast, the sauternes with the dessert, the brandy with the demitasse to the postprandial liqueurs and the midnight highballs. But whatever course a party takes, its source begins with bottles and a bar.

Whenever a few congenial people meet privately to bend elbows, the first thing the host asks is simply and correctly, "What'll you have?" He then turns to his liquor cabinet and prepares his potations one by one. In the free play that follows, someone is bound to ask for an extra rock, a splash of soda or a sprinkling of salt on his tequila-sour glass. It's all completely *gemütlich* and easy. But for mass drinking parties, the proceedings must be changed. If a man's to be a host and not a walking computer, he must eschew the drinking whims of each of his assorted visitors. It may be gallant for him to run to his bar or kitchen and carefully mix a not too sweet gimlet with a twist of temple orange for the second lady on the right-hand side of the fireplace, but when 17 other fierce thirsts remain unappeased, the only kind of bar to set up is one with all of its offerings—or a single offering, as the case may be—prominently in the spotlight atop the bar. This virtually guarantees that the assembled imbibers will adapt themselves to the available liquors just as naturally as they accept their host's creamed-chicken hash or lobster salad at the buffet table. If, for instance, there are several bottles of vodka on view together with pitchers of orange juice and tomato juice, the crowd, without any prompting, will call for bloody marys and screwdrivers. When they see bottles of gin, they'll ask for martinis or gin and tonic. While all drinks are theoretically poured with the advice and consent of the entertainees, there's usually a minimum of advice, mostly consent, while the host and his guests settle into the same happy groove.

Party pourings are either straight or mixed. How diversified each kind should be depends on the kind of entertainment you've planned. Generally, the bigger the party, the more limited the selection. Consider the mixed libation first. One of the best examples is the punch bowl—a single offering that's often the master key to the happiest kind of big drinking party and that frees the host from the constraint of serving and his guests from the constraint of being served. At smaller parties, if you or some of your crowd are known to have a whale of a time with zubrovka martinis, you might place a bottle of zubrovka as well as a bottle of gin alongside your vermouth. But you must set reasonable limits on your martini variations. You could conceivably place on your party bar an American gin, an English-style gin made in America, an English gin made in England, a Dutch genever gin and a German Steinhäger gin. You could, that is, if you were running a gin-tasting party and nothing else. But if you're tempted to match your gin assortment with a similarly expansive whiskey assortment, rum assortment, brandy assortment and vodka assortment—all for converting into mixed drinks—you'll be running a party with all your bottletops as well as your reason unscrewed. Keep in mind the fact that a host often catapults into fame during a single party, not by serving as many mixed long and short drinks as possible, but by serving one drink so superb, so perfectly balanced in flavors, so numbing cold in the summer or pleasantly hot in the winter, so lively with the best liquors and freshest juices, in such handsome drinking vessels, that none of his guests can possibly forget its excellence.

When you're serving straight drinks at parties, it's thoughtful to take into account your guests' drinking preferences, but again, don't go overboard, and don't jump to easy conclusions too hastily. For example, if you're throwing a party for a group of visiting Frenchmen, you might assume that wine apéritifs like St.-Raphaël, Dubonnet or Lillet would be ideal preludes. Your guess might be right, and it would be sensible to have at least one such apéritif ready for pouring. But it would also be a good idea to have a bottle of Scotch on tap, since many Frenchmen, particularly those on the international circuit, regularly take Scotch and soda before mealtime. If you happen to know of some members in your party whose eyes always dance when they see a bottle of 12-year-old Scotch, as well as others who are happy only with the lighter Highland dew, you might place a bottle of each on your bar table to add to the general enchantment. If, at a buffet table, you're serving a standing rib roast and you know that some of your crowd have always had a special partiality for dark brews, you might offer bottles of both stout and dark Münchener. If you're serving espresso and even though not a single guest knows of sambuca, the Italian anise-and-elderberry-flavored liqueur served with coffee beans, this might be the perfect opportunity to introduce the velvety sweet liqueur to everyone. If there's a simmering casserole of beef *bourguignon,* then bottles of red wine, anything from California-mountain red to French beaujolais, would be perfect.

As a practical guide for party potables (excluding the wines or spirits served with food, and champagne, which is in a class by itself), the ingredients for two short drinks and two tall drinks should be the outside limit for any party above a dozen people. The short drinks may be one mixed (sidecar) and one straight (bourbon on the rocks). The tall may be one mixed (tom collins) and one straight with a carbonated water (brandy and soda). Often the short and the tall are combined. Thus, if you're offering frozen daiquiris, which are made with rum, then rum and tonic in tall glasses would be a cool way of burning the candle at both ends. If you're offering rob roys, made with Scotch and vermouth, orders for Scotch and soda or vermouth on the rocks would be simply a matter of pouring the spirits already on hand. The important thing to remember is not to try to serve too many different drinks at one party. At the same time, if you can possibly introduce one original or offbeat mixed drink along with the standard cocktails or highballs, you'll kindle the pulse for additional party fun.

BARS

The qualifications for a party bar are two: It must be big and it must be reachable. It may be a corner bar, a bar on wheels or built-in saloon with foot rest. If it's a liquor cabinet, it should be high enough for mixing, pouring and serving. If the ends of the cabinet have drop-leaf extensions which can be raised or lowered to fit party needs, so much the better. The bar may be a medium- or large-size dining table covered first with a pad and then with a snowy white linen or other attractive tablecloth. If the space under the table is to be used for reserve spirits and carbonated waters, the covering should be floor-length. Using bridge tables for bar mixing purposes may be adequate if your bartender happens to be Toulouse-Lautrec, but for any man of normal height, they're entirely too low. Breakfast tables or dining-room sideboards can both be put into service at the party bar. A long, narrow table with all liquors, bar equipment, glassware and carbonated waters on top is preferable to a wide table with limited access. Chafing-dish or platter food is best offered at another buffet table. At really big levees, hosts sometimes set up two bars strategically placed so that the crush of traffic at any one spot is never too great.

BARTENDERS

Just when a small crowd becomes a big one is one of those twilight distinctions that depend on your own party experience, your bar space and your floor space. If, as the host, you're also your own bartender, chef, maître d'hôtel, waiter and coat-check attendant all rolled into one, then a party of 10 to 12 people is just about as large as you'll want to handle alone. If the drinking party is 18 to 24 or above, you'll find it best to hire a bartender-waiter, i.e., one who mixes and serves drinks and takes care of the normal cleanup as the party proceeds, as well as the after-party cleanup. Sometimes the owner of your favorite bistro or manager of your club restaurant will suggest one of his staff who's willing to work on a day or evening off. Perhaps a friend or a friend of a friend will know of an available party bartender. Public agencies as well as college employment services are both sources of supply for single engagements.

When you hire a bartender, remember to spell out beforehand precisely what his duties will be. Fifteen minutes' or a half hour's orientation will pay off well. If a special mixed drink is to be offered, it's a good idea to actually go through a test run beforehand. For mixing any offbeat drinks, the bartender should use a measuring jigger, following proportions exactly. For standard martinis, manhattans and on-the-rocks drinks, he may pour freehanded only if his hand is sufficiently trained to pour with accuracy. He may ask guests to "say when." But nothing—absolutely nothing—at a drinking party will cause guests to feel as ill starred and unhappy as drinks poured freehanded that are irritatingly weak or unmercifully strong. If the bartender is unsure of his pouring hand, it's a good idea to have him use the measuring jigger, and then simply and quietly ask each guest served if he'd care for a dividend or a double.

ICE FOR PARTIES

Knowing that you're about to prepare for a wet holiday, you should begin making and collecting ice cubes several days (not hours) in advance of your party. If you don't have sufficient ice-making equipment or ice storage space, arrange with a local ice dealer to get ice from him or have him deliver it—as close to partytime as possible. If you're in need of an ice block for your punch bowl, the iceman will supply it, or you can make your own punch-bowl glacier (see page 31). Time and again at otherwise fine parties, the host finds himself scraping the bottom of the ice bucket, draining cocktail shakers for used ice, while his freezer works furiously to keep pace with his party's demands. At any cocktail party, count on at least a half tray of ice per person. For long, drawn-out parties or for outdoor parties in warm weather, count on a full tray per person. If you're buying ice cubes, count on a minimum of $3/4$ pound and a maximum of $1^1/2$ pounds per person.

PARTY DRINKING EQUIPMENT

Priming the pumps for a drinking party is more than playing with the multiplication table. If you own only one of those cozy cocktail shakers or mixing glasses with a capacity of two cocktails, you'll obviously need a more commodious piece of barware for a dozen or 18 people. If, on the other hand, your mixing glass has a capacity of six drinks, and assuming you've invited 18 people for cocktails, it doesn't follow that you must rush out and hastily buy two more mixing glasses. Most likely the 18 celebrants won't arrive en masse. Batches of drinks can be quickly stirred or shaken from time to time for those present. But if you plan to offer a choice of martinis and rum sours, the same mixing glass can be used continuously only if your bar is in the kitchen or right alongside a sink where the mixing glass can be washed as often as necessary. Two mixing glasses with strainers or one martini pitcher and one cocktail shaker are indicated.

Assume, again, that 18 drinking comrades are coming for a fling of tall coolers or on-the-rocks drinks and that you own six highball stirrers. Here, you *should* shoulder drinking arms and multiply six times three at least or, to be more practical, about six times ten. Stirrers—like cocktail or canapé spears—disappear fast and irretrievably. There should always be legions of them along with coasters and cocktail napkins for any possible deluge. There should also be mountains of cocktail napkins not only for drinks but every time you serve hot or cold hors d'oeuvres for hand-picking.

If you're planning party libations made with fresh fruit juice, then your small hand squeezer should retire in favor of the latest electrical equipment.

At least two large ice buckets should be on hand for any party above ten. At patio and picnic parties, plastic-foam ice buckets are completely serviceable and acceptable, but for indoor use you'll probably want to use something more elegant.

Finally, you should have two or three bottle openers, since this piece of bar gadgetry is inevitably misplaced. Whenever a party brings large numbers into your drinking circle, check the bar equipment in the color illustration section for mass imbibing.

PARTY GLASSWARE

Not even Lloyd's of London would be likely to bet on the glassware needed for a bachelor party. When the bride's health is being toasted and retoasted and all the glasses are dutifully smashed in the nearest fireplace after each round because they cannot be raised for any purpose more worthy, the amount of glassware needed obviously becomes astronomical. It's the only drinking occasion where cheap dime-store glassware might be justified. For the usual cocktail party, there should be at least two glasses per drinker. Caterers who supply glassware for private parties will furnish from three to five glasses per person on the theory that it's not practical to wash glasses after each round of drinks. But in your own kitchen, particularly if you've hired someone for glass washing, the two-per-cocktailer is a practical formula which allows ample time for washing, refills, etc. If you're serving tall drinks, from gin rickeys to rum collins, you can again safely count on two glasses per person. For other merry-go-rounds, the host should set special sights for his glassware needs, depending on the particular kind of liquid cheer which is being offered. If, for instance, you're mapping out a wine-tasting party, there should be a complete set of clean glasses for each different wine, so that tasters making the rounds of pleasure from one wine to the next can sip comparatively without running into their neighbors' drinking vessels. Thus, eight people sipping four different clarets should have access to

32 wineglasses. Consider the opposite extreme. At a midnight hot-grog party, a single mug per person, with a 25-percent surplus for possible breakage or spur-of-the-moment guests, will usually be enough. Guests particularly treasure their mulled or blazed drinks. They sip them as slowly as possible and will very peacefully wait for refills. At a punch-bowl party, most of the crowd wanting seconds or thirds simply take their own punch cups to the bowl and ladle out their refills. The same formula of one glass per person (plus a reserve of 25 percent) also goes for table wineglasses at a dinner party, brandy glasses and liqueur glasses.

DRINK CALCULATOR

As a rule, the drinking curve rises headlong on holidays and weekends and descends at other times. Also, as men get older, their capacity for hoisting and draining the glass increases. Seniors drink more, and can hold more, than freshmen. The class of 1940 at its annual midwinter reunion polishes off considerably more than the class of 1970. The '70s raise more thunder about their drinking, but at the end of the evening, when the actual liquor tally is made, the older imbibers will be far ahead of the more youthful alumni. A party around a punch bowl will normally drink at least 50 percent more than a party where the host laboriously mixes drinks one by one to order. Often, the place where one cracks his bottles determines the amount of liquid cheer consumed. The liquor downed at a dockside party is of far greater volume than the drink dispensed from a boat's galley. Ale or beer drinkers cavorting at an outdoor lobster barbecue will kill kegs rather than the bottles of an indoor seafood party.

Before estimating how much liquor to buy for any party where mixed drinks are served, you must start out with the specific recipes you have in mind. If, for instance, you plan to serve brandy sours, you must decide beforehand whether each drink will have a 1½-ounce or a 2-ounce base. If you're serving tall coolers with rum and other spirits, you must go back to the base recipe, check each kind of spirit called for, and then expand it to any number up to infinity. Even when your goal isn't infinity, it's always best in your calculations to err on the side of too much. Certainly, if you're buying for your party the same spirits you'd normally stock in your liquor cabinet, additional bottles left over are good liquid assets. And in buying a half-dozen or dozen bottles at a time, you can usually tuck away a noticeable saving under the single-bottle price.

A useful guideline for parties, tested over and over, is simply this: Most of the crowd will consume two to three drinks at the usual cocktail hour at sundown, before a buffet or before a sit-down dinner. After dinner, if you're serving highballs, you can again reasonably estimate two to three drinks per person, depending on how long guests remain after the dinner table has been cleared. At a knock-down, drag-out bachelor party, the two-to-three formula will expand to four-to-six. At a pre-theater party, where everyone wants to keep an especially clear head, the formula may dip to one to two drinks per guest. The following guide covers cocktails before dinner or postprandial highballs. If you're serving both, calculate both.

If you're the host for a party of	As a rule, they'll consume	If drinks are 1½ ozs., you'll need at least	If drinks are 2 ozs., you'll need at least
6	12–18 drinks	2 fifths	2 fifths
8	16–24 ,,	2 ,,	2 ,,
10	20–30 ,,	2 ,,	3 ,,
12	24–36 ,,	3 ,,	3 ,,
20	40–60 ,,	4 ,,	5 ,,
30	60–90 ,,	6 ,,	8 ,,

To be on the plus side, quarts may be purchased instead of fifths; often there's a saving in the larger bottles.

In buying wines for a party, the host should allow three ounces for a serving of an apéritif wine, sherry or port. Red and white table wines, including champagne, are usually poured in four-ounce portions, assuming that you're using generous 11-ounce tulip glasses or wide-bellied wineglasses. If a single wine is served throughout the dinner, count on two or three glasses per person. If several wines are served with individual courses, count on one or two glasses of each wine per person.

If you're serving predinner apéritif wines, not apéritif cocktails, or if you're serving sherry or port for a party of	your guests will generally average	You should buy or have on hand ready for serving
6	6–12 drinks	2 fifths
8	8–16 ,,	2 ,,
10	10–20 ,,	3 ,,
12	12–24 ,,	3 ,,
20	20–40 ,,	5 ,,
30	30–60 ,,	8 ,,

When serving a single red or white table wine throughout the meal and your party consists of	Your guests will generally average	You should buy or have on hand ready for serving
6	12–18 drinks	3 fifths
8	16–24 ,,	4 ,,
10	20–30 ,,	5 ,,
12	24–36 ,,	6 ,,
20	40–60 ,,	10 ,,
30	60–90 ,,	15 ,,

The above wine schedule also applies to champagne or other sparkling wines served during the dinner. If the bubbly is served before the dinner as cocktails or after the dinner for toasting, the same guide may be followed.

Brandy and liqueurs are in a special category when served straight and not as an ingredient in dessert cocktails, liqueur frappés, etc. The usual serving in the small brandy glass as well as the larger brandy snifter is one ounce per person; the same goes for liqueurs served straight.

When pouring brandy or liqueurs as after-dinner drinks for a party of	As a rule they'll consume	You'll need the following fifths of brandy or liqueurs
6	6–12 drinks	1 fifth
8	8–16 drinks	1 fifth
10	10–20 ,,	1 ,,
12	12–24 ,,	1 ,,
20	20–40 ,,	2 fifths
30	30–60 ,,	3 ,,

Note well: Many small bottles of imported liqueurs are odd sizes like $^{23}/_{32}$ pint or 11.8 fluid ounces. The American fifth is 25.6 ounces. Make adjustments, if necessary, when calculating your party needs.

In estimating carbonated waters such as club soda, tonic water, ginger ale, cola drinks, etc., a generous guideline is to allow a 28-ounce bottle for each two persons. Thus, a person consuming three gin and tonics would usually pour from 12 to 14 ounces for his three drinks. The smaller 12-ounce bottles of carbonated waters are easy when guests are pouring their own drinks at cocktail tables. Larger-size bottles are used when a bartender is doing the honors. If you're using your own soda water made with soda charges, keep plenty of charges in reserve. The usual charge makes one quart of soda.

At an all-beer party—a picnic, barbecue or steak party—count on an average of three bottles of beer, ale or stout per person.

So much for a general guide to successful party planning; we now recommend to you several specific party ideas that we've found enjoyable. The following fêtes don't, of course, represent a comprehensive listing of all party plans—they're merely intended as a sampling of the many possible courses to follow. And this is as it should be. Our purpose is to suggest enough ideas to spark your own imagination. Glean those that complement your style of living and then embellish them with personal touches that will make each party very much your own thing.

24
PARTIES FOR PLEASURE

THE BRUNCH PARTY

Of all formulas concocted to cast off the post-Saturday-night pall, none is more likely to recapture the previous night's camaraderie and smooth the rumpled features of the late-rising night owl quicker than a festive early-afternoon array of good food and drink. There are winter brunches before a blazing log fire, spring brunches for inaugurating the new cabin cruiser, summer after-tennis fêtes held at courtside, and autumn brunches offered either indoors or on your terrace, to mention just a few of the species and subspecies.

Although your agenda may be scheduled for a noonish kickoff, the whole day's docket should be as flexible as possible. A bon-voyage brunch, for instance, before a sailing or a plane flight may be given on the midmorning or midafternoon of departure. And brunchers who love the pleasant preamble of a walk, a swim, a short drive or just the indulgence of breathing in the cool morning zephyrs before brunchtime are entitled to the privilege of eating when they're hungry and drinking when they're dry—in either order.

One of the first duties of the brunchmaster is to set a sumptuous table, and the first step toward that end is to acquire tableware that's vivid and inviting. A single glass of orange juice or a screwdriver is a somewhat humdrum sight, but the same drinks become munificent and inviting when they're served from deep glass pitchers resting in an iced champagne bucket. Highly burnished Sheffield platters and coffee sets, once of interest mainly to antiquarians, are now sought after as modern graces of the brunch table. At an alfresco brunch, a hibachi or a portable charcoaler with a smoker top is perfect for conquering early-afternoon appetites with mixed grills of lamb chops, sausages, tomatoes, ham steaks, mushrooms and kidneys. Scrambled eggs should arrive on imposing platters or nestled in warm chafing dishes. Corned-beef hash or chicken hash-browned should be kept warm on hot trays or in casseroles over a trivet flame or candle lamp.

One of the most auspicious sights at any brunch table is a commodious breadbasket piled high with warm quick breads. Today, this kind of prodigality is merely a matter of shopping at the right bakeries. If you've access to a French baker, you can garner fresh *brioches,* the richest and silkiest of soft rolls, flaky *croissants* so tender they seem to float away when you sample them, long salt sticks and crisp club rolls. Italians will revel in their huge *panettone,* a billowy mound of a yeast cake with raisins and candied fruit. For partisans of Americana there are blueberry muffins, corn muffins and pecan buns, all from the bakery or frozen-food counters. All quick breads or buns require no more toil than brief baking or warming in the oven. And the best coffee in the world will taste even better if you own an electric grinder and use it just before brewing.

Many dedicated brunchmen look to the Scandinavian smorgasbord for inspiration: cold rare roast beef, ox tongue, ham, rolled pork, sautéed kidneys, herring with boiled potatoes, hard and semisoft cheeses and a selection of rich fruit jams. One of the best things about a smorgasbord brunch is that it can take care of itself; after the platters are set out, you simply join your guests in the waiting line.

Sunday brunches start with pick-me-ups that have the effect of alternately stimulating and soothing; the usual screwdrivers with vodka may be varied with rum, sherry or Pernod. And be sure to lay in a stock of after-brunch liqueurs—especially a fine coffee liqueur with a float of heavy cream, served ice-cold. We know of no potion that so gently makes the clock stand still.

The Post-Football Fête

For one of October's most inviting recipes, take a cool Saturday afternoon, stir in approximately two hours of gridiron grandstanding, moisten to taste with *eau de vie* from a hip flask, then simmer down to a leisurely evening repast in the mellow light of your own digs. Ever since Englishmen in the 11th Century engaged in the manly sport of kicking around old skulls on battlefields. *futballe* has been one of the most uninhibited forms of ordered mayhem known to man. Happily, it has its own highly civilized safety valve—the convocation at cocktails and dinner following the game, when the afternoon's formations and strategies are all relived calmly in the vicinity of home bar and ice bucket. Only a fiercely loyal alumnus returning home from his own campus can appreciate the rich colors of the fall—the scarlet of a bloody mary, the harvest yellow of a 16-ounce mug overflowing with frosty ale, the autumnal haze surrounding a double old-fashioned glass filled with whiskey and rocks.

One of the best things about football is that it starts with the September oyster season and its fried-oyster platters, oysters on the half shell and creamy oyster stews. Coolish nights bring out the carnivore in men, best satisfied by such hearty fare as rich oxtail stews, calf's liver sautéed with calvados, and Swiss steaks simmered with Spanish onions, peppers and tomatoes.

Every chef planning to tackle an after-football party is automatically guided by one obvious ground rule: All preliminaries for the party must take place either before or after the game. You can't retire to the kitchen between halves. A dinner that's cooked before the game and held for serving time can be as elaborate as you wish as long as it doesn't keep you from reaching your seat before the first whistle blows. An after-game menu naturally must consist of ready-in-a-minute foods. Wise kitchen strategists often combine both styles into winning combinations. An oxtail stew, for instance—cooking time, four hours—may be simmered a day or two before the game; stews always taste better when reheated, anyway. Hot smoked-oyster canapés can be broiled while guests are still making their first sweep toward the ice bucket.

The protracted cheering and jeering that goes on at any big tilt always creates a special symptom diagnosed as pigskin thirst. The most obvious kind of first aid is the double highball. Very prominently favored in the postfootball pharmacopoeia is the rob roy, served either cold or hot—in an old-fashioned glass or in a mug with boiling water and stick cinnamon. For those of pure Scotch blood who'd rather skip the vermouth, a hot old-fashioned made with two ounces of Scotch will provide instant comfort. Many college men, past and present, simplify the whole problem of entertaining both their friends and some of their gridiron adversaries by offering the oldest of Anglo-Saxon potables—liquid malt. It was no accident that, for many centuries, breweries were located right on the campuses of English colleges. But even today, as the fall deepens into winter, a thirst doth rise for nut-brown ale and creamy stout. Both of them blend beautifully when poured together into tall seidels. Gambrinus' brew may flow with any food when men move from gridiron to groaning board.

AN APRÈS-SKI PARTY

Few things on this earth put a more ravenous edge on a man's appetite than a bracing, frost-nipped day on the slopes. When the day's skiing is over, Valhalla seems near at hand as the mountain air becomes suffused with the aromas of hot seafood chowder, strong coffee and steaming rum toddies.

There are a number of techniques for hosting a ski feast. You can muster the whole meal ready-made, from quiche Lorraine to cognac, using any first-class restaurant or club kitchen as your commissary, and then transport it intact to your lodge, where the simple chore of reheating is all that's required. Of course, if your lodge's larder and kitchen facilities lend themselves to on-the-scene cookery, you may prefer starting from scratch. Or you can cook a stew or glaze spareribs in your own kitchen beforehand, pack them in wide-mouthed vacuum jugs and insulated picnic bags, then simply unpack when you're ready to serve the hungry snowmen and their snow bunnies. If you're a ski host of the one-day-sojourn-to-a-nearby-slope persuasion, you might take along the raw ingredients in your station wagon, drop the tail gate for a buffet table, light the hibachi or gasoline stove and broil the teriyaki or sauté the steaks to order.

There was a time when buying cooked collations meant a lot of bother. Advance shopping these days requires about as much effort as a trip on a chair lift. If you've access to a Swedish foodshop or café, Swedish meatballs as well as sweet-and-sour baked beans seem especially designed for modern appetites. Neapolitan Italy may not be the habitat for skiing, but any of the small pastas in rich cheese sauce or tomato sauce are perfect for relishing under the open sky. For cooking on the station-wagon barbecue, tender meats such as tournedos or shish kebab are all quickly done over a crackling fire. Turn such foods frequently, since the frigid air above the fire cools them quickly.

If all this begins to sound like a summer picnic, it's not coincidental—but you'll soon discover major differences. There are no ants, for example, in the winter, and there are some ski stamping grounds where Klondike temperatures cause cutlery,

dinner plates and mugs to become so frostbitten they can hardly
be handled. To avert such a cold fate, it's wise to protect your
dinnerware in an insulated picnic box—the kind that's used in
summer to keep things cold. And if you're carrying hot grog,
remember that winter drinks are made with boiling water, and
the mugs in which they're served make for really tall drinks;
consequently, a gallon vacuum jugful is just about enough to
warm the cockles and soothe the muscles of four to six skiers. To
keep the grog hot, of course, you should preheat the jug by
pouring boiling water into it and letting it remain for about five
minutes before replacing it with your hot potation. For hot-drink
recipes, see pages 277 to 284.

THE INTIMATE SUNDOWN PARTY

Americans are generally agreed that the best way to watch
the evening sun go down is through a cocktail glass. The most
frequent and fashionable way to celebrate that heavenly event is
the small, intimate cocktail party, where a few friends gather to
skoal each other in the congenial setting of one's home, rather
than at the kind of mass drinking session where cocktailers are
as crowded as the hold of a slave ship.

For such an intimate assemblage, no radical rearrangement
of furniture is necessary. But if your studio or apartment is the
scene of frequent predinner gatherings, it's a good idea to own
cocktail tables that are alcoholproof or else cover them with glass
tops. So that each guest will have a spot within arm's reach
where he can easily rest his glass, small folding tables or stack
tables should be distributed wherever necessary.

If you're addicted to spur-of-the-moment cocktail parties,
your basic bar inventory should be well stocked at all times.
Take a quick check of your hard and soft bar supplies once or
twice a week, particularly before weekends. Don't be caught in
the all too common spot of the host who undertakes to mix three
frozen daiquiris only to find that he has about two ounces of
light rum left in his bottle, or plenty of sweet vermouth but an
embarrassingly small supply of dry vermouth for the six guests
who opted for martinis.

As for the finger food, millions of toasties, tidbits, hot and
cold hors d'oeuvres, canapés and quiches are sold all ready for
the oven, bowl or tray. When making your selection, simply ask
yourself, are they decidedly provocative in flavor, salty, peppery
or in some way piquant? They needn't be so spice-laden that
they take your scalp off, but they should spur rather than
dampen both the thirst apparatus and the taste buds. Ordinary

boiled ham, for instance, merely pacifies the taste juices; genuine razorback Smithfield ham, cured with pepper, sets them flowing.

If you want your canapés or hors d'oeuvres to be as showy as possible, buy them already prepared. If you're an hors d'oeuvre hobbyist and want your appetizers to bear your own culinary signature, consult pages 287 to 305. In any event, remember that hot hors d'oeuvres should be so hot as to make you hesitate before you take the second bite; cold hors d'oeuvres, with the exception of cheese, which should be at room temperature, should taste as though they were just removed from an ice block on the North Pole.

A sensible custom is to place on the buffet or cocktail table two or three platters of really distinguished sundown goods such as Stilton cheese, *pâté de foie gras,* beluga caviar, Westphalian or prosciutto ham, smoked turkey and other high-stepping dishes that don't normally appear on the boarding-house table. Guests can then scoop out the cheese or pâté and spread it on crackers or toast while the host sits Buddhalike in the background.

When you ask your friends to a simple cocktail party and not a cocktail supper, be sure to tell them in the clearest terms that they're invited to cocktails *before* dinner. Cocktail parties sometimes lead to spur-of-the-moment expeditions to a restaurant or potluck parties in your own pad, but a host should encourage such spontaneous suggestions only after a down-to-earth assessment of what's likely to be both practical and pleasurable for both himself and his guests.

THE BACHELOR DINNER PARTY

Judgment day doesn't necessarily coincide with one's wedding day; it often occurs several nights before the nuptials are celebrated, during the trial by alcohol, the riotous rite identified as the bachelor dinner party. Seldom is a bachelor dinner a do-it-yourself bacchanalia in your own pad, however; it is a pay-it-yourself affair, although sometimes the prospective father-in-law or the best man and some of his buddies will pick up the tab. In any case, a private room in a hotel or club is infinitely more practical than your own digs for absorbing the shock of baked Alaskas crashing on the floor, martinis poured into grand pianos and champagne glasses sailing at supersonic speed into fireplaces. Those about to give up their bachelorhood should be guided by the following straight steers on the last supper.

Choose a private dining room in a club, hotel or restaurant that can best be described as clubbable—that is, a *gemütlich* room with absolute privacy where the dinner and service are handled by top-flight pros. Avoid the type of men's clubs that have always been inhabited by live corpses. In many cities there are university clubs, among others, where the atmosphere is intimate, easy and jovial. A nonmember of a particular club may often use the club's facilities simply by asking one of his acquaintances who is a member to sponsor him as a guest. Some clubs and all hotels include bedroom facilities, where guests who lose all power of locomotion can be quietly transported and stashed away until their heads resume normal size.

A bachelor dinner, in spite of all the ribbing and riling, should allow trenchermen to get together and enjoy an evening of reminiscences and sociability. Although the party may start with martinis, switch to beer or wine with the steak, champagne with the dessert, cognac with the coffee, and resume with champagne, toasting on into the night, it shouldn't be designed to turn men into human drainpipes. One way to divert the drinkers to eating is to escort your guests vigorously to the table right after the second round of cocktails. Additional drinks may be served at the table, but they'll soon be phased out by the crab-meat or jumbo-shrimp cocktails as serious eating begins. Offer the kind of soup guests simply can't ignore—bowls of velvety black-bean soup or baked onion soup au gratin. Avoid a fillet of sole marguery with its opulent sauce and order instead a simple broiled striped bass or Kennebec salmon. Beefsteak is the traditional meat course at a bachelor dinner. It can be dressed up as a planked steak surrounded with vegetables, but the most impressive and practical is the thick shell steak, a boneless cut of about six portions, which is sliced before serving. Draw the dinner to a close with a platter of assorted cheeses and salted crackers or, if you have a sweet tooth, with a warm wedge of apple pie topped with cheddar cheese, or vanilla ice cream and warm brandied peaches.

The old custom of toasting the bride by breaking the glass against the fireplace symbolizes a number of things—the love of the bride and groom, which will continue to last until the glass is made whole again, or the fact that the glass can't possibly be used for any worthier purpose. Whatever tradition lies behind the custom, there's no doubt about its consequence: It costs like hell. Most clubs and hotels will furnish inexpensive glasses for breaking rather than hand-blown crystal etched with their own crest.

Young grooms who receive a bill for their bachelor party sometimes go into a state of deep shock. The best way to avoid being rolled is to ascertain all possible charges beforehand. Ask the steward or manager if there is any reduction when drinks are ordered beforehand in volume. Frequently there is. Ask for sample menus. When you make your choice at a stated price, ask what charges there will be for room rental, if any, the number of

covers you must guarantee, how many additional covers the
kitchen can take care of in the event there's a last-minute
increase in the number of cronies attending, the cost of flowers,
cigars, cigarettes, glassware breakage and other so-called
incidentals. Count on the usual 15- to 20-percent tip. It's a good
idea to slip the headwaiter a five- or ten-spot before the dinner,
explaining that he'll receive the main gratuity later for dividing
among the help. A prepayment of this kind not only encourages
him to give the best possible service during the dinner, but often
is an insurance against later hijacking. Remember simply that
while marriages are sometimes made in heaven, bachelor dinners
require more earthly considerations.

AN ALFRESCO PARTY

Something marvelously metaphysical takes place when an
indoor meal, no matter how magnificent, is carried outdoors.
Simply by crossing the threshold between living room and
terrace, vichyssoise suddenly becomes creamier, champagne
bubblier and fruit juicier. An alfresco dining room can be a
terrace high above a city street, a stretch of bluestone beside a
swimming pool or a grass carpet beneath a patio umbrella. There
were terraces long before there were tranquilizers. Guests
stretched out on your leisure chairs, feeling charitable toward the
whole world, may be predisposed to find whatever food and
drink you proffer to be perfect. No effort must be spared, of
course, to make the menu match their expectations, but there's
no reason that a host can't enjoy his own hospitality. To help
keep him as carefree as possible, there are now many models of
food carts available, all designed to quickly and quietly transport
food and drink from indoors to outdoors. Some come with
movable shelves and drawers, some with hot table surfaces that
merely require plugging in to keep soup marmites and casseroles
bubbling hot. There are others with recessed condiment racks,
with insulated compartments for crushed ice, or even with beds
for charcoal fires.

Quite often a meal served under the heavens will include an
old classic, such as cold chicken Jeanette—boneless cooked
breast of chicken in a velvety jellied sauce, flanked with slices of
pâté de foie gras. It's not literally new but, like the charm of
baroque music reaching ears for the first time, it comes as a fresh
discovery whenever it's served. Alfresco menus on the grand
scale tend to be an appetizing amalgam of hot and cold. Hot
consommé with a feathery garnish of spun eggs will provide all
the benefits of a kitchen comfortably beyond the range of its
heat. Cold peaches in champagne will take the edge off the most
torrid summer day.

Like coffee and cognac, alfresco dinners and summer wine cups glorify each other. Two good examples are raspberry claret cup page 231 and white wine cooler page 237. The Spanish are past masters at this art, as anyone can testify who's ever slaked his thirst with the countless species of *sangrías* in the Iberian Peninsula. See page 272. All good wine cups in the summertime seem to share one common fault: They're never big enough. Even non–wine drinkers find themselves drinking on and on. Hours will pass, and the wine cup is still *fresco*.

THE COCKTAIL SUPPER PARTY

The cocktail supper is based on the theory that it takes more than peanuts to make a party. As a meal, it stands midway between the tidbittery of a mere drinking session and a full-fledged sit-down dinner. The appetites that always stir wherever drinks are served may be temporarily appeased with hot and cold hors d'oeuvres, but the most satisfying provender the gods can possibly provide is casseroles of chicken, bowls of herbed rice, beef stew in red wine—the cordial elements of an easy buffet. In planning a cocktail supper, the host must make sure that his guests are otherwise uncommitted for the evening. He should clearly spell out the fact that hunger as well as thirst will be exorcised, and he shouldn't draw the line for winding up the party at any particular time.

At a cocktail supper, let your food be ample, your menu brief. Instead of caravans of rich canapés with more garnishes than you can shake a cocktail spear at, the appetizers should feature a single cold and a single hot hors d'oeuvre of unrivaled goodness. The main dish that follows may be hot or cold or a seasonable combination of the two. Cold glazed ham, for example, and hot Swedish brown beans form a compatible partnership along with a mushroom-and-asparagus salad with curried mayonnaise. Or a hot beef or veal goulash may be served with hot buttered noodles or with a cold noodle salad and a julienne of radishes, green peppers and scallions, and a French dressing with Parmesan cheese. Desserts should be the noncooked type such as strawberries Romanoff or a fresh-fruit compote with kirsch, supplemented with a tray of assorted small specialties from the best pastryshop within driving distance.

As for the drinking at a cocktail supper, anything goes. If you want to accompany food with wine, of course you may, but it's not necessary; American devotees of the cocktail will find a sazerac or a bourbon mist quite gratifying with their food as well as before it. Wine-oriented conservatives from the Continent may

writhe, but Americans who blissfully drink their 11-to-1 martinis
with the appetizers will be gloriously happy to continue
downing them with the meal.

Hosts should also face the fact that at the cocktail hour these
days the most important things aren't necessarily cocktails. They
may be highballs, lowballs or drinks of any variety from fino
sherry to shandygaff. Finally, men who confidently offer one
main dish at a cocktail supper shouldn't hesitate to offer one
main drink, perfectly balanced and served, for which they've
won their bar spurs.

THE GALLEY PARTY

It's hard to imagine surroundings more felicitous for a party
than topside on a boat moored in a quiet cove, the summer
stillness broken only by the gentle lapping of gin and tonics
against frosty tumblers.

The kind of victuals you stow aboard depends for the most
part on the length of your cruise and the size of your galley. If
you're speedboating from one yacht club to another, of course,
you can pick up food and drink wherever you happen to tie up.
Slightly longer trips are simply floating picnics. You pack your
portable cooler with unsliced rare roast beef, corned beef brisket
or barbecued chickens, fill a deep bowl with German potato
salad, stack the fresh rye and the pumpernickel, remember the
mustard, add the necessary amount of cold lager to your cargo,
and shove off. But for an all-day or weekend cruise, you'll want
hot and hefty fare from your own galley. The sailor assigned to
the job may have a misgiving or two when he or she lights the
ministove, but when the aroma of crisp bacon or hashed brown
potatoes or hot clam chowder first rises on deck, all hands will
know that the real master of the vessel is stationed below.

Cruising schedules on rivers, lakes and seas all over the
world are alike in one respect: The best-laid schemes gang aft
agley in the face of becalmed waters or ailing engines.
Anticipating these normal delays, an experienced commodore
sees to it that there are always extra rations in cans. The entire
crew will welcome a canned cured ham as readily as a fresh one.
Buy the type, if possible, that requires no refrigeration. Canned
Canadian-style bacon—another name for smoked boneless pork
loin—is equally good hot or cold, at sea as well as on land. In
the canned-chicken department, large cans containing whole
birds are a better bet than the small cans or jars filled with
trimmings. Corned-beef hash or roast-beef hash, both staunch
nautical standbys, can go into the frying pan without any
additions, although you can enhance them mightily with a few
beaten egg yolks, cream or melted butter and a spray of

Worcestershire sauce. Among canned meats and seafood, the field is unlimited—from galantine to gaffelbiter. Just remember, though, that some of the foods that sound exotic—kangaroo steak or canned wild boar—aren't likely to satisfy a ravenous seafaring party as readily as generous helpings of chili con carne, meat-stuffed ravioli and other time-tested pleasures. There are days when nothing, not even 151-proof rum, can warm a crew like mugs of hot thick soup, many of which now come in foil envelopes.

Since most cruising for party purposes takes place in warm or comparatively warm climates, tall coolers fit in perfectly with offshore outings. But the gross tonnage of corkscrews, cans, bottles, ice buckets, tongs, racks and ice picks can sometimes present a formidable obstacle course twixt the gent who's drawn the duty as bartender and his wares. To avoid this kind of overstocking, carry one superb totable potable, premixed on land, needing in some cases only the addition of carbonated waters. If you decide on straight drinks, try to carry no more bottles and glassware than fit into a mounted bar rack. Finally, insulated unbreakable bar glasses conserve ice and are the mainstay of many a waterborne party.

THE INDOOR PICNIC

The best season for an indoor picnic is late winter, after you've recovered from end-of-the-year revelries and before the promise of a warm outdoors has become more than a pipe dream. The most natural site for such a celebration is directly in front of a glowing fireplace. Guests can gather near the hearth, preferably picnic style on the floor, and grill to their hearts' content.

Like any well-bred picnic, your party should be a communal cook-in. Too many cooks can spoil a broth, but not a picnic. In fact, to keep a picnicker from joining in the cooking is an implied insult. While some of the party thread shrimp onto skewers, others can be basting the split squabs, the sirloin or tenderloin steaks. Martini mixers can twirl away while others open bottles of wine, and the couple in the corner, oblivious to the world, brew their own version of Irish coffee. Skewered beef, ham or spareribs, even chunks of boned and skinned breast of chicken are all magnificent fireside fare, basted with soy sauce, barbecue sauce or olive oil flavored with herbs, mustard and garlic.

On such occasions, the hibachi is perfect for the man who likes to play with fire. You'll need two double-size grills for a picnic party of from eight to ten. If you lack a fireplace, the best technique is to light your hibachi outdoors. When smoke no longer gets in your eyes, bring the fire equipment inside and place it on a stove or near a ventilating fan or hood. If your barbecue party stretches into several hours, build a double bed of charcoal two inches thick. Stack extra coals on the right and left sides of each brazier to provide even fire at the flared ends.

As host, it's your job to supply at least the main course; co-picnickers can be called upon to furnish a tasty bean salad or a box of delicious mignon éclairs. You should also furnish all the necessary accouterments—the hibachis, tableware, bar tools, brushes for basting, extra-long tongs, spatulas and forks for scooping food from the grill.

Guests bearing liquid gifts will probably show up with whiskey, gin and vermouth, which do yeoman's service on any bibbing occasion. But you'll be prepared for all comers—with or without bottles—if you have a gallon vacuum jug filled with bloody marys that have been premixed with ice, then drained into the jug for subsequent serving on the rocks in old-fashioned glasses. Chilled all-purpose wines such as Sylvaner should come to the party with the cold bloom still on the bottles. Among reds, the eye-opening flavor of zinfandel is the perfect complement for charcoal-broiled meats and seafood.

THE CATERED PARTY

Sheer numbers aren't in themselves a guarantee that a party will be a howling hit, but for mounting a saturnalia featuring both food and drink, a crowd of a dozen or so well-matched pairs is just about big enough to be unbridled in a civilized way. The host who wants to have as good a time as his guests, however, keeps in mind that when the guest list goes above a score of people, party planning should be turned over to the pros. Caterers are masters of movable feasts. An experienced caterer is always happy to listen to the most inquisitorial host, confer with him, guide him, and even on rare occasions yield to him, provided he accepts the caterer's guiding philosophy: Don't do it yourself.

Hosts in search of caterers are usually guided by that oldest and most dependable of media—word of mouth. Some caterers are justly renowned for their pasta dishes. Others are luau specialists. There are hors d'oeuvre monarchs and canapé czars. So don't hesitate to ask a caterer which dish he considers his finest opus—and invite him, if possible, to offer samples. Many caterers have specialties such as beef stroganoff stashed away in their refrigerators or freezers. Naturally, no caterer will be able to snap his fingers and produce an instant 12-pound cold stuffed lobster in aspic while you're waiting in his reception room. But many of them keep on file a gallery of colored photos and slides of their decorative culinary art. And most caterers are usually more than pleased to display their china, silverware, linen, chafing dishes and other components of their *mise en scène.*

Prices for a catered affair will, of course, depend on your locale and your caterer, but one can figure on a minimum charge of about $8 per person for a simple dinner (including drinks and hors d'oeuvres) on up to $16 per person for the caviar route. In terms of time, temper and money saved by not having to make all of the arrangements yourself, it's a sound investment.

If it's your first adventure in large-scale regalement, you'll want the caterer's counsel on how many celebrants your apartment or town house can comfortably hold for party purposes. In warm climates, terraces are often put to use. An adjoining study can sometimes be opened as an extension of the main party room, but the best parties are those that are not fragmented too noticeably. Keep in mind that you needn't provide seating for all your guests, since practically all large at-home parties today are combination stand-up and sit-down affairs. Guests help themselves and are helped at bountifully stocked buffet tables. Bar waiters circulate among both sit-downers and standees. The informal wall table and the light movable chair are indispensable for easy conversational islets and for keeping hot food and coffee on an even keel.

When the caterer's truck pulls up to your digs, one of the first pieces of equipment he's likely to deliver is a portable bar. In apartments where space is at a premium, however, it's sometimes best to eliminate this option in favor of additional dance-floor or dining space. A working bar can always be improvised in an adjoining room, where drinks are prepared out of sight and passed by waiters to the merrymakers.

In choosing your drinks, the simplest of all bar services is naturally the punch bowl—a perfect choice when drinking is the main focus of attention. But for rejoicing around a buffet, where stacked platters and bubbling chafing dishes are the big centers of interest, the punch bowl is frequently bypassed in favor of the regular bar repertory. In some cases, you may supply the bar stock yourself, but the caterer usually provides all the necessary makings and mixes—as well as the bartender.

As your professionally prepared party moves into high gear, it will take on a special warmth as the catered spirits raise those of the assembled celebrants. It's a glow that will be more than matched by the one you get when, in the midst of your limited duties as master of the revels, you realize that you're not only unruffled and unharried but are enjoying yourself immensely.

AN URBAN LUAU

Staging an indoor luau is as easy as poi. Even being sky-high in an apartment can have some built-in blessings: Guests don't have to scour about for volcanic rocks, ti leaves and palm fronds, and you don't have to dig a pit to roast the traditional whole suckling pig. Instead, just ask a butcher to wrap up his juiciest pork-loin roasts, which you can start sizzling on an indoor rotisserie. If naught but the entire pig on a platter will suffice, you can order one from a professional catering service.

Don't get hung up adorning your pad with fishnets and colored-glass globes. Concentrate on laying out a properly Polynesian bar and buffet, which is, after all, where the action is. Begin by visiting your friendly florist. He won't be able to duplicate all 4000 varieties of hibiscus growing on Oahu, but he can supply you with quantities of lush greenery. Tell him the size of your luau table and ask for enough flat ferns to cover it. Order one or two centerpieces of short-stemmed flowers—long-stemmed beauties are quite acceptable as buffet decorations, but at a sit-down feast they invariably create a junglelike atmosphere that inhibits cross-table conversation. Scatter fruit among the flowers and fronds. Pineapples cut lengthwise, with the meat removed, sliced and returned to the shells, stalks of yellow and red bananas, grapes, citrus fruits and mangoes all make for delicious tropical tidbits that can also serve as decorations. Set the stage as well with plenty of condiments such as chutneys, some mild, others peppery hot. As sideshows, include chopped hard-boiled eggs and chives, tomatoes with basil, cucumbers in yogurt and dill, sliced bananas sprinkled with lime juice and brown sugar, and green salad with avocado and papaya chunks. Tiny morsels of browned coconut meat, called Coco Bits, taste great with coconut-cream or curry dishes.

The potable to proffer at any luau is rum. A stock of light, dark and 151-proof rum will be the base for the rum cocktails, chapter 18, as well as many of the tall coolers, chapter 19. For a special after-dinner tipple, try a sweet Polynesian change of pace such as a pineapple–crème de menthe frappé. Fill saucer champagne glasses three-fourths full with finely crushed ice and pour in a shot of undiluted frozen pineapple juice. Stir it in the glass; then add an ounce of green crème de menthe.

The key to a luau feast is neither pig nor poi but *hoomanawanui,* which means "take it easy." Let the party choose its own speed. A luau isn't an organized affair that requires careful supervision by the host. If you've done your preplanning well, the night can virtually run itself. As you and your guests dream and dance after dinner, you'll find that a luau never really seems to end but slowly drifts off into the moonlight.

THE PROGRESSIVE DINNER PARTY

For those who may not have yet caught up with this kaleidoscopic form of culinary sport, it's a party in which the hosting chores are divided into courses. Everybody may meet at one house for the hors d'oeuvres and cocktails, travel to another for the guinea hen and champagne, to a third for the crepes and demitasse, to a fourth for dancing and highballs, and finally, as the rosy-fingered dawn creeps round, gather in a breakfast room for the comforting stimuli of ice-cold bloody marys and soft-scrambled eggs on toast.

Nobody is ever really invited to a progressive dinner; a compatible crowd—eight or ten usually—gathers together and agrees to an eat-and-drink party. It may be necessary for a ranking member to take phone in hand and make a few initial calls. Some planning is needed—deciding whether it's to be black tie, for instance—but the preliminary huddle around a cocktail table invariably turns into the kind of relaxed fun that the party itself always generates. Each host has the right to select his own course, lest the preliminary planning session turn into a gourmandial Great Debate as smoked salmon is voted or vetoed, Bibb lettuce sent back to the salad committee, or the main course filibustered into the night. Each host, of course, is responsible for one of the five acts in the dinner drama. The provider of the main course takes on a somewhat disproportionate share of work, but in this case the unequal division of labor is one which is coveted by every devoted amateur chef who enjoys showing off.

Too many martinis have been known to seriously stall a progressive dinner at its very first port of call; so moderation in pursuit of the progressive dinner party is no vice. Let all those who have doubts about leaving a cozy apartment after the hors d'oeuvres be assured that the cold, bracing air will only make the *pièce de résistance* all the more irresistible. Appetites are worked up anew, and while the canapés may have been wonderful, the main course will be even more appetizing at the next way station. For long distances, a chauffeur-driven limousine is a worthwhile luxury. The host of each party segment should see to it that the troops leave his predecessor's within a reasonable amount of time and arrive at his own digs en masse. The old, hardened rule that the dinner and diner shall both be ready at the same time is here thrown overboard. Only the dinner waits. The acid test of a good host at a progressive dinner is doing so much in advance that he has practically nothing left to do when his guests arrive.

The host for each course is also the libation pourer for that course. Glassware for the cocktails should be prechilled, frosty

cold. The champagne or white wine to be served with the main
course should have been chilled beforehand, or the château red
wine decanted if necessary. With the dessert and demitasse,
brandy snifters or liqueur glasses or both should be within arm's
reach. At the fourth anchorage, the highball host takes over. If
ever a highball should be commandingly tall, it's late at night,
during the witching hour, when thirsts are at their peak. The
party reaches its happy apogee by the dawn's early light at
breakfast headquarters, where vodka and gin, orange juice,
tomato juice and clam juice (a nifty addition to your bloody
mary) should be ready alongside the bowl of eggs, the electric
skillet and the coffeemaker.

THE THEATER PARTY

Modern epicures have a perfect definition of theater. It's the
interlude between the snack before and the supper afterward.
The idea of pre-theater appeasement rather than a full
trencherman's dinner bolted down in time to make the curtain
gets a big hand from performers and audiences alike. And for
generations the midnight supper *after* the show has been one of
the most gracious of all ways to entertain.

If your theater party is to be really successful, you'll first
pick a play cued to the tastes of your guests. You'll offer them
the prologue of cocktails and the kind of food that takes the edge
off their hunger but still lets them sit through Ionesco or Beckett
with a clear head. Your potables should allow them to roll in the
aisles with the play's fun rather than with the aftereffects of five
martinis. And when the show's over, your party will taxi to the
armchair comfort of your own hearth, where fine food and wine
will help make a bomb tolerable and a superb play bewitching.
In the fall and winter, there are all kinds of dialogues for
fireplace suppers, but none more engaging than the chatter over
cast, staging, sets and story.

While one man can manage this kind of party, there are
times when dual hosting works out best. The first producer gets
the tickets and is responsible for the early snack and for taxi or
limousine service. The second impresario hosts the leisurely
after-theater supper and drink. The division of labor needn't
follow these specifications to the letter, but it's the one we've
found best for intimate theater parties of 6 to 12 people. If you
belong to a theater subscription club, members naturally take
turns throughout the season in hosting the party.

Ironically, the scene of action that hangs up most hosts the
first time they stage a two-act theater party isn't the sumptuous
supper after the show but the small snack before. Bachelors in
the land of plenty still seem to suffer from a pronounced phobia

of not appeasing the belly slave that theoretically rules every civilized man about town. The question of how to allay the appetite without overwhelming it can be answered in very practical terms: Serve the first course of a dinner. Would you normally offer cherrystone clams and an onion soup, a mulligatawny or a cheese fondue? Present any of these, and the first mouthful will assuage the pangs of hunger. Another delightful solution is the smorrebrod—or Danish open sandwiches—eaten with knife and fork. The toppings range from boneless sardines and sliced tomato to smoked cod liver with scrambled eggs and raw chopped steak with onions and capers.

In planning your after-theater menu, the first rule is to avoid duplicating the party of the first part. If there were lobster cocktails beforehand, don't serve coquille of seafood to the captive crowd at midnight. Let your supper program fit the changed mood with dishes of substance such as chicken breasts in a cream sauce flavored with bourbon and sherry, or filet mignon garnished with mushrooms and artichoke bottoms and a red-wine sauce. Avoid avant-garde cookery, dishes that require elaborate carving, and food conversation pieces that try to steal the scene from the show itself. Last-minute preparation, even in your black tie, is perfectly feasible, provided all behind-the-scenes work has been put out of the way beforehand and your labors are limited to little more than simply sautéeing and reheating of sauces.

Before the theater, those who want light cocktails will elect the negroni, vermouth cassis or white-wine cassis. Cocktails on the rocks will appease those who want to make long drinks of short ones. When you return to your apartment after the theater, throw open the full resources of your bar. And for the final program note, what could possibly be better than a tray of liqueurs such as Chartreuse, Benedictine or Grand Marnier poured over rocks or finely shaved ice?

THE 12-to-12 HOLIDAY PARTY

There are festive times round about the holiday season when you and other merrymakers wish the jollification could somehow last and last—as if one wished that time could really be made to stand still. What we here propose as a means of accomplishing this miracle—or something close to it—is a 12-o'clock party, or, more precisely, a 12-to-12 one. The idea is this: Thanks to global time zones, it's midnight—or noon—somewhere in the world every hour on the hour. What you do as host to prolong the pleasure of the holiday is to follow the sun around the world, arresting time by celebrating 12 o'clock—wherever it may be—every hour on the hour for 12 hours. Practically speaking, you serve forth food and drink to your guests hourly, each offering reflecting the ethnic best of some part of the world where the hands of the clocks are pointing straight up. There's no set cocktail time, no set dining time. Your guests may nibble and swig as much or as little as they wish, when they wish, for as long as they wish, and the variety of victuals and potables you proffer will keep the most sylphlike birds and the huskiest trenchermen returning to your bar and buffet for renewed refreshment and high spirits from first arrival to last departure.

Sound like a hell of a lot of work for beleaguered hosts? Rest ye merry, gentlemen; the fun eclipses the toil, and preplanning precludes your being a kitchen slavey. And the stopped-clock informality of your fête (the fact that your guests may drop in, drop out—and return as the holiday moves them) guarantees that your party participants, at any given moment, are *chez vous* because they want to be, not because they've accepted a time-binding invitation.

The wise way to invite friends to your party is to send out written invitations two or three weeks in advance. On each, list the dishes you'll be serving at the hour they're to be offered. By letting your guests know that there will be new manna from your kitchen every hour, your batting average for acceptances will come close to a thousand.

The best plan for most bachelors who've earned their own personal *cordon bleu* is to whip up a few of the 13 courses that have won your friends' loudest bravissimos in the past and purchase the balance of the feast. Buy or prepare enough food for two-thirds the total number of guests invited. Hors d'oeuvre portions such as shrimp or pâté should be larger than normal. Chefs d'oeuvre, meats and poultry, should be smaller than normal. Leftovers can be converted into frozen assets.

To complete your preparations, bedeck the table with candles, flowers or centerpieces, and a fruit bowl or basket. Food plates should be no larger than salad size. Provide the largest

possible stockpile of forks and, at midnight, enough fondue forks
for all present. Napkins should be amassed at the buffet table
and other strategic spots throughout the apartment. There should
be trays of assorted small, split, buttered rolls or small
bread-and-butter sandwiches, allowing one and a half servings
per guest. Store most of the bread and rolls, covered with
moistened towels, in the refrigerator. You'll want to hire three
helpers or recruit some of your friends—one who will act as
custodian of the punch bowls, bar and buffet table; the others to
take care of cooking and cleanup.

At 12 noon you should start the buffet with something like a
cold glazed ham, a potato-and-apple salad flavored with
calvados, and a chafing-dish specialty such as wild rice and
mushrooms. These standbys should be kept available through the
whole party, replenished and refreshed from time to time, to be
enjoyed for themselves or combined with subsequent courses.

Among foods which make their hourly appearance, and
which you can buy in one grand taxi circuit, are: gnocchi, the
Italian dumplings, with Parmesan cheese from your favorite
trattoria; *pâté maison;* quiche Lorraine, warmed just before
serving; cooked, shelled, deveined shrimp on a platter with
Russian dressing and cocktail sauce; cold smoked turkey, sliced
thin but not transparent; Chinese roast duck and roast pork; beef
bourguignon; beef stroganoff; cheese fondue all ready for the
chafing dish; curry of chicken from Indian and many American
restaurants; caviar platter of fresh beluga and red-salmon caviar,
supplemented with a sturgeon-and-radish salad with sour cream.

Courses which might be prepared at your own range could
include: whole filet of beef, roasted in a very hot oven for 30 to
40 minutes; thick shell steaks, broiled, sliced crosswise and
served on toast or buns; crab meat *diavolo,* cooked in a
brandy-flavored, unstrained tomato sauce; sausages, small links
browned in the oven and then simmered in a brown sauce with
white wine.

For the bar, provide a fish-house punch, page 271, and a
champagne punch, page 270, and/or the standard ingredients for
hard drinks, as well as assorted light and dark beers.

A WINE-TASTING PARTY

There's no reason in the world why a party-bent host
couldn't throw a whiskey-tasting party or a rum-tasting party or
even a vodka-tasting party, since vodka, along with everything
else that enters the mouth, *does* leave a taste impression. But it's
doubtful if any of these hypothetical events could whip up the
fun, the wild, hilarious prattle, the endless sippings and

soundings off, the mellow feeling of having become well versed bacchanalogically and the pleasant afterglow that are the natural result of every wine-tasting party.

Note if you will the happy judicial grin of people arriving at a wine-tasting party, each guest knowing that he holds the scales of judgment in his own mouth. There are, of course, self-conscious and sometimes pretentious wine drinkers—especially in England and America—who look upon a wine-tasting session as a court trial. (Some French and German wine promoters encourage this kind of mumbo jumbo in the interests of foreign trade.) The trial hopefully tests the sipper's ability to agree with the price of the wine. But let the host in any blind wine tasting pour his treasured Piesporter *Trockenbeerenauslese* 1959 costing $28 a bottle, and if the wine creates no more excitement than a Bernkasteler Doktor costing $7 a bottle—as may well happen—the host, if not his guests, learns that a wine costing four times the price of another wine doesn't necessarily multiply the pleasure by four. The price of wine, like other things, depends on its supply and the thirsty demand for it. In a blind wine tasting, the mouth sees no dollar signs. There are home-grown grapes in Italy and in this country, pressed into home-made wines, for instance, and the pleasure they generate can't possibly be expressed in lire or dollars.

From a practical standpoint, wine tasting not only serves party purposes well but gives the host the chance to test candidates for his own cellar. In setting the sights for your party, invite those friends who don't mind forsaking hard liquor for the pleasures of the noble grape, and shun the sort of man whose concept of Nirvana is a half-dozen martinis in a row. Eight to twelve guests is a good number for a wine-tasting party. More than a dozen tends to cloud the issue and befuddle the tasting. Invite as many people as you'd normally ask to a buffet supper, since a supper normally follows a private wine tasting in a studio or apartment.

The best time for a wine-tasting party is sundown. At that time the taste apparatus will be at its keenest—freed from the cantankerousness of the breakfast table and fully recovered from every trace of lunch or dinner fatigue. Don't serve the elaborate assortment of hot and cold hors d'oeuvres that normally goes with cocktails at this hour. Provide instead, in modest quantities, breadsticks, unbuttered slices of thin French bread or whole-wheat Italian bread, soy crackers or small wedges of mildly aged hard cheese such as Edam or cheddar. Avoid rich, pungent cheeses such as gorgonzola which stick to the palate. Provide pitchers of cold water. In other words, offer palate-clearing rather than palate-stultifying items: the kind of food that will clean the taste between sips of different wines and tempt the guest to sip and sample more.

For your first wine-tasting party, you may have to buy or
rent glassware. If you've invited eight people, you should have at
least 32 stemmed wineglasses so that guests can compare three
or four wines at one tasting. They should be tulip-shaped with a
minimum eight-ounce capacity, preferably larger. At a
champagne-tasting party, glasses should again be tulip-shaped
rather than the common saucer-shaped glasses, to conserve
bubbles as well as bouquet. For red or white table wines,
round-bellied Burgundy glasses serve well, permitting
comfortable nosing. For sherries, Madeiras or ports, the smaller
dock glass is preferable. Glasses should be thin, crystal-clear,
without the ropelike edge of glasses designed to prevent nicking.

At wine tastings in public eating places, a battery of four
glasses is usually placed before each judge. When the four have
been used, the contents of the glasses, if any, are then dumped
into a container on the table. The glasses are sometimes rinsed at
the table, readied for a second tasting. It's reminiscent of the
rough-and-ready brass-spittoon era. In your own digs, an
infinitely more gracious way is to hire a kitchen helper, if you
need one, for washing glasses between tastings. He or she can
later help with the buffet supper and cleanup.

In selecting wines for a tasting party, you can range from
spicy apéritif wines through red and white table wines, rosés
and sparkling wines on to the sweetest cream sherries, vintage
ports and Madeiras. But when your party becomes a
jack-of-all-wines, it often leaves your guests feeling like masters
of none. Infinitely more fun is to cover one or two segments of
the huge wine scene with a selective sampling of the most
interesting bottlings you can find.

Discuss your plans with your wine merchant—assuming
you've found a reliable one who really knows his wines and isn't
just another neighborhood dispenser of package goods. Choose
new wines you're curious about as well as some you've already
tried. You might have to visit the shelves of several stores to get
three different Cabernet Sauvignons or three tawny ports. The
wines to be judged should be both alike and different. One
wouldn't compare a sweet Hungarian Tokay and a sweet
Marsala. But one definitely would compare a French sauternes
with a California made from the same grapes. As a general
guideline, you can select for party tastings:

Wines of the same grape: Rieslings from the Alsace,
Germany and California, and perhaps the Rieslings now
being bottled in New York State, made from European
grapes grown in an Eastern state.

Wines of the same region: French red Graves and French
Médocs.

Nonvintage wines versus vintage wines, assuming the latter
aren't too hoary with age.

The same wines of different vintages: 1959s, say, versus
1964s.

Wines of similar processing: French versus California
champagnes, or German *Sekts* versus Italian Asti Spumantes.

Before the party starts, be sure that red table wines are at
room temperature, not higher than 70° F. (Some people like reds
at a cellar temperature—about 60° F.) Beaujolais, rosés and
sherries are often served chilled. White table wines and white
dessert wines, as well as champagne or other sparkling wines,
should be chilled to about 40° to 50° F. Place them in the
refrigerator for one to two hours, or chill them in a champagne
bucket with ice for 15 minutes to a half hour. Red wines should
be opened about an hour before serving to permit them to
"breathe," that is, to allow their bouquets to expand. Old vintage
reds or vintage ports should be decanted if necessary.

Set up a rectangular or square table with a snowy white
cloth. Space bottles between glasses or on a large lazy Susan.
Wines should be uncorked, and corks placed beside the bottles
for those wishing to inspect them. The corks should smell of
wine, not cork. Naturally, any wine that might have been spoiled
because of a defective cork—a very rare occurrence—wouldn't be
on the table for sampling.

If your wine tasting is to be blind, then all bottles should be
covered with paper bags, each numbered for refills and later
identification. At home, the hide-and-seek game of a blind wine
tasting may be fun if it doesn't make the guests feel that *they*
rather than the wines are being judged. By exposing the labels in
an open wine tasting, guests guide themselves from one pleasure
to the next rather than engage in the mumbo jumbo of
identification. For some people, it may be interesting to be seated
in a Porsche racer blindfolded and driven around town to test
the car's riding qualities; for others it's much more instructive to
see and feel what's going on.

Don't worry about unfinished bottles as a result of your
wine-tasting party. Recork them or empty them into decanters.
Keep them chilled until served at another time. Some may be
used for cooking. Naturally, once any bottle of wine is opened
and the wine is exposed to the air, something of its original
glamour evaporates. There are sherry experts who will always
insist on opening a fresh bottle for tasting purposes. But sherry
and other fortified wines can, in fact, last for weeks or months
on the shelf after being opened.

Finally, when the tasting is completed and second-guessers
as well as Monday-morning quarterbacks have had their say, the

wine-tasting party should continue with buffet food or a sit-down dinner, along with the wine that the host selects as *his* prize specimen. There's a whale of a difference between tasting wine alone and tasting it with meat or seafood. A soft white Burgundy, for instance, like a Meursault, will be both velvety and nutty in its flavor impressions. But the same wine later with a roast stuffed duckling or a dish of terrapin will be remembered for its odd, romping dryness. The quality of any wine is a marriage of the human palate and a subtle combination of alcohol, pigments, aromas, bouquets, acids, tannins, sugars and countless other components that Bacchus himself couldn't name. When food is added, the list of components grows. The fact that they're seemingly infinite and infinitely arguable simply means that a wine-tasting party can never be dull. The more differences, the more opinionated the reactions, the merrier.

INDEX

This Index is designed to guide the reader to specific categories of wines and spirits. Numerals following a recipe are printed in Italics.

ABOUT THE AUTHOR

Thomas Mario has been Food and Drink Editor of PLAYBOY since 1953. His wide range of knowledge in the history and practice of the culinary arts has made him an internationally known authority in the field; his frequent overseas travels keep him up to date on the latest developments concerning food, wine and spirits. Through Food Science Associates of Rye, N.Y., Mr. Mario has served for more than a decade as a consultant to the food and food-services industries.